INFRASTRUCTURES
OF IMPUNITY

A volume in the series
Cornell Modern Indonesia Project
Edited by Eric Tagliacozzo and Thomas B. Pepinksy

A list of titles in this series is available at cornellpress.cornell.edu.

INFRASTRUCTURES OF IMPUNITY

New Order Violence in Indonesia

Elizabeth F. Drexler

SOUTHEAST ASIA PROGRAM PUBLICATIONS

AN IMPRINT OF CORNELL UNIVERSITY PRESS

Ithaca and London

Copyright © 2024 by Cornell University

All rights reserved. Except for brief quotations in a review, this book, or parts
thereof, must not be reproduced in any form without permission in writing from
the publisher. For information, address Cornell University Press, Sage House,
512 East State Street, Ithaca, New York 14850. Visit our website at cornellpress.
cornell.edu.

First published 2024 by Cornell University Press

Librarians: A CIP catalog record for this book is available from the Library
of Congress.

ISBN 978-1-5017-7309-9 (hardcover)
ISBN 978-1-5017-7310-5 (paperback)
ISBN 978-1-5017-7312-9 (pdf)
ISBN 978-1-5017-7311-2 (epub)

For Jacob

Contents

Acknowledgments

My interest in transitional justice for New Order violence began in 1998 when I was swept into the postauthoritarian euphoria with students, journalists, activists, and many others. The struggle for justice has been long, and I admire the individuals who have persisted. Over many years, countless people have provided myriad forms of invaluable assistance to my process of research and writing. I am grateful to all the individuals who talked to me, some for hours at a time and many repeatedly, during interviews and conversations over more than two decades.

I appreciate the time, ideas, support, and friendship extended by Suraya, Yati, Marsillam, Sumarsih, Suciwati, and Usman. Aghniadi answered numerous questions and tracked down many media references. A number of organizations generously contributed to my research: KontraS, JSKK, Amnesty Indonesia, ELSAM, the KKPK, LBH Jakarta, the IPT, YLBHI, AJAR, Komnas HAM, and Komnas Perempuan. I appreciate the opportunity to attend Sehama, Kalabahu, Rabuan, Kamisan, and countless discussions and meetings over the years. I cannot name all the individuals who have assisted me in Indonesia, but I would like to thank Agnes, Artidjo, Arsil, Atnike, Ayash, Baskara, Bedjo, Bivitri, Dolo, Fai, Febriana, Galuh, Haris, Hariwi, Ichsan, Ifdhal, Indri, Jati, Lexy, Martin, Nani, Ndari, Nezar, Ninies, Nursyahbani, Pak Kus, Pak Oki, Pak Putu, Pretty, Prodita, Puri, Putri, Robert, Roro, Sandyawan, Stanley, Tumiso, Uci, and many others. Alan Feinstein and John McGlynn also provided support and insights.

Beyond Indonesia, the friends and colleagues who have contributed to this project in different ways over its long development are too numerous to name, but I especially thank Dave Akin, Chris Duncan, Steve Esquith, Elaine Gerber, Bob Hefner, Yazier Henry, Alex Hinton, Doreen Lee, Mara Leichtman, Sharon Lowery, Deborah Margolis, Al McCoy, Mary McCoy, Eric Montgomery, Elisabeth Ida Mulyani, Kerth O'Brien, Sebastian Pompe, Geoffrey Robinson, John Roosa, Helen Veit, and Saskia Wieringa. Conversations with John H. Davis Jr. helped me to articulate the contribution of the infrastructure of impunity beyond Indonesia. I am grateful to Melissa Charenko, Jamie Davidson, Tyrell Haberkorn, Ed Murphy, and Dave Sheridan for reading parts of this manuscript and providing insightful commentary. I especially appreciate the generous and thoughtful comments provided by three anonymous reviewers who read the entire manuscript with great care.

I am grateful to a number of institutions that invited me to present earlier versions of this work, and to audiences who offered valuable feedback, in Indonesia: Atma Jaya; University of Indonesia, Depok; Universitas Pelita Harapan; Sanata Dharma, Yogyakarta; Universitas Islam Negri Sunan Kalijaga, Yogyakarta; and, in the US, the University of California, Los Angeles; the University of Michigan, Ann Arbor; the University of Notre Dame; Rutgers University, Newark; and the University of Wisconsin, Madison.

I thank the Indonesian Ministry of Research, the Institute of Sciences, the Department of Anthropology at the University of Indonesia, AMINEF, and the American Institute for Indonesian Studies for facilitating my research in Indonesia. I am grateful to Suraya Afiff, Yosef Djakababa, and Suzie Sudarman for their sponsorship. This research was funded by an AIFIS Henry Luce Fellowship Grant, a Fulbright Senior Scholar Award, and, at Michigan State University, awards from the Dr. Delia Koo Faculty Endowment and Muslim Studies Program. Support for writing was provided by a Michigan State University Frank and Adelaide Kussy Scholarship for Study of the Holocaust and Its Legacy and for Study of Genocide, as well as the Dr. Delia Koo Faculty Endowment. I appreciate the support provided by the Department of Anthropology, especially in funding Jarad Whitney Cornett's outstanding research assistance in the final stages of completing this book.

Peter Agree's friendship and wisdom have been constant and indispensable over the long course of this project. I appreciate Pamela Haig's skillful edits and excavations. I was fortunate to work with my editor, Sarah Grossman, her colleagues Jacqulyn Teoh, Karen Hwa, and Eric Levy, and other members of the Cornell team on the publication of this book.

No words can properly express the depth of my love and gratitude for my family, especially my son, Jacob, who was resourceful and adventurous during the years we lived in Indonesia as well as the pandemic years spent writing and homeschooling. His love, hugs, and humor make everything possible and worthwhile. My husband Nazaruddin's enduring confidence in me has been a source of strength over many years and miles. My mother and father and my brother have provided invaluable love, support, and encouragement. Thank you all for believing in me and this project.

Portions of chapter 6 have appeared previously in "Impunity and Transitional Justice in Indonesia: Aksi Kamisan's Circular Time," *International Journal of Transitional Justice* 16, no. 3 (2022) 298–313.

I am grateful to John McGlynn and the Lontar Foundation for permission to reprint portions of *Home* appearing in chapter 1 and *The Mysterious Marksman* appearing in chapter 2.

Abbreviations and Terms

ABRI	Angkatan Bersenjata Republik Indonesia (Armed Forces of the Republic of Indonesia)
Aksi Kamisan	Thursday Action silent protest
Bakorstanas	Badan Koordinasi Bantuan Pemantapan Stabilitas Nasional (Agency for the Coordination of Support for the Development of National Stability)
BIN	Badan Intelijen Negara (State Intelligence Agency)
BM	Bathi Mulyono
CAVR	Comissão de Acolhimento, Verdade e Reconciliação de Timor Leste (Commission for Reception, Truth, and Reconciliation in East Timor)
DKP	Dewan Kehormatan Perwira (Officers' Honor Council)
ELSAM	Lembaga Studi dan Advokasi Masyarakat (Institute for Policy Research and Advocacy)
ET	eks-tapol (former political prisoner)
G30S	Gerakan 30 September (September 30th Movement)
Gerwani	Gerakan Wanita Indonesia (Indonesian Women's Movement)
Golkar	Partai Golongan Karya (Party of Functional Groups) (Suharto's party)
ICC	International Criminal Court
Ingat 65	Remember 65 website
IPT	International People's Tribunal for 1965
islah	restitution
KIP	Komisi Informasi Publik (Commission for Public Information)
KKPK	Koalisi Keadilan dan Pengungkapan Kebenaran (Coalition for Justice and Truth Telling)
Komnas HAM	Komisi Nasional Hak Asasi Manusia (Indonesian National Human Rights Commission)
Komnas Perempuan	Komisi Nasional Anti-Kekerasan Terhadap Perempuan (National Commission on Violence against Women)
Konfrontasi	Confrontation (Sukarno's campaign to oppose the formation of Malaysia, 1963–66)

KontraS	Komisi untuk Orang Hilang dan Korban Tindak Kekerasan (Commission for the Disappeared and Victims of Violence)
Kopassus	Komando Pasukan Khusus (Special Forces Command)
Kopkamtib	Komando Operasi Pemulihan Keamanan dan Ketertiban (Operational Command for the Restoration of Security and Order)
KPK	Komisi Pemberantasan Korupsi (Corruption Eradication Commission)
KPP HAM	Komisi Penyelidik Pelanggaran Hak Asasi Manusia (Investigative Commission on Human Rights) (formed by Komnas HAM to investigate cases to determine whether gross violations of human rights occurred)
kriminalisasi	criminalization
LBH	Lembaga Bantuan Hukum (Legal Aid Institute)
Litsus	penelitian khusus (special review)
Lubang Buaya	Crocodile Hole, name of the area near the well in which the seven victims of the September 30th Movement were found
Mahmillub	Mahkamah Militer Luar Biasa (Extraordinary Military Tribunals)
Masyumi	Majelis Syuro Muslimin Indonesia (Consultative Council of Indonesian Muslims)
MPR-RI	Majelis Permusyawaratan Rakyat Republik Indonesia (People's Consultative Assembly of the Republic of Indonesia, or Parliament, consisting of two houses: the DPR [Dewan Perwakilan Rakyat, or People's Representative Council] and the DPD [Dewan Perwakilan Daerah, or Regional Representative Council])
MPRS	Majelis Permusyawaratan Rakyat Sementara (Provisional People's Consultative Assembly)
Pancasila	Five Principles (Indonesian national philosophy)
PDI	Partai Demokrasi Indonesia (Indonesian Democratic Party)
PDI-P	Partai Demokrasi Indonesia Perjuangan (Indonesian Democratic Party of Struggle)
pemuda	youth
petrus	penembakan misterius (mysterious killings)
PKI	Partai Komunis Indonesia (Communist Party of Indonesia)
PP	Pemuda Pancasila (Pancasila Youth)

PPP	Partai Persatuan Pembangunan (United Development Party)
PRD	Partai Rakyat Demokratik (People's Democratic Party)
reformasi	period of transition after the resignation of Soeharto in 1998
Semanggi 1	November 13, 1998, incident in which government forces killed seventeen demonstrators who were protesting the SI-MPR (Special Session of the People's Consultative Assembly of the Republic of Indonesia) at the Semanggi cloverleaf traffic interchange near the parliament building in Jakarta
Semanggi 2	September 24, 1999, incident in which government forces killed twelve demonstrators and wounded more than two hundred who were protesting the emergency security bill being debated by the Parliament
Supersemar	Surat Perintah Sebelas Maret (Order of March 11 Letter, transferring power from Sukarno to Suharto)
Tanjung Priok case	Gross violations of human rights case named for the port area in North Jakarta where security forces killed over twenty-four civilians in 1984 after an army sergeant ordered a mosque leader (Amir Biki) to remove banners and pamphlets critical of the government
TAP MPRS 25/1966	Ketetapan Majelis Permusyawaratan Rakyat Sementara No. 25, tahun 1966 (Provisional People's Consultative Assembly Decree No. 25 of 1966, which banned the dissemination and teaching of Marxism and Communism)
tapol	tahanan politik (political prisoner)
TAPOL	UK-based human rights group
TGPF	Tim Gabung Pencari Fakta (Joint Fact-Finding Team appointed to investigate May 1998 riots and rapes)
TNI	Tentara Nasional Indonesia (Indonesian National Armed Forces)
TNI AD	Tentara Nasional Indonesia Angkatan Darat (Indonesian National Military-Land Force) (Indonesian National Army)
TOR	terms of reference
Trisakti tragedy	On May 12, 1998, at Trisakti University, Indonesian soldiers opened fire on unarmed protesters demanding Soeharto's resignation, killing four students and two others, which sparked massive protests

TRuK   Tim Relawan untuk Kemanusiaan (Volunteers for Humanity team, which investigated the May 1998 violence, especially rape cases)

Note on Names, Spelling, and Translation

I refer to individuals by their nickname, first name, or only name, as is common practice in Indonesia. Following anthropological conventions, I have used nicknames, initials or pseudonyms or not named individuals to protect their identities. I have used modern Indonesian spellings—for example *u* instead of *oe* (*Sukarno* rather than *Soekarno*)—with the exception of cases where I am quoting or citing other sources that use old spellings. All translations from Indonesian are my own unless otherwise noted.

TRUTH AND INFRASTRUCTURES OF IMPUNITY

This book is about the creation and persistence of impunity for a Cold War genocide (1965–66) and subsequent state violence, direct and indirect, in the name of
development and stability in Indonesia. This impunity persists in the realms of
law, culture, and common sense, and involves the dehumanization and eradication of (suspected) political opponents and an intricate bureaucracy developed
to stigmatize their family members over multiple generations and secure the
silence and complicity of others. It involves many forms of violence, complicity, and complacency, and produces subsequent generations that both know and
unknow about past state violence.

Through these themes, I explore why truth telling and factual revelation have
not succeeded in redressing human rights violations. *Infrastructures of Impunity*
critiques a foundational belief that the documentation of history and past state
crimes prevents their recurrence. After periods of state violence and authoritarianism, "transitional justice" interventions are often initiated to develop the rule
of law and support transitions to democracy. They may include institutions such
as truth commissions, tribunals, and policies such as lustration or purges, amnes-
ties, and days of remembrance, designed to support incoming successor states
as they address the crimes of previous repressive regimes.[1] Transitional justice
advocates have produced a wealth of documentation about past cases and yet
have had very little success in achieving accountability for state crimes or changing public perceptions of the past. Human rights and justice projects in Indonesia
have drawn on survivor testimony, documentation, and truth seeking in a global
posttruth era. Meanwhile, those in power use historical narratives that have an

enduring affective hold, and this affective resonance disrupts activist history and truth-seeking projects. Thus, the lack of success of these efforts is not a failure of the transitional justice advocates; rather, it is an indication of the power of affective and infrastructural forces that support impunity in the present.

An important theme of human rights work is the power of stories about the past, but in the case of Indonesia we see that past propaganda has a long half-life. Finding, using, and making effective the "truth" about the past is a long and circuitous process in which documents and evidence are important but are also subverted by the very institutions and processes that promise to authorize their validity and make them consequential. These are all elements of what I call an infrastructure of impunity. And the truths bend to that infrastructure more than the infrastructure bends to the truths.

The key protagonists in this story are those who struggled for justice and against impunity, and those who perform small acts of consistency, creativity, and repetition that subvert the infrastructure. Since the mid-2010s, activists of the millennial generation have engaged the power of affect and micro or experiential truths to reconsider the violent past.

In 1966, General Suharto and his New Order regime took power in Indonesia. The New Order made its version of history enduring and affectively powerful into the present. Official Indonesian school histories, films, and policies say that Suharto took power after a supposed coup attempt by suspected members of the PKI, the then-legal Communist Party of Indonesia. These histories mention only in passing the killings of a million or more suspected members or supporters of the PKI, and they omit the New Order's widespread violations of human rights, repression of political dissent, stigmatization, systematic propaganda, and campaigns of terror, which followed these inaugural killings for more than three decades. The genocide and associated bureaucratic efforts to eradicate the Left were abetted by the United States and other countries during the global Cold War.[2] The New Order regime remained in power for over thirty years, creating rich dividends for US corporations through resource extraction, the creation of a class of oligarchs, and a widespread system of corruption. It delivered significant development and modernization to a tactically depoliticized population.

The euphoria that marked the end of President Suharto's authoritarian New Order in 1998 was followed by notable reforms: passage of human rights legislation and the establishment of new institutions and policies that promised to address authoritarian-era violence and corruption. Early efforts led by those with direct experience of New Order repression focused on documenting violations and violence, gathering testimonies, organizing victims, raising awareness, "straightening" history, and advocating for human rights tribunals and other legal forms of justice. Although the country has not had an official transitional justice process, and though some say political reform has allowed Indonesians to successfully forget Suharto-era authoritarian violence and move on, Indonesian NGOs since 1998 have launched numerous campaigns against unresolved cases of violence. Technical and political ruses have been used to prevent evidence from entering the court, and there has been little moral outrage in public discourse, where past state (authoritarian) narratives remain affectively and politically powerful. State institutions, especially the police, have failed to protect victims from nonstate groups that extend patterns of extrajudicial violence into the present. The military's territorial command has remained a feature of everyday life everywhere. Military and political elites and cronies still dominate the political field, and the infrastructure of impunity has continued to shield perpetrators, institutions, practices, and especially cronies and beneficiaries from accountability.

In 2014, Joko Widodo, commonly referred to as Jokowi, was elected Indonesia's first president who did not belong to a prominent political family or a have a military background. Jokowi campaigned on his status as someone unburdened by the past, and on a vision that included addressing past human rights violations.[3] He successfully attracted the votes and enthusiasm of youth. Despite decades of human rights documentation, however, Jokowi's vision and voters' apparent support for it, even when augmented by public truth telling, did not lead to resolution or accountability.

Many responses to state violence, including international human rights advocacy and transitional justice practices, are founded on the premises that exposing violations compels the world to stop them; that acknowledgement and truth telling are healing for survivors; that documentation and truth telling promote justice; that ending impunity with the prosecution of individual criminal perpetrators prevents the recurrence of state violence; and that political transitions, reconciliation, and the public legitimacy of institutions depend on settling the historical accounts. Key to all of these strategies is the importance of investigating, documenting, and making public the truth of state violence. In the literature on transitional justice, scholars and practitioners have advocated for different kinds and forms of knowledge and truth, but their perceived importance, and especially their relationship to law and to the international community, is a vital assumption in many strategies.

The urgency and imperative to witness has become a widespread, almost universal response to atrocity. For instance, scholars and literary figures have pointed to the Holocaust's effort to erase its own witnesses.[4] Military dictatorships have used tactics such as disappearances to terrorize critics and their families and often incorporate the prospect of oblivion into torture.[5] The pattern of disappearances have given rise to strong demands for information by family members and human rights workers. Governments have often masked state repression with the rhetoric of national security. The literary scholar and translator Marguerite Feitlowitz analyzes Argentina's dirty war to demonstrate that language was used in public to obscure intentions, actions, and meanings; to "inspire trust, both at home and abroad"; to "seal . . . complicity"; and to "sow paralyzing terror and confusion."[6] She notes that "even if one doesn't agree, the language— to some extent—gets internalized."[7] In clandestine contexts, "language became a form of torture."[8] Disappearances, state denials, and doublespeak all create conditions in which revelation of the truth and an end to deniability are seen as imperative in and of themselves. At the same time, state denials often find the power to endure even after the facts have been exposed and corrected.

In transitional justice, the power of truth telling relies on the attachment of forensic facts to meaningful terms, and especially to legal norms. This advocacy work holds that there are universal human rights that apply to all individuals, and that the international community has a responsibility to protect them.[9] Documented acts can be measured against universal standards and norms that have been violated. The lawyer and legal scholar Ruti Teitel points out that "demands cast in rights language become claims that cannot otherwise be rationalized away in the domestic scheme, such as in terms of war or national security."[10] Revelation of truth has the promise to reverse the official doublespeak and propaganda that justify state violence.

Some forms of speaking truth to power, particularly those advanced during the Cold War, rely on local actors smuggling irrefutable evidence of state violence out of the local context to be publicized by international networks, in hopes of ending the secrecy in which state abuse occurs and is thereafter obfuscated. Transnational organizations such as Amnesty International and Human Rights Watch and networks of local human rights defenders have circulated urgent actions and coordinated letter-writing and media campaigns in the name of individuals whose human rights have been violated, in order to pressure state officials to release them or update family members on their whereabouts. In other cases, such as the long-running effort to counter the Indonesian government's denials about atrocities committed in occupied East Timor, activists have sought to end military aid and arms sales by the United States to repressive governments. Some of these campaigns have succeeded. Governments do release certain prisoners after public outcry, and arms sales and military aid are occasionally suspended. The idea of truth telling, however, promises much more than these specific outcomes—and perhaps because of these successes.

In his analysis of how human rights naming and shaming works, Thomas Keenan writes about the presumption of human rights advocates that in the absence of a functioning legal apparatus, representation works as an informal mechanism: the exposure of silenced or hidden violations enforces compliance with shared norms and laws through shaming perpetrators.[11] This belief in the power of truth to enforce, and even create, norms shapes the institutions and practice of transitional justice. In the late 1990s and early 2000s, truth commissions were the most prominent institutionalization of truth seeking.[12] Advocates of criminal justice tended to see the truth commission as a vehicle for amnesty and a process that would replace the pursuit of legal justice, and that stood almost in opposition to justice.[13] For example, South Africa's Truth and Reconciliation Commission, which operated from 1995 to 2002, was empowered to provide amnesty in exchange for truth. In some cases, state perpetrators have advocated for truth commissions to avoid accountability. Because of this, analysts worried that there was a trade-off between truth and justice.[14] Since 2009, this concern is no longer as prominent and has been replaced by ideas of complementarity.[15]

Scholars have highlighted intersections between truth and justice strategies. For example, legal studies scholar Jamie Rowen argues, the "quasi-judicial nature" of truth commissions are central to their appeal.[16] Narratives about the past that are authorized through commissions can undermine past justifications and logics that made individuals tolerant of or complicit with state repression. Such narratives can drive further accountability (that is, criminal processes) or can serve as a form of historical justice.[17] In terms of historical justice, following Hannah Arendt's analysis of Eichmann in Jerusalem, legal scholars have debated the limitations of the trial for generating larger truths about historical violence.[18] And yet others see trials as sites for the social construction of knowledge that play an important role in collective memory.[19] Ruti Teitel emphasizes the importance of "legal rituals," including both trials and hearings, to enable the production of histories that "perform critical undoings that respond to prior repression."[20] For some Indonesian activists I spoke with, a judicial process was necessary to authorize information that had been documented or to demand the release of state files believed to contain relevant information that would presumably facilitate such undoings.

Despite the promises of transitional justice, scholars and practitioners have critiqued its processes and results. The political theorist Bronwyn Leebaw argues that the "truth" produced in transitional justice institutions is legalistic, depoliticized, polarizing, and unable to appreciate acts of resistance and ambiguous gray zones.[21] Zinaida Miller points out the shortcoming that transitional justice, like human rights, focuses on violations of civil and political rights while failing to address social and economic rights or structural violence.[22]

In addition to the critiques of political theorists, anthropologists have analyzed ethnographically how transitional justice principles and institutions are localized.[23] They have challenged assumptions about the nature of the truth captured in these institutions by paying particular attention to issues of gender and gendered violence, the complex political and social dynamics associated with collective memory after violence, issues of public secrecy, and the nature of silence and social forgetting, as well as past contexts of collaboration and betrayal.[24] Work with survivors has also challenged assumptions that providing testimony in a transitional institution is therapeutic.[25] Taken together, this anthropological work demonstrates that transitional justice interventions are falling far short of the promised results. The anthropologist Alex Hinton has pointed to a "justice facade" that "masks power and the complexities of everyday experience."[26] And yet, the desire for justice through formal transitional rituals persists among various groups in societies that have experienced violence.

Despite these institutions designed to produce truth and justice, scholars and advocates have shown that impunity persists. To end impunity, specifically, these advocates demand individual criminal prosecutions for perpetrators of human rights violations and more serious crimes, arguing that prosecutions "deter future abuses, promote the rule of law, restore the confidence of citizens in government, guarantee respect for human rights, and ensure justice for victims of atrocious crimes."[27]

The historian of human rights Samuel Moyn notes that ending impunity draws on the intuitive concept that there is a class of infractions for which there must be zero tolerance, and which nation-states have "internationalized as punishable when domestic justice fails."[28] Moyn and other scholars have noted that the current movement to "end impunity" through the International Criminal Court (ICC) prioritizes one definition of justice—individual criminal accountability—and excludes others: most notably, structural, racial, economic, and collective justice.[29] Many scholars have pointed out that claims about the utility of international tribunals and ending impunity are rarely articulated or evaluated.[30]

In addition to marginalizing other visions of justice, the mobilization of international institutions, such as the ICC, designed to combat impunity have "reinforced a structure of global governance premised on exploitation and inequality," according to the legal theorist Vasuki Nesiah. Nesiah suggests that anti-impunity efforts have provided impunity for the more powerful in some cases or obscured systemic injustices and the repeated failures of international justice processes.[31] This critique of the global movement against impunity focuses primarily on cases the ICC has pursued, but the powerful rhetoric of ending impunity circulates internationally and informs justice campaigns even in countries that are not signatories to the International Criminal Court.

The historian and political scientist Tyrell Haberkorn analyzes prolonged impunity in Thailand, a country that, like Indonesia, has not been a focus of the ICC. She examines how impunity, defined not simply as the lack of justice but as the failure to see something as a crime, is normalized and "takes place in plain sight." Concludes Haberkorn, "The public nature of impunity makes it pedagogical for both state perpetrators and citizens."[32] Likewise, I explore how victims, family members, and activists in Indonesia persistently demand justice (most often defined in legal terms) despite repeated failures to achieve it, and consider whether these failed attempts at accountability implicitly "teach" seekers of justice about the power of the state and its control over law, and thereby extend impunity into the present. At the same time, I argue that even where impunity is blatant, there is a value in repeatedly naming it as impunity—as a crime and a deviation rather than as a defense of nationalist ideals.

International campaigns and institutions tend to construe justice as prosecution for discrete events with clear perpetrators, but this definition does not adequately capture cases of prolonged and widespread impunity that occur in the aftermath of sustained state violence. In Indonesia, for example, the genocide not only occurred over the years of killings but was extended over a half century through new incidents and types of violence abetted by the infrastructure of impunity.

Indonesians often talk about a "red thread" that connects many factors into one unit that produces particular effects. It is a common expression that I heard from activists during the authoritarian period to suggest how disparate elements worked together and could be understood with a single narrative, but I heard it in other ordinary contexts as well. Anthropological analysis of "infrastructure" helps us understand and untangle the red threads of social and political life in Indonesia. Brian Larkin describes infrastructures as "built networks that facilitate the flow of goods, people, or ideas and allow for their exchange over space.... They comprise the architecture for circulation, literally providing the undergirding of modern societies, and they generate the ambient environment of everyday life."[33] Infrastructures also make promises for the future. They mobilize affect and "the senses of desire, pride, and frustration, feelings which can be deeply political."[34] Like the red thread, an infrastructure is both material and immaterial.

Other scholars have described how particular kinds of infrastructure include and exclude individuals, which produces direct as well as indirect violence, abjection, and abandonment.[35] The anthropologists Dennis Rodgers and Bruce O'Neill write that infrastructure is "not just a material embodiment of violence (structural or otherwise), but often its instrumental medium."[36] In the case of Indonesia, the violence of impunity has not simply continued, but has grown. The anthropologist James Ferguson argues that infrastructural violence eludes efforts to specify individual perpetrators because the harms come from large-scale systems that incorporate human and nonhuman elements. Infrastructures, Ferguson observes, can also naturalize, make invisible, or make "to seem inevitable" massive inequalities.[37] As such, infrastructure is a particularly useful concept for examining how impunity extends, repeats, and grows in Indonesia, beyond the agency (or prosecution) of discrete, identifiable perpetrators. The infrastructure of impunity circulates throughout the entire archipelago through the army's territorial command, bureaucracy, laws, law enforcement, media, and culture. This infrastructure is built out of a variety of elements: bureaucratic, military, legal, political, educational, social, and affective. Although some of these elements are occasionally dormant and others have been used at different times and in different cases, they can be described as a unified entity whose elements, both singly and in concert, help explain and account for the persistence of impunity. The infrastructure transforms over time. Violations of civil and political rights over multiple generations are transformed into structural violence and economic deprivation. The logic and bureaucratic mechanisms for enacting stigmatization and exclusion remain available to be applied to other groups and individuals, thus shaping how resources and rights flow through society and keeping alive the affective force of propaganda.

Bureaucracy is an important element of the infrastructure of impunity. The civilian bureaucracy is shadowed by the army's territorial command and its ubiquitous posts.[38] In addition to depriving citizens of legal rights, stigmatization as enacted through bureaucracy deprives individuals of public services and excludes them from social belonging, and has far-reaching economic and social consequences. The bureaucracy creates a ubiquitous system where one's rights as a citizen can always be revoked. The logic of association means that an individual's status can always change and thus must be maintained by constant vigilance, especially by avoiding "contamination" through association with a stigmatized group.

Violence that is implemented through bureaucracies is often analyzed in terms of Weberian models that emphasize flawed operations or procedures, or bad agents. In their analysis of the Abu Ghraib prison abuse scandal, Steven Caton and Bernardo Zacka argue that the Weberian model is insufficient and that the "system" is better understood as one that institutionalizes "arbitrariness."[39] By their logic, accountability processes that rely on written records of procedures or documentation of individual acts that violate clear norms and procedures follow Weberian models and are not well suited to understanding this kind of bureaucratic violence. Pervasive and prolonged impunity allows for improvisation and arbitrariness; indeed, this is a key element of the infrastructure and how it extends. For example, local power holders (civilian and military) are able to inflict myriad forms of dehumanization, exclusion, and exploitation on former political prisoners and their families, while in other cases, violence is perpetrated by criminal groups that are both linked to and disavowed by the security apparatus. In their analysis of the Brazilian police forces, sociologist Martha Huggins and her team analyze the creation of a "climate that powerfully structures not only the business of state violence but also social accounting of it."[40] Understanding violence and impunity through an infrastructure that has dynamic, intersecting elements sheds new light on the conditions that enable both the perpetration of violence and the subsequent evasion of accountability for it.

The historian Jess Melvin's work demonstrates the Indonesian Army's intention in 1965–66 to annihilate leftists, including but not limited to actual and suspected members and supporters of the Communist Party of Indonesia (Partai Komunis Indonesia, or PKI), a then-legal political party. This intention was expressed in the creation of institutions, offices, and declarations ordering the mandatory involvement of civilians in the army's campaign to exterminate other civilians.[41] Melvin describes in careful detail the "mechanics of mass murder," diagramming the institutions, documents, and policies enacted by the army to orchestrate the killings. The army's territorial command that shadowed the civilian bureaucracy was critical. The historian John Roosa explains that "by building its own bureaucracy and firmly latching it onto the civilian bureaucracy, the army mangled the lines of jurisdictional authority within the state. The army was free to intervene in the work of all other state officials while remaining outside the control of any other department." It is important to understand the scale of this apparatus: in addition to army officials who were assigned to civilian posts, approximately a "third of the army's troops were stationed in [the territorial command structure]." Roosa further notes that "in the army's logic, the task of 'managing' Indonesian society was a necessary corollary of the army's duty to defend society from external attacks."[42] The territorial command provided a formal structure, but its powers were outside the law.

Melvin shows how the existing territorial command was put to a new use to carry out the killing and ensure that all of the other elements of the state complied. Melvin's work in Aceh is one of the few cases where extensive documentation has been uncovered. Other authors describe a less structured but no less damaging system of winks and nods whereby criminal gangs were engaged by the military and its proxies to commit the killings.[43] To both orchestrate the genocide and create impunity for it, a system of institutions, laws, policies, and bureaucracies was created or adapted.

The bureaucracy shaped the daily lives of communities across the archipelago. The mobilization of individuals as intelligence informants or as perpetrators of direct and indirect violence extended the bureaucracy beyond the military posts and the institutions and policies of the state. A climate of impunity structured both the killings and the social and legal accounting of them; the perpetuation of impunity created both a climate and a bureaucracy that repeated and compounded this socially and legally accepted form of dehumanization. The system of detention and discrimination and the ways in which stigmatization spread through families was regulated by official policies that ensured that political prisoners and their relatives would be denied access to basic rights as citizens and consigned to a space of "civil death."[44] In Indonesia, impunity happens blatantly in public, but also in slow motion, over generations.

Infrastructure can be spectacular, like modernist construction projects, but also nearly invisible and noticeable only when it breaks.[45] Likewise, the infrastructure of impunity has also acquired mundane and ubiquitous forms as individuals have attempted to navigate Indonesia's bureaucracy and the army's omnipresent territorial command, which structures everyday life down to the most minute practices and the level of neighborhood governance. The territorial command posts are a key component of this bureaucracy and an omnipresent part of life across the archipelago, always there should one fail to be vigilant. Impunity's infrastructure has assumed nearly invisible, or all-pervasive, forms as families reinforce stigmatization in the most private and intimate realms. While impunity does occur in plain sight, the infrastructure also includes unseen elements that have extended impunity over time, all but intractably.

And in Indonesia, law itself became part of this clandestine infrastructure.[46] It appeared to be a route to resolution and justice but has often functioned to extend impunity. The law's capacity to secure, extend, and perpetuate impunity depends on its superficial appearance as the opposite—a site of transparency and consistency in the service of accountability and justice. For instance, trials for partial and minor elements of large-scale campaigns of violence can provide immunity against future trials in the name of due process. Certain laws and policies have dehumanized particular citizens and subjected them to civil death, while the system of law has continued to function and has created the appearance, and experience, for other citizens that the rule of law functions and that they are law-abiding citizens rather than complicit beneficiaries. Invisible yet ordinary forms of human rights violations, enabled by subtle everyday laws, institutional cultures, and practices that dehumanize and stigmatize individuals or groups, have extended impunity beyond the initial genocide. Even so, the idea of legal solutions remains compelling for human rights advocates in Indonesia, and the effort to resolve impunity within the legal system actually extends the infrastructure of impunity over time and space.

Historical narratives provide the affective force that allows the system of law and bureaucracy to clandestinely function for impunity rather than justice. These narratives are an indispensable element of the infrastructure of impunity. In Indonesia the state has built its impunity with the use of affectively powerful propaganda, cemented by bureaucratic processes and an omnipresent military command structure that shape everyday lives. Narratives of a nation and culture under threat, traitors to be eradicated, and national values to be upheld have rationalized questionable legal policies and bureaucratic practices and have justified violent practices by local army command posts and their proxies. Historical narratives also shape memories; they condition citizens to feel visceral disgust at the threatening others. Repetition and dramatization have made state narratives affectively and enduringly powerful.

By *affect*, I refer specifically to a force that includes and yet goes beyond emotion, one that is individually and socially experienced in an emotional or embodied manner that exceeds or bypasses conscious, rational narratives and logics, and at the same time infuses these narratives with a visceral element.[47] Affect moves individuals and societies. The genocide and performance studies scholar Kerry Whigham highlights that affect is dynamic and a social phenomenon.[48] Scholars have noted that affective forces move between individuals in a way that is beyond the grasp of conscious engagement.[49] Affect creates felt realities and allows people to make connections between logically disparate events.[50] It can also motivate forms of collective action and provide social legitimacy for authoritarian policies.

Theories of trauma and transitional justice focus on the importance of narrating past harms and shaping collective memory. The cultural theorist Kaitlyn Murphy notes the importance of memory in eliciting affect, which she notes is about "unseen but felt—sensed—connections . . . the way of being in one's life that is brought on by the ongoing act of remembering and, in a sense, living with memory."[51] These sensed connections are especially powerful and difficult to articulate in situations where past genocide or conflict may appear to have been "forgotten" but powerfully linger, often beyond language and logical discussion, or even experience and conscious memory.[52]

The "belated" power of trauma in continuing to inflict damage many years after the fact is intensified by the infrastructure that compounds impunity and extends its harms to new individuals and times with myriad practices that shape everyday life.[53] Understanding the intersection of affect and more concrete elements of the infrastructure of impunity helps to make sense out of the long aftermath of collective trauma and the failures of otherwise promising interventions.

In addition to historical narratives and the experience of policies that concretize propaganda, the law itself mobilizes affect. This is not a feature of an unsophisticated legal system in Indonesia; instead, as the legal anthropologist Kamari M. Clarke argues, despite its representation as a neutral objective process, international justice also relies on the mobilization of affect. In particular, Clarke points to the importance of narratives of "victims to be saved" and "perpetrators to be held accountable" in campaigns for international justice.[54] These narratives circulate globally, but in Indonesia, enduringly powerful narratives undercut the valence of those that Clarke describes. The literature on historical justice emphasizes the importance of reclaiming language and recontextualizing actions outside state narratives in which they are justified in terms of security. But these narratives are not simply substantive falsehoods to be corrected—I argue that they have a visceral, affective power that helps explain why truth-seeking and transitional justice initiatives in Indonesia have failed to disrupt the continued power and endurance of the infrastructure of impunity. This affective power endlessly renews the sense of insecurity, which, in an endless loop, feeds back into institutional, bureaucratic, and social processes.

Cumulatively, the infrastructure of impunity describes the "red thread"—all of these material and immaterial elements that shape the discussion of past state violence, the distribution of the resources of citizenship, and national narratives and memories of the nation. This infrastructure explains why simply "telling the truth" or giving testimony to historical fact hasn't resulted in greater justice. In Indonesia we see powerful exculpatory propaganda and narratives, true, but also the incandescent affective force that imbues them with enduring and mutable power, and we see how the law itself, rather than providing a forum to emend the propaganda, actually structures and supports persistent impunity.

The infrastructure of impunity is composed of elements from law, law enforcement, and the courts but extends well beyond them. It includes bureaucracy and policies that stigmatize certain citizens and relegate some to civil death, as well as bureaucracies that render others numb and complicit with the regime and unable to see dehumanization as wrong. It further includes the army's territorial command and its role in daily life; changes in the built environment, historical narratives, and the monuments, commemorations, and films that popularize them; and intimate realms of family, culture, and religion. Efforts to document the truth of state violence, to rewrite false historical narratives, to seek legal justice, and to create new social awareness and end stigmatization are stymied by this multifaceted, often invisible infrastructure that perpetuates the past system.

Drawing on field research conducted between 2014 and 2019 and longitudinal work with key actors since 1998, this book explores how the infrastructure of impunity developed through unresolved cases since 1965 and how engagement with knowledge, memory, and truth telling about Indonesia's authoritarian past has evolved over the last twenty years.[55]

The first chapter examines the origins and the persistence of affectively powerful histories of the genocide and considers how they were made emotionally and viscerally compelling. It considers the bureaucratic and legal elements that enforced the "truth" of the state's narrative: namely, the systematic arrest, psychological evaluation, and imprisonment without trial of suspected Communist Party members, and the subsequent discrimination against them. It describes several elements of the infrastructure of impunity: the bureaucracy, in the form of identity cards and practices of social stigmatization; the territorial command and its direct, indirect, and potential violence or intimidation; the built environment, at sites of memorials and museums; and powerful narratives, as conveyed through propaganda films and state histories. All of these elements help to mobilize enduring affects of betrayal, shame, stigmatization, fear, and vengeance. The chapter focuses on how subsequent generations encounter the propaganda, knowing that it is false but nonetheless affected and shaped by it, to reveal more about how the state built this infrastructure after 1965 and why it persists. I also consider the undiscussed role of economic beneficiaries from the 1965 killings and how policies and stigmatization over generations have transformed civil and political rights violations into structural violence and economic disparity.

From 1982 to 1985, regional police, military, and their proxies across Indonesia implemented a coordinated campaign to kill what they described as criminals, recidivists, ex-prisoners—in fact any individual who posed a threat to the regime, leaving tattooed corpses by the side of the road. In 1988, Suharto claimed responsibility, saying the killings let people know that someone was in charge. This was a case of blatant impunity and points to the state's nebulous relationship to criminality. Chapter 2 examines how the violence and brutality of extrajudicial killings renewed the terror of the regime, just as official historical narratives about the events of 1965 were being reemphasized and systematic policies of discrimination toward family members of suspected Communists were being extended. In this context it became socially acceptable, even beneficial and justifiable, to kill people who disturbed stability, a move that implicitly justified past killings of Communists and renewed the power of the state to eliminate people seen as traitors to the nation (and also renewed the complicity of the public). The chapter examines surreal short fiction written in the mid-1980s about the killings as an archive of affect that highlights complicity and ambiguity, and inversions of state narratives that justify the killings. We see how impunity undermines truth, and that the archive of fiction in this example more accurately tells the truth of the killings and public complicity than official narratives or archives.

From the 1980s through the end of the authoritarian period in 1998, there were multiple cases of state violence. Chapter 3 examines the powerful hope that documenting state violence might lead to justice and accountability, showing that official investigations, policy, and institutional reforms have failed to produce a sense of justice in the decades following the official end of authoritarian rule. The advocacy organization KontraS and its allies initially produced, cited, and circulated documents, and then attempted to use new institutions—such as an ad hoc Human Rights Tribunal, official investigation teams, and the Commission for Public Information—to make the state liable for what it "knows." In one specific case, KontraS demanded that the state, and the citizenry, recall the substance of past cases and resist forgetting what had been acknowledged in public and yet disappeared from public discourse and state archives, seemingly without any consequence. This chapter examines early documentary victories: for example, investigations that implicated the Special Forces in the rape of women who appeared to be of Chinese descent during the May 1998 riots, and the State Intelligence Agency in the 2004 murder of KontraS founder Munir Said Thalib. And yet the disappearance of these reports and supporting materials reveals how documents and public knowledge do not automatically produce accountability, which calls into question human rights assumptions about the effectiveness of ending deniability and writing new histories. Likewise, the legal framework established to address the past authoritarian violence—the ad hoc Human Rights Tribunals (Pengadilan HAM) and a Commission for Truth and Reconciliation (Komisi Kebenaran dan Rekonsiliasi)—became ineffective. Activists continue to engage existing legal and institutional infrastructure to combat impunity and to make documents have consequences. This chapter looks at truth in its documentary form (who knows what, and where this knowledge circulated), as well as the information disclosed and how it can or cannot be "used" by activists, depending on its provenance.

In Chapter 4, we see how the infrastructure of impunity, especially the process by which narratives of betrayal and endangerment secure citizen complicity in a system of law that does not recognize the equal rights of all citizens, is threatened by both new historical disclosures and an international verdict. In 2015, the International People's Tribunal (IPT) expert judges determined that the 1965 killings were crimes against humanity and qualified as a genocide, which provoked an unprecedented emotional response by political and military elites. It was not new evidence of state violence that provoked outrage, but rather new interpretations of evidence of acts that had not been denied and were widely known—and that were even considered legal in many accounts, according to Indonesian law or interpretations of it. The IPT was an affront to the perpetrators and their ability to control the parameters and implementation of the law.

While the IPT made moral claims through the language of law, many people involved claimed that the tribunal was inspired by Joshua Oppenheimer's important film *The Act of Killing*. I suggest that, taken together, the film and the IPT problematize impunity in new ways by focusing on perpetrators and the legal system rather than on the (contested) humanity of the victims. Together, the surreal film and the review of earlier, established evidence in a new legal framework demonstrate how the infrastructure works affectively through both law and history.

The state responded with a national symposium that sought to create an "understanding" (a combination of knowledge and affective and visceral truth) that could reconcile the information that could not be repressed or denied with the political impossibility of accountability for the past. Despite fears that this symposium would amount to whitewashing, the day was moving, and survivors and descendants felt that they had been part of a historical moment. The hopefulness and success of this effort, however, was interrupted by a countersymposium and the mobilization of criminal elements to attack survivors.

Chapter 5 analyzes a campaign that Indonesian NGOs launched in 2015 to name the use of criminal law against activists *kriminalisasi*, usually translated as "criminalization." Begun in 2015, seventeen years after the end of authoritarianism, this alliance of activists focuses not on the innocence of victims but on visible but unseen and ordinary forms of human rights violations enabled by subtle everyday laws, institutional cultures, and practices that dehumanize and stigmatize individuals or groups of citizens. Being named a suspect triggers a presumption of guilt and social stigmatization for the victim of false or malicious criminal charges, who then draws on both legal and political channels to assert his or her innocence. An array of elite and ordinary cases demonstrates a pervasive pattern by which evidence, facts, and truth are no longer the issue in legal cases brought against critics, and in which the law is being used for ends other than justice. The chapter shows that law and politics are core elements of the infrastructure.

The activists described in this chapter approach criminalization as a problem that can be resolved legally, and retain the belief that law is the only avenue for justice for those with less money and power in a corrupt and oligarchical political system with legacies of authoritarianism. Activists may have started from the assumption that criminalization was a corruption of the law, but they ultimately came to a troubling realization: law itself is the means to impunity for the powerful, and despite efforts toward transitional justice and legal reform, the system allows for stigmatization and marginalization of the less powerful and minorities that it should protect. Some of the human rights literature sees campaigns against impunity as being in opposition to those against structural (economic) injustice, but in the cases described here, we see how the infrastructure of impunity leads to and is itself a structural injustice.

In chapter 6, the demands for legal justice shift and evolve, from naming shaming and the call for legal justice to a more affective, embodied, and aesthetic practice that engages youth. Every week, a silent protest, called Kamisan, at the state palace in Jakarta and in other Indonesian cities demands justice for victims of state violence. Kamisan is supported by various NGOs and activists, but it was initiated by families of victims of New Order violence. The organizers frame their demand as justice (through legal processes) and directly appeal to the president in weekly, hand-delivered letters. As it has continued over more than ten years, Kamisan has also created a stage for new aesthetic and affective responses to injustice. Kamisan demonstrates ongoing impunity and unifies some otherwise polarized victims' groups and cases. The protest highlights different "micro" elements of the infrastructure that are in the president's power to change. Its repetition and consistency over more than a decade have become symbolically important in a context where political discourses, alliances, and promises shift rapidly. The experience here is not only about the facts or historical links between cases but also about feelings and affect. I also look at Kamisan as a model for understanding how the history of state violence appears not in chronological narratives, but in repetition and connection of different events, past and present. In this way, Kamisan demonstrates the role of temporality in impunity. While Kamisan provides weekly demonstrations of the state's power to repeatedly avoid accountability, it repeats the people's demand for accountability. The network of diverse individuals with a sense that injustice has been going on too long and that the victims of stigmatization are human beings has the potential to challenge elements of the infrastructure of impunity.

Discussions during the 2010s and 2020s have hailed the creative arts as promising ways to grapple with the shortcomings of official transitional justice strategies. Authors point to the power of the arts to make visible that which was previously unseen or imperceptible, to open new spaces for engagement, especially affective engagement, and to imagine new futures.[56] In addition, as the transitional justice scholar Clara Ramírez-Barat writes, the arts create a context for victims to deal with trauma, facilitate symbolic commemoration, and raise awareness about past.[57] Many of these promises, significantly, echo earlier promises of truth and revelation, but with key differences. Unlike truth commissions and trials, which by definition are backward looking and designed to create official narratives of past events, creative acts, arts, and performance collapse linear time—the past and present—into repetitive circular time and embrace the ongoing effects of the past violence in the present. In the case of Indonesia, state propaganda and official histories, in order to keep citizens constantly vigilant and guarded, mobilize the notion that perceived past threats, such as Communism, might return. Kamisan inverts that narrative. It demonstrates the repetition of impunity itself, and the persistent marginalization of particular communities. Shifting attention from the past to the present makes the acts and elements that create the infrastructure of impunity visible, specific, and contingent.

The conclusion reflects not only on how insights from Indonesia might apply to other cases of transitional justice but also on how an infrastructure of impunity might gradually take hold in established democracies as well.

1

BUILDING THE FOUNDATION FOR IMPUNITY

Indonesia is a sprawling archipelago with many religions, ethnicities, and languages that gained its independence from the Dutch in 1945. It was united by resistance to Dutch colonialism and founding president Sukarno's charisma and nationalist rhetoric.[1] In April 1955, leaders and high-ranking officials of twenty-nine newly and nearly independent countries in Africa, Asia, and the Middle East gathered in the Indonesian city of Bandung for the Asian African Conference hosted by Sukarno. The conference produced Third World solidarity and inspired efforts to resist imperialism and engagement in power struggles between other countries. Sukarno embodied the "spirit of Bandung"—the feeling of political possibility as the formerly colonized, as Hilmar Farid puts it, sought to "assert their role in the new global order as an alternative to both sides of the Cold War divide."[2]

This was a vibrant period for arts and culture initiatives that resisted neocolonialism and imperialism. Many older Indonesians I spoke with in 1998 recalled this period fondly, noting that they may not have had prosperity and development, but they had dignity and national pride. Sukarno called 1964 "The Year of Living Dangerously"—a nod both to the revolutionary spirit and to the external threats from countries like the United States and United Kingdom that he had antagonized.[3] Other dangers included the precarious, fragile balance of opposed forces in the country. Sukarno's rule depended on balancing the power of the Communist Party (which was both popular and legal at the time), religious parties, nationalists, and the army. Sukarno called this the policy of Nationalism, Religion, Communism (NASAKOM), and factions of the army thought the policy had allowed the Communist Party of Indonesia (PKI) to gain too much influence. The 1955 elections demonstrated that the PKI had strong popular support and a clear program of significant issues.[4]

In 1957, in response to regional rebellions and other instability, President Sukarno imposed martial law, which delayed elections and consolidated political power in his hands. Delayed elections eliminated one of the PKI's opportunities to expand its power legally. Similarly, Sukarno drew on a tradition that male elders guide discussion to suggest that Guided Democracy was part of Indonesian culture.[5] In 1960, the newly passed Basic Agrarian Law led to unilateral actions (*aksi sepihak*) and land occupations by peasant unions and rural poor.[6] Sukarno invoked an ideology of Marhaenism, which drew on Marxism and socialism but was also presented as indigenous to Indonesian (Javanese) culture. Sukarno was flamboyant. He took a strong stance against neocolonial forces, and told the West to "go to hell with your aid,"[7] threatened to invade the western half of Papua New Guinea in the name of liberation (and nation building), and engaged in a policy of violent *konfrontasi* (confrontation) with Malaysia. In the early 1960s, currency devaluation and massive inflation led to unrest, and news spread of Sukarno's ill health. He had personally played such a pivotal role in keeping forces in balance that this news, and discussions of his successor, destabilized Indonesia.

In 1965, with support from the United States and other Western powers, General Suharto seized control of Indonesia following a purported coup attempt that had been quickly extinguished. In the early hours of October 1, army soldiers kidnapped six generals from their homes in Jakarta. Three who resisted were killed in their homes, and the other three were brought to an area called Lubang Buaya (near an air force base on the edge of Jakarta) and killed, their corpses left in a well and discovered several days later. One general was injured and escaped, although his daughter was killed at his home. Suharto and his associates named this coup attempt the September 30th Movement (Gerakan 30 September, or G30S, on which intelligence agents imposed the incorrect acronym GESTAPU) and blamed it on the PKI.[8] This occurred at the height of the Cold War, and the coup attempt became a "pretext for mass murder," according to the historian John Roosa.[9] The widespread and systematic killings of suspected supporters of the then-legal PKI in 1965 and 1966 left more than five hundred thousand dead and effectively destroyed the cultural, political, and intellectual Left in Indonesia. After these genocidal killings, Suharto's New Order regime formally took power in 1966 and remained in power until 1998.

Many mysteries remain to this day about the actions, intentions, and identities of those planning and executing the 1965 coup, and Indonesian and international scholars have offered a number of interpretations. Historians diverge most notably in how they interpret the link between the September 30th Movement

(G30S) and the PKI. Those in the movement claimed that their actions were taken to defend President Sukarno and prevent a coup attempt by the "Council of Generals" (Dewan Jendral) backed by the CIA. Official New Order propaganda treated the G30S and PKI as interchangeable, and unified the two with a virgule, as G30S/PKI.[10] It held the PKI responsible for the coup attempt, which in turn justified actions taken to eradicate the Left and explained the mass killings as a spontaneous running "amok," as the people acted to avenge the nation.[11] This narrative never established any clear motive for the PKI national leadership to risk a coup when they were doing very well as a legal, nonviolent movement.[12] In the 1970s, international scholars argued that the coup attempt was an intra-army affair and that the PKI was not involved at all.[13] John Roosa has suggested that PKI leader D. N. Aidit was in fact involved, but that other leaders and the Politburo were not.[14] The problem of motive and the reliability of a key infor-mant, Sjam Kamaruzaman, who might have been a double agent, complicates this scenario.[15] Another interpretation promulgated by the Suharto regime was that President Sukarno himself was the mastermind, by the logic that he did not immediately blame the PKI.[16] Others theorize that Suharto masterminded the coup, which would explain why he was not targeted and became the senior surviving general. There are plausible explanations to suggest that the planners were confident that Suharto would support them and therefore did not include him.[17] According to the historian Geoffrey Robinson, "Available evidence points at least as strongly to Suharto as one of the plotters of the movement, as it does to either the PKI or Sukarno."[18]

Still others have suggested that the coup was a foreign plot. The United States, concerned that Indonesia was on the way to becoming a Communist state, encouraged different elements to work against Sukarno and the PKI. In the 1950s, the US had backed regional rebellions in hopes of destabilizing Sukarno.[19] Based on analysis of declassified documents, the historian Geoffrey Robinson highlights the similarity between proposed US and UK strategies and actual events: "The PKI should be accused of an act of treachery, which would then provide a pretext for massive army retaliation. The perfect mechanism for set-ting such a chain of events in motion would be an act of provocation in the form of a rumor or document purporting to show plans for a right-wing coup—that would lead the PKI and other progressive forces to take rash action that could be construed as treacherous and threatening to national security."[20] The US media declared the decimation of the Left a "shining light" in Asia and celebrated Indo-nesia as a bulwark against the domino fall of Southeast Asia to Communism.[21] For decades, the US and other Western countries overlooked the mass killings and the policies that stigmatized critics and suspected leftists. Indonesian state narratives elided the mass killings, focusing on the "treachery" perpetrated by the

PKI and reiterating the threat of a Communist vengeance and resurgence. These narratives celebrated that Communism had been destroyed down to its roots by the people and the army.[22]

For the next thirty-two years, Suharto presided over an Asian development miracle underwritten by many other cases of gross human rights violations that targeted any perceived threat to the regime from religious, ethnic, political, or other sources. The New Order period was characterized by widespread violations of human rights, repression of political dissent, the stigmatization of accused Communist Party members or sympathizers, pervasive propaganda, and campaigns of terror about a "latent" Communist danger.[23]

For more than twenty years after Suharto's rule ended in 1998, the official historical narrative has been critiqued; nevertheless, it remains powerful and has left indelible marks, even for generations of Indonesians born after the New Order period, and even for those in school after Suharto's fall, when the propaganda was less systematically applied. Although the official narrative is no longer monolithic, its logics, including the Communist threat and the stigmatization of suspected Communists and leftists, still structure common sense and inform many legal, political, and bureaucratic policies and cases. The narrative took hold and persists through various elements: the built environment, museums, media and film, policy, memory, history, education, and, crucially, the mobilization of affect and sentiment. It persists even in the bureaucracy and the law itself. The infrastructure describes how these elements form a network of tangible and intangible, affective elements that circulate things, ideas, feelings, and power through time and space and make this narrative and its ramifications persistent, even when they are challenged half a century later.

Collectively, this can be further specified as an "infrastructure of impunity," and it helps explain why efforts to remember and redress historical wrongs and to "tell the truth" about the past do not necessarily lead to more just outcomes. Over half a century, truth and revelation have not transformed the infrastructure so much as they have themselves been shaped by it.

At the end of the New Order in 1998, Indonesian civil society groups sought to implement transitional justice processes. There were no international interventions, though many organizations in the country received international funding. Many survivors of 1965 testified about their experiences, and many analyses also demonstrated the falsity of the New Order narrative.[24] The state narrative about the events of 1965 has been challenged, and new information about the time, while not endorsed or disseminated by the state, is available. Victims and survivors have even launched successful cases to challenge the effects of stigmatizing policies.[25]

And yet the false narratives remain viscerally powerful and structure everyday life, even fifty-seven years after the original events and twenty-five years after the end of the regime. This paradox—of truth telling and the stubborn persistence of false narratives that render the state impervious to accountability—happens through the work of building an infrastructure of impunity, and challenges the expectations and suppositions of transitional justice. The state-crafted propaganda supported it with false evidence, embedded it in annual rituals and commemorations, enshrined it in museums, and broadcast it in films. The affective power in the narrative—the ways that it is rendered visceral—is achieved through repetition, experience, embodied realities, and social and familial pressure, and it is structured by state institutions, policies, and practices.

The genocide studies scholar Kerry Whigham describes "resonate violence," which captures the importance of affective processes—for example, the gradual introduction of stigmatizing legislation prior to the Holocaust and the justification of genocidal policies and physical violence—but also the "residual, felt aspect of violence, which continues to perform long after the initial genocide or physically violent act."[26] Likewise, the creation and extension of the infrastructure of impunity involves affective elements that reach back and project forward in time, especially in legal concepts and bureaucratic practices. For example, state policies and legal or pseudolegal processes that encourage or mandate discrimination, stigmatization, dehumanization, and violence are both incremental and spectacular. Over time, these policies, actions, and injustices are normalized, even by targeted individuals and groups.[27] Bystanders and beneficiaries fail to see how their ideas of law and nationalism are grounded in the denial of rights to massive numbers of citizens.

Historical narratives—protean and malleable as they are—about the events of 1965 formed the foundation of the infrastructure of impunity. Some individuals and groups challenged the official versions of history throughout the New Order years, but despite factual challenges, the logics and ramifications of the official narrative persisted unchallenged, even after the acceptance of some new facts. The historical narratives were challenged and countered on factual grounds but not on affective grounds.

Visceral, affective, and common-sense residues of state propaganda persist even after their official broadcast wanes or ends and their content has been challenged factually. The history commissioned by the New Order has had a long postcoup half-life. Political feelings and realities may be built on ghosts of the past and the specter of future threats, but their consequences are tangible and immediate.

The histories crafted by Suharto's regime celebrated his role in rescuing the nation from cruel Communists, renewed the threat of latent Communism, and demanded vigilance from all citizens. These New Order histories provide very little context for the period between independence and 1965. Instead, New Order official histories reductively interpreted regional rebellions, tensions in the new nation, and instances of violence as part of an ongoing threat of Communism that was present at the start of the nationalist struggle.[28] They effectively erased the Left's contributions to national independence and nation building, and young professionals studying abroad and training in nonaligned countries were forced into exile after 1965.[29]

The official narrative of the coup attempt holds that the PKI was responsible and that on the night of September 30, 1965, members of Gerwani, the PKI-affiliated women's organization, danced naked for the generals and then savagely mutilated them: castrating them, gouging their eyes out, and smashing their bodies into a well. Scholars have proven that generals were not castrated and argued that the role of the PKI is not clear.[30] Nevertheless, falsified media reports became the evidence for (New Order) state histories,[31] which in turn became the basis for propaganda films, museums, national rituals and commemorations, and school history texts—cumulatively, a narrative that has obdurately resisted the force of facts and truth telling.

Work on the Sacred Pancasila Monument at Lubang Buaya (Monumen Pancasila Sakti Lubang Buaya) began in 1967, and the monument opened in 1969 and was formally dedicated in 1972. *Pancasila* refers to the "Five Principles," the founding ideology of Indonesia articulated by Sukarno as an amalgamation of monotheism, nationalism, and socialism.[32] The New Order state built the museum and monument at the site where the generals' bodies were found in a well, Lubang Buaya, which translates literally as "the crocodile hole" (or "pit"). Lubang Buaya is an important site for the infrastructure of impunity, as it shapes the built environment to validate and authenticate the state's narrative. For example, the site is wide open and a visitor can easily imagine the women's dance. At the time of the "coup attempt," it was owned by the air force and was being used as a site to train youth and other organizations (including women's organizations) to participate in the low-intensity, ongoing war against the Federation of Malaysia (1963–66). The PKI was an enthusiastic supporter of Sukarno's "Crush Malaysia" campaign (Ganyang Malaysia).[33] The New Order narrative used the fact that the bodies were found at this site to implicate the organizations present there, as well as the air force, in the killings of the generals.

In the fifty years since the killings, Jakarta has grown up around the site and it has become a large and open area in the midst of an otherwise densely populated sprawl typical of Indonesian cities: mosques, markets, strip malls, office buildings, bus terminals, and traffic. The museum is set off from the main road by a long and shady entrance road that in the early morning bustles with visitors there to exercise. The spot is a green space for recreation and meeting as well as pilgrimages and elementary, middle, and high school visits.

As visitors pass through the gate to the complex, they must pay an entry fee and buy a small guidebook that provides a condensed version of the state narrative for visitors to take home. Despite new historical analysis, the guidebook, revised in 2013, reproduces the New Order propaganda. A passage in the short foreword describes the events of 1965 as a coup by the September 30th Movement of the PKI. "As a first step," it reads, "they kidnapped and then murdered several officers and high-ranking officials of the Indonesian National Army [TNI AD] who were seen as their political enemies. In a relatively short time, the rebellion was successfully annihilated by the Armed Forces of the Republic of Indonesia [ABRI] and the people who follow Pancasila [Pancasilaist]"—as if the ideology itself eradicated the opposing ideology and the people who believed in it. The narrative then moves further back in history: "From the PKI rebellions in 1948 and 1965 we agree that Communism is an ideology that is dangerous and that we must be continually vigilant [waspadai secara terus menerus], especially in conditions like this." These open-ended "conditions" are perpetual and omnipresent. According to those who built it, the museum will "build the people's caution and resistance by presenting several treasons and betrayal done by the PKI since 1945" as well as demonstrate "the destruction of Communism by the People of Indonesia along with the armed forces."[34]

Opposite the museum, steps lead down to a long, tiled path and then up again to the well and monument. The monument consists of enormous bronze statues of the martyred generals towering over an open tiled area with a bronze relief around the base that depicts Indonesian history from independence to the beginning of the New Order. The relief portrays early independence through to the Sukarno years as chaotic and violent, in contrast to the prosperous, orderly times after Suharto came to power. The plaza leading up to the monument features the well, covered with an ornate roof and carved pillars, where the generals' bodies were found. Adjacent to the well, a small building labeled in English, "Torturing Verandah," with large open windows to view the inside, features life-sized mannequins and audio recordings of the alleged torture of the generals by the Communists and especially Gerwani, the women's organization.[35] The sign states that the diorama is based on evidence presented at the Extraordinary Military Tribunals (Mahkamah Militer Luar Biasa, or Mahmillub).

The Sacred Pancasila Museum, or Paseban (Paseban/Museum Pancasila Sakti) was opened in 1982. The Museum of the Betrayal of the PKI (Communist) (Museum Pengkhianatan PKI [Komunis]) was formally opened in 1992.[36] In 2003, a Relic Room (Ruang Relik) was opened that displays clothes that the generals were wearing the night they were killed, as well as their personal belongings, including tennis rackets, golf clubs, and photos. The Sacred Pancasila Museum was renovated in 2013.

FIGURE 1.1.   Students viewing the Sacred Pancasila Monument at Lubang Buaya (Monumen Pancasila Sakti Lubang Buaya) in 2017. Photo by the author.

Sites and objects are important to how individuals remember. Jonah Rubin writes about how "nonliving actants"—by which he means material, nonhuman elements—affect the dynamics of memory.[37] The Lubang Buaya site is an important actant: it connects past with present, and individuals' personal memories with national scripts. The site is significant in national myths as the place where multiple acts occurred that supposedly prove the evil of the Communist Party. In his discussion of genocide memorial sites, Kerry Whigham writes, "Sites of memory aim to generate individuals for whom the past becomes an orienting force in their lives, one that influences the way they view the world and the decisions they make. They do this not only through pure transfer of factual knowledge or history, but by engaging . . . the series of practices that provide embodied ways of feeling and knowing—a knowing that exceeds that which can be learned from reading a book or watching a film."[38] Demonstrating that the New Order was adroit at creating a sense of place, Lubang Buaya is designed to provoke a visceral disgust at Communist betrayal and a persistent threat of future recurrences. The monument and museum attach the narrative and propaganda to a physical place.

In addition, October 1 has been declared the day of Sacred Pancasila. On this day, the media and public attention focus on the site and its ceremonies. Students might visit the sacred site a few times on school trips, but politicians visit it repeatedly. Its events and ceremonies are broadcast on TV to trigger the memories of those who have visited there before, to convey the importance of visiting for those who have not, and to awaken vigilance against the PKI.

Throughout the late New Order (1985–97), the importance of place, and of this site specifically, was reinforced through the official narrative, and especially through mandatory viewings of a propaganda film that is woven all but inescapably into the site. The site reproduces the film's confabulation of history, and the film seamlessly prefigures and shapes visitors' experience of the historic site. In the mid-1980s the New Order regime commissioned the film *Treachery of the September 30th Movement/PKI* (Pengkhianatan G30S/PKI).[39] The film was based on histories written by Nugroho Notosusanto, the primary army historian. It won various awards in Indonesia and held box office records for more than a decade, which is not surprising since the New Order government required students of all ages, civil servants, regional elites, and others to pay admission and watch the film every year on September 30.[40] It was shown annually on screens set up in fields, as well as on the state-run television channel. The regime prohibited discussion of the film, even in classrooms. Without discussion, illogical elements of the film and narrative were repeated, memorized, and internalized viscerally. The film circulated throughout the archipelago and established a shared national narrative.

The film powerfully connects viewers to the monument and museum and anchors the dramatic events of the film to a specific location. It also connects distant viewers across the archipelago to the monument and historic site so widely featured in school texts and national narratives. By 2015, the propaganda narrative was so deeply embedded in place and historical text that clips from the film were played as actual documentary and archival footage in contemporary televised programs related to 1965.[41] Visitors remember the film's "documentation" of the past (which is reproduced in the museum's dioramas of the past and reinserted into national discussions in place of actual archival footage of events) at the same time that the film establishes a false narrative about the site. Both the film and school visits to the museum became collective experiences for most Indonesians that established a national script and a false screen memory.

The film—over three and a half hours long—is in color with foreboding music and dramatizes the official version of the coup attempt. The film opens not with documentary footage but with a shot that looks up at the bronzed statues of the martyred generals at the Lubang Buaya monument, followed by a slow pan over the bronze relief that depicts the New Order version of history. It concentrates on the days before and after September 30, 1965, in Jakarta and begins in earnest with actors playing PKI leaders in a smoke-filled room, plotting the violence and their premeditated intent to torture and kill. According to the film, the PKI planned to kidnap the seven generals presumed to be part of the army's Council of Generals and use the initial coup attempt as a pretext for its own coup, to take over the city and "secure" Sukarno.

Suharto is the hero of the film. When he hears that the Communists have assassinated the generals, he counters the Communist leaders, portrayed as bloodthirsty, by proclaiming that the army will crush the rebellion and avenge the generals' deaths. The film closes with the burial of the generals at the Lubang Buaya monument and an exhortation to the people of Indonesia to carry on the struggle and remain vigilant (against Communism). Despite the lack of histori-cal referents, aside from the location of the monument, the film's genre, use of sound effects and music, visual elements, and dramatic reenactment of events all make the story emotionally powerful.

The site and the film have become self-referential and mutually reinforcing. Many of the dioramas at the museum are based on scenes from the dramatic film, where actors representing the generals are abducted from their homes. Conversely, when students go to the museum, they remember the narrative and feelings from the film, but in a context where they are primed to believe that the film depicts actual historical events that occurred at the place they are visiting.

Together the film, museum, and monument site are the foundation of the infrastructure of impunity, and one that hasn't been dislodged by efforts at human rights truth telling or counterfactual narratives for the millennial gen-eration. They are inescapably annealed, the site amplifying the affective power of the film by creating the sense that it is based on actual historical events that occurred at an actual place.

In 2017, Suraya Affif, an anthropologist at the University of Indonesia, and I took a group of twenty-two students to the monument as part of a three-day work-shop on human rights and ethnography. The previous year, I had visited the site with her semester-long ethnography course and we had decided that a field trip would be an excellent conclusion to our workshop. On the day of the workshop visit, I was stopped at the entrance. I had been to the monument several times before without any difficulty, in conjunction with the ethnography class, always traveling by taxi and meeting the students at the entrance area. This time, I was told that because I was a foreign citizen, I was not allowed to enter. Suraya was waiting by the entrance gate in her car, where I joined her. She insisted to the guard that we were there for a university workshop and that we did not want copies of the booklet included in the admission fee. Eventually we were taken to see a uniformed major inside. Suraya explained that if it was a museum, then it needed to be public. He surprised us by citing UNESCO information related to museums and public access, acknowledging that it should be open to the public. He produced an official document noting that the park was now closed to international visitors. After a longer back and forth, he said that if I were to visit again, I would need an official letter in addition to other permits I had secured— a specific permit from the armed forces. He finally conceded that we did not have to buy the booklets and waved a hand so that I could enter and join our students.

Before we entered the park, we had students write about their memories from earlier visits, and afterward we had them record their impressions from this visit. This exercise revealed the affective force of the film and museum, mutually constituted, and the narrative of impunity that both support, which explains the persistence of impunity even in the face of facts and truth telling. While the place provided a link to ostensibly authentic historical material, the film, although less authentically historical or factual, shaped and even prefigured students' experiences of the site. One student wrote, "This place is neatly arranged, with many trees and the atmosphere is green, but for some reason, this place reminds me of a cemetery or a photo of the 'forest' atmosphere at the time of the kidnapping that we can see on the internet [in the film]." Another student commented on her reaction as she walked down the tree-lined road into the main area of the museum: "Since I arrived at the front gate of the museum, I had begun to feel dizzy and my stomach was not good." Several other students noted different bodily sensations related to their memories of past visits to the museum.

While we did not purchase booklets this time, I had several copies from previous visits. The book encapsulates key elements of state propaganda. The cover proclaims, "Be careful . . . and watch yourself so that events like this are not repeated again." In their field notes, several students highlighted and copied a similar injunction that appears in bronze below the monument. The rationale for the museum, commemorating but also conjuring a future threat, is stated plainly: "By visualizing a few stories of rebellion both on the monument relief and in the form of dioramas in the museum, along with preserving places that have a connection with the rebellion, we hope that visitors will know the tragedy which once befell [*menimpa*] our nation that was done by the Communists, and it is hoped that vigilance toward the danger of Communism will increase."[42] The place is summoned to authenticate the historical narratives, conveyed through repeated viewings of the dramatic film, through the embodied and affective experience of actually being at the historic site.

At the same time, the powerful affect of vengeance is simultaneously introduced and disavowed. The epigraph of the booklet reproduces General Nasution's words from the ceremony moving the corpses to the hero's cemetery: "Betrayal toward all of us and all our brothers and sisters has been perpetrated, but we can't take the desire for revenge into our hearts." The creators of the park demand vigilance but exhort visitors not to seek vengeance. Since Communism has been destroyed (without any mention of the people who were killed by the people and the army), there is always the unstated possibility that Communists might seek vengeance, which in the official logic increases the looming threat and justifies repressive measures taken against those who might pursue it.[43]

On another visit in 2016, I was in the museum when a large group of senior high school students (*sekolah menengah atas*) entered. They went through in groups, some reading the captions and looking at each diorama and each episode of history, narrated to show the treachery of the PKI. They had selfie sticks and were eager to take their photos in front of the sometimes quite gruesome dioramas. They were very excited to see a foreigner there and immediately began to request photos with me. When I asked them what they thought of the exhibits, they laughed, and they became less interested in talking to me when I asked them if this was accurate history. The question itself rendered them momentarily speechless, as they understood that I was asking about historical events rather than sharing in the same moment of fear, national pride, and a school field trip adventure that should be celebrated by all visitors, even foreigners. I sensed that they were aware of the challenges to the narrative and facts, aspects of which had been questioned in the media, and yet the excitement and heroics of the national myth were still compelling and sensational—or they understood, at least, the danger of questioning that myth. As other interactions demonstrated, it was possible to remain committed to the national myths and heroics even as their details were interrogated and challenged. These students had made it to the site and wanted their souvenir photos within the national myth, not a factual debate over the accuracy of the scenes depicted.

On another visit, I was shocked to see a group of about fifty prekindergarten or kindergarten children with two adults gathered at the meeting point, lined up with their water bottles slung over their orange and white batik shirts. I had heard that the guidelines had changed and younger students were no longer visiting Lubang Buaya, and yet these students clearly did not meet the new third-grade minimum. These kinds of class trips mixed pleasure (school trips often combined the museum with a visit to the Ancol Dreamland and Fantasy World aquatic theme parks in Jakarta), adventure, and a group context in which kids were vulnerable to teachers and other authorities as well as to peer pressure. On the day of our workshop, extended families were visiting with young children, and many of our students commented that they were sad to see young children playing in a park dedicated to violence.

The museum is designed to provide a visceral experience. The indoor museum is dimly lit and has one path that wends through a historical chronicle, broken up by a few rock installations. Visitors enter the museum in a dark room with backlit mosaic photos and purplish collages of other historical photographs. These composite images are presented as evidence to authenticate the fabricated dioramas that illustrate the state narrative in the rest of the museum. The first image, titled "The Betrayal by the PKI of Their Own Country in 1948," includes documentary images from a PKI rebellion in 1948 to suggest the PKI's recurrent and persistent threats to the nation. The second, "Exhumation of the Corpses of the Generals Who Were Victims of PKI Cruelty during G30SPKI," uses grainy images from the well to ground narratives about the evil deeds of the Communist women said to have tortured and killed the generals and dumped them in the well at this site. The third and last, "The Trial of the PKI at the Extraordinary Military Court," suggests that the actions of Suharto and his associates were legal and followed due process. These images all have some tenuous connection to past events, but they are tied inextricably to the patently distorted interpretations in the dioramas and narratives.

When they leave this room, visitors are led through a long, dim pathway lined by chronological dioramas on the walls that display exaggerated scenes of betrayal by the PKI since the early nationalist years, effectively distorting or reversing historical evidence that leftists contributed significantly to the early nation. Almost all of the incidents are bloody, and the terse three-line captions reduce much greater complexity to a redundant narrative of the PKI's violence and betrayal of the nation.

The upstairs dioramas depict the abduction and murder of the generals based on the propaganda film. Our workshop students reflected on how the drops of blood scattered in the dioramas provided evidence that helped them to imagine PKI cruelty as they recalled their earlier school visits: "This museum showed how vile the PKI was toward national heroes. I still remember there were spots of blood and facts that made me imagine how cruel the PKI's actions were. From the trip, my teacher said the national heroes were murdered and tortured by Communists. At that time, of course, I believed and swallowed the information given. History books also solidified the confirmation of that story. Honestly, this story gave me imaginations [nightmares] for the next years."

The dioramas acquire historical legitimacy and certification because they are presented in the museum at the very place where the violence and betrayal were said to occur. While the park has the surface effect of historical fact and certainty, visitors experience it as prefigured through an influential and all but ubiquitous propaganda film that shapes how they experience the putatively more historically grounded and factual site. To walk through the museum, in other words, is to walk through the film. The dioramas depicting the supposed coup attempt reproduce scenes from the film's version of history. History, this site, and the propaganda film are mutually reinforcing and inform each other. And this is a foundation of the larger infrastructure of impunity, because that impunity relies on an affective-historical narrative that emphasizes perpetual, forever threats and plays on the emotions to elicit equally visceral responses from visitors and viewers. These kinds of narratives, which rely on affect more than on historical facticity or authenticity, can never really be debunked or dislodged by subsequent restorative or transitional efforts at truth telling or setting the record straight. As generations of schoolchildren, film viewers, and visitors experience it, the story was never "about" the historical facts to begin with; rather, it acted on them emotionally and became embodied in powerful affects of fear, vengeance, and vigilance. This apprehension and sense of a continuous threat in the past and future is a core element of impunity. The depiction of the past events, tied to a projection of future threats, enforces a logic that endlessly justifies the treatment of those accused of being Communists. The complicity secured here for inhumane treatment extends impunity and the cycle of knowing and not knowing further into the future, thereby diminishing the effects of survivor testimony.

Impunity for 1965 entailed looking further back in history to project the threat of Communism further into the future. "There have been threats to the unitary state of Indonesia throughout history," the museum booklet narrates. "These rebellions have sought to replace Pancasila with other ideologies including Communism."[44] Tensions emerged between Islamists and leftists or socialists in the early years of Indonesian independence. Significant regional and religious rebellions occurred between 1945 and 1965. But these various issues are not described, and the threat from Communism is projected both backward and forward in time and across the archipelago, so that all citizens can recall the violence they have witnessed, experienced, or heard about and attach it to state narratives. Those narratives consolidate memories of past violence as solely and entirely Communist violence and project that threat endlessly into the future, as in the booklet's statement that "the efforts to implement the ideology of Communism in Indonesia have never stopped."[45]

For example, in the Lubang Buaya museum, the first wall-sized photo, "The Betrayal by the PKI of Their Own Country in 1948," refers to the Madiun Incident, which has been used as evidence in public discourse to justify the continued exclusion of leftists from public life, to justify past violence, and to project future threats. In 1948 in Madiun, East Java, leftist officials and military units clashed with republican forces and declared a "National Front Government." Evidence suggests that this action was not coordinated by the national Communist Party.

Republican and international leaders accused the PKI of trying to overthrow the nationalist government. In response, Masyumi, an Islamic party and organization, called for a holy war against the atheistic Communists. Affiliated civil defense units arrested thirty-five thousand PKI members and killed many of them, including prominent leaders.[46] National PKI leaders insisted that this was a "provocation . . . to entrap and annihilate" the party; nevertheless, it was seen as evidence of PKI "treachery" and provided ready proof of the PKI's disloyalty in 1965.[47] The affair was politically and militarily devastating to the Left and profoundly damaged its relationships with the Muslim bloc.[48]

In 1953, a group of Muslim veterans demanded that the Madiun anniversary be commemorated. PKI leader Aidit defended the PKI, and according to the sociologist Saskia Wieringa and the human rights lawyer Nursyahbani Katjasungkana, the "court agreed that the PKI should not be accused of treachery."[49] Politically and legally, the affair was closed in the early 1950s, but the specter of PKI betrayal, as evidenced by the history of Madiun and 1965, is still cited today. Wieringa and Katjasungkana argue that there were great losses in the years of violent struggle for independence and the early nationalist period, and that forces from other armed regional rebellions were offered amnesty; however, there was no discussion of amnesty for the PKI. While other issues that inspired rebellion, such as regional autonomy, have been addressed, they write, "there is no longer any space to fight for the issues the PKI stood for."[50]

As the Madiun issue suggests, the feeling of threat, fear, endangerment, and victimization for the majority Muslim population is especially strong and affectively powerful. Wieringa and Katjasungkana argue that prominent representations of the Muslim point of view of the Madiun Incident see Muslims as victims and ignore the complex political dynamics of the time, including tensions within the Left and various republican groups over how to respond to the Dutch, as well as the legacies of the Japanese occupation.[51]

Historical narratives are part of the infrastructure of impunity, and falsified narratives, omissions, and distortions are the foundation for propaganda and policies; nevertheless, correction of the historical facts does not necessarily remedy half a century of propaganda and policy justification, because that remedy is not simply a matter of correcting the facts or contextualizing the difficulties of the time. It is a matter of the affective power of the narratives and the concrete policies of stigmatization and widespread social complicity justified by those narratives. The propaganda film *Treachery of the September 30th Movement/PKI*, for instance, like the artfully fabricated and curated museum dioramas, reminds audiences that the PKI had staged a coup in 1948 in Madiun and links this coup to other violence experienced in the early years of independence, to imply that the PKI had killed people throughout the country. The film features scenes such as the burning of religious books, designed to enrage Muslims, and graphically depicts violence and desecration against Muslims. These scenes are not based on documentary evidence but were created for the movie by the renowned Indonesian director Arifin C. Noer.

The second wall-sized compilation image features another distorted historical referent: the exhumation of the corpses from the well. The propaganda narrative held that Communist women were waiting at the airfield, dancing naked, when the kidnapped generals arrived. Media reports depicted a depraved, immoral atmosphere. According to press accounts and later narratives, the women immediately began to torture the generals, gouging their eyes out and castrating them. Saskia Wierenga observes that media reports evoked *kuntilanak*, the evil spirit of a woman who died in childbirth and appeared as a beautiful woman, to trigger culturally resonant associations of fear, and that they claimed that women had received injections to increase their energy as they competed to engage in the greatest number of sexual acts. PKI leader Aidit allegedly encouraged them to discard religious teachings and to compete for a golden horse award by killing a general.[52] These narratives built disgust at the idea that the PKI, and especially affiliated women, were beyond humanity, and they linked the amoral activities to a plan by the party leadership. And since the army closed down the press, with the exception of the two daily papers it controlled, the media became a tool for spreading propaganda and hate and discrediting Sukarno and the Communist Party.[53]

Access to archival documents is limited in Indonesia. Scholars have demonstrated that the story is not true and even that the creation and perpetuation of this lurid and grotesque narrative was shaped by CIA interventions in the creation of literature and films.[54] The rest of the narrative, designed to inspire disgust and fear, drew on religiously and culturally powerful tropes, fabricated evidence, false testimonies, and documentation extracted under torture. The women were detained, tortured, and slandered without any charges, trial, or other elements of due process. Wieringa has interviewed survivors and carefully gone through the propaganda from the military newspapers and notes that the story about the women's organization, Gerwani, took some time to develop, but once it did, there were clear indications that the army must have been widely distributing the same story, because it was repeated almost verbatim in different media. Wieringa suggests that the narrative about Gerwani resonates with conservative male, religious fears of women's power.[55] The affective power of the fabricated narrative is intensified though imagery and parallels to Javanese epic drama (*wayang*) and cultural symbols as well as religious elements. *Wayang* performances adapt Sanskrit epics such as the *Ramayana* and *Mahabharata* and furnish ubiquitous metaphors for daily and political life in Java and nationally.[56]

FIGURE 1.2.   The bronze relief below the monument at Lubang Buaya depicts the chaotic atmosphere described in the propaganda. Women are scantily clad and wear proud expressions as one dances beside a body being forced head-first into a hole with an open-mouthed crocodile below. Photo by the author.

As Wieringa explains, stories of sexual depravity at Lubang Buaya resonate with the *gara gara* element of the *wayang*, in which disturbance of the natural equilibrium is resolved by the hero, whose mastery in part relies on control of lust and lower impulses. The sexual slander, she observes, also triggered "Islamic fears of uncontrolled sexual powers of women" and in Bali prompted Hindu obligations to purify the land.[57] Roosa notes that Sukarno attempted to calm the nation and underscore the absurdity of the army's claims, but his remarks were silenced and distorted.[58]

Taken together, the perceived historical evidence of the Madiun Incident and narratives that the Communists were evil, castrating atheists created an unsettling and threatening mood for Muslims. The propaganda film dramatizes this atmospheric menace and reproduces it for subsequent generations. One scene in the film depicts a Gerwani woman slicing the face of one of the generals with a razor blade, and another features a general's daughter crying hysterically as her father is shot and killed while she watches. In one especially memorable scene for university students who participated in our trip (a scene recalled in the museum context),

Pierre Tendean—General Nasution's assistant—confronts those who came to abduct his superior and states that he himself is Nasution, thus allowing the general to flee while his assistant is killed. Scholars have noted that the film and monuments, in addition to graphically demonstrating the barbarity and cruelty of the Communist Party and its followers, conjure scenes of chaos to highlight the contrast with the order and calm of the New Order.[59]

Even younger people who are distant from the original events and may not have been subjected to mandatory screenings of the G30S film nevertheless have absorbed its ambiance and have been instructed by religious leaders on how to respond. One student did a miniethnography that examined collective memories of 1965 with members of two "hard-line" Muslim groups. Demonstrations by the Islamic Defenders Front (Front Pembela Islam) are widely publicized in the media, so she asked her interviewee (a young member of the group) if he had ever participated. He described the few he had attended and, unprompted, mentioned the money he had received for participating. As he described the reasons for the demonstrations—food stalls that remained open during fasting month, discos and other sinful activities, or the West and NGOs—she followed up to ask whether he had demonstrated against the PKI. He had not specifically, but his reaction illustrates how easily a link was forged between other causes and the PKI: he told her there is always a banner that warns of the latent dangers of the PKI. She concluded that "they never demonstrated specially about the PKI and Communists or atheists, but every action, whoever and whatever they protest, is always connected to Communism. According to them this is a way to remind the society of the latent danger of Communism." She asked the man whether there really still are Communists, and he acknowledged that the actual PKI are no longer there but said that their influence remains, and that the sins he enumerated "originate from the PKI." He became emotional as he said that the important thing is that the "PKI have no god. . . . If there is a PKI again, in Indonesia everyone will become atheist." Anxieties about piety, morality, and the role of Islam, explicitly and implicitly connected to the narratives about the PKI, animate public discourse and justify various policies that limit the rights of minority groups. Such anxieties are easily mobilized by political parties and leaders to consolidate their power.

The myth that Gerwani women castrated the generals is so powerful and pervasive that most students at our workshop were surprised to read Benedict Anderson's 1987 article that analyzes the autopsy report and shows that the generals were not castrated.[60] In fact, Roosa notes, Sukarno had also urged journalists to publicize the autopsy report in 1965, but the papers that reported his remarks noted only that he had scolded journalists and urged them to write the truth.[61] The army's papers went further, finding counterevidence in the form of false testimonies extracted under torture from women alleged to be Gerwani members to support its propaganda story.[62] Anderson's article was widely discussed in activist circles in 1998 as the New Order ended, but it has not changed popular memory. (Even without access to international scholarship based on autopsy reports, the castration narrative could easily be questioned. The new building built in 2003 that displays the clothes the generals were wearing at the time show blood stains on shirts but no damage to their pants.)

The New Order state's version of 1965 was never exclusively about the transfer of factual knowledge or propaganda in schools, history books, and state broadcasts. It was also about embodied ways of feeling, the creation of a logic in which fear governs but is also abstract, mutable, and easily mobilized for an endless array of threats and can become an orienting force in the present, influencing how people view the state, their neighbors, policies, and expectations. When students visit the monument on class field trips, the propaganda film, history lectures, and history books have already stimulated their emotions. In addition, most students have already been instructed by their families about the dangers of Communism. Even when their families did not believe state propaganda, students recalled that they were cautioned against asking questions or voicing dissenting opinions.

Our students remembered their school visits as contexts where movies came to life in their minds. Some of them experienced resurgent trauma as they entered the monument, even more than a decade after their visits as elementary school students. As kids, they were primed both rationally and viscerally to believe a particular narrative, reinforced in most cases by families and authorities at schools. At the site, they felt as if they were seeing ground zero. As one of the students put it, seeing the dioramas and propaganda there made it *bulat*: that is, complete, or round. One student who visited Lubang Buaya for the first time with our group noted the congruence between the museum and monument and the official history: "Everything is as told in history books and films. The dioramas were created to be like the branding of the authorities to support the stories that had been published."

The well, called the "crocodile hole," where the women allegedly threw the mutilated corpses, was memorable and terrifying for the students. One student recalled the fears conjured by the name of the place: "When I actually visited Lubang Buaya in elementary school, I thought of Lubang Buaya as a dark hole that was filled with crocodiles, ready to eat the generals." Their teacher's words only intensified this fear: "At that time, I felt scared of the PKI assassinators of these generals. This fear was strengthened with a statement from Pak Kusno, who was our IPS [social studies] teacher, when we arrived at Lubang Buaya. He stated that the symbol of the PKI was a hammer and sickle because of this sickness that the PKI used to slaughter and kill Muslims. [Another teacher] also stated that 'a number of women danced on top of the generals' dead bodies.'"

Other students recalled that teachers instructed them to pray after viewing the well. Even long after the events, they remembered the fear provoked by their teachers, other students, and their memories of the film. The film links the violent capture of the generals at their homes to the crocodile hole. One student said, "Before leaving for Lubang Buaya, we [students] watched a screening of the film *Pengkhianatan G30S/PKI* in school. . . . [T]here was one scene that I vividly remember, which was when Ade Irma filled her face with her father's blood."[63] Another student recalled fears of possession: "Me and my friends felt scared. The jokes during the bus ride about the hole that contained a crocodile that could devour its prey instantly disappeared, replaced by images of the bodies mutilated and thrown into the hole. I still remember how my friends and I felt scared when we tried to see the crocodile's hole and the inside of the hole. One of my friends boastingly said, 'Don't stare into it for long; you might get possessed.' Maybe it's because our teacher said to pray once we saw Lubang Buaya." The instruction to pray reinforced the students' identity as religious people (in contrast to atheist Communists) and suggested that if they strayed for a moment from religion, they could become possessed. The students reflected on the compulsion as well as the dares from others to look in the well, which glowed red from a light bulb inside, symbolizing the generals' blood.

Another student had involuntary chills as she reflected on the well and how it terrified her: "I remember one of the generals was thrown in alive, to the point where I felt the chills imagining how they would have felt, squeezed and distressed. At that time, what was on my mind was that the PKI was a cruel party. I remember in elementary school, it was compulsory to watch the G30S/PKI film in school. I still remember the Tendean shooting scene and the scene of an eye being scooped [by the Gerwani]. Since elementary school, even until high school, I still thought that Communism was an ideology that was evil and inherently opposed to the Pancasila."

The torture house located near the well, our students remembered, also provoked fear. Some recalled and commented on its affectively powerful sound recordings, so realistic as they entered the building (or, after the renovations when visitors could not enter the building, looked inside through the windows) and confronted life-sized replicas of violent Communists in the act of torturing the generals, all of which was said to have occurred at this very place. None of them recalled the actual words, but many of them recalled the sounds of shooting and yelling, and the cries of pain. One of the students was old enough to remember the original museum, before it was renovated, from a 1985 visit when he was in third grade and entered the building. The original experience was immersive, he said: "In the past, the torture house had not been renovated . . . but it was still shaped like the old house and we could go inside, complete with the sound of the atmosphere of torture which was fear inspiring for years. Now it is different because we only see from the outside, so the ambience is not felt and does not make us carried away." In the past, he said, "it was more traumatic due to the sound ambience at the torture site."

The current (renovated) exhibit still features life-sized mannequins, which many students who had not seen the original exhibit also saw as particularly powerful and traumatizing. One said, "I vividly remember the exhibit that displayed the torture of the generals, located not far from the death hole [well]. The figures and the event were enough to make me feel traumatized." Another commented again on the power of the recordings in the torture house: "The recordings are old recordings that have never been replaced since they were first installed there. The security seems to intentionally never replace them to pull visitors into the past, making the visualization of a tortured and bloody statue become increasingly real. The recording was also filled with sound effects such

FIGURE 1.3. Inside the yellow house of the "torturing verandah" at Lubang Buaya, life-sized mannequins depict the beating of Major General S. Parman. A window in the background shows where visitors can look in to the building. Photo by the author.

FIGURE 1.4. Students from the workshop and families visiting Lubang Buaya crowd together to look into the "torturing verandah" building to see the exhibit demonstrating the torture of the generals at the site. Photo by the author.

as gunshots, punches, and shouts." Sound is a powerful medium for conveying affect.[64] The "background" noise of gunshots, screams, and yelling makes visitors feel they are in another moment. It is like stepping into the movie, powerfully conveying verisimilitude without truth.

The propaganda narrative remains viscerally powerful more than fifty years after the supposed coup attempt, and more than twenty years after the formal end of the regime empowered by it. It has endured and survived numerous attempts to correct the historical record, challenge the narrative factually, and speak the truth as an antidote to the propaganda. As part of the infrastructure of impunity, the narrative is made affectively powerful in public screenings of the film, visits to the museum and monument, and broadcasts and commemorations screened on television that trigger memories of the immersive propaganda experience from elementary school.

In 2012, the National Human Rights Commission (Komnas HAM) completed a report over one thousand pages long, which concluded that the detention, forced labor, stigmatization, and killings that followed the supposed coup attempt were gross violations of human rights.[65] An International People's Tribunal has ruled that these violations constituted a genocide.[66] And yet the museum has been expanded and the original exhibits remain without any emendation or acknowledgment of these findings. After the New Order ended in 1998, the film was no longer screened annually on the night of September 30. The minister of information stopped the screenings four months after Suharto's rule ended, because it emphasized "a cult of personality" (of Suharto).[67] Although the film was no longer required viewing, a 2002 survey by the popular weekly magazine *Tempo* indicated that at least 97 percent of 1,101 students surveyed had seen the film, and 87 percent had seen it more than once. Even after years without mandatory viewings, the film remains a powerful and widespread screen memory. School history texts were rewritten in the early 2000s to redact the link between G30S and PKI. Before these texts could be adopted as curriculum, however, the enthusiasm for reform diminished and they were burned.[68] Nevertheless, many historical sources are available to download online. While not endorsed by the government, counterhistories and media articles have challenged New Order narratives both as a whole and in particular details. Eventually the government sponsored an official symposium (see chapter 4) to craft a new narrative about this "dark page of Indonesia's history," and survivors and advocacy groups continued to publicly demand justice and challenge propaganda narratives.

Even so, the propaganda narratives immerse participants in an emotional and moral relationship to history that outlasts and defies truth telling. Joshua Oppenheimer's film *The Act of Killing* captures one executioner stating, "For me, that film [*Treachery of the September 30th Movement/PKI*] is the one thing that makes me feel not guilty."[69] For the population more removed from the killings, the film and propaganda extend the moral justifications and logics of a Communist threat against which the military is the national hero. In 2017, the military required all soldiers to view the original state film because "history was now being distorted."[70] *Tempo* ran a story consisting of facts that the generation of youth aged twenty years and under (who grew up after screenings of the film had stopped) must know, especially those who had never seen the film. The facts included, "Many people doubt the accuracy of the film, especially the air force," and the assertion that the film "deviates from history."[71] The examples given did not directly address the 1965 propaganda; instead, the article confined itself to observations such as the film's referring to East Timor as part of Indonesia when in fact, in 1965, it was not part of Indonesia.[72]

A group of about twenty middle-aged professionals were visiting the monument on the same day that we were. Some of them said hello to Suraya, who thought the group was from the Ministry of the Environment. Our students saw them as they listened to the presentation by a uniformed army man, who spoke through a megaphone under the roof by the well. The ministry group was serious and attentive to their guide. Our students sat on the edge of the platform and took notes, and they seemed surprised to see the tour. The guide noted the "controversy" surrounding the G30S narrative but dismissed it as analysis rather than historical evidence, and suggested that it was the work of the university—an elite bastion of student activism and antistate criticism.[73] One of our students wrote, "A group of KLH [Ministry of the Environment] members who attended the TNI [current acronym for the Indonesian Armed Forces] training program came, all official, and were guided by a tour guide. . . .. It is ironic. Lies continue to be reproduced to the next generations. In the end, the story of the 'winner' wins." Another student wrote, "After I left the museum [building], I suddenly saw a group with a tour guide who explained the version of history he has memorized; he memorized inaccurate history to explain it to the public. . . .. In my opinion, the stories we heard were incoherent in one part and the other part of the story presented was inconsistent. My friends and I were able to spot the irregularities of the story, but uniquely, the group seemed to agree with it and did not ask questions." If this was indeed a group of state employees, then they had likely taken the field trip together to demonstrate their allegiance to the military version of history. They all appeared to be old enough to have been educated during the New Order, and they were likely to have absorbed the narrative and, more importantly, the emotional elements of the propaganda on display at Lubang Buaya.

One student's miniethnography project illustrated this gap between the new "facts" and the enduring power of the official narrative to justify, explain, and orient common sense in the present. The project considered how the museum worked to "other" the Communists and explored what happens when this othering becomes "normal." The student invited friends to the museum and monument as "informants" to discuss their experiences. He told me that he had selected one friend because he was the son of a military officer, old enough to have been educated under the New Order. But over the course of their day at the monument and the process of ethnographic interview and observation, the student came to see his friend's complex position. The friend was intellectually engaged with new literature and ideas and yet still believed the spirit of the narrative, that the army had saved the nation. But belief in this narrative requires a threat, and thus perpetuates the widespread and often unconscious stigmatization of variously defined "Communists."

Challenging or correcting historical facts without attention to the affective power of earlier false narratives does not produce enough dissonance to undermine the narrative of impunity. The student with this ethnography project went on to join a research unit that worked extensively with the army, and met many younger military members who were also personally skeptical of the facts presented in the official narrative of the museum and monument. But he told me they adamantly believed the conclusion that the nation needed to be protected from future threats and had been saved by the military.[74] Even acceptance that the narrative might have been false did not undermine the sense of danger or the importance of the military. The justificatory power of the narrative remains, despite counternarratives and factual challenges.

The students who came with us to Lubang Buaya were university age and older and had all self-selected to join a three-day workshop on human rights that included critical readings and discussion and culminated in the visit to the museum and monument. Nevertheless, one of the participants admitted in an anonymous statement that the propaganda version was still powerful. This student recalled a fifth-grade field trip in 2005, describing it as the place where the "the cruelty of PKI/Communist Party Indonesia buried seven people inside one hole that was only a few meters in size." The student went on to say that "seeing that hole when I was in elementary school has fixed in my memory until now the conclusion that history has demonstrated the low value of human lives. Until now, in my view, I see the PKI's action as atrocious. Even though this is wrong, we tend to repay atrocity with more atrocity. A lot of things are not remembered, only the atrocity that was done by the PKI that has been written down in the history of Indonesia and, of course, my memory. Even though at present there are a lot of stories that try to reveal more on the G30S PKI event." This comment reveals how the logic of vengeance structures common sense and moral judgment.

Others in our workshop who were visiting the museum for the first time with us found it less compelling. One student described having wished to visit the museum, which had featured so prominently in school texts, and having "heard and imagined the horrors since elementary school, about 2003, when I first tasted PLKJ subjects [civics] in the third grade. . . .. So every time I heard the name of the Lubang Buaya area, I immediately was suspicious of and cursed the Communists because they had been so cruel to this nation. Because of that, I also hated Communists. The story put this place on my wish list to visit since I was young." But these beliefs, developed from reading and watching the propaganda film, seemed ridiculous when the student actually visited the museum: "Interestingly, after reaching the site on a visit today, I felt a story that I once knew and all my impressions and attitudes at that time were very ridiculous. The name is ridiculous: the PKI (Communist) Betrayal Museum. A reflection of a regime full of hallucinations and false memories." This student was among a very few who had not been to the museum before. One recalled that her mother thought it was not appropriate and had her stay home when her elementary class took the field trip. I knew others from civil society organizations who had learned a critical version of the history from their parents but had been instructed not to ask questions in school, and recalled their discomfort on class field trips.

One student acknowledged having had access, along with others, to extra information and materials that deconstruct the state propaganda—and yet an affective response still survived, and transcended, this new knowledge. Like most others in the workshop, this student had shifted from a frightened student inspired to hate the PKI (usually around second or third grade) to a more critical observer: "This place feels paradoxical. On one hand, I know almost everything (if not the whole thing) that I will see here has been proven not valid, nevertheless the terrifying effect that this place deliberately provides can still make me feel unconscious as if drugged. I am not hypnotized by the historical story [told in the manner of a] gory film and anger at the PKI (and 'communist group' [kaum komunis]) because they betrayed my 'nation,' as I once imagined when I was in elementary school about G30S." When the student revisited the museum at a different time, with a different group, and equipped with different knowledge, they had different feelings about it as well: "Oppositely, now I feel a kind of irony mixed with surprise, along with feelings of frustration and regret, about this place and the aftermath of the regime's lying to many people. I'm pretty lucky because I'm in a group that has special access to deconstruct, also because we have access to reach toward what we call 'justice.'" The student's empathy or identification had shifted from martyred generals and the wounded child to those who might still be under the influence of the propaganda, or those who had been stigmatized by the false version of events enshrined in the museum: "But what about . . . those who don't have this privilege [to deconstruct and access legal justice]? What about those people who were accused of evil acts, even though they didn't do anything? I think of the G30S matter and its manifestation in this place to be the biggest lie with the heaviest implications that has lasted very long throughout the history of this nation."

Even where there is an understanding that the story is wrong—that it has caused suffering to wrongly accused victims—most students did not take the next step to consider the violence that was justified by the narratives. The park does not commemorate the suffering of victims of the killings and repression; rather, it serves to "other" them, to emphasize the necessity of subsequent actions against them, and to renew the threat of their latent danger, so malleable that it can be applied to the present and future. One student noted, "As a reconstructed historical site, the Sacred Pancasila Monument Complex at Lubang Buaya is not only a place for preserving collective memory about the 'latent danger' of the PKI but also a device that selects the national memory of Indonesia so that it fits with what is narrated by the regime in power at that moment, the New Order.'" As this comment suggests, the national memory still conforms to the propaganda of the

New Order, despite the shift in governments and the challenges to the monument's historical narratives.

For some younger people, doubts or confusion about what actually happened leads to the appearance of apathy or disengagement. The millennials' understanding that some elements of the story may be unknowable subtly decenters and undermines historical narratives generically, and their authority to dictate morality and justify behaviors. Jessica Widartha, a writer for the website Ingat 65 (Remember 65), draws a connection between this putative millennial apathy and the impossibility of knowing some parts of Indonesian history: the narratives and counternarratives are emotionally wrenching, and eventually it is hard to know what is credible, so finally she gives up and stops asking. She recalls the messages she heard from her family and elementary school teachers about the PKI's "evil" but also their unsatisfying answers to her "why" questions. She demands to know why these authority figures said such things to her if they did not know the answers. The link between the "facts" of the 1965 narrative and what that narrative justified is rarely examined. She remembers not just the information but also her emotions and bodily response to the propaganda. The torture of the generals provoked nausea and fear. She recalls holding her breath and closing her eyes during the propaganda film. Hearing that the film was required viewing for her mother's generation, she declares it "cruel," thus likening the repeated viewing of the film to the actions that it depicts. She repeats her question of "for what?"[75]

Reflecting the post–New Order generation's experience with the propaganda, Widartha has watched the film and visited the monument and museum, but she has also heard that individuals suspected of being Communists were killed on the spot. She calls this cruel as well. She poses various questions about the supposed coup attempt, the story of which she was exposed to at college, but rather than focus on the questions and controversies, she zeroes in on the possibility that no torture was visible on the generals' bodies (drawing on the autopsy report that our students had also read). Films and articles that counter the propaganda are widely available, but she is still unable to discover the facts behind the events of September 30: "The answer was not in my old history textbook. I found an article and documentary films about the testimony of the perpetrators of the killings in 1965 but not about the facts behind the events of September 30 itself. I found lots of articles and opinions filled with hypotheses of other people." The availability of material online does not resolve questions of authenticity, and conditions of uncertainty eventually result in the apathy that she first described: "Lots of things tweaked what I believed so that I stopped thinking about it. The more I looked, the more I did not know what I believed and what I did not. My feelings were mixed [campur aduk]; the history that terrified me since I was small, it turns out in fact—maybe—was a lie. *Afraid, terrified [ngeri], disappointed, angry*—at one point then I stopped looking for an answer."[76]

The impossibility of finding out what actually happened on the fateful night—the interpretations, narratives, motives, and plans that have been expunged from records or were never there to begin with—coupled with the weight of all that has happened based on the founding myth, engenders profound distrust toward the government. Widartha continues:

> Don't be mistaken. I have lots of questions. I want to know the answers. We have a right to an answer. Who has to answer? Who has to be responsible; those who refuse to atone for their sins [*menus dosanya*]? My country, step forward. Say the truth. Government, witness, or someone, tell us the truth. Give us clarification. Which one is true, which one is false. Why is it true and why is it false. Answer or slowly, we will no longer trust the state [*negara*]. All people have a right to know what actually happened. Nevertheless, in this situation, I don't want to act as if I know [*sok tahu*] and I also don't know, do you still want to call me apathetic?[77]

Activists from the 1998 era that I spoke to tended to blame the apathy on a spoiled millennial generation that "only cares for its gadgets" and does not value the freedoms it enjoys, secured by the risks taken and work done by their generation, which resisted the New Order. But millennial "apathy" is more accurately seen as a byproduct of the New Order narrative itself and the correspondingly weak power of historical fact to revise or diminish that narrative. Paralysis or inaction among millennials also has sources in their complicity with the narrative—their belief that the defeat of evil Communists allowed Indonesians to feel proud of their country and led to successful development, even when they are aware of the 1965–66 killings or have even been affected by them within their own families. This complicity with the emotions of triumph and success also makes it difficult for them to internalize that the grounding narrative of national life is false, especially when the truth of it was so deeply felt. It can be a paralyzing realization.

And even as young people are disaffected and mistrustful of the state, they also still seek clarification from it. The state responses that attempt to address the killings and other revelations (especially the historical symposium discussed in chapter 4) have failed to provide an affective counterweight to the first narrative, partly because they have failed to clarify and account for the founding lies, but also because the propaganda is still resonant. Among other things, the museum and monument are still open and the film is still shown in some contexts, all without any official clarification or information regarding the killings or other facts. For example, in 2015, the Islamic Defenders Front staged a public screening of the film in Jakarta, and the chief of Indonesian police warned in his opening speech that efforts to rehabilitate the PKI would only lead to its reemergence.[78] In public discourse, "efforts to rehabilitate the PKI" include efforts to clear names, efforts to address past violations of rights and due process, or even efforts toward truth seeking as part of national reconciliation—in short, anything that might challenge the affectively powerful propaganda. In 2017, given the new information online that might cause millennials to reject the narrative, President Jokowi suggested making an updated version of the film that could easily be understood and accepted by the millennial generation in order to convey the danger of Communism to them.[79] Coordinating minister and retired general Wiranto then clarified that the president did not want to change the content of the film, calling it a historical document.[80] The film is considered "historical" because it has endured and shaped understandings of history for so long that challenging it would be akin to challenging a triumphant national history. In 2018, military spokespersons stated that it was up to individuals to decide whether they wanted to watch the film.[81]

The film and the site are inextricably linked. The film prefigures the history and is integrated into the historical site as if it is history; the resulting narrative is viscerally powerful. For some students, the visit to this site provoked almost embodied memories: involuntary bodily responses such as shortness of breath and dizziness. This demonstrates the affective force of the narrative that supports impunity. For others, the feelings, especially of fear, were recalled but from a distance, and were prompted by the location. "When I was on the site," one student said, "my faded memories when I first arrived, strengthened again." His knowledge that the history was fabricated somewhat reduced his fear, but he still felt overwhelmed and confused by the narrative, even if it was fabricated. "My remaining memories regarding the [earlier, elementary school] visit were only how dark the museum was, [and] the gripping atmosphere and the exhibits that illustrated the PKI's cruelty. The earlier memories and feelings came back when I was standing, fixated on one of the exhibit displays that illustrated the cruelty mentioned." He noted how the "faded memories" from the museum were strengthened by the indoctrination process in school. Like many at our workshop who were critical of the history presented, this student noted that his parents were brave, and critical of the propaganda, and consequently he had not fully or viscerally absorbed the narratives as a child. Later, when he was undergoing interviews for the Military Academy test, he did not retell and perform the correct emotions of the "official" narrative and therefore was denied admission. Despite the fact that this student's parents did not reiterate the indoctrination at home and did not instill the deep fear characteristic of other families, he had still absorbed enough of the story that it returned to him, in his words, as a faded memory.

Narratives that make policies, as well as policies that make narratives, have strong and lasting effects. The concept of an infrastructure captures how these elements—narrative and policy, especially—work in concert as part of one system to enforce and then reinforce impunity. The state formalized its narrative of the foundational events of September 30, 1965, not only through the museum, monument, film, and historical lessons and narratives just described but also through a number of legal and bureaucratic elements that systemically stigmatized and isolated those accused of being PKI members, their families, and their descendants. Institutions and agents of the army's territorial command structure were distributed throughout the nation and implemented, or directed others to implement, these laws and policies. Along with the territorial command, elements of law, policy, and bureaucracy resulted in the systematic arrest of suspected Communist Party members, as well as their psychological evaluation, their imprisonment without trial, and their detention with forced labor on the island of Buru, along with subsequent discrimination against them. These became critical components of the infrastructure of impunity. This system unfolded not simply across space—networking various sites across the archipelago—but also over time, ensnaring past as well as future generations in the web of dehumanization and impunity.

The New Order regime built a legal apparatus that justified its takeover of power and enforced its narrative about the supposed coup attempt. Policy and narrative reinforced each other and helped to prevent investigations of past killings or a critical examination of the transition of power from Sukarno to Suharto. The rule of law itself, building on the foundational narrative, provided impunity and legalized the actions of Suharto and his regime, both retrospectively and prospectively. For example, the erasure of the rights of individuals accused of being Communists allowed others—neighbors, family members, and state institutions—to expropriate their land, positions and jobs, and labor. Discriminatory policies sentenced many individuals to detention and forced labor that benefited other individuals and enriched institutions (for example, the conversion and clearing of state land). Using a flexible if not capricious system of categorization, the New Order state suspended and denied pensions to employees who were not "loyal" to it, marking them without any due process as complicit with the Communists. Young professionals who had been abroad for missions or training were forced into exile.

Most of these policies were disputed on legal grounds, some during the New Order period but primarily after it. Nevertheless, stories of everyday life under these conditions show that powerful affective narratives bolstered by arbitrarily enforced laws and policies allowed many individuals and groups to continue to exploit, humiliate, and manipulate the stigmatized to their own economic

advantage and to justify these behaviors. Over time, this infrastructure of impunity was extended and compounded: future generations were required to provide evidence of a "clean [family] environment" for four generations in order to
secure positions in numerous fields, especially in military and state institutions.
This legal and social machinery could be set in motion against any critics, to
ostracize and undermine or even attack them.

Law is an important element of the infrastructure of impunity because it circulates throughout the vast archipelago, and institutions have branch offices and
local representatives across the nation that can arbitrarily implement and enforce
laws. Law, including the policy framework and the institutions of law enforcement (police and courts) and their bureaucratic and social effects, is an actant:
an institutional, material, and nonliving agent that actively distributes impunity
across time and space. The law further extends impunity, even as it should be
the remedy for it. The hope and expectation in much human rights literature is
that law remedies past injustice, but as the case of Indonesia shows, the law can
become an accomplice to past injustice and propaganda more than its remedy.
State and nonstate perpetrators collude with a great deal of flexibility in the system. This subverts the transformative force of law as an instrument of restitution.

The appearance of legality and due process was important to the New Order. As
an ally of the West during the Cold War, it was keen to present itself as a democracy. That the PKI was a legal organization in 1965 at the time of the killings
and detention has been forgotten after five decades under a policy that makes
Communism illegal. Suharto and his allies took a number of steps to ensure the
appearance of a lawful transition of power rather than a (violent) coup. Suharto
led an institution, Operational Command for the Restoration of Security and
Order (Komando Operasi Pemulihan Keamanan dan Ketertiban, or Kopkamtib),
that was tasked to do anything necessary to establish security and order in the
aftermath of the supposed coup attempt. Kopkamtib operated outside judicial
or political oversight and worked through local and regional military and police
commands to carry out its plans to cleanse society of the PKI's influence and to
annihilate the Left.[82] The role of Kopkamtib is difficult to overstate. The military
intelligence analyst Richard Tanter writes, "Kopkamtib was a concept more than
an organization, an ideological formulation that allowed the re-organization of
Armed Forces resources for total internal warfare and social engineering without legal restraints."[83] Members of the ubiquitous territorial command structure
mobilized its resources in the service of eradicating any threats, however vague,
to stability and development. Tanter concludes, "Through Kopkamtib, the nominally civilian government apparatus was bypassed at any point deemed appropriate by the head of state, to allow direct military rule. Moreover, the procedures

under which Kopkamtib operated allowed it to work free of the existing legal restraints on the armed forces itself. By the employment of its considerable military resources in the service of extraordinarily vague and broadly defined political ends, Kopkamtib was the means by which Indonesia was ruled by what amounted to permanent martial law, intermittent and uneven in application, but constant in doctrine and potential."[84] Rather than operating outside the law, it *became* the law, and it disseminated policies that remain effective today, even after the dissolution of the institution and its successor institution in 2000.[85] The Extraordinary Military Tribunals pictured in the museum composite image were also established under Kopkamtib, and PKI leaders as well as other influential allies of Sukarno were tried.

The "legal" transfer of the presidency to Suharto was completed by 1966 and required several other (pseudo)legal elements.[86] The Order of March 11 Letter (Supersemar) was reportedly signed by Sukarno and handed power over to Suharto. The original signed letter itself has not been found, and some suggest that it was signed under duress.[87] Although his power had been undermined, Sukarno was still president, and Parliament called on him to explain the alleged coup attempt. Based on Kopkamtib policies, leftists, Sukarnoists, and nationalists were removed from Parliament and the armed forces. A parliamentary order (TAP MPRS 25/1966) passed in 1966 banned the dissemination of Marxism-Leninism and Communism and made the PKI and related organizations illegal. A legislature cleared of Sukarno allies named Suharto acting president and then elected Suharto in 1966. Although Kopkamtib was dissolved, the prohibitions on the dissemination of Marxism and Communism were renewed in a 1999 law on state security,[88] and they were incorporated into the 2022 revision of the penal code to provide a pretextual or quasi-legal framework for the ongoing stigmatization of survivors and criminalization of critics and the ongoing impunity for perpetrators and beneficiaries of the genocide and transfer of power.

An army-led campaign of mass killings, detention, forced labor, sexual violence, and torture that annihilated the Left began in October 1965 and continued through 1966. There are still no reliable data on how many were killed, but one early official estimate suggested one million, while an Indonesian class action lawsuit put the number at three million dead and seventeen million more as victims of its policies.[89] The New Order ignored and silenced discussion of these killings, as national mourning was channeled entirely to the martyred generals. The taboos on discussion of the killings were strong and effective in both public and private discourse, and many millennials are surprised to find that their families were affected by the killings and subsequent stigmatization. I recall from my dissertation research during the New Order that these killings would occasionally get mentioned in discussions with activists focused on other human rights issues, but they were not frequently referenced, even among those at the forefront of campaigns for East Timor, labor rights, and human rights, or those who covertly studied Marx.

Individuals who were children in the 1960s recall a terrifying time, one that I frequently heard described as a time of chaos. The danger, however, was ascribed to Communists, especially the threat of their seeking vengeance, and to the "masses" and the specter of chaos and a lack of discipline or order. Most people I spoke with vocally criticized the New Order, but some remained apprehensive about the PKI and didn't entirely view them as "victims." Some told me that I didn't know about the PKI's horrible deeds and was not hearing about them in post-*reformasi* times. One woman told me that her father had been a village leader in Sumatra and had repeatedly received death threats, and that it was an atmosphere of "kill or be killed." Other individuals born in the late 1960s from eastern Indonesia recalled the cruelty that played out locally.[90] Some people wondered why there was no concern about human rights back then, implying that the retroactive application of a human rights framework did not address (or redress) the PKI's violence.

John Roosa describes how, as part of the army's psychological war, "Operation Mental," indoctrination teams went from village to village to spread the army's propaganda, further disseminated by the army-controlled media, that "built an alternative universe unmoored from the reality on the ground where PKI supporters were not waging war or even resisting arrest. It encouraged people to believe in events that never happened and to perceive dangers that did not exist."[91] Significantly, the sense of endangerment later recalled by many individuals and organizations was a key component of the propaganda, and as Roosa explains, the propaganda did not blatantly urge killing PKI members. Rather, it emphasized that the threat must be "crushed" through the systematic attribution of collective responsibility for the coup attempt to the entire party and all its supporters, who were dehumanized by lurid stories nested in a logic of ongoing and past threats.[92] The sense of threat was deepened by the sensational reports of secret documents discovered in PKI strongholds of blacklisted names to be killed, especially members of the Islamic organization the Revival of the Ulama (Nahdlatul Ulama).[93] Roosa emphasizes that the army's propaganda was spread by commanders with megaphones to those who were illiterate or not able to access media, and that violence was organized by the indoctrination teams through face-to-face meetings.[94] Geoffrey Robinson notes that the army wanted more than statements of loyalty: it demanded concrete action. Army policies stated that "if in the [village] you find members of the PKI, but do not kill them, it will be you who we punish."[95]

Although the army rhetoric of the time and later narratives attributed the killings to preexisting social tensions, the army itself created the "kill or be killed" conditions. And while the threat may be remembered as the PKI's violence toward others, in fact the military was coordinating the murder of those it determined to be active supporters of or insufficiently opposed to the PKI. Despite regional variations in killings, recent scholarship has demonstrated that there was a consistent pattern: the army would disappear and execute those who had been captured, thus contradicting the idea that the killings were perpetrated by civilians run amok, with some support from the army.[96] People were occasionally executed in front of villagers even though there were not large-scale public spectacles of the killings; the media was filled with lurid stories of PKI violence and threats. Certainly, particular stories may have been disbelieved,[97] but overall they created an atmosphere in which the PKI was seen to be an enemy that must be eliminated. John Roosa notes that the *preman* (local thug) executioners were discreet but also did not hide their terror-inspiring role in the disappearances and executions.[98] It was likely far more traumatic to live alongside those who executed or disappeared loved ones as an open secret and with obvious impunity than to have previously witnessed or participated in any PKI or guerrilla violence.[99] Nevertheless, later generations and public discourse recounted the threat and danger as a social conflict between "sides," and not as violence perpetrated by an army directly or through its proxies. The army's policies were rarely discussed; much more frequently discussed, and performed, was the tension between religious factions (primarily Muslim, but also Catholic) and the Communists—a tension dramatized in the propaganda film and projected into future threats.

In the days and weeks following the supposed coup attempt, as suspected Communist Party members and leftists were rounded up, arrested, interrogated, tortured, and sometimes killed,[100] the army leadership, with the later involvement of Indonesian and Dutch psychologists and other academics, began to categorize prisoners.[101] Category A prisoners were "clearly involved" in planning the coup or failed to report it to authorities. Category B prisoners were not involved but were "know[n] for certain" to be "traitors," even if "there is not enough evidence to bring them to court"; and those in Category C "may reasonably be assumed to have been directly or indirectly involved" in the coup.[102]

Significantly, when this categorization system was designed and implemented, membership in Communist and other organizations was still legal, and it remained so until the passage of the 1966 parliamentary order. And yet being a member of these organizations was grounds for arrest and detention. Many accounts, testimonies, and memoirs disclose that individuals who were arrested were often not even members of such organizations—they may simply have known someone involved or attended a meeting. During the New Order era, an environmental activist that I met in Flores, an island in eastern Indonesia, recalled that in his community many people had signed a list to receive rice subsidies, and that list was later declared to be a membership list for the Communist Party. There was still a great deal of repression when he told me this in 1996, but he was explicitly angry with the Communist Party for "duping" all those who signed, who were then later considered to be part of their organizations. As Robinson notes, guilt in this system was determined not by action but by association and presumed ideas, attitudes, and intentions.[103] Category C was so flexible that the army could ensnare many individuals who were only indirectly or not at all involved with Communists. It provided a legal veneer for indiscriminate arrests of individuals barely affiliated, if at all, with Communism and leftist organizations.

Arrests and detentions were also carried out by militias and other groups, thus diffusing accountability, as well as resentment, across society rather than concentrating it on the army. This involvement of mass organizations and militias supports the state's narrative that violence was carried out by angry mobs and that detention was to protect leftists from attacks, but documents, policies, and the widespread and systematic nature of arrests and detentions, as well as the official statements to support them, demonstrate that the army orchestrated widespread and systematic crimes against humanity.[104] Rather than consider justice for victims of the killings or those wrongly accused, the attorney general in November 1973 instructed local prosecutors to not prosecute any cases of killings of suspected Communist Party members and affiliates, as they were the result of "spontaneity" and the "anger of the masses." Pursuing the cases, the attorney general argued, would "give rise to psychological effects among G30S/PKI remnants, emboldening their struggle, could be used by international organisations affiliated with or under the influence of the international Communist movement, and would cause apathy in society towards helping the government and state instruments in the future."[105] Furthermore, relevant military units would supply evidence that those killed were in fact members of the PKI or affiliated organizations. The justifying propaganda inscribed in the attorney general's memo and the failure to prosecute these cases essentially conscripted local legal apparatuses into the infrastructure of impunity, both rendering the law an accessory to state murder and reifying the propaganda narrative across the archipelago.

Law also contributed to impunity in cases brought before tribunals. Category A prisoners were tried in military tribunals—these tribunals are depicted in the third composite photo at the entrance to the museum. According to later military reports concerning the latent dangers of Communism, 1,887 prisoners were classified as Category A, and 1,009 of them were tried by several types of courts. The balance were transferred to Category B and were not tried.[106] In July 1985, at about the same time that the regime was producing its propaganda film, expanding the museum, and developing new social studies, history, and civics curricula, three Category A prisoners charged with involvement in G30S and subversion and tried under Kopkamtib were executed, despite international campaigns and requests for clemency. They were arrested in late 1968 or early 1969, tried by the Extraordinary Military Tribunals seven years after their arrests, and then executed after seventeen years of imprisonment, when the minister of justice declared that they had exhausted both due process of law and requests for clemency.[107] The appearance of due process allowed Indonesian officials and allies to claim that their procedures were lawful. A bureaucracy was built on the pretext of law and (unconstitutional) institutions that spawned extensive policies and extended "states of emergency" for three decades. Kopkamtib was the heart of this bureaucratic and policy apparatus: it had no constitutional basis or standing, and no parliamentary or judicial oversight. It was created as a temporary, transitional institution, but it persisted,[108] justified by the ever-renewable threat of Communism, variously styled as "new-style Communism," "latent Communism," "silent movements," and other terms the regime deployed to attribute any critique or unrest to the vilified Communist Party and in turn activate the legal and institutional systems to take harsh measures against them.

The three Category A prisoners faced numerous violations of due process and of the Indonesian Criminal Code. Kopkamtib issued an order (5/1969) that allowed for indefinite detention of those being held on charges of subversion or for violating the ban on disseminating Marxism. But the testimony of one of these prisoners exposes vividly how the system worked. Gatot Lestario's defense statement made on December 26, 1975, consisted of eighty pages handwritten in an exercise book.[109] Despite being unable to access lawyers and in full awareness of the flawed court system, Lestario still mounted his own defense, critiquing the basis for the trials and appealing to the "court of history."[110] He had "no illusions" about the trial, arguing that the "so-called G30S cases" were "show-trials which are designed for political consumption by those in power."[111] Lestario noted how the trials were arranged to support the New Order version of events: "As many people as possible have been accused of playing a leading role, and each of them is expected to testify against others."[112] The pattern of fostering betrayal through interrogations continued throughout the New Order.

Lestario outlined the inhumane treatment and violations of the UN charter in detention, imprisonment, and the use of law to support extralegal power—to discriminate based on belief—and accused the victors of a slow genocide. They detained individuals on inference or guesswork and forced them to state their involvement in G30S or the PKI.[113] These points have been made by human rights organizations in the fifty years since 1965; however, the lack of testimony from PKI leaders who were knowledgeable and well regarded, the lack of documents and evidence, and the manner in which the regime orchestrated things so that individuals testified against each other has left profound gaps in the historical record. All of this, in turn, fortified the regime's propaganda narrative and the infrastructure of impunity built on it.

Lestario denied that PKI members knew anything about the "military adventurism" (the supposed coup attempt) planned by a small group of PKI leaders. He tried to narrate the politics of 1965 with respect to the law, and deftly revealed its nebulous state: "My comrades have told the court that the PKI did not wage a rebellion or coup, that the dissolution of the PKI is illegal, and that the South Blitar Affair [an armed rebellion] was an inevitable consequence of the fact that communists and other democrats were placed outside the law, becoming people who could be murdered at will, with impunity."[114] By design, this history would not be revealed in the trials, and he lamented that the judiciary was not independent, that the right-wing coup attempt (the rumored Council of Generals to which the PKI was reacting) was not investigated, and that PKI leaders who knew the truth were not allowed to testify.

Much of the defense relied on arguments about the PKI's effort to support Sukarno and the legitimately elected government, while Suharto and other army members were insubordinate to President Sukarno. Lestario testified that the palace was surrounded when Sukarno was forced to sign the Order of March 11 Letter (Supersemar) that transferred power to Suharto, and he indicted this ostensibly "legal" transfer of power as the real coup.

Lestario's case, and his exceptional defense as a Category A prisoner, highlights how the system was built and extended. Kopkamtib was justified in a "state of emergency" but had endured far longer and had resulted in numerous decrees that overrode the criminal code and human rights conventions. As Lestario's testimony eloquently articulates, Suharto did not circumvent the law so much as he appropriated and claimed it: he drafted unconstitutional laws. For example, Lestario called the Supersemar "neither a law nor a piece of legislation, it is an order." He continued: "The MPRS decree endorsing the Supersemar was unconstitutional, it was an infringement of the 1945 Constitution."[115] Nevertheless, the bureaucracy built on these orders and the trials of the PKI repeatedly reinforced the impression that the state was acting legally.[116]

In the conclusion of his defense, Lestario reversed the roles: he accused the military regime of crimes against humanity. "This court of the Indonesian military regime may regard me as the accused, but in the court of history, with the entire people acting as witnesses, I stand here as the accuser for all the crimes against humanity already committed, now being committed or still to be committed by the present regime against the Indonesian people, against members of the PKI and the mass organisations, against the so-called 'remnants,' in short, against all Indonesian patriots and democrats of whatever group, wherever they are."[117]

As his case shows, the symbolic narrative of G30S/PKI worked in concert with the law. The legal, bureaucratic, and policy elements of the state apparatus were used to silence political analysis that might undermine the state's propaganda narrative. Conversely, the state's propaganda narrative justified the laws and policies that made it impervious to critique or dissent.

In the 1980s, political prisoners clearly understood the regime's very effective manipulation of the language and symbols of nationalism. Mira, a political prisoner, wrote in *TAPOL Bulletin* (*TAPOL* is an abbreviation of *tahanan politik*, or political prisoner) in 1985 that "the patriotic forces of the people will not be able to restore democracy in Indonesia as long as the G30S/PKI symbol still clouds their vision" and that "the Suharto military regime can only be thrust aside if the democratic forces can shake off the influence of these disruptive and misleading symbols."[118]

Lestario implied that trials of key leaders were designed to give the appearance and pretext of law but were conducted as stagecraft and done in such a way as to ensure that leaders could not explore the truth. He and Mira faulted the PKI for not speaking out about its own mistakes. Many Indonesians are beginning to learn about the killings, the innocent victims, and the thugs who perpetrated violence, but the actual political and military machinations of the supposed coup attempt remain unknown. Mira lamented that no one in the PKI had issued a document that could shatter the symbol of the G30S/PKI, and in the "court of history" that Lestario envisioned, this lack of documentary evidence is all the more problematic fifty years later. Yet the affective elements in the infrastructure of impunity that support the law and policy, and vice versa, are not apt to be easily dissolved, even with the documentary evidence he sought. The affectively powerful narrative of the past that justifies actions in the future undermines the very possibility of a court of history.

As for Category B prisoners, they were sent to Buru. It is a relevant part of the infrastructure of impunity that these prisoners were isolated on this island, supposedly for their own protection, but were also forced into labor and starvation, and their efforts at clearing the land enriched the army, not just on Buru but elsewhere.[119]

At many events from 2014 to 2017, I spoke with a man who had been imprisoned on Buru. Before 1965 he had been a schoolteacher. He said that those who went to Buru knew nothing about politics or the PKI. He left Buru with one of the last groups to leave, the "die-hard group." He returned to find that his wife had remarried. Her second husband died after his release and she wanted to marry him again, but he refused. He had his dignity, he said. During a more formal interview, he passed quickly over his experiences on Buru and moved on to his thoughts about what should be done today. He had been part of one organization of victims of 1965 during the early *reformasi* years of 1998–2000,[120] but he had gotten into conflicts with one of the primary organizers over the use of funds. He opposed the travel expenses and high profiles of some former prisoners and went back to a horticultural job.

Many years later, as many of the more prominent victims passed away, he was active in meetings and demonstrations related to 1965 and lived in the shared house that had been established for former victims. In discussions in 2015, many of the self-identified victims (sometimes they are called victims, but later they were also called survivors—the state initially called them *ekstapol*, or ET, meaning ex–political prisoners[121]) were in agreement about the need to rehabilitate their names, and some wanted to have a memorial on Buru. But he said that before a memorial could be placed there, they would need to fix the land and the conditions on Buru to resolve a conflict with the local residents. He spoke at great length about his understanding of the land in Buru, of how prisoners who had spent time there knew what had grown and would grow there. If he could get the funds for it, he wanted to return and work on reforestation and land rehabilitation. He wanted to grow things there and to heal the land devastated by their relocation and forced labor at the site. He explained animatedly that fruit, such as a small lychee called klenkeng, would grow there, not just rice. The restoration had to involve both the people and the land, he emphasized.[122]

His stories are a glimpse at the lingering fear and vulnerability of the ex-prisoners, as well as their stigmatization, as he imagined that it would agitate local inhabitants if they memorialized their suffering without working first to restore the environment that was destroyed—with their *forced* labor—to fuel and build lucrative businesses for the army and its associates.

Elsewhere, too, penal colonies contributed to military business, and state policies were used to the advantage of regional military commands across the archipelago. Writing about South Sulawesi, the Indonesian historian Taufik Ahmad states that the military used the penal colony as a source of forced labor that could be exploited to establish lucrative military businesses and build houses and structures for military institutions and personnel. State forests were declared prison camps, and once the land was cleared it became the property of the military, either personally or institutionally. Thus, in addition to benefiting from prisoners' forced labor, the army appropriated national assets as individual or institutional resources.[123] Subsequent investigations disclosed practices of forced labor and enslavement across the archipelago, including sites not only in Sulawesi and Maluku but also in Kalimantan and Java.[124]

The state-sanctioned appropriation of the Left's assets by the military and, in other cases, religious groups or individuals was an important element of the infrastructure of impunity for the long term: in 2016, I was told by activists that seized assets posed more of an obstacle to resolution than political will. The benefits and beneficiaries of the 1965 killings and the development that followed are rarely discussed. While land reform was most closely identified with the PKI, it was actually mandated by the national government, as the Indonesian historian Roro Sawita notes, and in Bali tensions around land reform were exacerbated by elite politics and the army's mobilization of executioners.[125] *Tjidurian 19 Rumah budaya yang dirampas* (Seized culture house), a short film made in 2009 about the Communist Party–affiliated literary and arts organization Lembaga Kebudayaan Rakyat (Institute for People's Culture), was screened as part of the Rekoleksi Memori festival in 2015.[126] It made clear the extent to which the army seized valuable properties in 1965–66 across Indonesia and in the center of Jakarta. Some activists were working with victims to document this seizure of property, but one person involved told me that many victims were still afraid to speak up, and still others were concerned that a database of reports could also be used to terrorize individuals and families. As long as the stigmas and propaganda remained effective and past cases were not reopened, the assets remained comfortably and securely with the families or organizations that had seized them.

Category B isolated a group of supposed "die-hard" evil Communists, but Category C prisoners were dispersed throughout society and became targets for exploitation, humiliation, and stigmatization. From the early New Order onward, individuals had to undergo mental and ideological screening to confirm that they did not have family members over the last four generations who had been involved in G30S/PKI or Communism. Presidential Order No. 28/1975 set the guidelines for treatment of those implicated by the G30S/PKI, Category C.[127] By the 1980s, the "clean environment letter" (which certifies no family involvement for four generations) was required for employment in many sectors.[128] In 1990, a subsequent presidential decree established the special review (*penelitian khusus*, abbreviated *litsus*) requirements for civil servants.[129] In addition to investigating the family and social background of individuals, these policies also tested the extent to which the individual could demonstrate allegiance to New Order propaganda, including the latent dangers of Communism. These policies, when applied, could bar individuals from their positions without legal process or evidence. Even after the dissolution of the institution of Kopkamtib,[130] which had labeled individuals as Category C, the label itself and the discrimination persisted. The Supreme Court as well as the National Human Rights Commission both sent letters to Presidents Megawati and Susilo Bambang Yudhoyono, and yet Category C prisoners have received no rehabilitation or compensation.

During the New Order period, they and their families were required to report (*wajib lapor*) to local authorities, who subjected them to another layer of stigmatization, humiliation, and arbitrary treatment. Children of PKI members were also subject to many restrictions and seen to be a dangerous threat, as they might seek revenge.[131]

I met Uciwati at an event organized by a consortium of human rights organizations to interest high school students in a graphic design competition related to information about past cases.[132] Many students, in high school in 2015, talked to Uciwati, or "Uci," after this session and at other times. They were surprised to hear her story. Uci's father had been an elected leader in Cilacap, and her mother had been linked to Gerwani because of her official state position as a supervisor of the different women's organizations, as stipulated by her father's elected role. Her parents were both arrested in 1965, and Uci went to live with her grandmother. She was forced to report to the police station twice a week because she had been involved in a youth organization.[133] When she reported to the police station, she took care to ensure that other students did not know what she was doing. At first she was able to continue at school, but then the school head was fired for being too lenient on the children of ex-PKI, and she was expelled.

She then requested permission to report to a subdistrict police station (*polsek*) closer to her grandmother's home. She traveled to the station through fields to avoid meeting anyone who might ask where she was going. She felt ashamed. She was the only child who had to report to police. At one point, the head of police ordered those required to report to bring materials (such as bricks, sand, and cement) for the construction of a new building that would house the ET on their release. She reflected on the experience in a collection of survivors' stories. She was worried because she didn't want her eighty-year-old grandmother to be burdened by the task. So eventually she decided to take stones from the village well to fulfill her obligation. When it was her turn to present her materials, the police chief (*kapolsek*) asked if she would steal from others when stones from the well were depleted. She replied that she hadn't stolen—she had been commanded to contribute the materials. The police chief then told her that she didn't have to bring anything, because this would just create more of a problem. She felt relieved but also sorry for the other *tapol* (political prisoner) adults around her, waiting to report and present their materials and knowing also that their uncompensated labor would construct the building. She stopped herself from pitying the others when she realized it would be the same as pitying herself. Her parents had raised her to have humility and dignity and not to be self-pitying.

Everyone greeted her parents fondly when they were released. Her mother performed midwifery services for village women for free, and her father was well regarded. Because he was still very popular, her father was forbidden by authorities from working in any field that would allow him to influence other people (and spread Communism). He had to seek permission from two levels of the military command to leave the city. Uci's father died five years after his release from prison, and she realized that she had to continue his struggle. She became involved with other children of victims and they initiated various activities, including a singing group, Paduan Suara Dialita, which she told me was healing. They sing songs from prison and songs from the 1960s that had been silenced. The group has performed many times and received honors and recognition.[134]

Students who listened, rapt, to Uci's story were surprised by it, but they also approached her afterward and confided that they, too, had family members who had been stigmatized. Her story affected them not because Uci corrected the facts of history but because it spoke to the wrenching tensions within families and the shame of being linked to Communism or stigmatized as Communist.

Most political prisoners were released in the late 1970s due to international pressure.[135] Many memoirs describe their difficult journeys home to their families, whom they had not seen for over a decade. Their release was not the end of their stigmatization or their problems, however. In fact, in many ways it increased them, as the former prisoners were in greater contact with society and exposed to the pervasive New Order concern about latent danger and ideological contagion. Official concerns about such contagion prompted numerous formal and informal restrictions on ex-prisoners and their families, which subsequently assumed various and widely stigmatizing social forms.

Policies that affected individuals accused of being Communists were extended and intensified in the mid-1980s, as a growing younger generation had no direct experience or recollection of the 1960s. At this same time, the state invested in the museum, monument, and propaganda film and extended policies such as the required reporting that Uci described, the stigmatization of family members, the marking of ex-prisoners with the label "ET" on their ID cards after release, and the stipulation of "clean environment" letters. This is where, and how, the bureaucratic translates into social practice, and how the infrastructure of impunity gets embedded in the micropractices of "legal" stigmatization that reinforce the threatening phantasm at the heart of the 1965 violence. The stigma of the ET, or ex–political prisoner, was clearly visible on the ID card every time individuals or family members attempted to access their rights or state services, or confirmed their name and address.[136] It was a redundant reminder that they do not have rights and are outside society.

The Legal Aid Institute launched a class action suit in 2005 that aggregated all of the data and characteristics from individual cases of discrimination to convey the massive scale of the New Order's systematic stigmatization of leftists and the

Left-affiliated. In addition to postrelease restrictions, the very circumstances of a prisoner's release solidified impunity, documented the ex-prisoner's guilt, and formalized the role of social vigilance, because as a condition of release, prisoners, notes Geoffrey Robinson, had to "confess that they had belonged to a banned organization, to condemn the September 30th Movement, and to swear they would be loyal to the state ideology, Pancasila."[137] According to the chief of Kopkamtib, "After they are released and returned to society, they still have to assure the Government through concrete deeds that they consciously have discarded their Communist ideology, and that they are faithful to the Pancasila ideology. . . . This adjustment is a social process in itself . . . which also requires supervision by the society in general as well as by the law enforcement agencies."[138] Deputizing society to supervise this demonstration of loyalty to the state dispersed opportunities to stigmatize others. The army's infrastructural imperative was clear, and according to Robinson, an internal document from 1974 described its goal of eliminating remnants of G30S/PKI by creating "an integrated system of surveillance and control of former [political] detainees and prisoners that is both efficient and effective."[139]

The policies and the social process of implementation restricted the lives of ETs and their families and friends, and formalized social and economic hardship into policy and law. Former prisoners were barred from sensitive occupations in order to further isolate them.[140] They were not able to get loans because they had no property—it had been confiscated when they were arrested and detained. Fear and suspicion grow when society is militarized and enrolled, or conscripted, into vigilance. This militarization of society and the social dispersal of discrimination to demonstrate loyalty and seek advantage fostered micro, or personal, betrayals that tore at the social fabric. These moves embedded the infrastructure of impunity more deeply not only in policy but also in ordinary social life and practice.

I observed survivors in Jakarta from 2015 to 2017 who were active in advocacy and attended meetings, seminars, film screenings, and demonstrations. Many testified to the conditions on Buru, and some spoke of their roles before they were detained. When I asked them about their experiences, they focused on the ongoing activism about 1965 and their view of national politics, especially the promises by the Jokowi administration to address past human rights violations. Most of them were well educated and had been politically engaged in the 1960s, or became so through their experiences during detention with other "hardcore" prisoners. One volume detailing the experiences of ordinary people and family members for Indonesian audiences is a 2011 publication of testimonies collected for an oral history project led by the historian and Jesuit priest Baskara T. Wardaya, in central Java.[141] One story ("Daughter and Wife of Political Prisoners") illustrates the gradual accumulation of stigma over time. It describes the lifelong suffering of the daughter of a musician who was arrested in 1966, after he declined to perform at the request of a village official. The daughter had to work very hard to help support her mother and younger siblings. Her father had contributed to the cost of building the school with the understanding that his children would attend free of charge in the future, but this agreement was not honored. The woman's older siblings went to live with distant family members, thus severing their association with the political prisoner, and ended up doing well. The stigmatization extended to her son, who endured repeated incidents of bullying, abuse, humiliation, and exploitation from children as well as adult neighbors. When her son began to work at a sand-mining business, he was continually deceived and cheated and accused of being a thief and beaten for it by neighbors, who happened to be in the air force and military police—and the actual thieves. The mother complained first to the air force office, which tried to buy her off. Then, accompanied by three lawyers, she complained to the local military police. They told her to go to her parents' home in a neighboring area. When she returned, her house had been completely ransacked by villagers.

This story illustrates how repressive state policies that fortify impunity become part of the very weave of social life in the village, where neighbors themselves exact the vengeance and repression enforced by state policy and narrative. Extensive evidence points to how state policies have systematically discriminated against detainees, but this story demonstrates how family members of political prisoners were discriminated against by neighbors and other family members, by security forces, and by local government officials. Even when they were able to have a day in court, the state did not protect people from the abuse of nonstate community members. Furthermore, economic discrimination and devastation that began with their parents' detention, loss of property, and lost wages were compounded and extended by bullying and exploitation by state officials who demanded bribes when the family members sought to visit the prisoners in jail or secure necessary documents and IDs, and by the fate of prisoners' children, who were forced out of school and into marginal jobs in order to survive. Stigmatized individuals themselves became scapegoats for the theft perpetrated by more powerful members of society.

The stigmatization of family members did not end with those accused in 1965 and their children. As Uci notes, even in 2015, high school students reported their families enduring similar treatment. Even after the institutions of screening were shut down in 2000, the decree that banned Marxism (TAP MPRS 25/1966) and that justified these practices remains on the books and rationalizes ongoing stigmatization. Even when individuals overcome the family pressure and stress and speak about their experiences, a legal element can be used to criminalize their testimony. For example, an account by Ribka Tjiptaning, the child of a PKI member, was published in the euphoric spirit of *reformasi* in 2002. It is literally titled *I Am Proud to Be the Child of PKI*.[142] Tjiptaning opens her memoir by clarifying,

> I did not write this book with a desire to show my bravery in resisting the authoritarian power of the New Order; I wanted to give an example to my friends the children of political and criminal prisoners. . . . To rise up from the shackles of oppression so that they can enjoy life as they should and at the same time they can play a role in developing democracy. My brothers and sisters who have the same fate, don't back up, don't lower yourself, don't be ashamed [or] afraid, but you have to feel motivated to rise up and resist, meaning oppose injustice, oppose crime and evil and these things that ruin our life along with [the lives of] our children and grandchildren. We have to say the truth is truth and say what's false is false even if we have to face the weapons of the powerful.[143]

The memoir discusses her family background but mostly focuses on how she came to be selected as an Indonesian Democratic Party of Struggle (Partai Demokrasi Indonesia Perjuangan, or PDI-P) representative. In a 2015 interview, thirteen years after the memoir's publication, the author told CNN that very few children of PKI members will speak about or acknowledge this background.[144] In 2018, members of the army who still held political posts stated that there was a group of PKI members in the PDI-P,[145] and those politically opposed to Tjiptaning used her published work, which declared her father's political affiliation, to implicate her as a member of a banned party and accuse her of spreading an illegal ideology and contaminating the whole PDI-P party by association. A party official had to defend Tjiptaning and her book by arguing that she was writing about her father's political affiliation, not her own, and that "she did not have a choice of who had given birth to her."[146] The accusation of having an association with the PKI is still a powerful political tool. As in the past, the military was treating the PKI as an inherited sin (*dosa keturunan*), and the PDI-P tried to refute that logic. It remains illegal to be PKI, but the PDI-P was engaging the long process of undoing the idea of an inherited sin.

Formal policy prohibitions on the discussion of Marxism or the dissemination of Communist ideals were sufficiently flexible threats that they could be mobilized against any number of critics of the New Order. Even more than two decades after the end of the New Order, the elements of the infrastructure, the policies and the visceral power of the narratives combined, can be deployed to stigmatize political opponents. To this day, allegations that President Joko Widodo, popularly called Jokowi, is sympathetic to the PKI are a significant political liability and have been used to attack him. They have forced him to

decrease his support for any reexamination of 1965 and to demonstrate repeatedly that he is not sympathetic to the PKI by adopting the older rhetoric of *gebuk*
PKI—attack the PKI.[147]

The New Order built a bureaucracy around the stigmatization of leftists and suspected leftists. Stigmatization circulated through the very capillaries of the state
and was imprinted on its documents and stamps. Likewise, the large and small
elements of impunity permeated daily life in its most quotidian, basic, and even
intimate dimensions. Even documents that purported to exonerate individuals
associated them with forbidden groups and thus became backhanded liabilities
and sources of stigma. Christina Sumarmiyati, called Mamik, was a schoolteacher in central Java.[148] In December 1965 she was arrested without a proper
warrant and tortured on suspicion that she was a member of Gerwani; her father,
a peasants' union leader, was arrested as well. She was detained for four months
and eventually released for lack of proof. She was given an official "certificate of
release." Two years later, in 1968, she was again forcibly arrested in the middle of
the night and accused, again, of being a member of Gerwani. Her presentation
of the certificate of release did not eliminate suspicion; instead, the certificate and
her student league membership card enraged the military police,[149] who brought
her into their headquarters for interrogation. She was asked whether she knew
various individuals, but she did not and said so. She endured repeated sexual violence and torture, as she did not know the information her torturers sought and
refused to implicate others to stop her own torture. She moved through various
sites of detention and was not released until 1978. Fifty years later, the certificates
of release are valuable evidence of innocence and wrongful detention, but at the
time they were a liability because even as they confirmed a prisoner's release, they
also proved that the prisoner had been accused of (and therefore associated with)
the dangerous contagion of Communism.

In another case, I asked one former political prisoner, Bedjo Untung, about
documents he had saved. He said he had received a similar letter of release but
had burned it to destroy any evidence that would link him to the PKI.[150] Documents played an important role in this process, but very few documents have
been recovered after the fact. In another interview, Nani Nurani described how
her saved documents and letters became evidence that she and her legal team
used to demand rehabilitation and compensation for her later arrest and detention.[151] The documentary record has also been deployed by the International
People's Tribunal for 1965 to demonstrate a widespread and systematic campaign
of crimes against humanity.

In 1965 and 1966, Operation Mental Teams and Indoctrination Teams were
dispatched throughout the country to enforce a policy of nonneutrality as part

of a deliberate psychological warfare tactic by the army to enroll communities in the mass killings of suspected Communist Party members.[152] These teams alienated community members from each other. In subsequent years, Kopkamtib developed policies yet more deeply embedded within the family, and yet more intimate and exhaustive in their bureaucratic intention to divide communities and affectively manipulate individuals who might not have experienced the killings directly.[153] Families benefited from relatives' good behavior and compliance with state policies, and by the same token suffered for any perceived misdeed or thought. The suffering was visceral and emotional, as community members teased children about their parents and ostracized them, but family relationships and stigmas got transmitted well beyond the immediate context. Even when family members were absent, imprisoned, or deceased, policies required that they be named on official documents. Many families of prisoners erased family members by burning documents and changing names.[154]

The tentacles of policies against suspected PKI members extended throughout family relationships and across generations. All of the postrelease policies and humiliations described here created suffering for family members, kept the threat of Communism alive, and created abject others against whom the nation and proper family could be defined. These policies originated from the state and bureaucracy but became more intense actants as they moved through social capillaries and became part of everyday practice in communities and even families.

As the testimonies above reveal, family members often inflicted painful humiliation on and withheld assistance from their stigmatized family members. Testimonies describe how state policies and impunity had profound and tangible social consequences, and how this condition of "civil death" was actively exploited in individual lives and families.[155] These policies and their relationship to family extended the reach and power of the state, as families themselves enacted the discrimination and fear. Almost imperceptibly, family got conscripted into the infrastructure of impunity itself, and not just as its victim but as a participant, when families consciously or unconsciously mobilized affects of shame and fear against stigmatized family members.

The fraying and even destruction of bonds between prisoners and their families occurred in many different ways. Some stigmatized individuals disappeared so that their families would not suffer by association. In these cases, family members tended to remain silent. Some escaped by being sent to live with relatives in distant cities and acquiring new family contexts, and later shunned other stigmatized family members. Some children did not know why extended family members were estranged or absent, or they did not even know that these family members existed.[156] They didn't know why some had more property than they did, and still others didn't know why family members had "abandoned" them to remain in exile for decades.[157]

Children taught the New Order propaganda in schools were often ashamed of and hated individuals who were involved in these monstrous organizations (including absent family members), which obviously reinforced the silences within families.[158] In other cases, parents disclosed family histories when students returned home from screenings of the G30S/PKI film in schools or asked about historical narratives.[159]

The shaming, particularly as it occurred within their families, was painful for victims.[160] Many with whom I spoke were deeply concerned about having their names "rehabilitated" or expunged.[161] Some second-generation victims I interviewed perceived name clearing to be an important prerequisite for other legal processes, especially the restoration of assets seized in 1965 or other reparations owed by the state.[162] Younger activists, many of them from legal aid and human rights backgrounds, found the concern with rehabilitation to be insufficiently political, but at the same time they also recognized that they needed to respect the wishes of the victims and their families. While, to these advocates, the clearing of names may have seemed apolitical and tangential to broader justice efforts, it does target the intersection of the affective and the bureaucratic that is fundamental to the infrastructure of impunity.

The case of Nani Nurani, a singer favored by Sukarno (and envied by other performers), exemplifies the bureaucratic battle of name clearing. She had performed at a 1965 PKI event. She emphasized that despite her arrest, she was not part of the PKI. I met her for the first time at the Legal Aid Institute in Jakarta in December 2015, having been introduced to her by her lawyers. She had just been to the National Human Rights Commission and a few other places to talk about her case. Though I had spoken to her only over the phone, it was obvious who she was. She walked in with great poise and was very elegantly dressed. Over the next two years, we met often and attended numerous events together. I had copies of her book and documents related to the case, she had invited me to her home for the holidays, and I had met with her singing group. I knew that she later worked for the family of a local gang leader widely rumored to have been involved in the killings—she told me she didn't know if this was true or not and they hadn't discussed it. She had been a deeply devout Muslim since a very young age, and as a child she had called non-Muslims *kafir*.

Even though she had succeeded in some of her legal cases (for instance, securing the right to have an identity card for life without the ET stamp), she nevertheless remained very concerned that her name had not been officially cleared. Her legal successes resulted in court rulings that she had not belonged to the PKI, but she wanted a letter to rehabilitate her name. Such a letter was less important in her ongoing legal case for reparation of lost wages, because she had meticulously saved early documents of her arrest and release (the sort that others had burned to avoid stigma), which provided evidence for her legal cases and a basis for the calculation of wages lost due to her wrongful arrest and detention. Nevertheless, an official letter clearing her name was important to her emotionally. She wanted to be able to say to her nieces and nephews that she was not a Communist. Rehabilitating her name would also ensure that false allegations in the past would not be used against her family members in the future: it would ensure their access to resources and full citizenship.

In addition to mobilizing shame, families also internalized fear. Soe Tjen Marching begins her collection of oral history accounts of the genocide with an apology to her mother. Her mother, traumatized by "witnessing her husband being dragged from [her] home by Suharto's troops one day in 1966," believes that Marching's revelation of survivor stories is "reckless, thoughtless, and dangerous for our family."[163] Marching's mother is not an isolated case; the author notes that those who shared their stories had anxieties about speaking about these events, especially because of pressure from families and relatives to remain silent. She writes that these individuals were not troubled and frightened by the laws per se, but by their families. I would argue here that it was precisely the infiltration of law and policy into social and family practice and relationships that made the affects of fear and vigilance as well as stigmatization so powerful. In other words, rather than an opposition between law and policy and family, the family *became* the instantiation of the law and policy, and the agent of the practices of stigmatization. And this accounts for much of the stubborn persistence of impunity. Its infrastructure extends into the law as well as social practice and relationships.

This nexus of law and family is a key element of how the infrastructure of impunity works inside and outside the home and across generations. Marching writes that the New Order "strategy was so effectively sustained that fear has become so powerful and is seen as ubiquitous, accepted and undetected."[164] She refers to a "mutation of fear" whereby "many former victims have been transformed into agents that preserve the very ideology that has persecuted them."[165] Even brave activist victims are occasionally susceptible to this fear.

Given silences and erasures, it can be difficult to delineate precisely how policies circulated through intimate and family relationships. Roro Sawita described her work in Bali with other millennials educated after the end of the New Order but conditioned, even so, by the propaganda narrative. They were surprised when they began to learn how the stigmatization around the 1965 killings had provoked ongoing tensions and inequities throughout their families.[166] The Ingat 65 website was created by millennials precisely to gather ordinary stories of how

1965 affected families. Essays published there most often reflect surprising discoveries made when children questioned their parents about the effects of 1965.

Leila Chudori's novel *Pulang*, or *Home*, tells of how the policies related to 1965 extended trauma and discrimination intergenerationally. Hers is not a work of grand narratives and ideologies; rather, she focuses granularly on the lived experience of exiles, their families who remained in Indonesia, and what all of this means for the next generation. Chudori worked for the Indonesian newsmagazine *Tempo* and drew on her extensive research as a journalist, in addition to interviews with exiles in Paris over many years, to research her widely popular novel. Henri Chambert-Loir has critiqued historical inaccuracies in the novel, especially its erasure of Communist ideology;[167] nevertheless, *Home* is one of the most compelling and affectively powerful reflections on 1965 for a younger generation of readers.[168] Chudori described her novel to me as a family story more than a political analysis.[169] Perhaps because 1965 and its aftermath were experienced primarily, even if unconsciously, through family ties, it resonates strongly for readers.

The novel presents various stories within an extended family, but it centers on a fictional journalist, Dimas Suryo, who was abroad in Cuba during the supposed coup attempt. Most of the novel is set in Indonesia in 1998 and focuses on the children of the exile and the relatives who remained in Indonesia. Dimas's brother, Aji, who remained in Indonesia, demonstrates what life was like for family members who tried to keep their heads down. They dropped shared family names and never spoke back, or up. Aji has succeeded in earning a degree in engineering and working as a scientist. His son, who has always felt insecure about the (direct and indirect) discrimination and the need to keep a low profile, demonstrates how the stigma is internalized, even after he succeeds in gaining a position at one of the state-run companies as an accountant. He passes the clean environment screening test by dropping his last name and ignoring his family. When he wants to marry the director's daughter, he asks his family to help him by meeting his girlfriend's family and remaining silent about their background. He promises his family that he will tell his girlfriend and her parents that he has hidden his family from them. He argues with his father that he is only doing what the family did—he's keeping a low profile—but his parents insist that concealment of his true identity from his future wife is much different and implicates a different realm of honor and integrity altogether, as if the family is insulated from state policies by emotional bonds and propriety—ironically, the same propriety that the regime valorized in its propaganda.[170]

This story meshes with my interviews, which suggest that not all families were open about these relationships, even with their own children.[171] The family has a degree of agency in how they hide or reveal distant family bonds, but however they resolve the matter, it suggests an insidious cultural encroachment of state policies into the family. While they could drop their name in screenings and to potential employers, social realms require being positioned in a family context, and in this case personal integrity requires not hiding relatives. Even after the end of the New Order, many people, especially millennials, did not know of their stigmatized relatives, which suggests the likelihood that many families buried these links. Chudori probes this ethical issue through the family story.

Aji's wife says the policy of a check is fine, since people deserve a second chance from a criminal check, and then introduces the key problem that readers in 1998 needed to see emphasized, as it had been omitted from state narratives and campaigns: "But all this time—and this is what doesn't make any sense—our only fault is our link to Dimas. Isn't that right? And why is it a fault when he didn't even do anything wrong?"[172] Not doing anything wrong here could be interpreted to mean that Dimas was not formally a member of the party—he was abroad in Cuba only because someone else at the newspaper had to stay home for personal reasons. He was friendly with the Left but didn't really know anything about the upper echelon's plans (and certainly not the coup attempt). After the end of the New Order in 1998, many advocacy strategies emphasized wrongful arrests in 1965 of victims who were not even actual members of the PKI.[173] After their arrest the original facts did not matter—they were ex-prisoners and stigmatized as such. Chudori interrupts the reflexive New Order narrative and logic that everything leading up to 1965 justified what followed. That Dimas was not doing anything wrong could also mean that at that time it was not illegal to be part of the Communist Party (he was not, however, and the novel does not linger on this possibility). The mother says that there is little they can do and that there will always be "a brand on our forehead: 'political prisoner family.'" Regarding the prospective in-laws, she tells her son, "You are entering a circle of people who view our relationship with Dimas with contempt, as a historical defect. How long will you be able to keep up your act with your future wife and in-laws? If your marriage begins with a lie, what kind of future home will you ever be able to build?"[174] Cultural tropes hold that the PKI violated stability and family ideology, but with this line of questioning, the novel demonstrates that the New Order itself and its policies have fractured families.

In a succinct challenge to family values the son tells his father (Aji), "All I want from you and Mama is for you to be my parents." Aji replies, "And all I want from you is to be my son; to admit to being the son of Aji Suryo and nephew of Dimas Suryo."[175]

The son asks his family to come to dinner at his future wife's parents' home the next night. Aji insists that Lintang be included—she is Dimas's daughter from Paris and is currently visiting Indonesia to make a documentary film. The scene at the fiancée's lavish home comes to a climax when talk turns to French food and Lintang states that her father is a chef. The hosts recall a time in France when the daughter had an upset stomach and needed rice and wanted to eat at an Indonesian restaurant, but they could not eat there because it was owned by Communists. He continues that despite all the high praise for the restaurant, the food was ordinary. This inspires Lintang to defend her father, the chef at the same restaurant, thus revealing herself as the daughter of a Communist and thereby implicating the rest of the family as coming from an unclean environment. Even though the Suharto regime is weeks away from collapsing in the novel's time frame, the relationship ends and the son is suspended from his job.[176]

Home demonstrates how state policies infiltrate family and social networks, the hold of New Order propriety, and how families collude, even if invisibly and silently, with state policies. The mother attempts to keep the public realm separate from the family realm, imagining it as insulated from the state, but *Home* illustrates the impossibility of this separation.

Most students and many millennials I talked to noted how their families spread fear. One millennial writer recalled that her family prohibited her from singing a popular song associated with Gerwani, but they never explained their extremely strong reactions. There are many other victims who confess that their relatives are ashamed of them, and there are strongly religious or army families that make adherence to national narratives a matter of family honor. But *Home* distinctively shows how the very definition of being a family becomes a source of fear. While there has been much emphasis on the testimonies of survivors of Buru and other detention sites, it is important not to overlook the suffering of family members of those who were accused of being PKI. Even when they were not imprisoned, they suffered greatly, as did those who lay low and managed to succeed under the New Order. The experience of political prisoners and their family members illustrates how a complex and multifaceted infrastructure protects illegality from exposure, invests family and community with the enforcement of law and stigmatization, and infiltrates intimate relations with affects of fear, vengeance, and shame—core elements of the founding narrative of 1965 on which the system was first built. The infrastructure of impunity relies on these families and their belief in the rule of law and adherence and participation in the system of bureaucracy to perpetuate itself, even as survivors testify and new historical evidence challenges the narrative.

In the New Order and afterward, "bureaucracy" was how the regime both acted as if what it was doing were legal and simultaneously displaced the implementation of violent policies onto others, which made them complicit in the system. This is a core characteristic of the policy and legal elements in the infrastructure of impunity, built on the narratives of 1965. These narratives, whether experienced at the monument and museum or in propaganda films or classroom lessons, rationalize bureaucratic violence, dehumanization, and stigmatization with reiterations of the latent dangers of Communism. In 1965–66, being a member of the PKI was not illegal; nevertheless, suspects were denied rights and recourse to the law. Subsequent policies and orders made Communism illegal. The constitution and existing legal framework in 1965 were disregarded and changed by presidential decrees, and then a new system of law and policy emerged to support the operations and retrospectively claim that due process had been fulfilled.

Initially, the powerful affective elements of fear and vengeance evident at the museum, for example, could single-handedly blunt criticism of killings, abuse of law, and rampant illegality. Later a new system—an infrastructure—of law and policies themselves enforced the stigmatizing affective narratives and lodged them deeply within institutions as well as everyday social practice and bureaucratic details. Rather than combat impunity, the law becomes its accomplice and agent. Interlocking legal, social, and political elements created conditions of compounding hardship and enduring impunity.

THE FORGOTTEN MYSTERIOUS KILLINGS

From 1983 to 1985, "mysterious killings" (*penembakan misterius*, or *petrus*) occurred most prominently in central Java but throughout Indonesia as well. Experts and scholars estimate that during these years, up to eight thousand Indonesians were killed.[1] Corpses were left by the side of the road. President Suharto claimed that the killings were a necessary social policy to stop crime and promote security, and military officials publicized that these operations had successfully eradicated crime, even as they simultaneously made ambiguous comments that blamed the killings on rival gangs. According to Suharto,

> There was no mystery to these events. The real problem is that the inci-
> dents [the mysterious killings] were preceded by a fear that was felt by
> the people. The threat came from evil people, criminals, murderers, and
> so forth. Peaceful stability [*ketenraman*] was disrupted. It was as if in
> this country it did not exist. As if what was there was only the feel-
> ing of fear. The evil people had already acted beyond the boundaries
> of humanity. Not only did they violate the law, but they also acted in
> excess of the limits of humanity. For example, older people were already
> robbed and then they were killed. That is inhumane. If stealing, OK,
> take something, but don't then kill. In addition, there was a woman
> whose wealth was taken and on top of that was raped by those criminals
> in front of her husband. That is too much. Do we want to just be quiet
> and cover this kind of thing up? We have to have a treatment, forceful
> action. Violent action. But that violence is not based on just shooting

them: Dor! Dor! Just like that. No, but those who resist, like it or not, must be shot. Because they resist, they are shot. Then there is a corpse just left there; that is for shock therapy. So that many people understand that there is still someone who will overcome these evil deeds.[2]

The president's comments rationalized violence as a security measure, but petrus did much more than that. I argue that these killings and the subsequent reorganization of the extralegal criminal and violent elements of the state affectively transformed ideas of security, rights, and citizenship into key components of the infrastructure of impunity. Rather than becoming antidotes to impunity, these elements were forged into its accomplices.

The mysterious killings—one of the "gross violations" cases investigated by the Indonesian National Human Rights Commission (Komnas HAM) from 2008 to 2010—occurred in the mid-1980s, when the state was expanding its museum and the New Order bureaucracy itself expanded. The category of "gross violations" includes violations of both civil political and economic rights that occur repeatedly in a planned, widespread manner and affect significant numbers of victims without government response. Yet despite the official investigation and the fact that the killings were reported in newspapers and claimed by Suharto, there has been very little discussion of this case by critics and NGOs, and very few victims have come forward to demand rights. There is very little detailed information available on the texture and specifics of the incidents or the implementation of the policy. Because social stigmatization of criminals and the affective power of narratives justifying the killings remain so strong in Indonesia, almost no family members of the victims have made public statements. There is also very little advocacy or discussion related to this case, even among groups that concentrate on justice for past cases.

The facts of the killings and the state's role in them were widely proclaimed, yet prior to Suharto's statement, the relationship between the state and criminal elements was a "public secret." An open secret is something widely known yet not stated, but the petrus phenomenon was a public secret: something widely stated yet not known. The killings were both known and unknown, and were quickly forgotten or normalized. This affectively powerful ambiguity of knowing and not knowing, and especially the perception that the law is served by its blatant disregard and through extralegal violence, is the governing paradox and a key element of the infrastructure of impunity.

In the 1950s and 1960s, Indonesia had vibrant political parties with organizations down to the village level that provided various programs for education and welfare. Before they were eradicated, affiliates of the Communist Party and related organizations, along with other parties, had actively mobilized rural and urban populations. Sukarno used his fiery rhetoric to engage everyone in politics.

Things changed under Suharto. His New Order government presided over unprecedented development that contrasted starkly with the economic conditions during Sukarno's rule. Much of the growth was funded by the extraction of natural resources and international aid. Politics was transformed: the people were depoliticized and mobilized only intermittently to participate in rituals of authentication for the regime, such as sham elections.

By the late 1970s, some of the forces that initially supported Suharto's rise to power, including students, elements of the armed forces, and Muslim groups, were critical of the New Order. The political engineering, the corruption, and the military's encroachment into all areas of social and political life troubled some of them. Nevertheless, it was difficult to contest the state, as it cloaked its violations in the powerful and all but unassailable values of family, tradition, and culture, backed by an insidious bureaucracy and pervasive army territorial command structure that penetrated all aspects of daily life. The New Order represented state and society as part of a harmonious family, which allowed intervention into most aspects of political, social, and economic life. Opposition to the New Order or development was presented as an affront to the Indonesian ideal of the harmonious and authentic village life.[3]

Suharto and his propagandist and intelligence aide, Ali Moertopo, developed and justified the notion of the armed forces' dual function (*dwifungsi*) and of Pancasila democracy—a consensual decision-making process with no opposition based on the Five Principles of the national ideology:[4] "Because the origins of Pancasila democracy are to be found in family values and mutual cooperation," Suharto stated, "it does not recognise the absoluteness of a particular group due to either physical strength, economic power, authority, or number of voices."[5] Citizenship is determined not by the nation but by the regime.

Suharto, however, needed to create the appearance of democracy and legality during the Cold War and to assure the nation (and international supporters) that Indonesia was not becoming a military dictatorship. He tasked General Moertopo to engineer this project. In contrast to the political and nationalist engagement of the Sukarno period, Moertopo developed the idea of the floating mass: "people who are not permanently tied to membership of any political party."[6] In short, this tactic of depoliticization meant that political parties were banned at the village level and that people were to direct their energies toward development. Moertopo disbanded nine opposition parties and formed two state-backed parties, one nationalist (Partai Demokrasi Indonesia, or the Indonesian Democratic Party) (PDI), and one Muslim (Partai Persatuan Pembangunan, or the United Development Party) (PPP). A third group represented itself as an association of functional groups in society and included civil servants and others who were required to join (Golongan Karya, or the Party of Functional Groups) (Golkar). The only permitted political activity for ordinary people was voting in elections every five years. The regime increasingly consolidated its own power and extended its bureaucracy so that it permeated all aspects of life. The bureaucracy had no checks and balances. Restrictions were imposed on the press, and the school curriculum taught propaganda and national values.[7] And, as described in chapter 1, Sukarno's supporters and suspected members of the Communist Party were systematically cleared from public life and stripped of their rights as citizens.

Through its dual function (*dwifungsi*), the military infiltrated deeply into civilian life at the most local level, and in all areas. *Dwifungsi* derives from the army's work for national independence alongside the people and asserts that the military has a social and political role to play, in addition to their national defense role, because of this history. Moertopo claimed legitimacy for *dwifungsi* not only in history, however, but also in the constitution and in law:

> The preamble to the 1945 Constitution says: "The struggle of the independence movement has now reached the hour of rejoicing by leading the people of Indonesia safe and sound to the gateway of independence of an Indonesian state which is free, united, sovereign, just and prosperous." The struggle to achieve national independence was carried over into the struggle to maintain national unity, sovereignty, and a just and prosperous society. Therefore the armed forces, which played an active role in the liberation of the Indonesian people and state from colonial bonds, also have a responsibility to join in the struggle in the social, political, economic and cultural fields in order to secure, defend and fulfil the promise of national independence.[8]

In his 1967 state address on Pancasila democracy, Suharto denied that the presence of the military in social and political life indicated a usurpation of power, noting that they could have seized power in the supposed coup attempt. He urged people to look first at the standing of legal institutions, and ask whether human rights and democratic rights are guaranteed by laws based on the constitution.[9]

Military statements on petrus, as well as Suharto's statement on Pancasila democracy, expressed the New Order ideology that valued society over the individual:

> We wish to emphasise that Pancasila democracy will continue to hold in high esteem the basic human and democratic rights of every citizen, who in exercising them must be loyal to a greater good, that of society,

the people, and the state. It would be ideal if in the implementation of Pancasila democracy one could always achieve a balance between individual and general interests, between the interests of groups and of the nation, and between the people and the state. But if a problem arises where there is a conflict between individual and general interests or the interests of specific groups and the national interest, then we must sincerely, voluntarily and unselfishly sacrifice the relevant individual or group interest for that of society and the nation. This is the just principle and law of Pancasila democracy[10]

Most importantly for the purposes of this chapter, these statements created a veneer of legality and constitutionality. They conjoined extralegal actions and violence to legal apparatuses, which is the essence of the infrastructure of impunity. In the case of petrus, the illegality of the operations was much more blatant, and yet the framing rhetoric—that the social good overrides Western notions of individual rights—eventually shifted the idea of "law" to something applicable only to an imagined national (patriarchal) family and not to individuals, and especially not to those stigmatized and deemed to be (Communist) traitors or criminals. Citizenship, in other words, applied only to those who supported the regime. Security forces blatantly used this rhetoric of the needs of the many over the rights of the individual to justify the mysterious killings.

The *preman*—freemen, or freelance thugs—played an important role in petrus and the politics of the New Order, and the state had a preexisting relationship with criminal elements. Preman had been part of the political scene since the early nationalist period and featured prominently in the 1965 executions.[11] The government mobilized preman as a source of violence, or security, when it implemented government programs and events, but preman also controlled various black markets and illegal businesses, as well as entertainment, prostitution, recreation, and transportation—all with the understanding that some of their profits would be kicked back to the army. Moertopo, architect of the floating mass policy and one of Suharto's trusted advisers, was a master of counterintelligence and relied on extralegal forces to bring many key policies of the New Order to fruition. As tools of the state, preman groups attacked and eliminated enemies of the state (including opposition), ensured security and the implementation of events and programs, and created chaos as part of counterintelligence. Often this chaos was used to justify the arrest of opposition forces. When preman were disloyal to the state, they were eliminated (killed) by the independent Special Operations forces under Moertopo. The landscape was divided into the turf of rival gangs.

Criminality increased in 1982. In its statements, the government blamed the violence, along with problems in the election campaign, on remnants of the PKI,[12] and a year later linked the sadism of criminals to possible efforts by the PKI to make a "come back" [English in the original]," thus reviving the core propaganda narrative.[13] On the instructions of the security forces, neighborhoods formed, and armed, watch patrols, and many criminals were shot as they (reportedly) resisted arrest during the initial phase of the operations. The military asked businesses and people not to give money to criminals demanding it, as this would only lead to more criminality.[14] Ironically, the police did not protect businesses from extortion in the name of security.

The police assured the public that the possibility of mistaken targets was extremely low, and noted that criminals had an opportunity to report to a station and receive a card to indicate that they had sworn not to participate in criminal activities.[15] Even as military commanders denied there was a shoot-on-sight policy, they declared that "sadism done by criminals would not be tolerated," and urged the public to "behave well so that no other people would be shot."[16] The joint security forces—police and military—undertaking the operations were concerned that criminals would move to a different area rather than turn themselves in or be shot. And subsequently, after success in Yogyakarta and Jakarta, the operations expanded across the archipelago.[17] Paradoxically, officials extended the operations to guard the safety of society, even after they claimed that the operations had succeeded.

Even religion was invoked to justify the operations. According to military commanders in Yogyakarta, these putative criminals were beyond law and humanity; indeed, the commander noted, God even permitted them to be destroyed (*memberantsnya*).[18]

The Jakarta chief of police said they were working to restore security and order to protect the interests of the great number of innocent people: "The people who are not guilty, or have never done any crime, will be protected according to the existing laws. . . . [I]n the process of enforcing security and order sometimes there is a victim, nevertheless what has to be prevented is any innocent member of society becoming a victim."[19] Categorically, then, and de facto, the victims were "guilty" by the state's tautology.

There were a series of named military operations (for example, Operasi Pemberantastan Kejahatan or Operasi Clurit) to address criminality. *Petrus* was the term used by the press and public that described the corpses and the totality of these operations. Even as the mysterious killings were linked to the government, military officials partially disavowed them. Moertopo's rival, General L. B. Moerdani, explained to reporters that the shootings occurred only when criminals resisted after being given fair warning, but then Moerdani suggested that it could also be that the mysterious corpses were the result of gang competition and turf wars.[20] After a meeting with the president and senior military figures regarding the mysterious killings, General Try Sutrisno (who later became vice president) told reporters that the people should not be influenced by rumors that security forces did not respect the law: "Those who are guilty are the only ones who need to be afraid. Those who are not guilty don't need to feel afraid."[21] The minister of justice asked, "What is the meaning of tens of criminals being shot dead in contrast to tens of thousands or hundreds of thousands of people who might become victims of their criminal acts?"[22] Echoing these statements, members of Parliament justified the killings according to Islam or the right of the wider society to feel secure and peaceful, and as a warning to anyone who opposed the law.[23]

The state was not monolithic, of course—some generals in the armed forces criticized corruption and were known to be "principled." The secretary of the Golkar faction (the functional group for civil servants, and Suharto's electoral vehicle), Sarwono Kusumaatmadja, said that "institutions of law enforcement must give the people a feeling of security, not acts of violence outside of law."[24] He captured precisely the paradox of lawlessness in defense of the law. He urged the courts to be bold and give harsher penalties to criminals, suggesting that the law itself could be used to resolve problems. Inverting the security forces' claim that criminals were remnants of the Communist Party, a People's Representative Council representative stated that the eradication of crime outside of the law, and the chaos (*kekacauan*) of the mysterious killings, was like pouring fuel on a fire for the Communist struggle. The head of the Indonesian Ulema Council (Majelis Ulama Indonesia) worried that this "shortcut" of extralegal violence would become habitual and engrained, that people did not know who was playing what role, and that it needed to end immediately.[25] Nevertheless, the dominant discourse held that the law was defended through the elimination of the legal rights of (certain) citizens.[26] It's not that the killings existed *outside* the law, but that they were rationalized as a *defense* of the law.

Ali Moertopo, who had fallen out of favor as Suharto's key intelligence strategist, made a public statement that there was responsibility at the highest levels for the policy, citing a Majelis Permusyawaratan Rakyat Republik Indonesia (People's Consultative Assembly of the Republic of Indonesia, or MPR-RI) policy that gave the President responsibility for the operations.[27] This was an emergency situation, he said, since conventional methods of addressing criminality were not working, but the policy would not last forever, as Indonesia was a country with the rule of law.[28] The policy did not go on forever, but it did leave profound legacies and shaped both the rule of law and the affective resonance of that law, making it particularly difficult for those accused to assert their innocence or their right to due process.

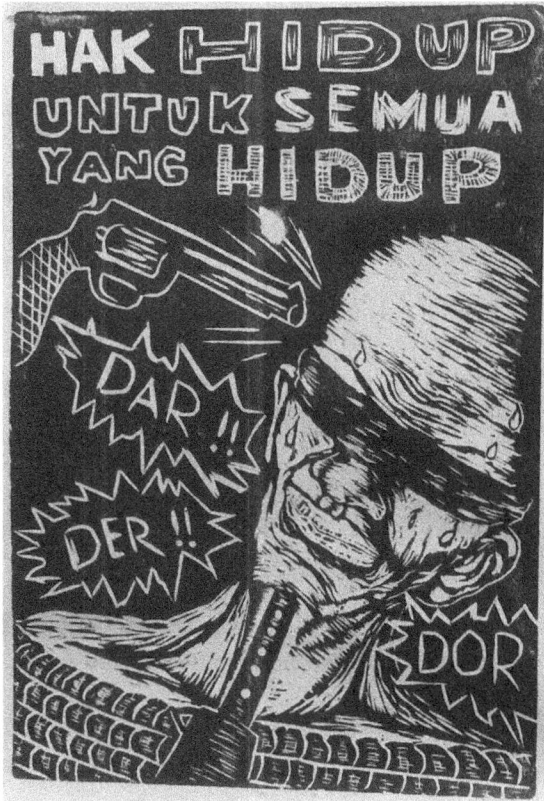

FIGURE 2.1. Wood block print image captioned, "The right to life for all those who are living." The phrase emphasizes that only those who were not killed had rights. The print was made at a workshop facilitated by the punk band Marginal at the Legal Aid Institute summer program, Kalabahu, May 10, 2016. Photo taken by the author, with the permission of artists at the workshop.

In Jakarta, criminals were told to turn themselves in, as they would be treated well in accordance with existing laws. This treatment would be better than being *kempesin*—blown out like a tire, but the word also means destroyed and penniless—by mysterious shootings.[29] For as much as they claimed success, security forces also asserted that they had to continue their operations or criminality would rise again. Members of the government, security forces, and intelligence agencies made public statements in support of the mysterious killings as necessary actions, albeit tough ones, before the country could return to handling the problem juridically.[30]

Since state agents made blatant statements that they either initiated or supported the killings (and a few spoke equally blatantly against them), much is known about the killings, which were themselves public and visible. Yet at the same time, these blatant claims coexisted with counterintelligence, deliberate ambiguity, and official duplicity and misdirection. The killings were not denied, but the qualities of their narration, and *how* they were narrated, maneuvered bystanders into a duplicitous status of knowing and unknowing. This phenomenon, not typically featured in human rights and transitional justice discourses, is key to understanding the infrastructure of impunity, especially in cases dominated by both blatant state violence and pervasive propaganda and duplicity.

A collection of short stories that appeared in prominent Indonesian newspapers in the mid-1980s powerfully challenges and defamiliarizes common-sense assumptions about petrus and speaks to themes of knowing and not knowing, complicity and ambiguity. All of these themes are elements of impunity. The author, Seno Gumira Ajidarma, known in Indonesia as Seno, worked as a magazine editor during the New Order and prolifically authored short stories throughout the mid and late 1980s that appeared in prominent newspapers, even during a time of heavy-handed news censorship.

In 1993, Seno's stories were republished under the title *Penembak misterius* (Mysterious marksman), which shifts the emphasis from the mysterious killings (*penembakan*) to the marksman (*penembak*) as the two meanings are fused in the acronym *petrus*.[31] The first three stories form an eponymous section that directly addresses the killings; the remaining stories reflect on the mid-1980s New Order and explore how citizens became numb to the regime and its bureaucracy. The stories highlight the hollow emptiness of the powerful symbols of family and tradition that the regime claims.

I approach these stories as an important archive of the violence in a context where the killings were a public secret. In climates of hostile political censorship, literature has been celebrated for smuggling out truths that can be read between the lines. The truth survives precisely because it appears in the guise of poetry, fiction, or fantasy.[32] Seno says, "When journalism is gagged, literature must speak. Because while journalism speaks with facts, literature speaks with truth."[33] And later he wrote, "Imagination is not capable of detaching facts from truth; it may become fiction, but it is still truth. Hopefully."[34] During the Cold War, literature was often a vehicle for testimony. It contributed to campaigns of exposure designed to end deniability and shame governments into accountability. These campaigns relied on the core assumption that knowledge produces change.[35] Similarly, retrospective narratives of state violence crafted in truth commissions provide stories of tragedy resolved, affirm the (national) value of (individual) suffering, and treat knowledge of past violence and injustice as transformational.[36] The political studies scholar Siphiwe Ignatius Dube concludes, "Within transitional narratives, knowledge is equated with transformation."[37] The promise of transformation through exposure of the truth is a core facet of human rights and transitional justice models.

In Seno's stories about the petrus, however, knowledge plays a different role because the killings themselves were not denied or covered up. On the contrary, the killings were designed to be seen and felt as part of social policy. In this context, Seno's stories challenge the premise that the knowledge of an atrocity is transformative, and that shaming perpetrators is effective redress. In their original context and time of publication, the stories could be read as an urgent wake-up call for the middle class to critically consider the mysterious killings and the benefits of development that implicitly justified this New Order violence and repression. More than three decades after their publication, the stories, as an archive of sorts, provide insights into how the killings, though apparently forgotten (or perhaps *because* they are forgotten), powerfully condition public acceptance of impunity in the name of law and order. Indirectly they speak to the habituation to violence, to stigmatization, and to a contradictory belief, undergirding the infrastructure of impunity, in the rule of law without rights for all.

Seno's story "Keroncong Killing" begins from a shooter's point of view, as he observes a lavish party through the scope of his weapon.[38] He describes how the scene would change if he pulled the trigger, especially if the body fell into the pool. In his earphone he hears the "sweet voice" of the woman who hired him to make the kill. It is part of the contract that he cannot know whom he is to kill. The woman tells the marksman only that his target is a "traitor of his country and nation." The marksman muses, "I swore I would be really happy if my victim this time was someone loathsome. A traitor to one's country and nation was truly despicable."[39] The shooter's inner monologue reveals that the status of "traitor" is nebulous and yet at the same time an ironclad justification for murder. Readers encountering the story in a newspaper in 1985 may have read this like the rest of the news, as confirmation that traitors deserve to be killed; or some may have read it as a statement of ambiguity about the identity of a traitor, perhaps even calling to mind those who were accused of being Communist traitors decades before. As many readers may have said about themselves, the marksman claims that he doesn't know about politics, and wonders about the family that would grieve the man's death. Still, he concludes unambiguously and categorically that as a traitor "he deserved his sentence,"[40] although there is no "sentence" per se: there has been no due process, but the familiar logic also held that the killings were quasi-legal.

The marksman reflects that he could shoot everyone at the party but won't do that because he works only "on contract." The contract, guaranteed by money rather than the rule of law, presumably harnesses and restrains extralegal violence.

The story, told as it is from his perspective, reinforces with every first-person statement the reader's connection to the marksman, who distances himself from the killing just as many Indonesians did at the time. The marksman kills explicitly for hire, but the wider population of silent beneficiaries similarly tolerates abuses for development and economic advancement.

As the story progresses, the assassin moves his scope from the target and follows the sounds of the musicians he can see on the stage, and the clattering dishes and background noise coming through his earpiece, until he is able to locate the woman speaking to him. With the woman in his sights, the marksman asks questions: "What kind of traitor? Why hasn't he been tried?"[41]

The woman reminds him that it is not his business and threatens to cancel the contract. He moves his rifle to her and asks whether the man really is a traitor. The woman persists in thinking she is in control, and even threatens him with death: "Shoot him now, you fool, or you'll die."[42] She thinks she is protected by her anonymity, but he describes her and her body betrays her terror: she pales and sweats as she realizes that her relationship with elite and economic power would not be enough to save her should he pull the trigger.

She protests that he has violated the contract, but he responds that he doesn't want to "shoot innocent people." She again tells him that it is not his business and then reminds him (and the reader who views the world through his eyes), "Last year you shot thousands of innocent people,"[43] effectively undermining his position of critiquing the regime (by reducing him to a criminal outside the national family and as such without rights), and demonstrating the power of the New Order state that has outsourced its violence. The nameless woman knows that his words will not be heeded because his relationship to the elite is unofficial, unacknowledged, and mediated by her. And yet it is precisely his skill as a marksman, the equipment prepared for his contract—the gun with a silencer—and his skills in disappearing that endanger her: he could kill her and vanish. He is of course already a killer and outside the social order, but his status with the regime exempts him from treatment as a criminal and makes him wonder with deep irony whether he would be called a hero for killing the target, since the target was a traitor.

Eventually the woman does disclose the reason for the death sentence: the target "slandered the name of our country abroad." The woman says that it is politics, and that it's not his business to decide whether this is reason enough to be shot, and she begs him not to shoot her. The shooter asks who ordered the kill; the woman again claims to know nothing. Finally she describes the person who gave the order, an older man talking to the target. The shooter evaluates his face as "cagey and full of deceit. Completely disgusting." The story ends with the shooter aiming at the older man who ordered the kill . . . but then calls it a *keroncong* fantasy.[44]

Keroncong music adapts Western instruments to Indonesian rhythms. It makes the marksman sleepy, as he shares at the beginning of the story. Thus, the marksman's powerful questions are tacitly diminished as a fantasy, prompted by the dreamy, soporific state produced by the popular music, not unlike the effects of the political refrains of tradition by the New Order.

The reader sees the world through the eyes of the unidentified shooter, who protests that he is not the killer; he just pulls the trigger. The story complicates the common-sense logic and morality of the New Order, as the marksman interrogates the idea that it is enough simply to label the target a traitor, and he, not the political elite, asks about evidence and trials. In New Order propaganda and practice, that label was indeed sufficient to precipitate and justify killing or stigmatization of the individual and his or her family, so the marksman invites readers, as well, to wonder whether the act justifies the punishment.

The story highlights moral ambiguity as well as knowledge. The limits of what can be known (the identity of the woman on the earphone; who ordered the kill; what the target did) ostensibly protect powerful individuals, or eliminate liability and moral deliberation. Yet at the same time, the marksman is able to easily locate the woman by following background noises, working affectively through sound rather than words.

The sequencing in the story is important and conveys feelings that go deeper than the news and the facts of the killings, all of which were blatant and publicized. At first the shooter appears to follow the New Order propaganda, doubtless familiar to readers: "He is a traitor, he deserves to die." But then the marksman's thoughts dissolve into ambiguity, and the story forces the middle-class reader's identification with the marksman. It does not directly challenge the emotionally powerful idea that traitors are loathsome and should be killed, but questions the evidence or grounds for labeling someone thus.

It also invites a critique that extralegal violence could get out of control. The state's involvement in the killings was at first a public secret and then a widely known fact, and Seno's story questions whether the state could actually control its criminal proxies—a particularly difficult matter to discuss straightforwardly in public. Finally, the marksman provokes questions of motivation and money. Part of the state's entanglement with criminal elements had to do with economic enrichment: the state was developing the bureaucracy to serve itself, increase its power, and enrich itself. By contrast, for a dangerous moment, the marksmen subverts that entire logic. He demonstrates that he could use his power to kill the greedy person who ordered the kill just as easily as he could shoot the target, and that he could disappear without the payment promised by the contract. (Two other stories reflecting on the New Order culture and values similarly make visible and question the common-sense logic of that period: "Semakin" and "Sarmen.")

The marksman ends by calling the story a fantasy. The details of the story are all factual and logical. There are no monsters or fantastical elements, which do appear in Seno's other stories. But the idea that one of the regime's hired assassins would speak is somewhat fantastic in and of itself. Very few marksmen testified to their experience as petrus left thousands dead or disappeared. Like the gun in this story, they were silenced.

One criminal, however—Bathi Mulyono, or BM, as he prefers to be called—escaped and did testify as to how the system worked.[45] BM was recruited after he murdered another prisoner while serving a prison sentence for murder.[46] After his release from jail, he worked with the elite and the military to build a good business of brokering activities on the street, including parking and managing security payments for food stalls and other vendors, as well as shady fields of economic activity.[47] As a convicted murderer, he had a reputation and was powerful and respected on the street. He was asked by Ali Moertopo's group to make and lead an organization of recidivists and youths to serve as part of Suharto's floating mass during the late 1970s.[48] BM was able to mobilize as many as five thousand youths for local and regional government and the national Golkar party. He was trained by intelligence agents to create violence. In the 1977 election, the new Islamic party (PPP) did well. Suharto wanted to besmirch its reputation, and he dispatched BM to a PPP campaign rally before the 1982 election to do so. BM describes going to the sanctioned rally at Lapangan Banteng, the plaza in central Jakarta, dressed in the uniform of Suharto's functional party (Golkar) with a T-shirt beneath his jacket that identified him as a PPP activist. He took off the jacket and created havoc and violence, and consequently the Islamic party was painted as anarchist, disorderly, chaotic, and a threat to society. The PPP did not win the election. The violence justified repression and security operations by the regime and also smeared the PPP as a disruptive, destabilizing force in society. BM notes that he never claimed this act, and Ali Moertopo was credited and then dismissed for it.[49] In this system, criminal elements created chaos to be resolved, worked in black and gray markets, mobilized masses of supporters, and assassinated rivals or critics, especially public figures who could interfere with the New Order regime's agenda of long-term power.[50]

BM disappeared in 1983 after motorcycles shot at the vehicle he was driving. As the petrus began, he was given a letter guaranteeing his protection by Moertopo, but he soon realized that the letter could not protect him.[51] Retrospectively it has become clear that the killings were about eliminating Moertopo's independent basis of power, which stemmed from the criminal gangs he controlled, and possibly erasing evidence of how the system worked. In this respect, the letter would have been a liability.

BM escaped by moving and hiding. He had five passports, each with a different name, and he moved through Singapore, Brunei, and Malaysia, as well as Java.[52] On one of his journeys, he hitched a ride with a pickup truck. As he climbed aboard, he saw sacks used to transport vegetables and men with long rifles. One of them cautioned him not to sit on a sack, as it was full of human heads. As they continued through the teak forest, the truck stopped every few kilometers and the men took the sacks down in turns, fired shots, and threw them into the forest. BM recalled seeing seven executions, and, fearing he would be recognized as a criminal, he asked to get off at a coffee stall by the side of the road, rather than continue with the truck.[53] In this way, BM witnessed the shift in the covert intelligence worlds as Benny Moerdani came to power.[54] BM understood his organization and work to be destroying labor organizations and ensuring that they were loyal only to Suharto's Golkar, and he speculated that rather than disband the organization in line with new intelligence priorities, they were simply killing off members.[55] "Maybe the powerful considered my job done and it was time to finish me off," he stated.[56] Because there was not "a reason to disband our organization, the pattern of planned, systematic killing" emerged.[57]

Read together, Seno's fictional "Keroncong Killing" and BM's nonfictional testimony demonstrate how impunity is both obvious and unseen. Since the killer works for the state and yet from within a space of civil death, analysis of ethics and morality is deflected and the state achieves impunity while simultaneously orchestrating violence. The criminal's word poses no true threat for the powerful because he is already a killer and a criminal and is therefore killable. Ingeniously, and paradoxically, the system creates an appearance of culpability—someone has been killed in punishment—but the powerful men in batik at the party Seno describes enjoy impunity. Socially and personally they feel distanced and different from the killer. Like all other infrastructures, the infrastructure of impunity does not serve all people equally well. Denial of impunity for BM effectively extends impunity for the powerful agents—the very agents for whom he worked. In this way, extralegal violence appears to support the law.

Victims of the mysterious killings were not all marksmen for the regime. Some were tattooed and possibly petty criminals; others were cases of mistaken identity; still others were human rights defenders or critics of the state. The overwhelming success of the stigmatization and dehumanization of criminals—and the vague or even nonexistent details about the victims, who were both seen and not seen at all—made it difficult to apply strategies of empathy or to see the victims as humans or citizens deserving of rights.[58] In this context, the few voices of victims from this time protest that they were not criminals.[59] None speaks to BM's drama or highly placed connections, but others tell that their friends were involved in luring them into police traps and describe the difficulties for those accused of being criminals, and their families.[60] The rhetoric that those labeled criminals had resisted and that there was no choice but to shoot them, coupled with the logic that they were guilty or else they would have turned themselves in and registered to obtain the police identity card (which would protect them from being shot on sight), created the illusion of a formal process,[61] one with which the individuals killed had simply not complied.

In this context of knowing and not knowing, Seno's stories create empathy for the dehumanized victims. In "The Sound of Rain on the Roof," for instance, the storyteller has been asked to tell a story of fear.[62] The sound of rain triggers an embodied response of fear: "Her chest would tighten and her heart pound heavily whenever the rain would stop."[63] The storyteller reminds middle-class readers encountering the story in the national newspaper that heavy rain could be frightening if a house has leaks or could be flooded or crushed. While the rain triggers the fear, it is accompanied in the story by the inevitable appearance of a tattooed corpse at the end of an alleyway. The story's protagonist, a woman named Sawitri, mostly does not hear anything, and yet the corpses always appear. She fears the rain, not the corpse. "She was always afraid," Seno writes, "but she always wanted to see the tattooed corpse's face."[64] The neighbors crowd around too, and if that makes it impossible for her to see by leaning out of her window, she "would always go outside and squeeze through the crowd until she could see the body." Even when she leaves her house to look, "she wasn't always able to see the face because sometimes the corpse had already been covered with a cloth, but Sawitri would feel relieved enough when she saw a part of the body."[65]

The reader in the mid-1980s may have identified with that same sense of relief, since the official and public record justified the killings as a means to rid the nation of crime and create a feeling of safety.[66] And yet, having lulled the reader into the familiar, comforting rationale for the killings, Seno emphasizes in the rest of the story the brutality of the regime and draws the reader to consider the humanity and individuality of the victims.

Sawitri sees some of the corpses as similar to sleeping people (distinguished only by the blood) and reminds readers that "not all of the corpses' faces are frightening."[67] Seno's reference to corpses as sleeping people invites a comparison to sleeping citizens, who perhaps may become corpses themselves.

While she sees the victims' souls and looks into their eyes, voices of the dead are hard to convey: "Sawitri felt as if the eyes told her many stories when she looked at them but it was difficult to retell them."[68] Sometimes she wonders about their families or perceives that their eyes are questioning or demanding their rights, and such empathy would have been extremely difficult for ordinary people to voice in a nonfictional context when the stories were first published. The stories may also be difficult to tell because of social stigmatization: her neighbors have become habituated to the appearance of the corpses; in fact, they are happy when they see them. She describes the scene: "The children would shout 'hooray, hooray. . . . Die! Go to hell! Now he knows how it feels! . . . Dog! Sometimes they would kick the corpse and step on its face."[69] Decades after the killings, the stigmatization remains effective, but it is difficult to acknowledge that society participated in sadism in the name of security, law, and order—and that the practice continues today with less physical and more abstract means of dehumanizing criminals.

In the story, the sadism started before the neighbors spontaneously defaced the discarded corpses, as Sawitri notices that the tattoos have been ruined by excessive and unnecessary gunshots: "Sawitri felt that sometimes the shooters of these tattooed bodies indeed had intended to destroy the images. They could have shot only the parts of the body that would cause a fatal wound, but they also shot at places they didn't need to shoot. . . .. Did they shoot at those places just to make the tattooed men suffer?"[70] Portraying the brutality of the regime that presents itself as civilized, legal, and proper reverses the discourse of the sadistic criminal used to justify the operations.

The tattoos described in the story depict the names and images of lovers with hearts. They are not criminal or gang markers. Through one tattoo, Sawitri recognizes someone she knew. His tattoo reads, "I love mama," demonstrating that victims also embody (in this case, literally inscribed on the body) the ideal bonds of family that the regime extols rhetorically (often to marginalize prostitutes, criminals, and others seen to violate family norms).

Here, the story shifts, as Sawitri recalls tattooing her name on Pamuji's chest. The reader is not immediately given any context about his identity, as she recalls that her name was not the only name there—other tattoos named different lovers. The reader then learns that Sawitri is a prostitute. It becomes clear that Sawitri is looking for her loved one, Pamuji, relieved that each corpse she sees is not her beloved, underscoring that she can't know if he is hiding or has been killed, that there will be no prayers or burial.

Seno reminds middle-class, urban readers that even though the policy is no longer prominently in the news, the practice continues, and there are victims in human relationships that the system, and policies, make it all but impossible to see: "The photos disappeared from the newspapers, but the tattooed corpses continued to appear."[71] The killings are more apparent and visible in the crowded neighborhoods (*kampung*) among the poor, whose houses, in the rain, "could be smashed by a medium-sized tree."[72]

Like "Keroncong Killing," this story questions the evidence that brands someone a traitor. Here the "evidence" of the tattoo is unsettled, and unsettling. Popular understandings of the mysterious killings surmised that those with tattoos were targeted and that youths without tattoos or criminal records could feel safe and immune from petrus operations.[73] Komnas HAM investigations disclosed reports of young men who came to the hospital to ask for their tattoos to be removed, but most were denied because they did not bring a letter from the police.[74] In an interview, Yosep Adi Prasetyo, the deputy chairman of Komnas HAM who headed the investigation into the petrus, recalled the period as terrifying and commented on the struggles to remove tattoos and the lasting scars after removal.[75]

Police denied that they were targeting young men with tattoos, and insisted instead that they were focused on weapons or suspicious vehicles.[76] BM's comments reveal that being on the list of preman, criminals, and recidivists—not so much having tattoos—endangered individuals. It was suggested that the authorities had a secret list of criminals (*gali*, or groups of wild youths) and those people had to come forward, register, or face the consequences. Paralleling the treatment of those branded as ex–political prisoners, once registered, they had to carry special IDs, report to the military every day (making it impossible to have a job), and report on their family backgrounds. There is less information on those who began to work for the military, police, and government as informants and agents as a result of these registrations.[77]

Official statements claimed the success of joint police and military operations where some agents went undercover as thugs to defeat recidivists.[78] Thus, someone who appeared to be a criminal may have been an undercover police officer. Amid the ambiguity as to which violence was from the state (to create security) and which was opposed it (to create insecurity), the idea of a difficult-to-remove tattoo was to reassure the public with the idea of a permanent, visible, and physically indelible identity for the criminal.

Official statements emphasized that no one who was innocent would be killed,[79] indirectly enforcing the logic that if you were killed or caught then you were, by definition, guilty. Beyond eroding the presumption of innocence in criminal justice, this process also led to social recrimination and brutality.[80] The public desecrated the corpses of victims—taken to be inherently guilty and thus beyond society or rights—and tolerated the denial of cultural and religious rites for victims. I spoke with one New Order activist (born in the late 1960s) whose own tattoos were dramatic and visible. She described her uncles, who were twins. One was a good kid and the other was a "bad" kid. Her aunt crocheted them gloves to cover the tattoos on their wrists and hands. One, the obedient son, worked as a bicycle cab (*becak*) driver, and he was killed—the wrong twin. Her family doesn't like to talk about it, and her own activism has focused on other instances of gross violations of human rights, rather than this one.[81]

FIGURE 2.2. "Tattoos Are Not Criminal" wood block print, made at a workshop facilitated by the punk band Marginal at the Legal Aid Institute summer program, Kalabahu, May 10, 2016. Photo taken by the author, with the permission of artists at the workshop.

Other evidence, in addition to the disfigurement of tattoos, may indicate the anxiety that security forces felt about the mystical powers of the criminals they sought to eliminate. For example, forensic evidence revealed the use of gold bullets for killings—beliefs hold that black magic can be used to establish immunity to all but gold bullets. Other forensic evidence indicated the use of an axe to hack open the chests of criminals, who appeared to continue to breathe after being shot.[82]

In 1987, a year and a half after the publication of "The Sound of Rain on the Roof," Seno published a surreal story titled "Grrrh!" from the perspective of a police officer charged with battling the zombies of tattooed bodies improperly buried.[83] Entwined in the more fantastic elements of the story are pointed and direct critiques of the government and the killings. The critiques were most likely directed to the readers of the Jakarta newspaper that published it. The story achieves a form of grotesque realism.

The story "quotes" a newspaper article report of living corpses appearing in every busy area of the capital city. Traditional defenses against this inexplicable, strange threat had failed. Seno writes, "Even weapons that were enhanced with sorcerers' spells were useless. . . . Even the missile strikes did not kill them. Pieces of meat still jumped around and maggots fell from corpses and multiplied in terrifying proportions." The newspaper alludes to the mysterious killings when it notes that the zombies "act like criminals,"[84] and the fictionalized article ends by pointing to the government: "We hope that the government will be able to overcome these truly strange events. Indeed, in daily life, in this country, there are too many illogical matters that are blindly accepted. . . . Living corpses that roam the streets are too terrifying for reality."[85] Seno deftly blends logic and illogic. While the descriptions of the corpses are designed to inspire revulsion, corpses in public and criminals shot dead are all factual, real, and justified on the grounds of security.

The detective in Seno's story looks for reasons why the corpses are rising up from the netherworld. He wonders whether they had been criminals when they were alive. He notices "the traces of tattoos on their decomposing skin" and the holes of bullet wounds. Seno contemplates once again the problem of social forgetting, or the refusal to draw connections. The detective, he writes, "was on the verge of recalling something, but then lost track of it."[86] Finally the detective finds a report that the opened graves are those of third-class criminals, and some of the zombies had originated in the "Big Hole." A zombie knocks on his door, and the detective recognizes him as one of the last victims of "that famous and controversial slaughter at the Big Hole."[87]

He tries to tell his commander that shooting the zombie won't solve the problem, and neither will a missile. The zombies are a collective return of the repressed, the people and events known yet not known, dead and buried except not buried. He begs his superior, "Don't you remember? Along with Ngadul, six thousand third-class criminals were secretly wiped out!"[88] They were buried at the site from which the zombies came, but the commander is unable to make the connection, and the detective introduces the problem that not only were some of the criminals reformed, but religious laws were not respected and there were not prayers or a proper burial for the corpses.

The detective concludes, "The slaughter was a big mistake, sir! Our generation is suffering the consequences! Those people weren't willing to die, sir! They're taking revenge!"[89] The fear of revenge animated the propaganda about Communism, and while the state disavowed any desire for revenge, the fear that others might seek revenge contributed to a spiral of violence and mistreatment as well as a tolerance for consigning some individuals to the space of civil death and dehumanization, beyond even religious rites of burial. In Seno's story, the superior finally asks what must be done, and the detective replies that they must have a mass prayer, that there are not enough missiles to destroy the zombies. But the superior dismisses his idea as dreaming and says they are importing missiles that will destroy the corpses. The story ends as a zombie eats the detective as he calls for help.

Seno's three stories that directly address the petrus are a kind of shock therapy to get readers, especially the middle-class, urban readers of the prominent newspapers that published them, to see and understand the brute violence occurring around them, without the cloak of justifications, duplicity, and rationalizing narratives. Social acceptance of this violence is a key component of how the infrastructure of impunity extends and endures: the violence is highly visible but is unseen or unremarked on. Fiction, however, achieves greater verisimilitude than the newspapers or factual narratives, and it creates a space for deeper knowing and understanding as well as the possibility of unconscious, affective movement. The stories interrogate the idea that the 1965 violence and the mysterious killings were necessary and imply that the violence, in the form of grotesque and indestructible zombies, will return to haunt subsequent generations.

All three stories play on knowledge, realism, and memory. Social knowledge—the tension of knowing and not knowing—distributes liability and complicity. The point of view and identification with characters and narrators disturbs and even inverts official narratives of morality. The marksman, for instance, is more ethical and thoughtful than the elite official who orders the kill. And even when the stories do not directly question these narratives, they do so indirectly—for example, what makes someone a traitor? What do tattoos indicate? The prostitute and criminal, for example, demonstrate genuine care as well as affectionate family and social bonds that are lacking in Seno's stories of New Order families.

As an archive of social knowledge, these three stories foreshadow why facts will seem to offer resolution but then fail to deliver. The reader who did not live through the events, or who does not remember them, can nevertheless experience retrospectively the ambiguity and uncertainty that fortifies the infrastructure of impunity.[90] In Seno's stories, several elements obscure knowledge and diminish the force of facts or truth telling: the popular music that induces the marksman's sleepiness, the warm yellow glow of lamps and fog that create the ambiance of a semiconscious dreamscape, a character's repeated failure to remember or grasp a truth just on the edge of consciousness, and contracts that delimit liability for knowledge. Even in cases where his protagonists and characters do manage to know, that knowledge does not lead to positive transformation and resolution;

instead the characters are eaten by the monstrous legacies of past actions, for example, or inhabit a world where logic becomes fantasy. The suffering in Seno's stories is not resignified or transformative: it is simply a fact. Even when the humanity of the victims is noted, their bodies simply remain on the pavement, getting wet. Through contradictions, surprise, irony, exaggeration, and surreal elements, Seno's stories provoke audiences to understand that they are complicit, that they could challenge the grounding logics of the New Order and must do so in order to avert future disaster.

Seno does not specifically hold out much hope for knowledge in these stories, which intimate instead the probable failure and limitations of the rational. The idea of "waking up" to finally question foundational logic and justifications of policies is in the end only a fantasy. Those with the power, the elite or the middle class, are shown as empty and unfeeling, and even the intimate domain of family is usurped as a site for the regime's propaganda. At the same time, other stories demonstrate how those who try to stay true to their ideals are changed by the regime and bureaucracy in nonrational ways that occur at the level of the body. Seno's stories, in their fantastically surreal as well as viscerally embodied moods, do not envision knowledge as a panacea, or a force for resolution, but seem to move far beyond it.

And in this sense his stories describe a core aspect of petrus: facts were conceded and known—criminals lacked rights, and people were violently killed—yet the facts weren't condemned or even seen as contrary to law; nor did they galvanize. The stories probe how people know facts and manage to evade their corresponding moral concerns and qualms. These elements contribute to the infrastructure of impunity, and that impunity is not necessarily challenged or dismantled by exposure and shaming—especially when the facts are abundantly known.

Other stories turn from victims and killers to consider bystanders—those whose fears about security are presumably allayed by the killings. These stories suggest how the regime numbs and ensnares individuals so that dehumanization and othering become normalized. They probe the contradictions between traditional values and development, and also depict the emptiness of successful families rent by the desire for position and status.

One of these stories, "Semangkin Formerly Semakin," tells of an ascending village official and the ways in which power disciplines and constricts his voice.[91] The official tries to puzzle out when the nasal sound began to creep into his pronunciation of "increasing," adding the *ng* sound that characterizes official speech. He has been elected village head of an administrative district in Jakarta and wants to speak correctly in his inaugural speech. "The wrong words could be misleading," he thinks. "If everything that was wrong was considered right, what would happen to the country?"[92] This is precisely the problem that other stories highlight, of course—how ordinary words and symbols have been used to justify practices at odds with their original values. After he repeatedly fails to pronounce the word correctly, a psychologist tells him that he has a syndrome that affects 2,500 people, all of whom have decided to accept it and pronounce the word with full conviction. A public official cannot avoid the topic of development and the correspondingly important word "increasing." Sukab protests that he doesn't want to "follow blindly" or "play it safe" and continues to try to practice the correct pronunciation.[93]

He finally pronounces it correctly and is ready for his inauguration. As he prepares his speech, he receives an urgent message with a decree announcing that the word *semakin* without the nasal pronunciation is forbidden, effective immediately. Try as he might, he is unable to return to the nasal pronunciation. His wife advises, "The truth did not choose to side with you. You must learn to read the signs of the times . . . that is the only way to live safely. Don't be too idealistic; don't be stubborn."[94] On the day of the official inauguration, his wife represents him, reading his text in her melodious voice that "sings reality to sleep,"[95] which recalls Seno's affection for metaphors of the soporific and sounds that lull people into acceptance of unacceptable realities, and realities at odds with their stated values of community, family, and democracy.

This story calls attention to how New Order bureaucracy corrupted people and generated impunity. While the New Order has ended, many elements of it that support the infrastructure of impunity persist into the present. The threat of violence alone does not achieve this—bureaucrats have managed to unknow and forget petrus—but is aided by the ways in which bureaucracy is mind numbing and constrictive and yet attractive and all-consuming at the same time. It sucks people in. This is an important element in the infrastructure of impunity: mundane boredom lulls people to accept its irrationality and illogic, until logic and truth become impossible.[96]

The stories portray the New Order bureaucracy as an inescapable and suffocating system: people are haunted yet cannot remember; the state infects and co-opts even the habits of their bodies (for example, involuntary pronunciation, which lulls logic until one accepts a wrong as a right). I dwell on these stories because they so vividly capture the inner, affective world and the truths of petrus, and because they are an invaluable archive of social knowledge—ironically, not a factual archive but an archive of affect that represents the duplicity and complicity and the emotional processes that create impunity.

The petrus operations were about more than the eradication of criminal gangs—they were also about shifts in how the military managed its relationships to criminal and extralegal elements. Suharto recognized that individuals such as Ali Moertopo had too much independent power through their gangs, and the killings were implemented by his one-time protégé and rival intelligence figure, General L. B. Moerdani. While the killings may have been responding to social anxieties about the violence of criminality, they did not resolve the issue or eradicate all of the perpetrators. Thousands of criminals registered and were thereby put in closer contact with the state. The personnel changed; for example, BM was an agent of Ali Moertopo, whose power others wanted to eliminate. The state did not eradicate the criminal element and its own reliance on it but simply reorganized and resignified it. From the demise of criminals emerged a new form of power and a new institutionalization and bureaucratization of other gangs.

Even before it was officially acknowledged, it was clear from statements in the newspaper that those who looked like criminals had the choice of turning themselves in (and then being given official ID cards with the stipulation that they report and do whatever the security forces required) or being shot on the spot. The involvement of the state in the killings was cast into doubt in official statements, but it was not denied—it was a public secret that the state was involved in engineering criminality as part of its counterintelligence operations, although it was very difficult to discuss this openly at this time. After the mysterious killings through the late New Order period (1990s), state proxies were transformed from criminal gangs into quasi-independent and formally bureaucratized organizations. In other words, criminals did not disappear so much as they were bureaucratized.[97]

The organization Pancasila Youth (Pemuda Pancasila, or PP), for example, worked very similarly to counterintelligence: it created the chaos that it was then well positioned to resolve. The political scientist Loren Ryter describes how the formalization and institutionalization of PP allowed it to claim that any gangsters caught were individual agents or rogue elements.[98] If they were not in uniform and in possession of their official PP membership cards, then PP as an organization was innocent, although there was widespread suspicion that PP or similar organizations were working with the state. Ryter suggests that by the late New Order period, the idea that the preman, and especially identifiable organizations such as PP, were behind violent incidents ironically allowed branches of the armed forces to commit violent acts out of uniform, making the violent proxies more necessary as a symbol than a force.[99] This institutionalized a mechanism for disavowal, ambiguity, and doubt. Any ties to Suharto and his generals were obscured by organizational hierarchies that limited liability.

PP continued despite the fall of Suharto and was mobilized to intimidate critics, while presenting itself as the putative face of patriotism. In the decades since the New Order, the relationship between the state, violence, and identity has further evolved and shifted. The anthropologist Laurens Bakker cites preman claims that in contrast to the New Order, when preman methods (extralegal violence, intimidation, and extortion) were used in the service of a patron, they are now used in the service of local society.[100] Societal control does not always prioritize the rights of minority citizens, and so the mobilization of mass organizations to intimidate victims of past state violence, particularly those of 1965, has proven particularly effective in silencing discussion and extending social stigmatization into the present. This often escalates into violence.[101]

The political scientist Ian Wilson demonstrates that some mass social organizations (*ormas*) have effectively drawn on civil society discourses, in addition to preman methods, to expand their constituencies and make themselves more acceptable, even with their use of premanisms such as thuggish behavior and criminality.[102] The *ormas* continue to enforce stigmas of the past and extend them to new target groups (especially sexual and religious minorities), and their popular support, augmented by the use of violence, means that social scapegoating continues and prevents legal or political efforts to hold perpetrators of state violence accountable. These proxy organizations have become influential elements in the infrastructure of impunity.

In terms of impunity, the killings worked on many levels: the appearance of corpses in public places (or in media coverage) demonstrated the state's power to eliminate individuals who threatened social order, in the name of a tough stance on criminality. Where corpses or formerly feared local thugs were turned over to communities to abuse, people become complicit with the killings. "Criminal" then became a new label for a stigmatized individual who was, literally, killable. More subtly, the killings undermined the rule of law at the same time that military figures stated that only those who resisted the law were shot on sight. Finally, the New Order eliminated evidence and witnesses of its own engagement with the criminal underworld.

The infrastructure relies on a transformation, abetted by the complicity of knowing and not knowing that Seno's fiction evokes so powerfully, by which law becomes something distinct from the rights of all. The mysterious killings, especially as encountered in Seno's surreal stories, provoke a basic issue: how is it that the killings are widely known and yet people still follow the rules and believe that they have a system of law? Social knowledge is part of the infrastructure of impunity because it is the process by which formal knowledge loses its transformational force as evidence.

During the New Order, state violence was blatant and acknowledged. Official statements and propaganda made violence heroic and necessary, while policies and laws justified mistreatment and the denial of citizens' rights. Violence and stigmatization were narrated as legal and nationalistic. The infrastructure of impunity relied on laws and policies as well as popular participation and belief. Perpetrators used national symbols as well as laws to ensure that they could not be held accountable. National mythology and propaganda enrolled bystanders and future generations into the same system of beliefs that the violence was necessary and justified. National development made them indirect beneficiaries. This infrastructure is widespread and mundane but also spectacular, as in the example of the Lubang Buaya Monument and Museum as well as the annual screening of the propaganda film.

As an archive of affect, Seno's short fiction highlights complicity and ambiguity in social knowledge—the nebulous identity of the "traitor," the unstable control of the state over its proxies and assassins, the blurred line between legal and extralegal violence, and the possibility that state narratives of morality may be easily inverted. Nothing is entirely as it seems. In the years after Seno's stories first appeared, these characteristics of the New Order intensified. Understanding Seno's stories not as "exposures" of repressed facts but rather as reflections on how societies know and unknow, and on the dynamic relationships that develop around knowledge of blatant state violence, foreshadows the difficulties that human rights and civil society organizations would face in drawing on transitional justice strategies in the aftermath of the New Order.

RESIST FORGETTING

After Indonesia's postauthoritarian transition—the *reformasi* of 1998—new forms of activism drew on victim testimony and other revelations to seek accountability for past violence. Twenty-five years after the end of Suharto's New Order in 1998, it is hard to recall the brave hope and confidence that revelations would produce meaningful changes. The postauthoritarian reformasi was a moment when it seemed that the critics and activists would win, equipped with the tools of data, facts, truth, and truth telling. It is hard to recall the energy and power of working around the clock in the face of death threats, murder attempts, and the murder of comrades to bring truths and revelations to light. Certainly, in some cases, these revelations produced concrete results and strengthened hopes for change. And yet, over time, the infrastructure of impunity has proven resilient, despite these apparent victories of acknowledgment, documentation, and institutional changes: for example, the dismissal of high-ranking perpetrators from institutions. Revelations are made but are also forgotten (or undermined); documents disappear, reappear, and inspire new advocacy as well as mutations and repetitions of past state propaganda. In this sense the experience in postauthoritarian Indonesia challenges the expectations of transitional justice and human rights literature, because its infrastructure of impunity diminishes the transformative power of revelations, facts, documents, and truth. The truth bends to that infrastructure more than the infrastructure bends to the truth. This chapter explores how this happened, and why it is so.

The reformasi era arrived in Indonesia near the end of a decade marked by fractures in the New Order regime and criticism by academics, nongovernmental organizations, lawyers, the press, and influential figures. As the mysterious killings had revealed, the New Order military had significant power, but it also had rivalries. In the late 1980s, to attract foreign investment, Suharto launched a policy of *keterbukaan,* or "openness." He relaxed controls on the press and allowed student activism and nongovernmental organizations to grow. In the 1990s students and NGOs became increasingly well organized and critical as they addressed issues of environment, development, economic inequality, and labor rights, as well as civil and political rights. The military tolerated more demonstrations and a critical momentum to expose Suharto's flaws and pressure him. But it would be a mistake to consider the openness policy a genuine effort to democratize; in fact, many observers suggested that General L. B. Moerdani, the author of the mysterious killings policy, devised the openness policy.

Nevertheless, openness did produce knowledge of state violence and a context for revelation as a form of critique and activism. The state also developed practices of engaging investigations and legal processes (and then undermining them). As the communications studies scholar Mary McCoy argues, the press played a key role in mediating these revelations, although its stance tended to mesh with economic and business interests.[1] McCoy's study of the press asserts that the problem of self-censorship is more devastating than violent or legal repression and cites one writer's description of it as "almost a disease from which no one is immune."[2] This culture of self-censorship was an important part of the infrastructure of impunity, muffling journalists and subtly delimiting the impact of truth telling and public debate.

Policies designed to depoliticize campuses restricted students' mass demonstrations; however, the anthropologist Doreen Lee has shown that critical writing practices, including the tightly controlled student press but also pamphlets, zines, and manifestos, helped to sustain opposition during a period that otherwise appeared to be uneventful and characterized by students who were silent or complicit with the regime.[3] Students built important connections with human rights, legal aid, and environmental NGOs during this period, directing their attention to national issues.[4]

Two cases demonstrate how both the state and its critics engaged in the exposure of facts, and with legal processes: the extrajudicial killing of the labor activist Marsinah and struggles for independence in East Timor. In 1991, journalists were allowed to visit East Timor, an event intended to display its successful integration into Indonesia after the violent occupation of 1975, which the United Nations had never acknowledged. But the journalists instead captured and internationally broadcast the military gunning down peaceful protesters in the Santa Cruz

cemetery. In response to international pressure, Suharto appointed two investigative commissions,[5] which eventually became the template for Komnas HAM,
the Indonesian National Human Rights Commission. This process also allowed
Suharto to restructure the intelligence agencies, where opposition against him
was strongest, to make them more loyal. The commissions established a pattern
of investigating but failing to effectively punish abuses by the military.[6] Indeed,
the Special Forces Command (Kopassus) unit began to train militia groups to
eradicate the Timorese resistance, which had intensified.

   In 1993 in East Java, students flooded the streets to protest the death of Marsinah, a young female labor activist sexually assaulted and killed by the military.
The protests expanded both because of the students' energy and passion and
because of the tacit support from the military, which supported the demonstration against Suharto.[7] The case was one of the first investigated by the new
National Human Rights Commission, whose report indicated numerous violations.[8] Six months after Marsinah's murder, civilian factory management and
one army officer were tried for the crime. At trial it was suggested that Marsinah
had evidence that the factory was making imitation trademark watches, though
the truth was that she was involved in labor organizing. The case demonstrates
issues that have plagued subsequent trials. Management personnel were tortured
and forced to sign faked confessions about the plan to murder Marsinah, and
when they recanted these testimonies in court, stating that they were made under
duress, their spoken testimony was discounted. The criminal code invalidates
spoken testimony in favor of written testimony, which supports the infrastructure of impunity because individuals can be tortured and forced to sign statements that ensure they will be convicted of crimes, and this effectively puts an
end to scrutiny. Human rights advocates argued that in addition to violations
of due process, the case hid the district military commander's involvement and
the military's interference in labor disputes.[9] The Komnas investigation raised
key issues, but legal technicalities (i.e., lack of permits) were used to silence the
commissioners from speaking in public, and the court completely ignored its
findings.

   Fractures within the state allowed for public demonstrations, occasional revelations, and sometimes the appearance that these revelations had consequences
for military personnel who had been caught violating the law. The exposure of
state violence and crime, and some resolution through the existing legal framework, further created an impression that public protest and demonstrations of
truth were effective and that the legal system itself could provide accountability
when confronted with evidence and public outrage.

   The military and elite spent the final years of the New Order with concerns
about succession, and the state combated demonstrations by students and

activists with both violence and laws designed to target dissent. In 1996 Megawati Sukarnoputri, the daughter of founding president Sukarno, was ousted from
her position as head of the nationalist party (PDI). Megawati's supporters, who
included many prodemocracy, student, and human rights groups, occupied the
party headquarters in central Jakarta, where they began an ongoing free speech
forum (*mimbar bebas*). I attended the lively and crowded forum with student
activists and recall the sense of power and the novelty of the gathering, but also
the sense of danger and suspicion: I was instructed on whom not to talk to and
how to avoid being followed as I took the orange Metro Mini bus to get to the
mall, where I was to meet my host family for a lift to their house in an outer
suburb.

On July 27, thugs (preman) backed by the military and dressed as supporters
of the government attacked Megawati's supporters. Police and military arrested
74 people and reportedly set fire to political banners. Five people were killed, 149
injured, and 74 went missing. Riots broke out around Jakarta over the next two
days and left much property destroyed. Jakarta's military commander ordered
troops to shoot on sight anyone disturbing order. The government blamed the
instigation of riots on prodemocracy organizations and labeled them "Communist." After arrests on July 27, 1996, at the PDI headquarters, the police released
the initials of 124 detainees. Those arrested included key figures in the labor
movement as well as the People's Democratic Party (Partai Rakyat Demokra-
tik, or PRD), whom the government accused of being Communists and mas-
terminding the riots. Parents and relatives of student activists were intimidated,
and the personal belongings of activists were seized, which led to further arrests
within activist networks. Those arrested were charged with violating Article 170
(use of violence against individuals or property) and Article 351 (assault).[10] PRD
leaders were tried for and convicted of subversion.

Following the attack on Megawati's headquarters and accusations that the
recently formed PRD was Communist, in 1997 and 1998 at least twenty-three
activists were kidnapped by the army; thirteen of them are still missing. Student
organizing and demonstrations continued, as did the violent repression of activists by security forces. In 1997 the Asian financial crisis shattered the justifications
of political repression in the name of stability and economic development. The
foreign exchange value of the rupiah fell precipitously, causing massive inflation.

From March 1998 onward, students filled the streets of major cities,
protesting not just a financial crisis (*krismon*) but a total crisis (*kristal*) and
demanding Suharto's resignation. In contrast to analyses that see these protests as
sudden, Doreen Lee carefully combed through the dispersed print, material, and
electronic ephemera of activism and other archives to map how the nationwide
protests built on student dissent during the New Order, which intensified after

the openness period when police became increasingly repressive and violent. Lee analyzes how the student movement claimed the mantle of the Youth Pledge (Sumpah Pemuda) as the latest generation of unified revolutionary youth that transcended ethnic and other divisions.[11] As a student at Gajah Mada University at the time, I witnessed firsthand how protests consumed the entire community. Protesters even boldly burned effigies of Suharto, and soldiers used tear gas, water cannons, rubber bullets, and sometimes live ammunition in retaliation. My previously apolitical roommates were in the streets along with seasoned activists and study group members. By May, students in Jakarta were organized into coalitions and the middle class was increasingly supportive of them, dropping off packaged rice (*nasi bungkus*) and bottled water for demonstrators. Lee notes how the student demonstrations and marches created new political subjectivities through their occupation of urban space and their aggregation of diverse groups into a "mass" that supported the students. She shows how they reversed the othering of the out-of-control mass and recast it instead as the people, and part of reform.[12]

On May 12, 1998, four students and two other civilians were killed at Trisakti University by snipers shooting into the campus from a high-rise building. This incident, which became known as the Trisakti Tragedy, sparked massive protests across Indonesia. For the next two days, Jakarta rioted and burned on national television. Many Chinese Indonesians, long scapegoated for their economic power and political marginality, fled to neighboring countries, inspiring a capital flight as well. Chinese businesses and homes were looted and burned. Women and girls of Chinese descent (or appearance) were gang raped, mutilated, and burned to death. More than a thousand looters, rioters, and urban poor were incinerated in malls. Witnesses described the actions of men with military boots, good physiques, and crew cuts who locked the malls from the outside before setting them on fire.[13] The widespread and coordinated nature of the destruction and violence, as well as the scale, confirmed for many people, before official evidence was presented, that the armed forces had been involved—it was impossible that they were not.

On May 17, student groups began to occupy the national Parliament building in Jakarta, some supported by different political or military figures. The next day even Suharto's most loyal cronies urged him to resign. Rival military figures urged protesters to remain at home; nevertheless they continued to arrive, carrying banners. Their demand for an end to corruption, collusion, and nepotism (*korupsi, kolusi, nepotisme*) unified diverse groups and became the cornerstone of protests, along with demands to "Bring Suharto to Justice" (*Adili Soeharto*) and revoke the military's dual function (*cabut dwifungsi*). At the same time, economic conditions continued to deteriorate, and protesters wanted a reduction in the price of *sembako*, the nine essential commodities.[14] This issue featured just as prominently in demonstrations and in my discussions with students and other middle-class intellectuals and professionals.

On May 21, Suharto resigned on national TV. Without the support of the powerful military, Vice President Habibie became the third president of Indonesia. Students, NGO members, journalists, academics, lawyers, and others I talked with were euphoric, and commentators frequently referred to a *reformasi*. But much of the New Order infrastructure still remained in place and functional.

By November the Parliament, composed of New Order figures, had convened a Special Session of the People's Consultative Assembly of the Republic of Indonesia (Sidang Istimewa MPR 1998) to discuss elections. Students again protested the dual function of the military, especially the practice of allocating parliamentary seats to its representatives, and challenged the legitimacy of Suharto-era legislators to set the parameters for the transition. On high alert, the military recruited auxiliary paramilitary (*pam swakarsa*) groups, provided them with uniforms and sharpened sticks, and asked them to guard the session. These units and other paramilitary, progovernment militias provoked violent clashes. On November 13, 1998, the security forces opened fire on protesters who were approaching the Parliament building from the Semanggi Highway. Four students and nine other civilians were killed. This came to be known as the first Semanggi tragedy, or Semanggi 1.

Economic conditions continued to deteriorate as institutions and laws perpetuated the New Order infrastructure, only without Suharto. As reformers moved to retract laws and policies, as well as to create new institutions, dramatic violence erupted in different places across the archipelago. More than one hundred alleged practitioners of black magic were killed in East Java (in Banyuwangi, late 1998); military spokespersons claimed that descendants of the PKI had exacted revenge against Muslim neighbors who had participated in the 1965–66 killings. As Mary McCoy chronicles, the media reported statements of Kopassus deserters, indicating that they had been tasked with destabilization and destruction in several cases.[15] Interreligious and ethnic conflict erupted in different locations across the archipelago (Maluku, Kalimantan).[16] A decade-long period of military operations in Aceh ended, but violence increased.[17] Some commentators described the atmosphere as one of long-simmering conflicts that were exploding in the absence of a strong leader (a discourse sufficiently popular that it was routinely repeated by taxi drivers I encountered at this time), but critics suggested that the military was orchestrating the violence in order to retain its security function and power. In addition to discussing key elements of the transition, particularly the elections, the session also intended to determine the number of parliamentary seats for the armed forces. The discourse that saw students as the conscience of the nation shifted: students came to be seen as manipulated, and their demonstrations and demands as a threat to the legal and constitutional process.[18] They might have forced the failure of the democratic process and possibly a military junta.

Tensions remained high as military figures and the political elite jockeyed to consolidate their power while appearing to be democratic. President Habibie's decision in January 1999 to offer East Timor a referendum on independence, on the grounds that the occupation had roused international criticism, was initially supported by the military in his cabinet who believed the Timorese would choose to remain with Indonesia; when they did not, there was a strong nationalist backlash. In May, the governments of Indonesia and Portugal and the UN Security Council agreed to have the Indonesian National Armed Forces (Tentara Nasional Indonesia, or TNI) provide security for the referendum.[19] On August 30, 1999, the East Timorese voted overwhelmingly to reject the offer of increased autonomy within Indonesia and to become independent. The TNI launched a scorched-earth campaign when the results were announced and caused extensive destruction until its forces withdrew. Discourses of national disintegration provoked intense fear among the elite. The state acknowledged the security forces' violence but seemed to be tottering on the brink of disaster. In June 1999, Indonesians elected a new Parliament, charged with selecting the next president.

On September 23 and 24, 1999, the Parliament debated a state security bill, which critics argued was more draconian than the recently revoked antisubversion laws and would have granted the military far-reaching powers. The parliamentary session unanimously passed the bill. Thousands of students and other protesters flooded the overpass leading to the Parliament. General Wiranto declared that these protests were engineered by provocateurs and hired masses,[20] a tactic often used by various intelligence units throughout the New Order and for years after. The military opened fire, killing seven, including a university student. Instead of signing the bill into law the next day as expected, Habibie delayed its passage, citing a need to familiarize people with new policies and rhetoric—another New Order propaganda technique. Protests continued. Finally, after the Parliament rejected his "accountability speech," which attempted to rationally defend his record (especially his granting East Timor a referendum), Habibie, failing to hold Suharto and his cronies accountable for corruption, and being implicated in a corruption scandal himself, agreed to relinquish the presidency by constitutional means.[21] On October 1, the newly elected Parliament convened to select the next president. Despite her popularity, Megawati Sukarnoputri was outmaneuvered by the prodemocracy critic and

Islamic leader Abdurrhman Wahid (Gus Dur), who was named president, with Megawati as vice president.

The reformasi era had arrived, and this might have been a time of reckoning with the past. While student activists had defended themselves in court under the New Order, producing strong rhetoric and political performance that circulated through networks of supporters by way of pamphlets and other documents,[22] I sensed especially strong hopes during reformasi that truth and documentation could be more meaningfully brought into the courts and bring about significant changes and an era of functioning rule of law and human rights. Yet several subsequent campaigns and incidents illustrate the ambiguous role of revelation, fact, documentation, and truth in postauthoritarian Indonesia, and the limitations of the same. In contrast to earlier cases, such as that of Gatot Lestario, where critics stood as the accused, in reformasi cases the military stood accused. And yet, even when individual agents were declared guilty and new laws and policies were passed, the infrastructure of impunity persisted and mutated into more insidious forms. The violence, inequality, marginalization, and stigmatization that were built into the New Order system were naturalized, made invisible, or made to seem inevitable, by laws on paper and laws in practice, the suspension of law, and the persistence of nationalist myths that justified violence and inequality in the name of security and development. Activists, legal reformers, and others hoped that a reformed system of law would expose the institutions and laws responsible for past violations, and yet even with new evidence and revelations, efforts to achieve justice through the law were subverted by technicalities, loopholes built into even reformasi-era laws, the application of the law, and many of the same elements that weakened the law in the New Order.[23]

On March 20, 1998, in the final days of the New Order, eleven NGOs and one student group founded the Commission for the Disappeared and Victims of Violence (Komisi untuk Orang Hilang dan Korban Tindak Kekerasan, or KontraS),[24] with the goal of "creating democracy based on the full sovereignty of the people with the basis and principle of a people who are free from fear, oppression, and violence."[25] This was not a legal aid organization, although the office occupied a room accessible from a side door at the Legal Aid Institute (Lembaga Bantuan Hukum, or LBH) on Diponegoro Street in central Jakarta. The LBH building was surrounded by a well-shaded yard and parking area; the street in front bustled with food vendors and motorcycle taxis. As the New Order ended, it was well established as a place for diverse activists, students, labor organizers, affected families and individuals, intellectuals, and others, including intelligence informants, to congregate and strategize or launch actions. Some KontraS members were employed by LBH, and most of those associated with KontraS and its founders had some experience with LBH's national network. While KontraS was part of the LBH milieu, and even though some individuals belonged to both organizations, they were distinct entities and each had their own style and methods to pursue democracy and freedom from fear, oppression, and violence. The focus on fear was significant: KontraS realized that to truly create democracy, it would have to challenge the New Order's affective infrastructure.

KontraS's office was busy but had a more focused energy and urgency than the LBH office. It sought to find missing activists, reveal truths, and secure justice for all the victims of the Suharto era. A row of file cabinets prevented anyone from walking directly into the office. Close to the ceiling, portraits of the missing were hung around the room. KontraS had also plastered the city with large posters that featured photos of twelve missing activists and the word *dicari* (searching for) stamped across them.

Human rights activists have been forcibly disappeared around the world, and this was especially true during and after the Cold War. In Indonesia, disappearance has been used since 1965 in a range of cases—the kidnapping of prodemocracy activists in 1997 was the final iteration of a process that had defined the New Order regime.[26] Disappearance, like torture, is a central element in the infrastructure of impunity. The legal scholar Lauren Dempster identifies silencing as a key motivation for perpetrators: silencing critics and dissent directly, but also indirectly silencing their supporters through fear.[27] Because disappearances seek to silence, revelation and memory projects are often seen as particularly effective antidotes. Unusually, many of the disappeared in Indonesia were returned, and thus efforts by KontraS and other organizations focused on finding the remaining missing persons and holding perpetrators accountable in court.

Munir Said Thalib was the leader and life force of KontraS. He had come to Jakarta from Surabaya with a history of labor organizing and legal aid work in East Java—he had handled Marsinah's murder case. He was of Arab descent, a devout Muslim, and a lawyer. Rather than approach particular cases in terms of legal aid or human rights, he targeted militarism, corruption, and rehabilitation for victims of state violence. He was articulate, critical, well informed, and trusted by activists, victims, organizers, and even some in positions of power.

Early on, KontraS was described as a "gang of data gatherers."[28] Upon reflection twenty years later, Usman Hamid, who coordinated KontraS in the early 2000s, emphasized how the organization did resemble a youth gang. They worked around the clock, didn't care if they were paid, and understood that they were facing the risk of death.[29] KontraS exuded a heroic, masculine, youthful mood, fueled by the energy of the student movement (in which many members had participated) and empowered by their victorious occupation of Parliament and Suharto's resignation.

KontraS epitomized the belief in truth telling, documentation, and evidence, and the promise of defeating state violence in the courts and through policy. Stefan Eklof notes that KontraS worked not just legally but politically, to campaign and embarrass the regime over its corruption, impunity, and violence. This was a new approach.[30] During reformasi, the political sphere held promise; over time, as we will see, it became part of the infrastructure of impunity.

In addition to seeking official documents and using legal processes, KontraS encouraged kidnapped activists and victims (and later their families) to give testimony and speak the truth publicly. After the 1996 attack on Megawati's headquarters, twenty-three activists were kidnapped, and in 1998, some of them returned from the death space of detention at secret military locations.[31] KontraS focused its early campaigns for testimony and truth telling on these activists and their families.

KontraS mobilized victims to protest at the institutions that had been the most powerful during the New Order: the headquarters of the military (MABES TNI), the Special Forces headquarters (Cianjur), and eventually at a weekly Thursday silent protest in front of the state palace (see chapter 6). Even as they campaigned for legal accountability, Munir also recognized the importance of the experience and feeling of fear. For Munir, "the most effective way to resist fear is to confront the source of the fear itself."[32] Munir commented on the important victory of working with victims to help them use their voices: "I really want people to be aware that the obstacle for Indonesian society to change and become critical toward authoritarianism is that there is a feeling of fear. . . .. [H]ow can people build a strong social system if it is only the mask of people who are afraid."[33]

Munir then described how he supported one mother, Ibu Tuti, as she went from thinking about how her child (Yani Afri) disappeared, to being concerned that the same thing might happen to her, to eventually speaking out at the army headquarters. He recalled that a magazine had asked her, "What have you gotten as long as you have been associated with KontraS?" and Ibu Tuti answered, "I am brave enough to give a speech." Munir reflected on the story and emphasized its importance: "The newspaper was cynical. [They wrote,] 'Whaaat. . . . Output [English in original] is only to make people give speeches. . . .' But for a mute society to give a speech is extraordinary. Even if it is only in the thought of one person, for me that work was a valuable investment in democracy, it was concrete."[34]

KontraS's successful campaign of revelation generated its own momentum. It was reported in the news, especially the historic demonstration by victims— hailed as brave—at army headquarters. The media then sought their statements, and they were acknowledged and heard in the public discourse. Longtime staff at KontraS acknowledge the importance of having victims speak as a campaign strategy for litigation as well as nonlitigation advocacy. Ibu Tuti understood that if journalists were present, even if official representatives would not meet with families, the newspaper would report on their activities. Usman Hamid recalls Ibu Tuti's bold style of questioning military spokespersons: "Be straightforward. Is my child already dead or is he still living? If he is dead, just say so. Then we won't be exhausted going around [to try to find his whereabouts]. I also can't bring my child back to life. The important thing is to be straightforward. God will respond later. The government is not just. My message is there is no law in Indonesia."[35]

The victims' brave testimony to the facts of state violence provided credible evidence, but it also mobilized powerful affects of bravery and sincerity in ordinary people. Mothers such as Ibu Tuti, seeking to know the whereabouts of their children, challenged dehumanizing and stigmatizing rhetoric and presented a different form of bravery than male activist students, who might have been construed and dismissed as opportunistic and allied with political interests. Engaging fear to further democracy was an important aspect of KontraS's approach. Even in 2015, KontraS staff pointed to the importance of activists connecting with victims. This was part of their "brand," one staff member told me.[36]

In the early period of reformasi, especially with the case of the missing activists, revelation seemed to promise resolution. In some cases, activists who returned stated that they had seen or heard the voices of other activists still missing. Inquiries made to the Special Forces unit were focused either on information about the location of the deceased or on the return of the living. In the heady postauthoritarian year of 1998, momentum seemed to be with the activists. They were heroes and martyrs, and even those who had been complicit with the regime were left unsure about how political power would get reconstituted.

In this moment of instability and uncertainty, revelations did lead to the dismissals of officers involved. On August 3, 1998, for example, the government formed an Officers' Honor Council (Dewan Kehormatan Perwira, or DKP) to review the forced disappearances. Munir and KontraS pressed for follow-up action after the council removed Suharto's son-in-law, General Prabowo, from his duties because of violations that included student activist kidnappings. Newspapers publicized Prabowo's removal; nevertheless, when KontraS tried to obtain a copy of the document in order to build a case that would implicate Muchdi Purwoparanjono and other high-ranking officers, the chief of the Armed Forces Legal Office (Kepala Badan Pembinaan Hukum, Kababinkum) stated that because it was only a recommendation and not final, they were not required to share the letter with the public.[37] While the letter has never been produced, its existence has not been forgotten, even two decades later. Two senior officers were disciplined: Prabowo Subianto was made nonactive military and Muchdi

Purwoparanjono was removed from his leadership position in the Special Forces. Subsequently, on April 6, 1999, the military headquarters held a military tribunal to prosecute the eleven members of the Rose Team (Tim Mawar), who were suspected of having committed the kidnappings.[38] The tribunal considered only the kidnapping of the activists who were released, and not those whose whereabouts remained unknown.

At this military tribunal, Nezar Patria, one of the returned activists, said he was appearing as a witness to "push the disclosure about the other kidnapping victims whose fate was not yet clear."[39] Justice in this case was always linked to the demand for others to be returned, and to the possibility that they might be. The tribunal limited itself to technicalities, however; for example, the police, and not the Special Forces, should have been responsible for the arrest of treason suspects. Munir noted that legally if, in the process of the hearing, new facts were revealed, such as a "witness stating that at the place of kidnapping he met other victims but in the indictment [*surat dakwaan*] that was not mentioned, then the trial can and should be ended, the indictment revoked legally, and then the process of investigation returned to the initial state to disclose new facts."[40]

But this did not happen. Nezar was one of the only activists to testify. KontraS and the returned activists criticized the military tribunal's indictments for failing to take into account the torture of the kidnapped while they were in military detention, although their graphic stories and personal testimonies had been widely publicized. The press, the NGO community, and activists seized on, and criticized, the emphasis on legal technicalities. Importantly, however, they saw this emphasis not as a flaw inherent to law or the legal process, but as something that occurred because the military tribunal was closed to the public.[41] They saw more revelation and transparency as the solution, especially to address the cases of activists who had been confined in secret spaces and might still be located.

The tribunal didn't focus on graphic stories, but they were certainly available to be included. Pius Lustrilanang was the first victim to share his testimony publicly. He had been released in April 1998 and escorted to the airport in Jakarta to return to his parents' house in Palembang. His captors threatened him, telling him that he should not speak of his captivity and should say instead that he had gone away by himself to seek quiet and to resolve his problems. He decided otherwise, and returned to Jakarta to testify to Komnas HAM. Eventually he would testify before the US Congress as part of the effort to end military aid to Indonesia. At the military tribunal he stated, "From the beginning it was clear, all the witnesses stated there was torture, beating, electric shocks, being held under in a tub of water, being burned with cigarettes and having to lie down on a block of ice. The indictment is not complete. As far as I remember, I stated all of that when I was examined [by the military police]."[42] Investigators were widely criticized for failing to conduct medical examinations, and another victim, Aan, added that signs of torture remained visible on their bodies,[43] even six months after their release, but this had not been included as part of the evidence gathered from the investigation.

In addition to criticizing the exclusion of evidence of torture, Munir criticized the tribunal's indictment for its inclusion of the irrelevant pretext for the kidnapping as a matter of patriotism.[44] Ever since 1965, laws, bureaucratic policies, and law enforcement had been used by perpetrators of state violence to justify their actions under the rubric of patriotism, so Munir was trying to subvert a deeply established and affectively powerful trope of the New Order. Without articulating it, he sought to use the trial and related campaign to undermine key elements of the infrastructure of impunity that had been built socially and legally during the New Order. At least momentarily, this logic was challenged.

After the military tribunal, eleven low-ranking members of the Special Forces were sentenced to between fifteen and twenty-six months in prison (though this was later overturned on appeal) and were dismissed from the Special Forces (though many later returned to military positions). After this verdict in April 1999, legislators and lawyers noted in the press that the verdict (*putusan mahmiliti II*) had not restored a "feeling of justice" because not all issues had been addressed and what should have been revealed (*terungkap*) was not.[45] In particular, lawyers and activists repeatedly noted that the court had covered up or omitted issues around the fate of the other kidnapping victims and the torture of the victims who had been released. It was suggested that the eleven members of the Special Forces were tried only to demonstrate nominally and symbolically, to both national and international observers, that the law was being enforced. In other words, this was more a theatrical performance of law than a substantive moment of truth or revelation. Munir also noted that the tribunal process merely trapped low-ranking soldiers who could not refuse the orders as those responsible.[46] Munir wanted the command hierarchy of those who decided and knew about the kidnappings brought to justice, but he also argued that the kidnappings were not just the problem of Prabowo or one or two individuals, but a political practice. The army needed to issue a public statement that this type of practice would not occur again.[47] When he distinguished between the implementation of legal technicalities and what was just and moral, he attempted to address narrative and affective elements of the infrastructure of impunity. The system of law needed to function, but there were also elements of justice extraneous to the law that would be undone only by political and narrative interventions.

The case of the thirteen still-missing activists was affectively powerful and conveyed an extralegal concept of justice. Victims testified to their mistreatment, even if it was not included legally or forensically in the tribunal, and even if the signs and traces of this torture on their bodies were not considered. The state's violence was known and unrefuted. More importantly, despite the impediments of blindfolds and circuitous routes to their detention, victims spoke about others they met there, or whose voices they had heard while in detention, in a heroic effort to discover the whereabouts of other victims. Popular accounts presented these activists as martyrs or heroes struggling to implement the reform agenda in all aspects, beyond simply the resignation of Suharto.

At the same time, in the trials, the military tried to counter this new narrative of heroism and martyrdom by reviving the power of its propaganda narratives, which had been so deeply and viscerally imprinted on all citizens after decades under the New Order. The military suggested that they had kidnapped the activists who had been returned, denied kidnapping the others, closed off the chain of command to higher-ups who had been implicated by the military honor board at the first moment of revelation, and, most importantly, did all of this by citing the imperative of national security. Munir had the analytic skills to see the big issues but also to embody these larger, abstract issues in victims' lives and voices. He critiqued the military tribunals for falling far short of the more expansive acknowledgments made initially by the DKP, but added that it was not just a few individuals: the kidnappings were part of a *practice* of violent politics, and that system needed to be examined, legally and politically.

During reformasi, much of what had been known to some individuals but was inarticulable in public was now widely known, expressed in public and broadcast on TV, which changed the terms of public discourse, especially for urban, middle-class Indonesians. Different forms of evidence and statements were available, and the gang of data gatherers and other activists eagerly collected them. They documented testimonies of the most marginal and inspired others to speak of their experiences on the record, in public and in a struggle for justice. The documentation efforts aimed for healing, truth, and history, but primarily they were an effort to gather evidence that would result in meaningful legal consequences.

Speaking truth to power like this was a common response to state terror, denial, and Cold War proxy violence in many countries.[48] The comparative literature and human rights scholar Thomas Keenan, among others, outlines the presumption of human rights advocates that in the absence of a functioning legal apparatus, representation and revelation work as an informal mechanism: the exposure of silenced or hidden violations enforces compliance with shared norms through the shaming of perpetrators.[49]

But the relationship between atrocities, violence, and the law in Indonesia was complex. The laws, especially the "emergency" laws, that Sukarno had put in place to maintain control of the nation remained in effect for decades after he was removed from power, and the legal infrastructure, as we have seen, had been used for extralegal agendas for years.[50] As violent and extralegal as its proxies often were, this veneer of legality had been important to the New Order, as seen in the laborious development of the Kopkamtib system and bureaucracy to classify detainees and to stigmatize them through extensive "legal" means. The sense that the violence was legal and necessary allowed for widely dispersed social complicity, and made challenges to impunity extremely perilous if not impossible.

This gap between law on paper and law in practice had stymied Indonesian lawyers in the New Order—and continued to do so during reformasi and beyond.[51] Lawyers themselves understood the pernicious influence of law in practice. In 1988, the prominent legal aid lawyer Abdul Hakim Garuda Nusantara wrote that law was a means to legitimize state power, foster economic growth, and facilitate the process of social engineering.[52] In 2000, another legal aid and human rights defender, Bambang Widjojanto, outlined succinctly and clearly the New Order's five steps to destroy the system of law in society: co-optation of the highest state institutions, including the Supreme Court; destruction of social institutions; the channeling of conflicts into the system the regime had prepared itself; the creation of a quasi-legal system for the resolution of social problems; and the introduction of not just a lack of independence but collusion and corruption.[53]

Despite awareness of these flaws in the system, activists persisted in their struggle to reclaim the law during the reformasi. For example, legal activists often used the term *engineered* (*direkayasakan*) during the New Order to indicate that powerful interests were manipulating legal cases for political and other reasons. Engineered cases were often made up, with fake evidence to frame an innocent person as a perpetrator. Even if the corrupt judiciary did not rule in favor of their clients, Indonesian legal advocates often scored moral victories and challenged the state's claims to the rule of law and legitimacy by compiling evidence to present in court and disseminate through international networks. In addition to presenting information, activists on trial used creativity and rhetorical strategies.[54]

If during the New Order, activists had to work to delegitimate the trials that sentenced them to years in prison, during reformasi, activists worked to reverse the system of engineered cases by bringing forth newly acknowledged, undeniable testimony, facts, and evidence of mistreatment by a violent military. They wanted to change the system of governance and demonstrate that law in practice could be just and effective. At the same time, they also worked to reform laws on paper that were used to target critics of the state. KontraS, in particular, sought to win cases in court to demonstrate that the regime had not in fact been ruled by law.

Activists knew that in reformasi the military did not want to be seen as flouting the law. Activists followed prevailing human rights and transitional justice logics, which held that evidence and truth can be brought into courts with sufficient political will. This may not have been a deeply contemplated strategy—they simply gathered evidence, tried to fight in court, and assumed that this was the way to defeat impunity, especially with public discourse momentarily on their side.

But much of the battle over law was undermined on the terrain of morality and justifying narratives, just as it had been during the New Order. As the following sections show, the power of the revelations was undermined in a variety of ways—sometimes through technicalities, as we saw with the tribunal, or through a reframing of indictments. But the power of truth telling was also undermined through the mobilization and revival of particular cultural attitudes and propaganda narratives, which worked affectively and viscerally. Unthinkable admissions and acknowledgments got absorbed into the infrastructure of impunity. This isn't to suggest that information, data, and documents simply disappeared—they will inform strategies later in this story. Nevertheless, during reformasi, they were neutralized and did not always lead to the desired results.

To recall, from May 13 to 15, 1998, Jakarta and other Indonesian cities were overwhelmed with violence, including gang rape directed toward women who appeared to be of Chinese descent and the incineration of hundreds of urban poor within a locked mall that they had been encouraged to loot. Not only did the military fail to prevent this violence, but later investigations determined that it helped orchestrate it. Observers suggested that the violence was part of a power struggle between different factions within the military (especially between Prabowo and Wiranto, who both occupied key ministerial positions in the 2019 Jokowi administration).

The May violence has been investigated by multiple teams, and yet the facts remain contested even today. Initially, the Volunteers for Humanity team (Tim Relawan untuk Kemanusiaan, or TRuK), a nongovernmental organization, collected testimonies from survivors of sexual assault. The team, led by the Catholic priest Father Sandyawan, reported 168 incidents of rape and sexual violence. In addition, international media and human rights organizations reported over one thousand cases of injury from the widespread riots. In July 1998, President Habibie (along with the ministers of defense and security, justice, internal affairs, foreign affairs, and women's affairs) established a Joint Fact-Finding Team (Tim Gabung Pencari Fakta, or TGPF) mandated to investigate the riots and specifically the rapes. The TGPF was led by Marzuki Darusman, the head of Komnas HAM, and included members of the armed forces, the police, the government, and the civil society and NGO community.[55] The team had only three months to investigate violence in multiple cities, lacked experience and precedents for data collection, and brought different methodologies and approaches to data collection.[56] The Indonesian studies scholar Jemma Purdey recalls that the struggle for truth was "a dual struggle to name the victims and name the perpetrators."[57]

In October 1998, an eighteen-year-old woman, Martadinata, was found murdered in her home. Many volunteers believed she was murdered because she was planning to provide testimony to human rights organizations internationally. The police insisted the case was criminal and arrested a male neighbor; meanwhile the media and official statements sexualized the case and the victim.[58] Despite its treatment as a criminal case, the murder had a chilling effect on testimony. Adding another impediment, the TGPF was divided about whether or not to require verification for cases of sexual violence. The military and police wanted to require verification by the Indonesian Doctors' Association, while other members accepted evidence provided by family members and eyewitnesses, to protect victims' identities. The final report included two sets of numbers, both significantly lower than those in the TRuK reports. Reflecting divisions among team members, the report stated that "it could not yet be determined as to whether the rapes occurred spontaneously or were part of the engineered violence" but included sexual violence as part of riot activities.[59] Remarkably, the report concluded that the violence was an "effort, which was initiated by the highest level of decision makers, to create an emergency situation that required the formation of an extraconstitutional government to control the entire situation."[60] It did not specify the relationship between elite military and on-the-ground agents.

The release of the TGPF report in November 1998 was significant. Many activists had long claimed that the violence had been engineered for political purposes, but it was unprecedented to have an official statement that confirmed it. And yet this statement and a report that confirmed the rapes was eclipsed by the problem that no victims were willing to provide testimony. The military rushed to deny that rapes had occurred, but female ministers and others also publicly doubted the findings, given the dearth of victims willing to come forward.[61] The controversy over the rapes that followed obscured other revelations of coordinated violence and destruction orchestrated by military factions.

Theoretically, this might have become a case where a report meaningfully contributed to high-level accountability, given the state agents identified. Unlike the missing persons tribunal, which both acknowledged and undermined the facts by reasserting familiar justifications, this report concluded that even by conservative methods of verification, fifteen rapes did indeed take place. But the affective resonance of the victims' silence undercut a potentially transformative, factual, and official admission of culpability. The silence is more accurately interpreted as a sound—the sound of state-manipulated constructions of appropriate family roles and behavior that were key components of the infrastructure of impunity and still consequentially resonant during reformasi.

Shortly after the completion of the TGPF report, the UN special rapporteur concluded that the rapes occurred, that the systematic involvement of the security forces should be further investigated, and that police investigation of Martadinata's murder was flawed and failed to take into account the threatening letters and death threats that her family had received.[62] The Indonesian delegation objected to these findings. The Indonesian government pointed to an official statement that expressed regret for the violence,[63] as well as the TGPF report itself, as evidence of its sincere efforts to address violence against women.

Komnas Perempuan (the National Commission on Violence against Women) was formed in response to the May 1998 sexual violence. Its mandate was to help eradicate violence against women and to support the rights of victims of violence generally.[64] Komnas Perempuan supported the law on the protection of witnesses and victims and a law on the elimination of domestic violence, and worked to emend the criminal code and procedure with regard to its definitions and procedures for rape and sexual violence. As part of its mandate, Komnas Perempuan coordinated memorials to the violence and reviewed the follow-up on the TGPF report recommendations. Ten years after the TGPF report stating that the rapes had occurred, Komnas Perempuan documented persistent denials that the rapes had occurred. These denials continued despite a methodology outlined in the follow-up report that included gathering testimony from victims and others who could represent victims who wished to maintain their anonymity. The Komnas Perempuan report reiterated stories both of the rapes themselves and of the suffering, discrimination, and psychological duress experienced in their aftermath, especially given persistent and widespread denial of the rapes.[65]

On the nineteenth anniversary of the riots and rapes, I attended a commemoration for victims held at the public cemetery in Jakarta. I also attended a session organized by students of Chinese descent that featured a doctor who had worked with many of the victims, and who once again testified to the veracity of the findings. Two years earlier I had attended the unveiling of a large-scale commemorative monument at the cemetery, and for several years I had attended meetings of survivors and NGOs to coordinate the commemoration. The nineteenth anniversary was designed to reassert the undeniable truth of the past revelations. Former president Habibie spoke at the anniversary event, along with Saparinah Sadli, a member of the TGPF and Komnas Perempuan.

They were not simply commemorating what had happened in the past but were still struggling in the present to have the official report's findings accepted and validated, notwithstanding the fact that it was, after all, an official report. This was a paradox of truth telling and revelation: even when the factual narrative was owned, acknowledged, and authorized in state documents, it was still subverted by affective, deeply lodged narratives that infiltrated reports, official commemorations, and public memory. And it was in these affective dimensions that the force of facts and truth telling dissolved into denial, impunity, and inaction.

Individuals involved in the TRuK report and some of those involved in the TGPF recognized that testifying or being identified as a victim in public was likely to trigger damaging social processes and mobilize older narratives that would revive impunity. While no explicit allusions were made to Gerwani, nevertheless, the anthropologist Karen Strassler observes, the only "official recognition of sexualised political violence in the nation's past was one in which women were figured as the perpetrators not the victims of violence."[66] It was also very clear that official channels of investigation, particularly those that might result in legal actions against perpetrators, required victims to engage precisely with the state apparatus that had failed to protect them in the past (and, even more

FIGURE 3.1.   Sandyawan bends over to shake hands with former president B. J. Habibie at the 2017 commemoration of the May 1998 violence at Pondok Ranggon cemetery. Commissioners of Komnas Perempuan Mariana Amirudin and Azriana Manalu stand, and in the background, Awan Simatupang's May 1998 Memorial monument depicts an outstretched hand draped with cloth and a needle and red thread repairing a tear in the fabric. Photo by the author.

so, had abetted the very violence that they endured) and that further victimized them in the present.

Meanwhile the TGPF report's factual acknowledgments were neutralized by the official military rejections of the report, the government's failure to implement many of the recommendations, and public discourses that made much of the victims' unwillingness to testify in public, which to skeptics called the rapes into question, even against the facts themselves. At the same time, the violence experienced by urban poor youth, especially those who were incinerated in the locked mall and others who suffered violence, was not heard or engaged socially, overshadowed as it was by the controversy over the rapes and the realization that only certain types of victims, such as student protesters, would be celebrated in public discourse—not the urban poor, who could be cast as looters and criminals. Finally, the force of early propaganda and patriarchy in Indonesian state, society, and culture was revived to undermine and stigmatize victims in the New Order style. This occurred in lieu of a galvanizing discussion about violence in politics and society, the marginalization of the Chinese minority, or the disregard for the lives of women and the urban poor.

Even though the report did not prompt punishments or prosecutions, it did inform institutional changes to end violence against women and became the basis for further investigations into the May riots by Komnas HAM. The TGPF truth telling was therefore important—but not in the anticipated ways.

Turning now to advances made in the law "on paper" during reformasi, we can observe how impunity for past crimes continued despite them. Following the dominant logic of human rights work, reformers sought to dismantle the past system by strengthening legal instruments to protect human rights and prosecute past cases, and to allow greater freedoms of the press and association, and civil political rights. They focused on key institutional reforms that they thought would end past patterns of governance, especially with regard to corruption, collusion, and nepotism; the military's dual social and political role (*dwifungsi*); violence; and militarism. In the past, critics were somewhat confined to revealing the gap between official rhetoric and actual conditions, but now, with strong social and political support, students and other activists sought to enshrine checks and balances against the powerful military in legislation, including legislation that would separate the police from the military in hopes that freeing the police from the military's control would facilitate accountability and change the law *in practice*.

Human rights defenders struggled to create strong laws and pass international conventions.[67] In the early reform period, I attended several sessions with NGOs and human rights groups to discuss the text of draft laws. The key elements of the human rights legislation were the 1999 Law on Human Rights, the constitutional amendment protecting human rights, and the 2000 Human Rights Court Law, which provides the basis for creating ad hoc tribunals for cases of "gross violations" of human rights.[68] Human rights organizations had specific foci, but many converged on the importance of addressing past New Order cases within some sort of transitional justice framework, arguing that this would be key to ending impunity and preventing future abuse.

Amendments to the constitution provided for an extensive list of rights and freedoms that encompassed most international standards; however, the legal scholars Simon Butt and Tim Lindsey analyze how the combination of two articles of the constitution limited these rights.[69] Article 28 I (1) establishes the rights to life, freedom from torture, freedom of conscience, religion, and freedom from slavery, and the right to not be prosecuted under a retrospective application of any law, as nonderogable—that is, not to be limited under any circumstances. Article 28 J (2), however, limits these and other constitutional rights in the name of public order and religious values. Other rights are similarly delimited; for example, state sovereignty delimits the right to self-determination, given secessionist threats from Aceh and Papua as well as the upsetting "loss" of Timor. Procedures of implementation and local regulations also attenuate these statements of basic rights.[70] The Constitutional Court, another new institution created in the reformasi period, has ruled that the first article cannot be applied out of context of the second article, which provides for limitations. The limitations have repeatedly been invoked to restrict the rights of religious minorities in the name of protecting the rights of the religious majority.

Similarly, while the human rights law (Law 3/1999) protects numerous specific rights, it also circumscribes those human rights with respect to the rights of others, morality, public order, or the national interest (Article 73). The human rights law stipulated the establishment of a Human Rights Court (Law 26/2000) to hear cases of genocide and crimes against humanity, with jurisdiction over Indonesian citizens regardless of where the human rights violations occur. The constitutional bill of rights includes the right to nonretrospective application of the law; however, the Human Rights Court law states that nonretroactivity does not apply in cases of gross violations of human rights.[71] Many components of the gross violations (individual incidents of extrajudicial killing, for example) were illegal under the Indonesian criminal code; the new laws were designed to include crimes of omission and implicate the masterminds further up the chain of command, rather than limiting culpability to lower-ranking field officers (as the criminal code would do). Indonesia was not a signatory to the International Covenant on Civil and Political Rights, which would have provided a basis to treat acts of commission and omission around gross violations as exempt from nonretroactivity provisions. As the result of a compromise with proponents of nonretroactivity, however, the Human Rights Court law states that gross violations that occurred before the passage of the law can be heard *if* the national legislature makes a recommendation and the president supports the establishment of a tribunal. The Constitutional Court ruled that this does not violate the constitutional right to nonretroactivity, as this process of establishing the court creates an institution that is the embodiment of the people.[72]

Significant attention has centered on the issue of nonretroactivity, but there are other problems with the human rights law as well. The Indonesian political scientist Ayu Sri Lestari Wahyuningroem notes that the law "complied with at least some of the demands of international law with the political compromises characteristic of Indonesia's time of transition. The mixture of these aspects resulted in a legal foundation for human rights trials that failed to address some of the most important aspects of justice in cases of gross abuses: command responsibility, crimes against humanity, and reparations for victims."[73]

The state expedited passage of the Human Rights Court law because it needed to establish a domestic court to avoid international prosecution of the Indonesian soldiers indicted for crimes against humanity in East Timor. According to the law, Komnas HAM must conduct preliminary investigations (*penyelidikan*) to determine whether an incident of suspected gross violations occurred. The attorney general and prosecutors would then pursue full investigations (*penyidikan*). But the prosecutor has most often returned the Komnas HAM reports as incomplete or in violation of various technicalities. Komnas HAM has investigated a number of key past cases, but as of 2023, the attorney general's office has pursued only the cases of East Timor and violence against Muslims at Tanjung Priok in 1984. In only one case, in 2012, has the national legislature recommended formation of an ad hoc tribunal, for the case of the disappeared activists. While demands for legal justice through these mechanisms remain strong, tribunals have a dismal record.

The first cases to be tried in ad hoc Human Rights Tribunals considered crimes against humanity perpetrated during the lead-up to the 1999 referendum in East Timor (now called Timor Leste). This is the case that had hastened the tribunal's formation in the first place. Under international scrutiny surrounding the Timor case, Komnas HAM conducted highly credible and swift investigations, to avoid the appearance that Indonesia was unable or unwilling to hold trials. The trials performed a simulacrum of justice and law to appease the international community, without embracing law and truth telling as remedies for the past. The report by the Investigative Commission on Human Rights Violations in East Timor (KPP HAM Timor Timur) concluded that the violence in East Timor was not "amok," horizontal violence as portrayed by the media and military sources, but a systematic campaign financed, coordinated, and encouraged by the Indonesian forces, with the knowledge and participation of the very highest levels in the chain of command.[74] According to members of the investigative commission, high-ranking generals responded to their summonses.[75] The initial investigations did not examine the violence of the invasion, only the violence in the lead-up to the referendum. Nevertheless, the report credibly established the criteria of "widespread" and "systematic" violence that define crimes against humanity.[76]

The tribunal's jurisdiction and time frame were severely limited, making it more difficult to demonstrate the military elite's systematic involvement and command responsibility.[77] Witnesses did not receive adequate protection, and special forces members were bussed to the court to fill the audience and intimidate witnesses as well as human rights defenders monitoring the court. The legal scholar David Cohen has powerfully argued that these tribunals were "intended to fail."[78] He diagnoses several key problems: the failure to use available evidence (including the report prepared by Komnas HAM, the report from the Investigative Commission on Human Rights [KPP HAM Timor Timur], or resources from the concurrent UN-supported hybrid tribunals in Dili), the failure to call witnesses (international observers and Timorese), and the failure to safeguard those who were called. The tribunal even further narrowed the indictments to particular acts, without considering larger contexts and chains of command.[79] Consequently, prosecutors did not sufficiently build a case for the widespread and systematic elements of crimes against humanity. Cohen notes that both the defense and prosecution understood the conflict to be one between two factions of Timorese with different outlooks on independence. Presenting the violence as horizontal rather than state violence succeeded as propaganda, since most Indonesians saw the conflict this way and the case did not significantly refigure public perceptions of militarism or human rights accountability.[80] The "Indonesian administration of the justice system is centralized and hierarchical," Cohen concludes, "such that the lack of political will at the highest levels is like a paralyzing narcotic that seeps downward through the whole system."[81] In short, the tribunals are best understood as a "performance" of human rights theater—aimed at the audience of the international community—rather than a commitment to reforming the law as a vehicle for justice and redress.

The very judicial independence that the tribunals were designed to provide was not delivered, aside from the personal efforts of individuals, especially judges, who faced significant intimidation as they returned guilty verdicts— verdicts that were swiftly overturned on appeal. Cohen points out that even if international observers focused on shortcomings, Indonesian journalists and experts emphasized the significance of a major general's having been convicted by a civilian human rights court, despite the fact that when confronted with judges who would not yield to pressure, the prosecution, even with its strong case, shifted and began to argue for his acquittal.[82]

Another ad hoc tribunal was formed in 2001 to prosecute the 1984 Tanjung Priok case, named for the port area in which security forces killed over twenty-four civilians. In 1984, an army sergeant ordered a mosque leader (Amir Biki) to remove banners and pamphlets critical of the government. When Biki refused, the sergeant did so himself and in the process trod on prayer areas without removing his shoes. The community was offended by this lack of respect and tensions escalated, culminating in the arrest of four Muslim figures who were detained at the District Military Command for North Jakarta. After strongly critical sermons, more than one thousand community members marched to the Military Command to demand the release of the detainees. The army fired on the protesters. Official investigations cite twenty-four deaths, though community witnesses cite many more and one recalled high-ranking military officials removing bodies piled four deep in trucks. At the time, the army claimed that the riots had been incited by someone in a fake military uniform, and later a highly critical general was arrested for inciting the riots. After the riots, 169 individuals were held and some tortured, and leaders were tried and convicted of subversion. Biki and others were killed.

During reformasi, victims' groups formed and lobbied the People's Representative Council and Komnas HAM to investigate the Tanjung Priok case. When the first report did not find evidence of systematic killings, the Islamic Defenders Front attacked Komnas HAM offices.[83] Islamic politicians criticized Komnas HAM for protecting the military and applying double standards—failing to investigate a case against Muslims while they did investigate cases against (predominantly Catholic) Timorese.[84] By October 2000, Komnas HAM had issued another report and recommended the formation of an ad hoc tribunal. The report implicated the current head of the Special Forces. But before the hearings began, several high-ranking military created islah (restitution) settlements of forgiveness with victims' families. The military did not admit to wrongdoing, but the families received cash payments in compensation. Subsequently these victims suggested that the case be dropped. In the hearings I observed in 2003, uniformed soldiers filled the audience. In addition to these soldiers, groups of family members of victims who wore islah T-shirts suggested that a cultural approach in line with Indonesian culture and Islamic values was more appropriate than the court. Clearly, the islah settlements had divided victims' groups and undercut the authority of law as a corrective to impunity.

The momentum of newly formed Islamic parties may have been a significant threat to the still-powerful military, particularly if this force could have been brought to bear on other cases of human rights violations. And so, the military effectively blunted the threat by providing cash and a settlement ostensibly more

FIGURE 3.2.   Uniformed Kopassus members fill the courtroom of the ad hoc tribunal for the Tanjung Priok case. Civilian individuals in the center wear T-shirts proclaiming, "Islah is our happiness." Photo by the author.

consistent with Islamic religion. Early organizers at KontraS recall the great difficulty of bringing victims together to create solidarity across all of these cases rather than on a case-by-case basis. The Islamic parties' portrayal of Komnas HAM as anti-Islam further undermined it and its investigations in the majority-Muslim country, where the political influence of Islam was rapidly expanding after its decades-long containment by the New Order. Ultimately, victims who pursued the legal case never received any compensation, and no perpetrators were held to account. The attorney general did not include high-ranking commanders in the investigation, and an appeals court acquitted the twelve soldiers convicted in the ad hoc process. Even as the legal process should have been a mechanism for accountability, it instead secured the military's impunity for the massacre, and the extralegal cultural-religious effort effectively undermined any religiously based moral condemnation by the majority-Muslim population.

In the early years of reformasi, the revelations generated by Munir Said Thalib and others at KontraS and kindred organizations yielded significant responses, and hopeful momentum, even if these revelations fell short of producing the justice imagined. All the while, the gang of data gatherers was well aware of the risk of death. Terror and intimidation happened often enough that they could never forget that forces opposed their work; for example, KontraS's offices were attacked, which underscored the importance of the data stored there as well as the desire to sow terror in these spaces of civil society.

On his way to begin a master's degree in international human rights law in the Netherlands, on September 7, 2004, Munir was murdered. He was poisoned by arsenic onboard a Garuda flight from Jakarta to Singapore to Amsterdam. Although there had been very little formal response to the information Munir uncovered, it made those in power—suspected perpetrators in military intelligence and their accomplices—uncomfortable enough to silence Munir by killing him.

The outpouring of sympathy after his death included the president and other leaders of the government and military, as well as Islamic public figures and ordinary citizens. Ministers, military generals, and the chief justice of Indonesia's Constitutional Court agreed that the government should honor Munir with an award to memorialize his contribution to the nation.[85] There were efforts to discredit Munir as not a nationalist, due to his work to defend human rights in Aceh and Papua against military operations committed in the state's name. Expressions of grief on banners urged the public to continue his struggle and rebuked stigmatizing remarks made about him.[86] Munir had a strong appeal to Muslims, and some commentators linked his human rights work to the universality of Islamic values—he was one of the few human rights defenders who enjoyed this reputation.

Within days of Munir's death, the armed forces spokesperson stated that the unnatural death was likely caused by an external or internal enemy. Suspicions were cast on the police, the military, NGOs, and foreign countries. Most of the rumors were preposterous. Munir's colleagues pointed out that he had been investigating the intelligence forces. An autopsy done in the Netherlands revealed a level of arsenic in his blood and organs that was three times a fatal level. The results were conveyed to the government of Indonesia, which did not share the results with his widow or the public. When the Dutch press reported the news, activists pushed for an investigative team that included international experts and a representative of Munir's family. The Dutch were hesitant to hand over results of their investigation to Indonesia without a guarantee that suspects would not face the death penalty (as allowed by Indonesian law). Eventually this letter was provided and Indonesian investigators accepted the autopsy results, although they declined to follow up on other elements of the Dutch investigation, declaring them irrelevant.

After the announcement of the cause of death, Munir's widow, Suciwati, received a styrofoam package with the head, feet, and internal organs of a rotting

FIGURE 3.3. The wall in KontraS's courtyard features a stencil of Munir's face and the words "We are still here and will double" (Kami tetap ada dan berlipat ganda), declaring to the security forces that even after his death, Munir's influence will grow. Photo by the author.

chicken and a printed message that read, "Be careful, don't involve the TNI in the death of Munir or you too will end up like this." Suciwati, NGOs, and the legislature urged the then president, Susilo Bambang Yudhoyono, a retired general who had earlier stated that the case was a test of Indonesia's history, to convene a team with the authority to investigate the murder and publicize the findings of the Netherlands autopsy.[87] Eventually he appointed a fact-finding team by presidential decree.[88]

The results of the report and autopsy have never been made public. Upon boarding his flight, Munir was offered a first-class seat by an off-duty pilot named Pollycarpus Budihari Priyanto. Pollycarpus allegedly put arsenic in orange juice that Munir drank during transit in Singapore. Munir boarded another flight to

Amsterdam in Singapore, and Pollycarpus returned to Jakarta. Munir became ill en route to Amsterdam, sitting in his original economy-class seat. He had stomach pain and diarrhea and died two hours outside Amsterdam—the plane did not make an emergency landing.

Pollycarpus stood for an ordinary criminal trial and was said to have murdered Munir because he had criticized the nation-state that Pollycarpus loved.[89] He was sentenced to fourteen years, which he appealed. The president asked him to expose the mastermind of the case, but he did not, and the president refused to establish another investigative team. Hendroprioyono, the chairman of the State Intelligence Agency (Badan Intelijen Negara, or BIN), was summoned for questioning by the team, but he failed to respond, foreclosing investigation into BIN's role. The police who were leading the investigation were not able to compel him to comply with the summons. The two human rights defenders on the fact-finding team (as representatives of Munir's family) used their credibility and media contacts to continue to question the role of BIN in the murder and urged the president to further investigate. In 2006, these two members of the fact-finding team were declared suspects in a defamation case brought by Hendropri-oyono, who claimed he had been tried by the media, demonstrating that even as the judicial process was failing to find those who had planned and orchestrated Munir's murder, other laws could be used to ensnare or cast doubt on the character of those seeking justice for Munir.[90] Eventually, in 2008, there was a trial that included the high-ranking BIN agent Muchdi Purwoparanjono, who, recall, had earlier been dismissed from his position. He was acquitted of involvement in the case. In another hearing, Garuda Airlines was found negligent for failing to make an emergency landing, and for its involvement in the murder, because it placed Pollycarpus on the flight in a manner that did not follow procedure. Executives were sentenced to one year, and Garuda was ordered to pay compensation of 600 million rupiah, which it did not pay. In 2010 Komnas HAM recommended another investigation, which did not happen, and publication of the fact-finding team's report, which also did not happen.

The report itself summarizes the investigative process. It describes the individuals interviewed and documents obtained (such as records indicating frequent calls from Muchdi's cell phone to Pollycarpus); highlights discrepancies in explanations; documents failures to follow up on potential sources of information; notes irregularities, such as the unavailability of CCTV footage for Munir's time in the Jakarta airport; and describes documents about firearms aboard flights to Aceh that had been destroyed (these last documents would have been relevant to proving that Pollycarpus was a nonorganic intelligence agent who had carried weapons on other flights, as flight staff had reported). The report also documents the compartmentalization of BIN, such that only deputies and the head would be aware of any plans. The notepad found in Pollycarpus's home with drawings of seat maps and notes about the flight time until arrival in Amsterdam were examined and attached to the report but not included in the evidence used in court.

The report argues that the murder drew on particular expertise: arsenic would be detectible only in an autopsy, its symptoms would present as simple nausea and diarrhea, and there would be no available in-flight medical assistance or antidotes for it. The planners of Munir's murder also demonstrated an understanding of international law. They knew that Indonesia would be responsible for the investigation because the murder occurred on its national airline. Finally, the report notes the terror and intimidation toward Munir's family and colleagues in the days before the announcement that the death occurred by arsenic poisoning. The report makes clear that the case was the work of several individuals from BIN and Garuda, and that there were higher-up "initiators" who could not be named because the fact-finding team's work was obstructed and because the police did not conduct thorough investigations. It states that the examination of BIN suspects occurred without all fact-finding team members present and that documents were not shared. It establishes a strong indication that the murder was connected to Munir's work for democratization and human rights and his criticism of the agents involved. In short, the report and legal cases fell far short of utilizing the information available, and that information was not shared with the public.

Clearly there was a lack of oversight and control over intelligence operations, protected as they were by compartmentalization and protocols of secrecy as well as by powerful lawyers and unofficial meetings with judges. These operations included the premeditated murder of an innocent human rights defender and public hero. The report's documentation of summonses refused demonstrates the power of the intelligence forces, and its documentation of interviews and records obtained demonstrates the complicity of state companies and others, and a detailed conspiracy.[91]

Testimony in the trial that acquitted Muchdi Purwoparanjono revealed further details not included in the report: because of Munir's work on the activist kidnappings case, Muchdi was removed from his post as general commander (*komandan jenderal*, or *danjen*) of the Special Forces after only fifty-two days, but in 2003 he became a division head (Deputy V) at the intelligence agency, a position that would have afforded numerous opportunities to threaten Munir. The trial also revealed that Pollycarpus himself typed the letter tasking him to be state security for Garuda on a computer at BIN, and that after he met with Muchdi, Pollycarpus bragged to another agent, Budi Santoso, "I got the job of finishing off Munir from Muchdi Purwoparanjono." The letter was given an official number and envelope from BIN and delivered to the director of Garuda, who then formally gave Pollycarpus the security assignment. This set of events suggested that Pollycarpus was connected to the highest levels of BIN, that the murder was planned, and that Garuda was following instructions from BIN. The trial also revealed that Pollycarpus informed Budi Santoso that he had "gotten the big fish in Singapore."[92] Nevertheless, the judge ruled that there was not sufficient and legally admissible evidence to suggest that Muchdi had planned to murder Munir.

Activists have also tried to demonstrate how many elements of the state were implicated in the cover-up by noting all the offices that received copies of the fact-finding team's report after it was handed over to the president in an official ceremony. Upon receiving it, various offices were to study it and meet with the president.

Without new evidence on which to base new indictments, NGO activists have turned their attention to publicizing the results of the fact-finding team's report. In 2016 Suciwati, Munir's widow, initiated a case at the Commission for Public Information (Komisi Informasi Publik, or KIP) to demand the results of the report. As we waited for the meeting with the commissioner to initiate the request, I asked Suciwati if she didn't have a copy of the report. After all, Usman Hamid and other colleagues of Munir's had been on the commission, and surely she must have read it. She said that of course she had it, but she couldn't *use* it, repeating a familiar refrain about reports and documents: many of the Komnas HAM reports circulated widely, and I myself had been given several reports and told that I could read them but not use them, as they were for eventual trials. Suciwati said that this process of demanding the results would allow her to use the results of the report in public. Her mood was optimistic at the start of the suit. Eventually the KIP ruled that the public had the right to the information and determined that the State Secretariat should provide a copy of the document. In 2017, thirteen years after Munir's murder, this was affirmed by the Supreme Court.

But at this point the State Secretariat reported that it did not have a copy of the document, and that it had been lost. Suciwati then reported the State Secretariat to the ombudsman, for maladministration. The government claimed it did not have a copy of the files (including the findings and evidence materials, which did not circulate as widely as the report's narratives).[93] The State Secretariat did not explain why the results of the report could not be publicized, as requested by Suciwati.

The legal cases punished the direct perpetrators as ordinary criminals and the executives at Garuda for their violations of procedures that allowed Pollycarpus to be on the flight. These trials did not review evidence of BIN's involvement. The later 2008 trial of BIN deputy Muchdi included a number of irregularities but resulted in his acquittal. In 2017, Wiranto stated that it was not "easy" for the government to reopen the case because Indonesian law forbids trying the case again when the field actor has already served his sentence, and Muchdi, indicted as the mastermind, had already been acquitted.[94] Ultimately, then, the case did not provide accountability but invulnerability from future trial, since Muchdi had been acquitted in the 2008 trial.

Although Suciwati won her suit at the KIP and the Supreme Court upheld the verdict, the state has still not produced the fact-finding team's document. It persists in claiming that it doesn't have it. Activists from KontraS and Komite Aksi untuk Munir (the Committee for Actions for Munir) have begun to "use" copies of the narrative report that they possess. In September 2019 at venues in Malang and Jakarta, on the fifteenth anniversary of Munir's murder, youth activists, social media influencers, and other artists staged readings of the "complete final report without cuts."[95] According to KontraS, the reading was designed to pressure the government to reopen the case. In addition, it was a "form of protest by civil society to demonstrate their disappointment with the state."[96] The state's response—that it cannot publicize the document because it does not have it— was "unacceptable" and all but absurdly surreal, especially since the existence of the document was demonstrated by the fact that protesters were reading it aloud. KontraS is clear that the public readings do not relieve the president of his obligation to publicize and follow up on the recommendations of the fact-finding team based on the 2004 presidential decree. The valuable "evidence" and supporting documents on which the narrative is based may have been disappeared, but the narrative as it exists in multiple, dispersed PDF copies remains and reproduces specific details, fragments of documents, and interviews. These findings have not been denied. The legal value of the findings for future trials has been undermined by Wiranto's statements that there are legal reasons that the case cannot be reopened given that the accused has already been acquitted. Wiranto served as coordinating minister for political, legal, and security affairs from 2016 to 2019 and was charged with addressing past cases. Legal technicalities once again trumped the spirit of the law; the law once again became a means to evade justice rather than fulfill it; and narratives revealed and openly disclosed—read aloud— once again became irrelevant to (legal) justice rather than serving as its agents.

Publication of the document at this point would show what the state knew, and how those implicated not only have escaped punishment but occupy positions of power in the current government, which ran its first campaign on promises to resolve the past. The investigation, the evidence that it uncovered, and the narrative summarizing "facts" of what happened and pointing to BIN's motive and role in the murder have not made a dent in the culture of impunity. Instead, the long process reported in the media has chronicled the state's, and especially the intelligence agency's, power to evade accountability. All of the changes presumed to follow from revelations did not happen. The infrastructure of impunity works in and through the political system: Even when public pressure forced the president to form an investigative team with some credible members, the political will required to name this an extraordinary case and activate an ad hoc tribunal was lacking. Even when forced to answer some questions, the intelligence agency did so in such a way that very little evidence was made available, and it was shared only with select members of the team and not entered into the record of the investigation. The undocumented and unofficial nature of these revelations made those who might repeat them vulnerable to charges that they were defaming people with political influence and power.

The infrastructure of impunity also works in and through the legal system: Even as fact-finding team members drew on the findings of their investigative team to demand further accountability, they were ensnared in a defamation case, unprotected and without the political and economic resources mobilized by their antagonists. Even when there was a trial based on the findings, the indictment prevented the conspiracy against Munir from being heard, and judges, under pressure and after closed meetings, acquitted Muchdi, thus guaranteeing that even though there remains a sense that justice has not been achieved, and even though information has been amassed for possible future trials (but key evidence has also been mysteriously lost), he will have legal immunity based on the laws that protect against double jeopardy. The web of laws that individually and on paper appear to support accountability and due process have, in practice, extended impunity for the powerful.

Human rights defenders and Munir's family have initiated a number of lawsuits in different venues—a civil case against Garuda, a public-access-to-information case to demand access to the report—but the legal channels for seeking justice and accountability have been exhausted. Even the wins remain unenforced. Without ongoing venues to struggle for justice, the efforts to publicize the case and remember Munir are less compelling: even if the information can be used to effectively generate political pressure to reopen the case, one of the primary suspects is immune.

In the case of the Munir fact-finding team's report, some evidence, such as whatever was said in the investigation of BIN by the police, was never made available to the team and was not included in the materials that formed the case files and attached documents handed over to the president in 2005. These statements and other attachments referenced in the report might provide valuable evidence for a new case, but they have disappeared. On the other hand, the narrative is readily available. The narrative demonstrates that there was a conspiracy to murder Munir, that the intelligence agency was involved, and that state companies were involved. And looking at the narrative alongside the results of the court cases, it demonstrates who has enjoyed impunity and who has not, what is known and who is not held accountable. But all of the information that the state should be liable for knowing is presented without any of the evidence that would make the knowledge legally actionable. And past cases that failed to take account of available information have now become a superficially "legal" means of granting immunity from future trials to intelligence agents—all in the name of due process.

The infrastructure of impunity has allowed the facts of the case to be widely known and yet not meaningfully known (or acted on) at all. Data and documents are at once mortal threats and ignored. Human rights assumptions that focus narrowly on documents as stable forms of evidence that can prompt justice processes overlook the importance of the figures animating the documents as well as the forces of impunity operating in and through the legal system. The documents themselves emerged but were undermined and later disappeared or were disqualified in the courts. Ongoing efforts to eliminate documents and statements previously acknowledged suggest that the data remain dangerous to the state, especially data related to Munir's murder. And yet the infrastructure of impunity has successfully undermined the data's power. Documents and truth matter, but then matter not at all. The actors who can mobilize the data and evidence, especially making it resonate affectively, are undermined, criminalized, and silenced by murder.

Over the course of my research I was given a lot of documents that I could read but not use, and I experienced firsthand the duplicitous role of data, documents, and evidence in post–New Order Indonesia. The phenomenon of reading but not using, actually, perfectly captures informally the state of knowing and not knowing described throughout this book, and that inoculates impunity from even the most explicit revelations of fact and truth.

These documents were not easily shared. Though many people I knew at different NGOs would ask whether I had read certain documents, they would always refer me to someone else to ask for them. I did not always acknowledge having the documents that I did possess, as I was interested in lingering more on the texture of the documents, of seeing what others knew about them, as they were absent yet frequently mentioned and widely known. In one interview in 2015 with a Komnas HAM commissioner whom I did not know well, we were reprising a familiar conversation about the files (*berkas*) going back and forth (*bolak-balik*) between Komnas HAM and the attorney general's office, and the files being returned. I asked whether she had read the reports or files. She did not answer. She noted that at one time the files had been returned to Komnas HAM and left at the gate without a proper sign-off. I asked what exactly the *berkas* looked like—were they envelopes or boxes of files? She said they were probably boxes, but the discussions of the back and forth did not usually specify *what* materials were going back and forth, or why and how.

I knew that the 1965 report was over one thousand pages long. I knew that the commissioner leading the investigation was a longtime and highly credible activist. Komnas HAM had instituted a system where victims making statements were given copies of their own statements (*berita acara pemeriksaan*). Various individuals suggested to me that one could ask the victims for these statements, which would make it possible to legally collect original, authorized pieces of the evidence, beyond the state sources. In one case, I interviewed a victim who was an organizer and had worked to collect oral histories from victims. I asked him about the documents he had and kept. He told me he had burned the earlier release letters, as he did not want them to be found and implicate him as having been connected to the PKI. He said of course he had a copy of his statement to Komnas HAM. I asked if he could give me a copy of his statement that I could use for my research. He was more concerned with the other documents that were issued after giving the statement, the ones that gave access to healthcare facilities, for instance. Eventually he admitted that he wasn't sure where his copy of the statement was.

Similarly, the commissioner was not able to answer when I asked what the *berkas* actually looked like or whether there were backup copies, emphasizing over and over that I was not asking to see or hear about the report because, after all, I had already read it. It became clear that these documents were talked about but not really engaged with.

The Komnas HAM documents are thorough, detailed accounts of events. They draw on interviews with state agents, print media sources from the past, and statements from victims. In some cases, I was given long transcripts of open-ended exploratory interviews with victims that were conducted early on to consider how to frame the case. They included documentation of team members, methodology, and timelines, as well as legal justifications for why the case was considered a gross violation case by applicable laws. Finally, they included a narrative version of events. They referenced various supporting documents that were not typically part of the PDF files that circulated more widely through activist networks. The reports indicated that there was evidence that a gross violation of human rights occurred and that there should be follow-up investigations and a tribunal. They did not include detailed statements or smoking-gun evidence from perpetrators (though these more interesting elements might be found in a review of supporting materials and interview transcripts).

As for the KPP HAM investigation of violence in East Timor, one senior human rights activist who had served as a member of the investigative commission told me that they had summoned high-ranking military generals who had provided videotaped statements. This person noted what had been said on tape to the commission in a case where it was later denied; however, when he tried to recover the video to challenge the reversal, the videos had disappeared—most likely after the threat of international prosecution had disappeared.

Similarly, in 2017, the public discourse denying that mass rape had taken place in 1998 escalated, even as former president Habibie stated at a public commemoration, at the mass grave site, that there had been findings that rapes had occurred. Even under these circumstances, "facts" of violence can melt into air. They were not irrefutable; they did not inevitably implicate or set a course toward justice or transformation. Instead they could be absorbed within the existing infrastructure of impunity, which proved stronger.

When I discussed the final report on the May riots with the head of the Joint Fact-Finding Team,[97] he noted how the secretary of the commission had been very close to the TNI (she occupied a similar role in several commissions; I had encountered her in 1999 as I sought information about a presidential decree team to investigate violence in Aceh). He asked whether I had a copy of the team's report. I said that I had been told that it was available at Komnas Perempuan, but that I had referred a student doing an undergraduate thesis on the topic there and she reported back that it was gone. The head of the team said that the documents should have been stored at what was then the Ministry of Law and Human Rights, but that they had not been kept there. They had vanished. Copies of the report findings are available in international libraries, internet sources, and personal collections, but the statements by witnesses and military members summoned, the names and addresses of victims, and other supporting evidence, he said, have all disappeared.

In March 2016 I spoke with Lexy after a meeting of victims at KontraS. A former communications major and a journalist and videographer, he has been working independently since the mid-1990s to create a video and audio archive of events. Initially he was interested in daily life as a student in Yogyakarta in the mid-1990s, but then he became interested in social justice after noting the growing importance of religion: in his view, everything, from the most mundane ordinary interactions to the machinations of elite politics, came down to religious affiliation and to a lesser extent political affiliation, which bothered him. So he began to look at problems of social justice and humanity through the creation of his archive.

I saw him often at events—hearings, meetings, protests, press conferences. Most of his work was unpublished, although he had a YouTube channel with twelve thousand subscribers who he says are ordinary people. He checks their names as they subscribe, and they are not the usual NGO types. He initially made films for the NGOs, but they were not very good at distribution, so he prefers to have his work available online to anyone who subscribes in what he refers to as the market distributing it. The short videos he has posted are a small fraction of what he has meticulously documented for future generations. He emphasizes that his archive will be intact and accessible two hundred years from now because he has taken care with indexing and storage and has also updated mediums so that the material will not become technologically obsolete. He feels that in the future, all of these "mysteries" (political intrigues, contradictions, statements of lack of knowledge or the impossibility of knowing made by those in power) will be solved by listening to the full materials in the archive. Unlike Gatot Lestario, whose testimony was described in chapter 1, he did not metaphorize this as a court of history, but the desire and impetus are similar.

I asked him what interested him from the material he documents, and whether he had noticed any discrepancies in the Munir case. He said there were some. For example, Ongeng, the long-haired preman whose testimony had led to Pollycarpus's jail sentence, had not also testified in the Muchdi case. He noted that by then the court was "already being much more unfair." Ongeng died very suddenly in 2012 after Muchdi's trial, and his nephew had identified a number of irregularities around his sudden death. He paused as he recalled and shook his head slightly. He said he just felt sad—Munir was so important, and if there had been five lawyers given access to all the interviews and documents the police had (not just the log of phone calls but the voice recordings that were supposedly unavailable), then they surely could have resolved the case. No one did enough. Now the star witness was dead, and records from the police investigation were probably lost. It was just sad.

The urge to gather the data, to document what is said for a future in which the truth will provide clarity and galvanize a response or resolution, persists. The quantity and content of data known to have been lost also increases, which indicates that it is not only the gang of data gatherers and their friends in the human rights and justice community who know the latent value and potential of data. Forcibly disappearing witnesses and data alike is an acknowledgment of its latent value, and possibly of a sense that the law may deliver a guilty verdict, a tenuous indication that the infrastructure of impunity is beyond the control of individuals and may fail. But more than twenty years after reformasi began, the initial hope that the documentation and data in themselves would provide

FIGURE 3.4.   The data storage room at KontraS in 2015 before the group moved to its current office. Some data have been digitized, but many have not. Photo by the author.

justice or the return of missing comrades has dimmed; the hope of a future in which the data are there and meaningful lingers among some of the activists. Truth failed to become an instrument of justice, even though it is at the heart of human rights and transitional justice discourse, because the infrastructure has conscripted even the tools of revelation and resistance, especially in and through the law.

Legal activists recognized that the law under Suharto was limited by a culture of corruption and engineering (discussed in chapter 5), but they had confidence in the law itself, with some modifications—the removal of bad laws, the addition of others to address past crimes and recognize international human rights, and so on. Activists hoped to use trials to move beyond individual cases to make larger structural points, to hold accountable the masterminds who plotted conspiracies against critics such as Munir or the PRD, rather than merely the individuals—the ones who made the kills—forced to implement their superiors' plans. And yet the reformed legal system, far from being a technical domain governed by truth, evidence, and rules designed to deliver justice, became part of an infrastructure designed to provide impunity for the powerful—past, present, and future.

NARRATING WHAT IS KNOWN

In 2014 Joko Widodo, known as Jokowi, narrowly won the presidential election against Prabowo Subianto, the general discharged by the military Officers' Honor Council (DKP) for his role in the kidnapping of the democracy activists at the end of the New Order. The youth vote was important in Jokowi's win, and many who had been students or youths during reformasi and still worked in civil society organizations told me that it was important to regenerate movements and engage these millennials who were "busy all the time with their gadgets." One of Jokowi's campaign promises and part of his vision (*nawa cita*) was to address past cases and strengthen human rights, and many of his supporters highlighted the fact that he was unburdened by the past. He had been a businessman in central Java who rose to become governor of Jakarta, and not a military or political elite—in contrast to both Prabowo (who ran against him) and Susilo Bambang Yudhoyono, known as SBY, a retired general who had served as president from 2004 to 2014. Komnas HAM had completed reports on the gross violations cases in 2012, and despite SBY's promises that they would be addressed, they were not.

The year after Jokowi's election was the fiftieth anniversary of the 1965 genocide, and significant attention was focused on it, beyond the community of activists and civil society groups. Indonesia was the guest of honor at the 2015 Frankfurt Book Fair, which led to articles that reflected on how purges of Communists and attacks on the Left had wiped out the vibrant literary scene in Indonesia.[1] The Ubud Readers and Writers Festival in Bali the same year highlighted works related to 1965 and the killings—yet despite proper permits, the Ubud sessions on 1965 were shut down.[2] The 2016 ASEAN literary festival took place in Jakarta and also featured a number of panels on 1965. Protesters claiming that the festival was a covert effort to disseminate Communist ideas and promote LGBTQ expression that threatened national values stood in front of the venue, but the festival continued. The Turn Left Festival (Belok Kiri Fest) explored the Left through discussions and cultural initiatives. It was also shut down and had to change its format from a large public gathering in one weekend to discussions at the Legal Aid Institute scattered over a series of weekends.[3] A temporary museum of human rights established in Jakarta and accompanied by proposals for a permanent museum captured the hope for human rights initiatives in the Jokowi era, but the permanent museum never came to fruition.[4] In May, a large monument had been installed at the cemetery where the victims of the May 1998 violence were buried.[5] Even as former elites remained politically powerful and vocally opposed these initiatives, the momentum seemed to be moving toward the resolution of past cases of violence.

Although these cultural efforts to address the events of 1965 and other instances of state violence appear to be independent of the state, many of them were intended to pressure the state or to attract its attention; in other words, they were designed to be political. I suggest that these cultural actions opened a new space of engagement and subtly challenged in new ways less visible elements of the infrastructure of impunity. In venues such as these, facts and documentation were converted not into legal evidence but into knowledge, stories, and feelings or sensibilities about the past. For activists, the state, the New Order generation, and millennials alike, culture and stories were important domains of struggle against the infrastructure of impunity, as suggested by an analysis of these commemorative efforts as well as the attempts to shut them down. Eventually millennials came to question past propaganda and often expressed outrage at being betrayed by the state and its propaganda. Both the activist campaigns to resist forgetting and remember 1965 (promoted using the hashtags #melawanlupa or #menolaklupa and #ingat65, respectively) and the state efforts to establish narratives about the past disclose the importance of stories in the infrastructure of impunity.

The Coalition for Justice and Truth Telling (Koalisi Keadilan dan Pengungkapan Kebenaran, or KKPK) was a coalition of NGOs that included many of the organizations involved in victim support, human rights, and transitional justice programs. Many of these same individuals had helped to draft the Truth and Reconciliation Commission bill (Rancangan Undang Undang Komisi Kebenaran dan Rekonsiliasi) in the early 2000s, and after the law was passed, they sought a judicial review in 2007 at the Constitutional Court to strike amnesty provisions from the law.[6] To their surprise, the Constitutional Court did not simply remove the amnesty provisions but nullified the entire law, leaving Indonesia with no mechanism for official truth and reconciliation processes.[7] The coalition sought to establish the truth of multiple incidents of violence during the New Order and to create more publicity around the cases to force the state to respond and resolve the cases, but also to regenerate the movement with new millennial youth engagement.

In contrast to other efforts to engage the state, the KKPK "Year of Truth" incorporated many elements of a truth commission, but without the support or involvement of the state. It elicited testimony from individuals across Indonesia who had suffered state violence and human rights violations. Modeled after the official truth commission in neighboring Timor Leste, the NGO coalition convened panels in multiple cities across the archipelago in which victims gave testimonies to public audiences.[8] The panels were formal, used the national language, and did not incorporate local cultural symbols or practices; however, they provided victim testimony and were moderated or officiated by powerful local figures to give their discussions local authority and legitimacy.

In addition to live community forums in the five cities, the KKPK produced edited videos for its website and social media campaigns. The short videos overlaid the narrative of past violence and everyday hardship onto contemporary life as well as the site of the historical violence. The Indonesian studies scholar Annie Pohlman argues that the network was doing the Year of Truth as a political demand for official recognition by the state of the truth about past state violence.[9] Many former civil society activists have become part of the political elite, and KKPK members have also lobbied them informally. There is very little research (from the KKPK or others) that describes the impact of the regional hearings on local social relations or their effect nationally. Even where local reconciliations occur, they do not effectively reveal the role of the state, especially in the 1965 killings.[10] The five-day hearings in Jakarta (in November 2013) were widely covered in the media, but one of the organizers told me in 2015 that it was difficult to gauge the campaign's effects and that likely it had circulated to too few people. While testimonies of individuals provide an archive for the future, they do not meet the requirements of judicial evidence, and it is unclear how the archive will be available for future generations. (In 2023, the KKPK website was no longer available, although videos of panels are available on YouTube.)

The KKPK's final report, titled *Finding Indonesia Again: Understanding Forty Years of Violence and Breaking the Chain of Impunity*,[11] describes patterns that caused violence: "Extermination" [*pembasmian*] includes violence to the PKI and the Left, Papua, Timor, and Aceh, and the failure to achieve justice. "Theft [*Perampasan*] of Natural Resources and Sources of Livelihoods" reviews forestry, mining, and plantations. "Homogenizing and Control" looks at how society has been silenced and forced to accept the state ideology, violence in the name of development and order, and militarism in politics. "Violence among Citizens" considers clashes between social groups not as spontaneous outbursts but as a military strategy, and examines the role of the state in perpetrating them. "Violence against women" examines specific cases of military operations (Timor, Papua, Aceh), communal conflicts, theft of resources, reproductive rights, and continuing violence. The sixth pattern considers the "Dead End of Law"—law as a tool of power, including the courts; law during the transitional period (1998–2005); the resolution of human rights violations of the past; and the problem of impunity. Rather than dividing victims by cases, the 370-page KKPK report supports victim solidarity by discerning patterns from multiple cases across geography and time, emphasizing state involvement. In addition to the report, a smaller book, which features the voices of the victims "freeing themselves from the shackles of past violence," includes color pictures organized by location, along with short summaries of testimonies.[12]

I talked to one of the report's team members at a KKPK workshop for regional participants in Jakarta. Galuh Wandita spent many years working for the Commission for Reception, Truth, and Reconciliation in East Timor (Comissão de Acolhimento, Verdade e Reconciliação de Timor Leste) and founded a transitional justice organization in Indonesia called Asia Justice and Rights. It was clear that she saw the final report as a resource for a new national history. She reminded me that history in Indonesia was taught by rote memorization and without questioning, and recalled her shock when she once lived abroad and her history teacher asked the class for their thoughts about the material. In Indonesia, looking into history meant that you might be labeled a "new-style Communist." She described her research on Buru, where the physical remains of the imprisonment of suspected Communists were strewn everywhere and yet never discussed. She underlined the histories of conflicts that families tried to hide from their children, to keep them safe. Advances had been made in the historical curriculum in the early 2000s, which were then reversed when new governments banned the books and once again lashed the supposed coup attempt G30S to the PKI, making it G30S/PKI. "At all levels from how we teach history to pop culture to the government, we are happily ahistorical," Wandita concluded. The KKPK's report was titled *Finding Indonesia Again* in order to encourage people to face their history and learn from it. The multiple footnotes on every page cite international and Indonesian scholarship related to historical events, official documents, and statements to the KKPK by victims and other historical figures (noted as in the KKPK's possession).

"For the next generations," Wandita said, "I don't see how we cannot be aware of this bloody past." She warned against ignoring it or sweeping it under the rug "because it is actually shaping the present very much. This whole culture of impunity, of allowing everyone to be corrupt, every man for himself, all that we learned from [the] New Order, and it is still shaping our future and will continue to unless we have a way to reflect on that wrong turn, or [the idea that] if you are different than me I can bully you to be [the] same." By way of example, she added that this applied to minority religions such as Ahmadiya and Shia Muslims. "I can use the power of state to convert, or force repentance [*tobat*] and if you don't, burn your [place of worship]. That is still happening in our culture and we have never looked at that."[13]

Narratives such as Anne Frank's diary are powerful, she reflected, "because of just one person's voice that is universal." She said Indonesians "don't have that one accessible story yet.... That is why it is important to keep finding the stories, and also, thinking of our workshop, we have to have alternative narratives that show humanity and show the human story . . . not only saying crimes against humanity or this was genocide." The "legal stuff" was needed, but so too was the "cultural stuff to reach out to the younger generation."[14]

As we talked about the KKPK report, she admitted that not enough people had seen it. They had tried to make it accessible and something that could be digested in smaller pieces, but more needed to be done to make it appealing to young people with their gadgets. The writing process had been exhausting and the report itself had been insufficiently "socialized" (the New Order term for disseminated or publicized).

Coalition meetings that I attended in 2015 confirmed that the KKPK was struggling with ways to promote its materials into a wider and more popular format. Its meetings included individuals who had been active in human rights since 1998 and older victims. Some members were active in lobbying for new institutions to protect victims and accessing state services to support victims of human rights violations.[15] Many others were dedicated to campaigns for justice and rehabilitation for victims. One of the KKPK's shared challenges was to expand the movement and the report beyond what many individuals called the pattern of "You again, You again" (Lu lagi, Lu lagi, abbreviated as L4),[16] meaning that the same people attended events.

The KKPK consortium worked with the famous Indonesian bands Superman Is Dead and Simfoni to perform songs by political prisoners set to new musical arrangements. These conveyed stories and information, interspersed with video clips of survivors narrating stories of daily life in prison. Other groups such as Dialita were composed of survivors and family members and sang a capella songs from the past. They saw gathering to sing as a form of healing for survivors and subsequent generations. In August 2015, these groups arranged a concert at Goethe Huis, the German Cultural Center, in Jakarta. Advertised through celebrity musicians' networks as a free concert, it was overwhelmingly popular; the attendance far exceeded planners' expectations. They had succeeded in attracting people beyond the "You again, You again" familiar faces, but many were concerned that fans came to hear the bands, which may not have changed awareness.

Another NGO of communications professionals took the KKPK's final report to different high schools, such as the one where Uciwati delivered her testimony (see chapter 1), and talked about graphic design techniques. This group encouraged students to design creative works inspired by the report for a nationwide contest sponsored by the KKPK and other organizations. I was struck by one comment in an art piece that said that the youth had to stop discriminating against those whom they thought were apathetic café-goers, in contrast to activists.

The KKPK was a start at attracting younger generations, both as consumers and as producers of a creative culture with different values and visions of the nation than in the past, and at offering a new cultural approach to activism that was shifting in ways not immediately perceptible to the older generation. The process is slow and contributes to a diffuse, cumulative effort of making new voices heard. I suggest that the KKPK also signaled a growing awareness of the importance of stories and narratives about the past—a shift away from facts and documents and toward the emotional valences that had always supported impunity.

Indonesia does not have a strong culture of literacy. Literature and films have been produced, especially about 1965, but they were not especially connected to ground-level civil society organizations and events until *The Act of Killing* (2012).[17] Joshua Oppenheimer's film documents *preman* executioners of 1965 and reflects on their role in the killings, their links to the powerful, and their continuing impunity in the present. *The Act of Killing* centers on the gangsters making a film—what they believe will be a heroic Hollywood film about their role in 1965. It has been presented internationally as a revelation of "dark secrets" and an act of "breaking silence," but as we've seen, the fact that the preman did the killing is not actually a secret in Indonesia.[18] The film's unique qualities are its focus on perpetrators (in contrast to many human rights films that focus on victims, and build empathy for them) and its consideration of how impunity endures into the present. Several forms of stigmatization support the infrastructure of impunity in Indonesia—the stigmatization of suspected Communists and other dissidents and the stigmatization of the criminal, among others—and Oppenheimer's surreal and exaggerated reenactment of violence in the film-within-a-film both denaturalizes ongoing impunity and allows audiences to shift stigmatization to the monstrous criminal perpetrators as they unapologetically revel in their past

acts of violence. The film has generated extensive scholarly analysis.[19] It also circulated more widely and became more mainstream than most of the other initiatives to reveal and narrate elements of the past.

The Act of Killing shows the past as very much present but only dimly acknowledged. It opens with a synopsis of history, which has been criticized as too brief
and simplified. Scholars have noted that the film is historically misleading because
the army is absent, and have suggested that the focus on individual executioners
is open to misinterpretation.[20] Likewise, the United States' role in supporting the
Indonesian genocide at the height of the Cold War and in response to fears of
domino-style Communism is invisible, save for the opening text.[21] Nevertheless,
the text does point to the undeniable fact that the military took power from the
government and that critics could be persecuted if labeled Communists.

The rolling text at the start of the film states,

> In 1965, the Indonesian government was overthrown by the military.
> Anybody opposed to the military dictatorship could be accused of being
> a communist: union members, landless farmers, intellectuals, and the
> ethnic Chinese. In less than a year, and with the direct aid of Western
> governments, over 1 million "communists" were murdered. The army
> used paramilitaries and gangsters to carry out the killings. These men
> have been in power—and have persecuted their opponents—ever since.
>
> When we met the killers, they proudly told us stories about what they
> did. To understand why, we asked them to create scenes about the kill-
> ings in whatever ways they wished. This film follows that process, and
> documents its consequences.[22]

This reminder is important for those long steeped in the propaganda narratives.
Pancasila Youth so successfully rebranded itself after petrus that the connections
between the preman who executed the killings and the nationalist Pancasila
Youth may not have been apparent to many viewers.

The film's protagonist, known by his nickname, Anwar Congo, a preman in
the city of Medan, reminisces about Hollywood movies that he and other preman
watched in the 1960s that made them happy as they went about their executions
and extortions. The film also follows the preman into the present to show their
continuing power, as it dramatizes the links between Pancasila Youth and the then
vice president, Jusuf Kalla, and follows the political campaign of a former executioner running for office, who imagines the moneymaking opportunities if elected.
The film also includes more reflective conversations between reunited executioners, and scenes in which they interact with their families as ordinary people.

Many young people I spoke with said that their opinion about 1965 shifted
after The Act of Killing, which engaged youth emotionally in ways that previous

documents and documentaries had not. The film was not banned, but some screenings were shut down in 2015 by paramilitary and other mass organizations. Activist networks distributed the film in a context of study-group-style screenings that involved viewers in meaningful group discussions led by experienced activists, more often than not against a backdrop of threats from mass organizations and even the state. Thus, as one senior activist and organizer reflected, students had the experience of watching together, having their questions answered, and being threatened for watching a film, which underscored the film's theme of the state's involvement with violence and heightened the emotional valence of hearing the story and watching the film.[23]

The film itself has drama, humor, and a cold, remorseless affect when it delivers its most incriminating testimony about the executioners' methods. The gangsters' admissions diverge from official narratives. They reveal that the violence was a business, not a spontaneous amok, and they hardly come across as heroic national martyrs. By showing the gangsters' cold and calculating affect, *The Act of Killing* disrupts the cultural and narrative foundations of the infrastructure of impunity that insulated killers from remorse. Further, it makes the remorselessness and continuing power of the preman into the present look grotesque and unacceptable, which shatters the propaganda narrative and has also alarmed elite military figures who would like to prolong the infrastructure of impunity. They have protested and disrupted screenings of the film and have tried to renew screenings of the state propaganda film.

Impunity itself proves moral rectitude in the killers' minds: in Indonesia, the infrastructure of impunity situates perpetrators of the violence on the side of law. Adi Zulkadry, one of the more prolific killers profiled in *The Act of Killing*, proclaims, "We were allowed to do it. And the proof is, we murdered people and were never punished. The people we killed—there's nothing to be done about it. They have to accept it. Maybe I'm just trying to make myself feel better, but it works. I've never felt guilty, never been depressed, never had nightmares." In contrast, the main protagonist, Anwar, appears troubled as he considers his past actions. In one scene he retches after a reenactment, although some have questioned whether the retching indicates genuine remorse or is a theatrical performance for the camera.[24]

The Indonesian film studies scholar Intan Paramaditha has reflected on how Indonesian viewers can recognize and situate themselves in relationship to the violence in *The Act of Killing*.[25] Like other analysts, she lingers on Joshua Oppenheimer's statement that he wanted people to recognize themselves in Anwar, but other scholars have observed that Anwar may or may not be genuinely troubled, and there are tens of thousands of others (like those who appear in the film) who are not troubled.[26] She notes that the killings were perpetrated not only by criminal preman groups, as depicted in the film, but also by Muslim groups, and that military campaigns were supported directly and indirectly by the fathers and grandfathers of most young Indonesians.[27] The role of Muslim groups in the killings is much more contentious in contemporary Indonesia, but in the film it is overshadowed by the preman killers' flamboyance and remorselessness. Consequently, middle-class and elite audiences can distance themselves from criminal perpetrators while also ignoring the many ways in which they are beneficiaries of their violence. For Paramaditha this is captured in the inappropriate laughter of middle-class audiences as they view the film.[28] At the same time, though, the spoils of post–Cold War development are featured in different scenes—in malls, and in collections of luxury goods—even if it has been difficult for middle-class audiences to recognize the link between Indonesian development and the killings.[29] Paramaditha notes that those who lived through the killings played active and less active roles but share a collective guilt: "The horror in *The Act of Killing* lies in our access, via Oppenheimer, to the perpetrators' confessions of their crime, expressed without remorse, and to their private lives in which they interact with their families like ordinary people."[30]

The revelation in *The Act of Killing* is a public secret, and the film's resonances, and dissonances, with the propaganda film *Treachery of the September 30th Movement/PKI* only deepens this ambiguous effect. Because it circulated in study group screenings and won international acclaim, the film attracted more notice and attention from both young people and the state.[31] As it became mainstream it created a space for discussion and a new urgency around the issue of state violence, supported of course by other efforts and revelations, and was an affectively powerful way to engage and reflect on impunity and its persistence. For example, Ariel Heryanto writes that he approached the widely regarded *Tempo* magazine to do a special edition on the executioners, and Oppenheimer facilitated contacts.[32] Heryanto describes this nonfiction magazine feature as more controversial than the film, but I would suggest that the *Tempo* nonfiction edition had this effect only because it came after the film had challenged the state propaganda *affectively*, with its surreal excess and emotional intensity. These elements of the film—excessive and fantastical—made the factual report more galvanizing and meaningful. The study-group-style screenings, much like previous NGO gatherings of victims, also wove the film into factual nonfiction and pointed young people to scholarly works available for free online (for example, Roosa's *Pretext for Mass Murder*).

As discussed above, critics have suggested that the film fails to create the audience identification with Anwar that Oppenheimer had hoped to achieve, and that in fact flamboyant gangsters allow middle-class audiences to distance themselves from the violence.[33] Whatever the case, the film does create a horrifying space where perpetrators are simultaneously remorseless and ordinary, well-respected family men. Although—and perhaps precisely because—it isn't factual or purely documentary, the film was engaging, especially for younger audiences. It advanced on earlier efforts by eschewing empathy for the victims in favor of a cold depiction of the perpetrators and the legal system.[34] Films and creative efforts that focused on victims' stories were important (including Oppenheimer's follow-up film *The Look of Silence*),[35] but shifting attention to the perpetrators interrupted the infrastructure of impunity and its exculpatory narratives of the perpetrators' actions in crucial ways and with a unique combination of factual perpetrator testimony and surreal fantasy reenactments. The film's inflection away from moral rationalizations about the danger of Communists and toward impunity in the law and widespread social complicity began to degrade the infrastructure. The affective work that the film performed made later factual revelations more significant.

By some accounts, for example, the International People's Tribunal for 1965 (IPT), founded in 2013, had its genesis in a screening of *The Act of Killing* for exiles in the Netherlands. Here, Oppenheimer reportedly told exiles that he had done what he could, and now it was up to them. In this case the surreal film mobilized individuals to gather hard facts and evidence for a tribunal to rule on past events.[36] The IPT was initiated by the Dutch scholar Saskia Wieringa and the Indonesian senior legal aid activist and political figure Nursyahbani Katjasung-kana, with the goal of "raising awareness of the events" and "promoting reconciliation in Indonesia," and with the further goals of "affirming that justice is still possible" and contributing to the rule of law and human rights in Indonesia.[37] The IPT did not have the authority to subpoena documents or statements; it primarily drew on victims' public testimonies and previously revealed documents. The tribunal hearings took place on November 10–13, 2015.

In 2014 I interviewed a number of different individuals and organizations that had been involved in transitional justice, particularly those who had worked on issues related to 1965. Many had doubts about the proposed International People's Tribunal, especially because they feared it would divide victims and organizations, and that it might also be too confrontational. Other groups worked on the ground in various ways to support the effort; in particular, they wanted to organize the victims in whose name the tribunal was working. Some of those victims wanted to prioritize rehabilitation instead of judicial processes, and a confrontational approach entailed risks. Some of the victims who remained in Indonesia thought exiles had enjoyed the good life in Europe, as much of the early propaganda had suggested. Around 2015, a number of initiatives demonstrated otherwise. These included Elisabeth Ida Mulyani's exhibit of portraits of exiles at the Rekoleksi Memori Temporary Museum, films that highlighted the life of exiles and were discussed on televised talk shows (*Letter from Prague*, for example), and works by writers such as Martin Aleida.[38] One exile, Tom Ilyas, attempted to return home in 2015 and was arrested, which put exiles' love for their homeland in the news.[39]

These groups also struggled over strategy: much of the NGOs' strategy had focused on those wrongly accused of being PKI. This was a safer strategy, but it left intact the vilification and cultural, social, and legal stigmatization of Communists. The tribunal, in contrast, considered not only those mistakenly identified as PKI but also the rights of political groups and the possibility that this had been a "politicide": the deliberate elimination of a group whose members share a political belief. Hard-liners interpreted this as the ominous return of revenge-seeking Communists.[40] This led to some tensions among victims as well. One that I interviewed thought that the tribunal's intent was to defend Communists, and this person most certainly was not a Communist and did not want to be identified with them.

As the tribunal conducted its work, however, these divisions diminished. The tribunal convened a weekly meeting called Rabuan (a Wednesday meeting that paralleled Kamisan, the Thursday protest discussed in chapter 6, and likely related to the term *Jumatan*, for Friday prayers). A small group of scholars, activists, and artists who had been involved with the 1965 cases for many years worked with the IPT to facilitate the meetings.

The group was called on to represent the voice of victims in various contexts. There were concerns over how victims were to be represented, because a number of regions had different organizations of victims. Some of the organizations had local branches in different areas, while others did not.[41] Eventually it was decided to create a new umbrella organization in whose name victims could speak in affiliation with the IPT. In addition to discussing matters related to the tribunal—how to livestream it or, later, the pros and cons of participating in a national symposium—the group was also a place for social support and the sharing of stories. By the end, one of the organizers, the artist Dolorosa Sinaga, had encouraged victims to write their stories in exercise books to create a makeshift historical archive. The group also collected small, voluntary cash donations from attendees each week and dispersed them to those who needed aid, especially for medical expenses. The group became a convenient entry point for victims to convey what they sought from the state.

The tribunal's fact-finding and sharing mission emerged out of a fictional film, but it generated factual narratives and stories as it went about its work. New data and documents were uncovered, but primarily the IPT reexamined existing evidence in ways that changed its affective and legal resonance.

The tribunal heard the long-silenced, marginalized, and discredited victims' voices, and these voices influenced the legal decision. Meetings like the Wednesday group had a clear purpose and provided an opportunity for victims, their family members, and supporters to meet and work together. The testimonies, for example—descriptions of sexual violence, delivered behind a screen—implicated well-known and powerful figures and institutions.[42] This meant that the monstrous violence portrayed in *The Act of Killing* that had for so long been sanitized in state narratives as simply the eradication of an ideology attached not only to the thugs but to the army and the state, and even to well-respected sociologists. Still, it would take more than individual testimonies to demonstrate genocide.

One of the Indonesian researchers working for the tribunal considered the Kopkamtib documents that described a widespread, systematic, and detailed plan by the army to kill leftists as the most surprising ones.[43] These documents and similar ones uncovered by the historian Jess Melvin in Aceh compelled scholars and activists to consider the mass killings as genocide.[44]

Another friend and longtime activist who had been involved in researching the killings for more than two decades told me that the Kopkamtib documents had been found in Sumatra's largest city, Medan, at a used book stall. He suspected that the military base there was getting rid of the documents and someone had scavenged these from their garbage. No documents of this kind have ever been procured from state agencies. Given the entrenched narrative of spontaneous amok killings, these careful and detailed plans are astonishing, as were the circumstances of their discovery. At the same time, most Indonesians would have known of some of the bureaucratic aspects of stigmatization—the classification system, the clean environment letter, or the category of the ET (ex-prisoner)—all designed to be very public (and humiliating).

While there were some fortuitous and stunning finds like this, the tribunal relied primarily on information that was already known; hence, the major innovation of the IPT was to situate its work within the context of international law and with an international panel of respected and credible individuals as judges.

After the hearing, which included testimony from twenty victims, the panel of judges published its verdict in July 2016. While the tribunal had no legal power over Indonesia, it confirmed that the Indonesian state and its proxies were guilty of nine counts of crimes against humanity alleged by the prosecution, including murder, enslavement, imprisonment, torture, sexual violence, persecution, enforced disappearance, and hate propaganda—and the panel of judges went further, naming the killings as genocide. This conclusion was more momentous than the presentation of facts or victims' stories. Although not a state organ, the tribunal recommended that the government of Indonesia follow up on the 2012

Komnas HAM report on 1965. The government had paid very little attention to the report, as it languished in the attorney general's office prior to the IPT. Together, Oppenheimer's film and the tribunal problematized impunity in new and different ways by focusing on perpetrators, and on the legal system itself. This verdict could achieve in the realm of law what *The Act of Killing* had achieved with its surreal reenactments: it could shatter narratives of impunity and inculpability.

The tribunal's finding that the killings, systematic and planned by the army, were genocide challenged public discourse and legal assumptions. As a crime under customary international law, genocide was not subject to nonretroactivity and could be prosecuted by using laws passed after the crime was committed.[45] The findings raised the possibility of international intervention if the state was unable or unwilling to hold perpetrators accountable. The fact that this was not new information also meant that everyone shared some complicity. Not surprisingly, then, the findings provoked very swift responses from the same figures and institutions that had ignored the Komnas HAM report for several years. The tribunal's examination of the evidence elicited a strong and emotional response from government ministers and especially retired and active senior military. Ministers announced that Indonesia had its own laws and would not bow to the IPT's demands. "Our country is a great nation," one said. "We acknowledge and we will resolve this problem [the 1965 tragedy] in our way and through universal values."[46] Social organizations and conservative groups targeted organizers and participants for their involvement with the tribunal.

Elites and vocal retired generals reacted to the tribunal in emotional and undignified ways on the television program *Indonesian Lawyers Club*. They berated the Indonesian coordinator of the tribunal, Nursyahbani Katjasungkana, attacking her as a traitor to the nation. She and the moderator reiterated that there was no legal consequence to the tribunal, but even so, its work deeply agitated the retired generals. After years of skillfully deploying emotionally resonant propaganda backed by a legal and bureaucratic system that had the power to inflict enormous harms and enforce compliance with the propaganda, as well as the resources and power to influence the outcome of trials and legal challenges related to what they referred to as the events of 1965, the tribunal threatened their control over the narrative. And there was the added threat of international prosecution if the state continued to be unwilling or unable to address the issue. Even without prosecutions, the plans designed to displace liability for the violence onto other groups now became evidence of the army's involvement and intent. The public record and scenes shown in *The Act of Killing* demonstrated that perpetrators had bragged with impunity about their acts. If the interpretation of 1965 shifted, this record would be an admission of guilt, and thus the narrative struggle was important in the legal battles.

Shortly after the broadcast of the *Indonesian Lawyers Club* episode, I met with an older man who had been involved in prodemocracy movements and held various posts in the government after reformasi. I asked him about the episode and shared my surprise at seeing a direct confrontation between the two sides, publicly televised. He bypassed the question and explained how badly the PKI had been treated. He related experiences from his time in prison: by virtue of his class position he had enjoyed privileges there, but he emphasized that the person who became his helper (servant) in prison had been arrested completely without cause on the grounds that he was a PKI supporter, based on suspicions about the family he worked for as a household helper. The man I interviewed had been part of the movement against Sukarno's Guided Democracy and was later jailed for involvement in the Malari protests against Suharto's New Order in 1974. I knew that he knew I was sympathetic to the victims—he had teased me on other occasions during reformasi after seeing me on a televised newscast at a 1965-related event, "with those Communists"—so I was surprised that he went to such efforts to explain this to me. I could only surmise that it was because so many others he knew were so easily provoked to act on recollected fear and resentment over what the PKI had (supposedly) done in the past. I myself had heard stories of past actions told as relativizing reasons why there could not be an examination of what had been done to the PKI without also examining what *they* had done in that chaotic period.

As the tribunal walked a fine line between challenging the state narratives and maintaining a legal focus, two cultural campaigns and events in late 2015 and early 2016 pushed back on the narrative of vilified Communism and reinterpreted the Left, both historically and in the present. The Turn Left Festival and *The History of the Indonesian Left for Beginners* explicitly engaged in and rehabilitated leftist culture and ideas.

The History of the Indonesian Left for Beginners was published collectively by thirty-two organizations and featured a graphic history, with comics by Yayak Yatamak and others. The Legal Aid Foundation in Jakarta hosted the book's launch event, which featured wall-sized illustrations from the book. Some of the millennials I spoke with found the cartoons too "vulgar," "frontal" (meaning direct and not nuanced), or "excessive." The comics conveyed the horror and reality of things glossed over or excluded from history, starting with the colonial era, and also restored the contribution of the Left to nationalism, earlier expunged by New Order narratives. Prominent human rights defenders wrote essays that imagined the Left in the present.

The Turn Left Festival (Belok Kiri Fest) was separate from the IPT, but they had overlapping constituencies. The festival was scheduled for a weekend at the Taman Ismail Marzuki Cultural Center in central Jakarta, but protesters brandishing signs about the threatening resurgence of Communism shut it down. Instead, organizers divided the festival into a series of weekend events with different speakers. Films and discussions highlighted the role of the exiles, their motivations for going abroad—for example, to learn skills to develop the young nation—and their painful decisions not to return home. Other moments recaptured the national pride and spirit of those later stigmatized as they sang nationalist songs together while younger students watched them or recorded them on their phones. Though Communism had been pervasively stigmatized, there was very little understanding of its ideology and principles (unsurprisingly, given prohibitions on teaching, reading, or discussing it). In a striking example, a later meeting with a group of survivors, convened by a journalist working with the tribunal, featured a journalist visiting from Cambodia. While most survivors asked about the perceptions of Communism in Cambodia, the journalist explained that things had moved on there, and that there was no real discussion of Communism and Marxism—even as the IPT prompted a national outpouring of anxiety over Communist resurgence in Indonesia.

Eventually the state had no choice but to address its history of violence due to the growing public pressure that resulted from *The Act of Killing*, the tribunal it inspired and its conclusion of genocide, the new initiatives to rehabilitate the history of the Left, and other creative endeavors about 1965.[47] The state convened a national symposium, "The 1965 National Tragedy, a Historical Approach," held at the Arya Duta Hotel in Jakarta on April 18 and 19, 2016.

It seemed clear to me that the symposium's timing, right after the tribunal, and the state's effort to engage academics and scholars were intended to undermine the conclusions drawn from the IPT's scholarly experts. For those who sponsored it, the symposium was an effort to find a narrative that could accommodate the truths and revelations about the past without upending everything that had been built on the propaganda narratives, including national identity, development, and the impunity that those narratives supported. This revised narrative might then become the basis for subsequent initiatives, especially national reconciliation. And it could be framed as a face-saving "Indonesian" way to address the past that did not force Indonesia to bow to international pressure.

The idea for the symposium and its realization were sudden and swift. Critical scholars who were interested in humanitarianism and human rights originally devised the idea for it. According to discussions with civil society organizations, the proposal for the symposium had been transformed from a truth-and-justice event supported by civil society to excavate truths into a state-supported, two-day symposium that emphasized social, cultural, and anthropological elements to address questions such as how people became killers. These kinds of questions speak more to "horizontal" killings than to coordination by the state.

The proposal was shared with Nani Nurachman Sutoyo, who was on the faculty of Atma Jaya Catholic University in Jakarta. Her father was one of the generals killed in 1965. Drawing on her training in psychology, she had extensively examined issues of trauma in her scholarly work and also reflected on her own experiences.[48] Nani's brother, retired lieutenant general Agus Widjojo (the former vice chairman of the People's Consultative Assembly of Indonesia and the military chief of territorial affairs), was regarded as a military reformer and intellectual. He had been involved in the bilateral commission for truth and friendship between Indonesia and Timor Leste.[49] Even as the son of a martyred hero, Agus had been accused of being a member of the PKI to undermine his reform work. Four days before the symposium, he had been installed as the head of the National Resilience Institute (Lemhanas). Both he and his sister had also been involved in an organization, the Forum for Solidarity of the Nation's Children (Forum Solidaritas Anak Bangsa), which brings together children of elite protagonists from a number of conflicts, including 1965 and regional rebellions.[50] The son of the executed PKI leader D. N. Aidit is a member, as are the children of other generals killed in 1965.

NGOs, tribunal participants, activists, and others were ambivalent and uncertain about participation in the symposium. On the one hand, organizations involved in transitional justice and victims/survivors and their allies were suspicious that it was an insincere effort at whitewashing. They also worried about its focus only on 1965 (and not the other cases of New Order violence). On the other hand, many also recognized it as an opportunity to be involved in the official process and to be heard.

Sidarto Danusubroto, a retired two-star police general and member of Jokowi's Presidential Advisory Board, was scheduled to attend one of the Wednesday meetings to encourage victims to participate in the symposium. Danusubroto was one of the key players who urged the president to follow through on plans to address 1965 and other cases. As one of Sukarno's key personnel (he had been a bodyguard and assistant, or *ajudant*), his own career had suffered as a result of the events of 1965. He had published several books related to reconciliation, and victims and activists held him in high regard.[51] Danusubroto was quite late on the evening that he was scheduled to address the Wednesday meeting, and many there worried that he would cancel. Nevertheless, they were willing to wait. Finally Danusubroto arrived, entering the room in his pressed batik shirt and out of breath, having just climbed four flights of stairs because the elevator was out. He'd taken a motorcycle to the office to navigate the jammed road, which was particularly impassable as darkness fell. After an uncharacteristically brief introduction, he launched into an impassioned plea that the victims gathered should attend the symposium on his authority and credibility, stating that it was a sincere effort and not a whitewash attempt.

An analysis of the reference document for the symposium—its terms of reference (TOR)—shows that the state response aimed to establish what it called an "understanding," as opposed to transitional justice notions of truth seeking. While the TOR set an agenda to understand the dynamic and the multifaceted ways that the past conflict continued to manifest in the present, it did not address structural elements and questions related to power, or the persistent resonance of 1965. Instead it took a psychological, individualized approach to the national context: "understanding" implies an action that is individual and private, and resembles the rhetoric of "making peace with oneself" (a common expression). The problem was distilled to a matter of managing individual emotions (and personal trauma) rather than structural, legal, or policy issues. It situated the problem in the realm of feelings about what is seen and known rather than considering how those in power manipulated individual and collective feelings and memories to secure impunity. Furthermore, it consigned concrete issues of policies, crimes, and rights violations to the realm of an irresolvable and unacknowledged past.

The TOR conceptualized the past not as a genocide or human rights issue but actually as having two elements:

> That event, in factual terms, was composed of two actions. The first action was the kidnapping of officers of the TNI AD on October 1, 1965, at about three o'clock in the morning, and the corpses were found in a well in the Lubang Buaya area in East Jakarta. The second action seemed to be the next stage of the 1965 tragedy, which was an operation hunting down [individuals, *pengejaran*], not just done by the TNI [here including all branches, not just the army] but also widened to be a horizontal conflict in some areas that resulted in the death of victims [who were] former members of the Indonesian Communist Party in great numbers.[52]

The TOR didn't disrupt the national narrative that those killed were PKI, but it did concede the lack of due process: "Some leaders of the PKI stood trial and were punished in the Extraordinary Military Tribunal. Nevertheless, tens of thousands of other people were thrown away, jailed, and tortured without a process of trial or chance to defend themselves and immediately experienced a long period of imprisonment and were called 'political prisoners.'" The document went on to specify the lack of due process and discrimination: "These political prisoners not only had their rights as citizens stolen with imprisonment without trial [and] experienced the theft [*rampasan*] of their basic rights, but they were also marked as ex-PKI and [suffered] several forms of discrimination and stigmatization in society, [and] they were blocked from intellectual work [and also faced] widespread fear because people were at risk of also being stigmatized only from talking to them."[53] This acknowledged much of what would have been common knowledge for those who lived through the period where those branded as Communists were consigned to civil death. The TOR interpretation ignored that many of those detained were not PKI—many were nationalists and Sukarnoists, but many others were victims of others' efforts to advance themselves or demonstrate their nonneutrality to the army. Furthermore, the TOR equated the suffering of the two groups of victims and thereby elided the vital role of the state in repressing or manipulating knowledge and inflicting suffering through law and bureaucracy. Framing the narrative as an ideological conflict between Communists and others actually takes away a common ground of rights, citizenship, and the rule of law; it also ignores differences in access to power and law.

The symposium aspired to move beyond these ideological interpretations and toward national reconciliation through a process of making sense out of data and information. Civil society activists and government officials alike have acknowledged that this flow of information cannot be stopped. Millennials and others have access to more information than ever before, and the cumulative efforts of civil society over the two decades leading up to the symposium had made it possible to undermine the government propaganda, notwithstanding efforts to intimidate activists and suppress challenges. But millennials and some students that I spoke to also noted the difficulties of trying to make sense out of the overwhelming amount of information suddenly available. In one sense the very *wealth* of information now available subverts or complicates the effort to find the "truth" or a narrative, and, along with the sense of betrayal, this overkill of information can create a sense of apathy. The TOR explained that the "tragedy of 1965 has made a thick fog for knowing what actually happened and what was the background that caused the tragedy." After asserting the impossibility of knowing, the document suggested that "the tragedy was a political event that occurred in the struggle for power at the highest level between President Sukarno, the Indonesian Communist Party, and the Armed Forces of Indonesia, especially the army. The situation was exacerbated by rumors of Sukarno's failing health."

"It is difficult to know [*mengetahui*] what happened," the authors of the TOR continued, and just as "difficult to understand [*memahami*] the background and explanations of the actors involved." One key strategy for "contextualizing" the killings was to insert 1965 into a chronology in which the killings were part of a long and chronic history of violence between opposed groups. The TOR noted that the 1965 "event did not happen suddenly" but "happened much earlier."

The authors elaborated the difficulties of knowing: "Different sides have different interpretations of the tragedy of 1965, and more attention is paid to the period after 1965 where many people became victims and there were various forms of discrimination and stigmatization of ex-members of PKI. Not many sides have given attention to the events before October 1, 1965."[54]

As the TOR saw it, knowledge of the past must come with an understanding of the context and justifications for the violence. The longer view in the TOR mobilized viscerally powerful narratives of the Communists' past violence and projected the threat of future vengeance as yet another chapter in a long and convoluted story of violence that could never really be understood or known.

The logic that both sides were guilty and the suggestion that "everyone is a victim" ignore not only differences in experiences but also differences in power and responsibility. Some in the military suggested that the army was just a cog in the global Cold War. Even if this were the entire story, the failure to explore the responsibility of the military closes off the chance for a more thorough understanding of how the United States and other countries were complicit in and responsible for the violence (foreign corporations, for example, extracted a massive quantity of resources under the Suharto regime as a direct result of the 1965 violence).

As the symposium hoped to create a new understanding, its organizers recognized the affective power of the propaganda film *Pengkhianatan G30S/PKI*, which "packaged the collective memory of the people of Indonesia with a black-and-white picture of the evildoers and heroes and ignored the complexity behind it." Organizers conceded that the film had been internalized in collective and individual memory: it "is constantly replayed in pieces in a confused mental state that maintains the trauma." They blamed the media for continuing to polarize victims and perpetrators, "creating animosity and bequeathing an ideological conflict that involves them [even though it] happened among their parents as the previous generation who directly experienced the tragedy."[55] Once again, the TOR emphasized individual and emotional facets of the problem but without any attention to culpability or responsibility.

The next paragraph, finally, mentioned victims: the generals who were killed and then the "ex-PKI" who were killed or had their rights stolen. While noting that one group of victims was called heroes and the other was stigmatized, the statement effectively homogenized and equalized their experiences, saying that they were both "struggling to resist trauma individually" and that "some have succeeded and some have failed and also some are still wrestling [*bergelut*] with ongoing trauma until the present."[56] Extending this logic, the TOR concluded, "In subsequent developments perpetrators and victims cannot be distinguished in a diametral way in the political conflict, where perpetrators were also victims and victims at the same time were also perpetrators." The authors continued, "With the passage of time, the majority of the victims and perpetrators have died, which transforms roles so that perpetrators become victims."[57] The fact that both perpetrators and victims were dying was often used as a justification to forgive and forget in public discourse, but this statement was more blatant than most in naming the perpetrators as victims and relativizing their roles in past political conflict.

The TOR distinguished itself from earlier efforts to "straighten history," because it acknowledged that the problem ran "deeper" than that: "History has multi-interpretations without a single truth. Each effort to construct a single truth [tunggal] about history will result in our collapse [terjerembab] in a game of power claims that position one side as 'true and winners' and the other side as the side that is 'wrong and defeated': a dichotomy that clouds history itself." Having established the impossibility of creating a "true" history acceptable to both sides, the TOR consigned the problem to the nation: "The point of the problem is not an individual one about individual perpetrators and/or victims, but a problem for the nation." The document asked, "Does this nation want to resolve this conflict and trauma that continues to shake the foundations [menggoncang bangunan] and spiritual life of the nation and also stimulates [merangsang] violence that still happens in a few forms until the present?"[58] Egregiously, this relativizing statement leaves open the interpretation that victims who gather to meet and are then attacked by mass organizations have provoked the violence they suffer, merely by gathering.[59]

The TOR nodded to past efforts, including the Komnas HAM report and victim-survivor testimony (this was the first time it added the word *survivors*), to conclude that a cultural problem remained unresolved: "From the experience of violence and efforts to resolve it which have been long, we must acknowledge with humility that this nation has not yet sincerely followed the process to become a nation that is civilized. A nation that is civilized will respect the dignity and value of humanity [harkat dan martabat kemanusiaan] and live based on the values of truth and justice, together with a balanced and healthy view of the past, which is very important to shape morals and ethics of living together for the future of the children of the nation."[60]

The TOR distinguished itself by adding psychological, anthropological, and cultural factors to the symposium to answer lingering questions, but these efforts tended to refer back to and bolster the propaganda narrative about the horizontal violence that communities perpetrated against each other. The larger context and overwhelming evidence of the army's deliberate, planned, and structural role in provoking this violence faded into the individual journey to make peace and reconcile with the past.

All of this is not to be overly cynical or to accuse the symposium organizers of bad faith. Instead, it strikes me that the discourse of personal healing and reconciliation could have been intended as a way to make the historical conflict less provocative, so that the symposium could take place at all.

The symposium itself on April 18–19, 2016, was heavily guarded. One scholar asked the police if they knew what they were guarding, and they did not. There were threats of "mass organizations" (*ormas*) disrupting and protesting at the event, and so the police had been deployed. In contrast to other cases, the event proceeded without disruption and the police managed to keep demonstrators under control.

I was encouraged to attend the symposium and surprised at how easy it was to be issued a formal letter of invitation by a member of the steering committee whom I knew through the Wednesday meetings. When I arrived, my name was not on the official list, nor were those of several others who came in at the same time, which suggested a decentralized approach, but we were welcomed and ushered in all the same. I attended both days of the symposium as an observer and met with many of the scholars who both presented and declined to present, and attended discussions before and after the event with human rights and victim support networks that both opposed and participated in the symposium. The IPT as an organization did not participate; however, many of the victims who gathered every Wednesday to discuss the tribunal and follow-up actions decided to go. Several of the activists who facilitated those meetings were also at the symposium. Many of the Wednesday group sat directly across from the speakers' table in the front row. Individuals who had ties to different groups ensured livestreaming and documentation of the historic event. Despite skepticism, activists made sure there were allies on the formulation team in the event that this turned out to be a significant initiative.

As presented at the symposium and in other public forums, the Forum for Solidarity of the Nation's Children hoped that children could come together to put aside the ideological conflicts of their parents to "make peace with the past" and "not be burdened in the future." Since its inception in the early 2000s, the organization had struggled to address what reconciliation would mean on a national level—who would reconcile with whom and for what—as well as more practical challenges of how to achieve it. While reconciliation has often been proposed, especially for 1965, the details are almost always contentious. Civil society and human rights organizations, often seen as "the Left" by conservatives, demand a full accounting of the events of 1965, with an emphasis on the rights and rehabilitation of victims killed, imprisoned without due process, and dispossessed of their civil rights. Others in the military, including Agus Widjojo and many speakers at the symposium, suggest that looking at the conditions that led to 1965 is important, and for many this includes the Madiun Incident as evidence of PKI violence.[61] Widjojo and others have argued that the definition of "victim" must be broader than what is usually understood in human rights frameworks, and the symposium's TOR emphasizes an ambiguous overlap of victim and perpetrator. The us-against-them perception makes clear why reconciliation is necessary but also why it is hard to achieve.

After participants had filled the tables around the edges of the ballroom, high-ranking government officials came in for a series of statements and photos. Coordinating Minister Luhut Panjaitan opened the symposium with a declaration that under no circumstance would the government issue an apology. The issuing of an apology had been contentious for some time. Several people with connections to (former) activists on Jokowi's staff told stories of how Jokowi was very close to signing a state apology for 1965, but it was derailed by pressure from a vocal group of conservative retired generals. In September 2015, as the fiftieth anniversary of the supposed coup attempt approached, the prospect of an apology had dominated the news and continued to do so subsequently, especially around anniversaries and at moments when it seemed there might be some effort to address the long half-life of 1965. The presidential apology was to be to the victims and to follow the Komnas HAM investigation; however, vocal hard-liners who opposed an apology had spun and misrepresented it as an apology to the still-illegal Communist Party. In 2015, standing at the Lubang Buaya monument for the armed forces ceremony to commemorate Sacred Pancasila Day on October 1, Jokowi stated that he had never had any desire to apologize to the families and followers of the PKI. Haris Azhar, who was then the coordinator of KontraS, interpreted the apology issue simply as a distraction. He told me that none of the civil society groups had asked for an apology, and the idea of an apology only served the purpose of provoking outraged indignation by vocal old-guard army elites, and possibly mobilizing mass organizations to protest. Distractions and polarizing rhetoric serve the infrastructure of impunity by drawing attention away from it.

At the symposium, Minister Luhut explained that it was important to make peace with the past, but that the government would never apologize. He invoked a "we"—presumably the nation, but possibly the military—that "knew what 'we' [*kami*, a form of *we* that does not include all listeners] had done." Belonging to this "we" already implied complicity. He then said that the same "we" "knew what was best for the country [*negri*]."[62] Other high-ranking government officials gave brief remarks as well.

I was stunned, and the people I knew in the room surely did not share his view that the 1965 violence was "the right thing to do." Up to this point, the atmosphere had been hopeful. I had been excited to see a wide range of people that I had met over two decades of work on past cases. But in the first, very brief set of appearances by elite figures, who left the room trailed by a pack of journalists waiting to question them in the lobby, it was suggested that there was no evidence of the number killed, and that the elite forces had killed only one person. Over the course of the day, other elite figures, in their brief remarks, continued to undermine and minimize the scale of the killings—the very killings that their predecessors had boasted of in the media and in *The Act of Killing*. They dismissed those earlier statements as exaggerations; they challenged those who thought otherwise to provide evidence of mass grave sites.

Organizers thought there would be an equal balance of audience from each "side" and later admitted to me that they were surprised by the overwhelming number of victims and supporters who attended. Their intention was to have each side speak to the other, although there were moments that many people I spoke with felt were too much. For example, one person involved in organizing the symposium told me later that they thought two poets would speak to each other, and those selected were representatives of opposed factions in the 1965 conflict. Putu Oka Sukanta, a Balinese author who had been part of the leftist literary milieu and consequently imprisoned, had initiated a number of projects with marginalized groups. He had won numerous international awards and had focused on dignity and humanity in his work, rather than explicit political messages. Putu's work considers the problem of marginalization, and not just for those accused of being Communists; he also considers how stigmatizing rhetoric attaches to new targets, including HIV-positive individuals, urban poor, homeless, and others. At the symposium Putu appeared calm and dignified, and, as requested, he had submitted his written comments to the organizers in advance.

But it was announced at the symposium that Taufiq Ismail would speak before Putu. Taufiq hated the PKI and Sukarno and had been a member of the movement (Generation of 1966, or Angkatan 66) that worked to oust Sukarno in favor of Suharto. Along with other writers, he had been a signatory to the Cultural Manifesto (Manifes Kebudayaan) of 1963, which had declared art for art's sake and not politics. He was strongly opposed to the Institute for People's Culture (Lembaga Kebudayaan Rakyat), which Sukarno had supported, that promoted revolutionary (Communist) themes and socialist realism. The institute was credited with attracting youth to Communist organizations.[63] As the scholar Wijaya Herlambang has shown, the United States was also involved in working through culture to undermine the Left.[64] Taufiq read a poem set as a conversation between a grandfather and his grandchildren about a massacre by Communists and used the name of an actual PKI leader (Musso). His reading was vulgar, graphic, and interrupted by loud booing. Finally the microphone was taken away. Putu got up to follow Taufiq's reading and said he would not comment on it, as he had pre-pared his poetry and submitted it as requested by the organizers, and he would read what he had planned. He said that as an individual he had tried not to become a prisoner (*pesakitan*). He outlined steps that the government should take for healing, beginning with "classifying" what happened in the early hours of October 1, 1965, acknowledging past violence, annulling the discriminatory poli-cies and the monitoring of the former prisoners, and subsequently rehabilitating all those who had been marginalized. Finally, he recommended a tribunal as part of a process of learning and healing.

In the days after the symposium I met with representatives from the Wednesday group and others as they debated whether or not they should hand over the list of gravesites, as challenged by Minister Luhut at the symposium, or if this was sim-ply a ploy to collect information about sites of evidence. On the one hand they were particularly worried that the military had asked for the locations of the sites so that it could dispatch thugs to destroy the evidence and terrorize the commu-nities living near the sites, who had protected and identified them. On the other hand, this was an opportunity to demonstrate the extent of the killings, especially after President Jokowi had ordered Luhut to follow up on investigations.[65]

I visited Komnas HAM with the victims' group from the Wednesday meeting. As we waited to enter a meeting with the commission's chair, they told me stories of what had happened in their communities. One man from central Java showed me a handwritten list of places where they knew that bodies had been buried in 1965 and 1966. The handwriting was precise and careful, done with a firm black ballpoint pen on lined white paper. After a long wait, we were ushered into a con-ference room. Victims had traveled from central Java; stalwarts of the IPT group such as Reza and Dolo were also there, and Lexy was documenting. The meeting was tense, as victims wanted to know what Komnas was doing to guarantee that these sites would be protected if they handed over the locations. In the end, 122 sites were documented that day.[66] There was very little follow-up in terms of investigations or protection of the sites; however, the mere threat of investigation and precise data provoked immediate political reaction from an association of retired military and police (Forum Komunikasi Putra Putri Purnawirawan TNI/POLRI Indonesia), which announced that together with Islamic organizations it would hold a countersymposium titled "Secure Pancasila from the Threat of a Resurrected PKI and Other Ideologies" (Mengamankan Pancasila dari ancaman rebangkitan PKI dan ideologi lain) a month later in June 2016.

The national symposium had still not issued recommendations by the start of the "anti-PKI" countersymposium. It was leaked that in acknowledgment of the gross violations of human rights that occurred before and after 1965, the state would issue an official statement of regret for 1965, offer general rehabilitation for all former prisoners, and, finally, establish an ad hoc presidential committee to coordinate the response.[67] A key point of contention was the idea that what happened in 1948 justified what happened in 1965. The countersymposium displayed graphic photographic evidence of supposed violence committed by the PKI in Madiun. Febriana Firdaus, a headscarf-wearing millennial journalist whose grandfather had been a victim in 1965, covered the event.[68] She posed challenging questions to the countersymposium: for example, what was Marxism? Most attendees were unable to answer. She was later subjected to intense cyberharassment. At the countersymposium, one vocal retired general demanded that the government not apologize and asserted that "this is also a symposium." He noted that his forces were ready to go to war, introducing a veiled threat of violence should Jokowi move forward to apologize or rehabilitate victims.[69] After the countersymposium, the political power of the former elites and military once again dominated and the original national symposium draft recommendations were never formalized or widely publicized, while the "anti-PKI" recommendations were widely publicized.[70] The military group wound its symposium around the ideas of the national symposium and in so doing swallowed up the first one and discredited it for "both" sides.

Ultimately, the first symposium demonstrated resistance to truth revelation and an unwillingness to pursue the implications of existing evidence. It also demonstrated an explicit effort to renarrate and affectively contain that which could no longer be denied. Recognizing the power of the IPT's narrative and judgment, the symposium tried to engage scholars and public figures in an exercise of "understanding" what happened, to create a narrative that could integrate and rehabilitate some of the revelations as something other than genocide. In this case the understanding was sought not to extend impunity (although the longer time frame that tied 1948 to 1965 was an effort to renew the justification of violence), but rather to create a context where a process of national reconciliation and rehabilitation could begin. The logic of impunity needs to be interrupted but seemingly cannot be. At the symposium and in other contexts we see that laws and policies and the narrative of impunity are deeply enmeshed and reinforce each other.

In this sense, *The Act of Killing* better mobilized engagement, especially among younger Indonesians, than documentation did, because it touched on the emotional and affective dimensions of 1965. The film focused on the perpetrators, highlighting their lack of heroism and vestigial power and respectability in Indonesian culture. In short it revealed the normalization of violence. The film inspired the International People's Tribunal, which generated more narrative, facts, and details about the systematic nature of the violence, undermining the sense that the violence was an emotional response by people (amok), and ultimately concluding that it was genocide. It also cast the victims as legal subjects capable of providing testimony about crimes committed by well-known figures, rather than as marginalized individuals consigned to civil death. Just as the film undermined the nationalist narratives and propaganda, the tribunal undermined the legal apparatus that justified it. Young people, activists, and media publicized the findings, especially the genocide verdict, and the lies that had been told; the monolithic history of the past was challenged. Yet the symposium (and countersymposium) held in reaction to the tribunal demonstrated once again how the infrastructure of impunity resists facts and narratives—resists even the pronouncement of genocide—and finds a way to reconsolidate and reassert itself. Even uncontested truth and fact do not dislodge it entirely. One powerful tactic in reconsolidation is to use a logic that relativizes the acts of both sides in the past, in this case drawing on the visceral sense of horror and threats of resurgent Communism to dilute the victim testimony and the narratives of the violence and crimes revealed and named as genocide.

By 2016 the propaganda narrative had eroded sufficiently to at least partially create a new narrative, perhaps even one that would further subvert impunity. Instead the national symposium gravitated toward an ambiguous narrative that "everyone" was a victim. I talked to Haris Azhar about a rumor that Komnas HAM would release its reports, but he pointed out that if they were released, even they would not alter history, because they would not be acknowledged by the state as valid (*sah*). There are ways beyond the impasse; for instance, acknowledging that both sides did commit crimes but severing the rationales for further violence. The first symposium tried to find a narrative that would be a basis for reconciliation, but it was overshadowed by those who sought to maintain the narratives that undergird the infrastructure of impunity. Narratives that look at guilt and at beneficiaries collectively and consider violence as a state-organized process rather than a nebulous culture, or the idea—as conveyed in *The Act of Killing*—that the killers were all monstrous, criminal others, might go further in highlighting and challenging the infrastructure of impunity.

In retrospect, it is easy to focus on the symposium as just one more failed effort to address the cases, but in the moment it was nevertheless a powerful experience for many victims and advocates. The event ended with an overwhelming feeling of optimism, and group selfies of those who had organized the symposium—the community of people who had been working on the issue for many years—and victims. It included a few highlights and some unprecedented statements. For example, Sukmawati, Sukarno's eldest daughter, powerfully took the state and elites to task for how they had marginalized her father and his legacy, along with his supporters. She emphasized that it was not all about Communism. A former member of Gerwani stood up and told those assembled that the propaganda film was inaccurate when it showed a PKI character smoking. She pointed out that the PKI were disciplined and did not smoke, and she underscored that Gerwani had been working for literacy in rural areas. After so many years of silencing and shaming, it was powerful to hear not simply that the women had been slandered but what they had wanted to contribute to the nation.

And Sidarto's closing at the symposium, a reflection in an official context by someone tasked by the state as its representative, was as close as the state has ever come to an official acknowledgment.[71] Sidarto said that the symposium had placed the 1965 tragedy in the context of history, but the state had not yet found a concept for reconciliation. He praised the symposium for being a civilized space

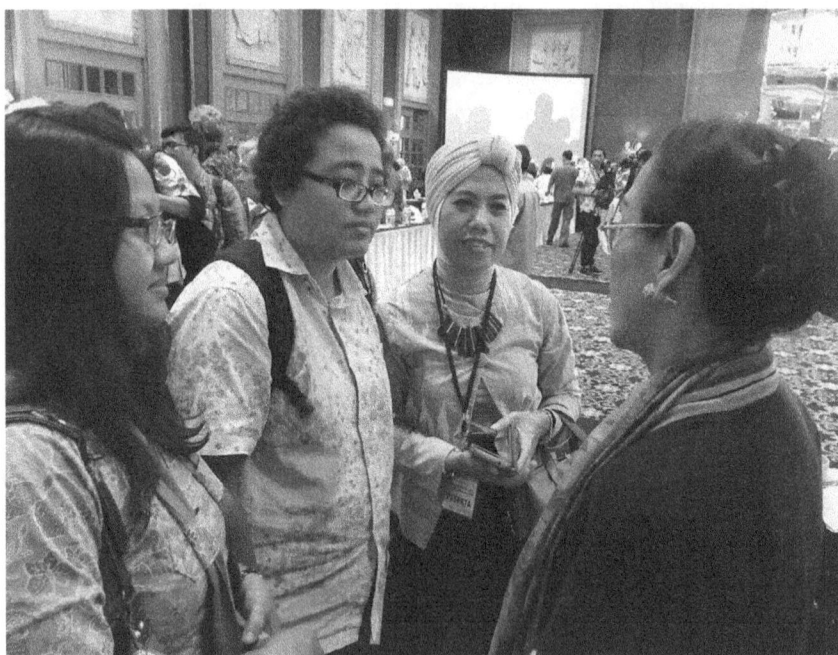

FIGURE 4.1. After the national symposium, founding president Sukarno's oldest daughter, Sukmawati, in profile, talks with younger activists working with 1965 former political prisoners across the archipelago. From left to right: Pipiet Ambarmirah (Yogyakarta), Roro Sawita (Bali), and Nurlaela Lamasitudju (Central Sulawesi). Photo by the author.

where opposing viewpoints could be heard, even if they were not shared. As evidence of its success he observed that on the second day, individuals still wanted to spontaneously share comments, without feeling scared or intimidated. He acknowledged the Cold War context but also granted that even so, Indonesia had not managed ideological differences well, and that this "haunted [the nation] until the present" as it managed "differences of race, ethnicity, religion, and other forms with violence." He conceded a horizontal conflict but said that "we also have to acknowledge the involvement of the state," and that, because of this, "we must reflect very deeply about how we administer the state and our nation." He continued, "We are aware [*sadar*]" that "in the past there were human rights violations that resulted in national wounds." He located the cause of the violations not in international human rights principles but in the basic principles of the Indonesian nation and state. There was a tragedy, and the heroes of the revolution (murdered generals) and their families were victims. But this tragedy had caused

> killing in great numbers, tens of thousands of other people thrown away, jailed and tortured without a judicial process or without being given a chance to defend themselves and detained for a long period of time and known by the term political prisoner. It is not only the theft of basic citizens' rights experienced by political prisoners in the form of detention without a legal process, but also the theft of basic citizens' rights for those branded as ex PKI members in the form of social discrimination and stigmatization, [and] prohibitions on intellectual work, along with fears about circulating it because simply discussing it put others at risk of being stigmatized.

The statement did not sever the relationship between the first event (the supposed coup) and the subsequent violence against suspected PKI members, nor did it rehabilitate the names of those stigmatized as Communists, but it did acknowledge forms of suffering and the violations of due process and citizens' rights. It introduced the idea that laws were violated, subtly unsettling the relativizing logic that all the violence and suffering was similar and that the New Order followed the rule of law.

In my conversation with three young activists—one from Bali, one from Java, and one from Sulawesi—at the end of the symposium, their excitement was palpable, and one echoed what many had said: that it had been a historic moment. Imagine, this activist said, if they had not participated. The event renewed the sense of possibility and hope that kept activists engaged and working with the state to address the cases. Even as they acknowledged some of the power of the symposium, activists remained vigilant against the possibility that this effort would undermine the use of existing laws to address other cases of past impunity, where there might be stronger evidence. The subject of the next chapter, a campaign against *kriminalisasi* (criminalization), demonstrates how the failures of due process have extended forms of impunity and have allowed the law to be used for ends other than justice, rendering the law a clandestine force for impunity.

5

LAW WITHOUT JUSTICE

In 2015, the same year as the International People's Tribunal and the year before the state's symposium, Indonesian NGOs tried another tack to advance human rights and justice in current cases. They launched an investigation to name and expose the use of criminal law against activists through *kriminalisasi*, which is usually translated as "criminalization." This alliance of activists shifted their attention from the innocence of victims to another core aspect of the infrastructure of impunity: the invisible yet ordinary forms of human rights violations enabled by subtle everyday laws, institutional cultures, and practices that dehumanize and stigmatize individuals or groups.

As activists struggle against corrupt or dysfunctional legal systems by publicizing repressed truths, they reinforce the idea that truth is the first step to justice and that law aligned with truth produces justice. Most activists and scholars are aware, however, that the truth on its own does not have effects without changes in key institutions, as the scholar Bruno Latour emphasizes.[1] In the kriminalisasi campaign, activists wanted to end the use of law for purposes other than justice. Their efforts raise questions about the connections between law and truth, problems of justice inherent to the law itself, and, perhaps most strikingly, advocacy strategies in cases where evidence and truth are not denied but simply irrelevant; where the law is technically applied accurately, yet for ulterior and extralegal motives; or where cases simply stall before evidence can be presented.

In short, criminalization speaks to the challenge of fighting impunity with the law. Being named a suspect triggers a presumption of guilt and social stigmatization for victims, who then draw on both legal and political channels to assert their innocence. Activists approached kriminalisasi initially as a problem that could be resolved legally and still believed that law was the only avenue for justice for those with less money and power in a political system where oligarchs, corruption, and legacies of authoritarianism threatened democracy. The discourse of criminalization started from the assumption that the law had simply been corruptly applied, but as we'll see, it ultimately led to the troubling realization that the problem was the law itself, which was the means to impunity for the powerful. This case demonstrates how the law is a key element of the infrastructure of impunity, one that is dynamic and transforms over time to extend impunity to ongoing cases.

In 2015, Haris Azhar, the coordinator of KontraS, invited me to attend a meeting with a group of activists to talk about a case that was changing their approach to human rights. Those present saw the case as part of a wider pattern: police were framing activists, whistleblowers, labor organizers, and others who seemed to oppose state or corporate interests. The case in question was against the former legal aid activist Bambang Widjojanto, for lying under oath in a past local election case. As vice chair of the Indonesian Corruption Eradication Commission (Komisi Pemberantasan Korupsi, or KPK), Widjojanto had initiated an investigation into the nominee for the chief of the Indonesian National Police on charges of graft. The police then brought a suit against Widjojanto, and he had to temporarily step down from his post with the KPK—and the police commander under investigation was confirmed as the head of the national police. One of the key unifying and mobilizing issues of the demonstrations that led to Suharto's resignation in 1998 was the widespread corruption, collusion, and nepotism of Suharto's regime. Activists, legal reformers, and others saw the establishment of the KPK as an independent institution with investigative powers as a key antidote to corruption in the judiciary and police, which had extended impunity. Two decades later, when Widjojanto was removed from his post, the KPK was a trusted institution and seen as highly credible.[2] The attack on Widjojanto and the KPK worried activists, particularly because he and his defenders were being viewed as criminals rather than as defenders of the law. As Haris put it, the police were using "law enforcement . . . for a goal other than justice."

In this case, the extralegal intention was to use the law to remove Widjojanto from his position and effectively end his investigation of high-ranking police officers. In contrast to past advocacy, the NGO group saw the verdict as irrelevant: if the police or prosecutor initiated an investigation, even without sufficient or valid evidence, it could still have the desired effect of making the victim unable to continue in his or her struggle or career. Such cases were unwinnable with the usual tactics of legal aid and defense. And NGO members highlighted the difficulty of rehabilitation for someone who had been temporarily removed from a position. Even if proven innocent they could not regain their former position, as they would have been replaced and their credibility damaged.

The group intended to redress the narratives that smeared victims of the state on the mere grounds that they had been arrested. Assembled that day were individuals working on law, human rights, labor, agrarian, and environmental issues.[3] Many had law degrees; some worked as public lawyers and legal aid activists or as labor or environmental advocates, others as analysts doing policy, research, or academic work.[4] In contrast to legal activism under the New Order, some activists had moved from purely apolitical and independent positions to engage in politics, leading to the impression that cases and campaigns could be instrumentalized in a variety of ways. At that initial meeting on the Widjojanto case, activists worked to define the problem so that they would not appear to be putting themselves above the law, and to find a solution that would not undermine the legitimacy of the law. They did not want to present the problem as one of corruption, since that theme was too politically charged and too easily devolved into accusations and counteraccusations that might undermine the very legal institutions they sought to fix. They wanted a label they could use to publicize the phenomenon and collect evidence.

At this first meeting, activists debated whether they should use the slippery term *kriminalisasi*. On the one hand, it was popular and widely understood, as the media had used it extensively to connote political intervention in criminal cases.[5] For example, the NGO group's campaign brochure pointed to use of the term in the coverage of the scandalous 2000 arrest of a labor activist for stealing rubber flip-flops. Activists suspected that he was arrested simply to reduce his labor organizing work.[6] On the other hand, the term had a different legal meaning, and the activists at this point wanted to situate their campaign in the legal realm. In fact, the popular meaning differed from the technical meaning: in the law, "criminalization" means to make something illegal that was previously not illegal. A campaign brochure cited as an example of the legal meaning of the term a law that made money laundering illegal in Indonesia. In meetings, the group wrestled with the idea that the term *kriminalisasi* was technically inaccurate in legal terms and that their goal was to create a concept that could be reviewed and used in criminal justice theory and practice. At their first meeting, the group emphasized that the standard of kriminalisasi that they developed must be objective and that they themselves had to follow the standards they set for the police. They sought to appear neutral and not political.

The term was made even more complex because powerful corruptors had used it to assert that they were being unfairly investigated and to present themselves as victims. The term risked making the activists sound as if they placed themselves above the law, just like the corrupt elite. In contrast, the NGOs wanted to restore the legitimacy of law and law enforcement. Thus, activists felt that they needed to align their struggle with the law, change the popular meaning of *kriminalisasi*, and encourage its use as a key element of policy review, legal reform, and advocacy strategy. Ultimately, in their campaign brochure, they adapted the popular meaning of the term and defined *kriminalisasi* as "using the authority of law enforcement for a bad goal or in bad faith" and a "betrayal of the trust the people have given to law enforcement."[7] Campaign materials later stated that the practices of *kriminalisasi* "crashed against of the principles of the rule of law."[8] The criminalization that the activists sought to address was not against an action, as the legal meaning of the term stipulated, but against the person. This criminalization was a threat to the rule of law.

FIGURE 5.1. Infographic that circulated proclaiming ten reasons that the Bambang Widjojanto case was kriminalisasi.

To prove that criminalization was more than a politically motivated claim, activists needed to make it visible in the public sphere by collecting a range of cases and examples. Kriminalisasi cases were not always the dramatic ones that culminated in spectacularly flawed trials, as had sometimes occurred during the authoritarian era. Kriminalisasi activists needed to shift their focus from individual cases to a technique of aggregation, whereby patterns once invisible could be made visible. If they could demonstrate systemic patterns, the conversation would be less likely to disintegrate into politicized discussions of particular cases. Activists hoped to present kriminalisasi as a problem that could be addressed through the law, a place where activists had more power than they did in political contexts. They also hoped that this systematic treatment would change public perceptions of victims of kriminalisasi and create a more critical understanding of the power of the police.

Activists began a yearlong process of convening public panel discussions to review cases. Out of these panels they produced a summary report that identified several types of kriminalisasi: "forced cases," in which evidence and charges were distorted or inappropriate; the use of torture; the "excessive use of law," when the application of laws and charges was excessive and disproportionate to the crime; and criminal acts by members of the law enforcement apparatus. Most of these cases fell into the first category.[9] They featured political officials or businesses that asked their employees to file false reports, and when the employees did not agree to be complicit in corrupt dealings, they were charged with crimes—often the same irregularities or crimes that they had tried to bring to the attention of their superiors or the authorities. For example, in one case a community member reported to the police that corporations had started unauthorized mining on community land. The police asked the individual for evidence, so he took a cable from the site—and then the police charged him with theft of the cable. The panel of experts noted that he did indeed take the cable, but obviously not for the purpose of stealing it and only to provide the very evidence demanded by law enforcement authorities. The panel noted that the police appeared to be working to protect the mining company rather than to enforce the law.[10]

Many other kriminalisasi cases involved torture. Police tortured suspects until they "confessed" to the crimes of which they were accused, reprising practices that had occurred in 1965 cases, where victims had to sign confessions for their release, or in the time of *petrus*, when criminals had to register as such to avoid an extrajudicial death. These kriminalisasi cases highlighted the problem that suspects could not retract statements even if their statements were extracted under torture and without legal counsel. One lawyer involved suggested to me that the widespread practice of torture by police (to yield false statements) had enabled the practice of kriminalisasi to develop in the first place. Those involved in the campaign construed torture not simply as a violation of an international human rights standard but as part of the system that enabled kriminalisasi. This gives us an insight into how the infrastructure of impunity works: accountability continues to elude activists, even while legal processes appear to be functioning.

These cases, gathered over several months, established a basis to criticize policing and legal practice, but in Indonesia, as elsewhere, the infrastructure of impunity uses the law as well as powerful affective experiences—what Brian Larkin might call the "poetics of infrastructure."[11] Although most of the lawyers involved in the kriminalisasi campaign were too young to remember the petrus cases or the authoritarian-era governance and human rights abuses, this past haunted them nevertheless.[12] Non-elite victims of kriminalisasi, who recall the pain of social stigmatization from the petrus era, did not name stigmatization as the problem. Nor did these activists link their campaign explicitly to the rights of criminals.[13] Rather, they focused their work on showing that people who were not really criminals, despite having done something that technically or formally violated the law, had systematically been made to appear to be criminals, without a trial or due process. In short, some of those criminalized did not belong in the category of criminal, even if they may have broken the law. The activists did not directly question the idea that others; namely, authentic criminals, could be treated violently.[14] Their assertion in this campaign was not that criminals deserve rights but that some criminals were wrongly and opportunistically categorized.

Decades of social and bureaucratic practices and policies that stigmatize criminals, as well as the fear of criminality and social ills that spread like a contagion, have made it difficult for most citizens to cultivate empathy for those charged as criminals or to view them as rights-deserving citizens. And this was clear even with a new generation of activists tackling kriminalisasi. The infrastructure of impunity relies on these affective, even unconscious, memories and visceral antipathy toward criminals, as well as the extensive network of laws on paper that can be utilized to initiate an investigation of a suspect. Indeed, one law student noted a presumption of guilt toward suspected criminals,[15] and a preference in Indonesian public discourse for corrupt police over public disorder or criminality.

I asked activists about the dangers of criminality, particularly in terms of how ordinary people balanced their need for police protection with their knowledge of police corruption. Several activists, in separate conversations, noted a recent case where a wealthy Chinese family had been killed in their home by burglars. They told me this story to convince me that Jakarta was dangerous, but also to highlight how the police misused their power—because in this case, police took valuable koi fish for themselves, rather than leaving them for surviving family members or depositing them with other evidence. Dangerous criminals certainly existed, but they were vastly different from the victims of kriminalisasi. Indeed, what makes someone a victim of kriminalisasi is precisely that they do not conform to the trope of the dehumanized, dangerous criminal other.

Avoiding empathy-based strategies seeking to demonstrate that criminals might be rights-deserving citizens, NGO members instead emphasized to high-ranking government officials that they themselves could easily become victims of kriminalisasi. One NGO member involved in drafting new regulations on criminal procedure and lobbying different ministries for support told officials that even if they were innocent, a mere accusation could ruin their careers. She smiled as she recalled the looks on their faces as they came to understand their vulnerability.

The kriminalisasi campaign focused on the problem that politics and power had infiltrated the law deeply through the conduit of the police. The disconnect between the ideal of justice and the realities of law and law enforcement was not new in Indonesia, and it has been a perennial issue elsewhere. Activists, lawyers, and scholars have critiqued the estrangement of law and justice from a number of angles. Theorists have pointed to the problematic connection between law and violence, especially in the figure of the police.[16] Numerous examples demonstrate the contemporary and historic relationship between law and state violence.[17] Anthropologists have focused on the practice of law in particular contexts. "Lawfare" names the process whereby politics are judicialized and the law is used for political ends.[18] Kari Telle has demonstrated how a range of actors can mobilize law to political ends in Indonesian cases of blasphemy.[19] Kamari Clarke observes how an emphasis on legal solutions blocks other forms of political action.[20]

Indonesian legal activists had to engage with the double-edged nature of the law as both a last resort for those without money or power and an instrument that the state can mobilize against critics to silence them and deflect criticism. They had to wrestle, in other words, with the gap between law on paper and law in practice. The *practice* of criminal law rarely comes into focus in discussions of transitional justice or human rights, and yet it should, because impunity is extended both by discriminatory laws that NGOs have contested in a variety of ways (the law on paper) and through criminal law as it is actually practiced (the law in practice).

In the kriminalisasi campaign, activists hoped to convey that the arbitrary nature of criminal law in practice was evidence of excessive police power, even short of direct police violence. The kriminalisasi cases differed from authoritarian-era "engineered" cases, where moral authority came from demonstrating the

gap between law on paper and law in practice. As activists approached kriminalisasi, they focused not on engineered cases that were completely fabricated
but, more specifically, on cases in which the goal of the police investigation
was not to solve the original crime (for example, stolen flip-flops) but to use
the law as a pretext for extralegal political goals (for example, reducing labor
activism). It needed to describe cases that were often dropped, such that, unlike
with engineered cases, victims rarely had the opportunity to defend themselves
in court.

Over the course of this campaign it became clear that both kriminalisasi
and the activists' new approaches to it highlighted a vital element of the infrastructure of impunity: efforts to eradicate corruption and increase law enforcement are often perceived internationally and in transitional justice discourse as
strengthening the rule of law, yet my analysis suggests that they may in fact be
deployed to further impunity and recreate invisible patterns of authoritarian
practice. Throughout the campaign, activists came up against the limits of the
law to combat kriminalisasi. The anthropologist Aradhana Sharma writes that
"instituting more laws . . . will . . . proliferate bureaucratic rules . . . that generate
corrupt acts."[21] In the case of kriminalisasi, additional laws on paper, no matter
what their content, proliferate the sites for individuals to be criminalized through
law enforcement. Close analysis of kriminalisasi reveals how the entire system of
law and law enforcement becomes part of the infrastructure of impunity, rather
than its remedy.

The kriminalisasi campaign moved from the specifics of individual cases and
possible rogue enforcement agents to the systematic nature of the problem, both
in law enforcement and in social perceptions. Activists worked simultaneously to
launch judicial reviews, to develop the social norm of the right to a fair trial, and
to humanize the criminalized. The campaign focused on future lawyers, potential victims of kriminalisasi, and the media to change social perceptions of those
who were criminalized, even as it stopped short of a campaign for the rights of
criminals.

It was a challenge to reconceive of a criminal as a rights-deserving citizen.
I attended the fair trial sessions at the Legal Aid Institute's monthlong training
program for those hoping to become public lawyers.[22] The students came from
across Indonesia, bringing their own backgrounds and contexts of local laws
and issues. Most of the students attending the program were law students, and
the training provided a social science and critical thinking curriculum as well as
practical discussions on writing, communication, and organizing. The program
was highly competitive, accepting only one in four applicants, and of those who
finished the program, only one in twenty would be offered an opportunity to join
the Legal Aid Institute.

The day consisted of a theoretical session in the morning and a session with expert community voices in the afternoon. In the theoretical session, students were asked whether someone still needed a fair trial if they were caught red-handed taking a bag. One person said that it might be the person's own bag. Several looked as if they might speak and then didn't. Finally, one of the non-law students in the class said, "Couldn't it be just for humanitarian reasons that they have the right to a fair trial even if they are guilty?" The hesitation and long pause among a highly select group of would-be human rights defenders demonstrated to me the power of the stigmatization of criminals that had begun during the New Order and continued to the present. Even when people know that the police are corrupt, it is still difficult, especially in drug-related cases, to see the "criminal" as deserving of rights.

The afternoon session paired groups of students with different resource people who had been involved as victims of kriminalisasi or victims of unfair trials.[23] Students were to figure out the normative, structural, and cultural issues from the testimony of the victims of unfair trials, as well as identify the actors involved. I joined a group of students whose expert source was a labor organizer who had been arrested and criminalized for failing to disperse at a labor demonstration. The organizer highlighted the difficult process of obtaining permits, the discipline of the workers, and the logistics of how they were prevented from dispersing, as well as their treatment by the police. The case was ongoing and involved not only twenty-three labor activists but also two public lawyers and one student. The students at the training identified issues of a culture of force and the arrogance of the police as well as, finally, the presumption of guilt that they had named in the earlier example of handbag theft.

Another group of students met with the mother of a young man who was wrongfully arrested (salah tangkap) and had gone from a witness for the police to a suspect in a murder case. She told me her son had seen the victim of a fight as he was dying and went to the police station as a witness. He was tortured and forced to sign a false confession. After a year, he was released, and in the high court he won his case for wrongful arrest and imprisonment. They now had a compensation case in process. The mother told me again and again that she knew he was not guilty; if he had been, she would not have defended him and would have asked only for an appropriate punishment according to the law. She said that she met with the murder victim's family and they knew that her son was not the killer; in fact, they knew the actual perpetrator and could have told the police that her son was innocent, but they said nothing.

I asked about social stigmas and her perceptions of the police. She said things improved after the case was written up in *Tempo* magazine and discussed on TV, and finally people said, "So he was not guilty." She told of how, when she was at court, she met other parents whose children had been framed on drug charges. They said that their children had been rounded up, told to lie down, and shot in the calves as if they had been running, while drugs were slipped into their pockets. Nevertheless, despite having seen that others had been criminalized or framed, she remained obdurate in her negative view of criminals, which was undiminished. She repeatedly emphasized her son's innocence, going so far as to say that she conducted her own investigation (what the police were supposed to do) into the case. She hated the police and it made her heart beat fast to see them, but now she was calmer around them. She said that in the case of her son they were just lazy and did not want to do any work. The myriad ways that his right to a fair trial had been violated, the torture during the interrogation, and other irregularities in his interaction with the police were not part of her narrative— she did not object to these practices per se, only to the investigations that wrongly labeled her son a criminal. Clearly, stigmatization has been effective and continues to do the work of impunity, to such an extent that this mother advocated for her son only because she was certain of his innocence, as gleaned from her own investigation. While she valued the law, the police were highly problematic in her account. Part of the problem, she said, was how much they paid in bribes to become police officers, and if they did their jobs (honestly) they would not make much money. Despite what she knew of the corruption of the police and court, the verdict nevertheless once again located the problem with implementation and corrupt agents of the law: at the end of the session, law students identified the problem of a "presumption of guilt" in this case, as they had in the earlier case.[24]

When activists used aggregation to demonstrate the pattern and common characteristics across various cases, they faced the problem that while formally and procedurally it may look as if law enforcement is working well, the motives for the application of law enforcement are not clear and may be extralegal and malicious. In interviews, I did notice a shift from trying to reclaim the law to an awareness that the law itself was part of the problem. In July 2016, I attended a daylong discussion session titled "Grounding Democracy," also held at the Legal Aid Foundation.[25] The room was filled with labor union members, identifiable by their uniform shirts. The director of the Jakarta Legal Aid Institute (LBH Jakarta) reviewed what kriminalisasi was and how it worked legally, but strikingly he also addressed the workers present as "candidates for kriminalisasi." He outlined strategies to avoid being criminalized, noting that as a lawyer he was suggesting that they be careful with their statements and use phrases such as "might have" to shield their criticisms from charges of defamation. Some of the audience members protested this advice because they preferred to make more direct and specific denunciations of their powerful antagonists.

A presentation by a member of the Indonesian Center for Law and Policy Studies (Pusat Studi Hukum dan Kebijakan Indonesia) noted that since the end of the New Order more than 1,500 new laws had been created. I thought of the efforts of activists whom I had talked to over the last fifteen years and their efforts to introduce new legislation and review existing legislation. But he noted that these new laws had created new opportunities for the state to intervene, to scrutinize individuals and their behaviors. It was unclear how this realization would change NGO practice in Indonesia, but certainly his comments indicated a shift even from the beginning of the kriminalisasi campaign toward an awareness that the law itself might be the problem.

The infrastructure of impunity challenges human rights advocacy models, because, as revealed in the kriminalisasi campaign, even technically correct applications of law may contribute to impunity and extend the authoritarian legacy or undermine democracy. The instigation of an investigation alone often had the desired outcome—it removed critics from their positions, ended their activism, and stigmatized them socially. Thus, even where legal procedures were followed and enforced, the problematic motive and practice remained and the damage to suspects was done before they had the opportunity to defend themselves in court. For example, regulations required that suspects be provided with legal counsel; however, lawyers told me that in some cases the police threatened to level more severe charges if individuals sought legal assistance. In other cases, the only lawyers that suspects were able to access were those "friendly" to the police. Requirements on paper (access to legal assistance) could be fulfilled in practice (lawyers friendly to the police are made available) without actually fulfilling the suspect's right to a fair trial, or the spirit of the law. It was difficult to find a solution on paper that could resolve problems in practice.

When I met with individuals a year after the conclusion of the public forums and the publication of the group's report, most members of the group said that the kriminalisasi campaign had demonstrated that the pattern was systemic and not the work of rogue elements, and yet their revelation of that pattern had not ended it. Many of the ideal solutions they imagined relied on the integrity of individuals who enforce the law (fair judges, ethical police, and dedicated investigators) and a commitment by all citizens, even well-regarded advocates such as Widjojanto, to submit to the legal system and accept its process and verdict without seeking political interventions. One member of the kriminalisasi group explained that in the Widjojanto case, there was a possible pretrial mechanism by which a panel of judges would evaluate police evidence to determine whether it was sufficient to charge Widjojanto.[26] But at the same time, he knew that if Widjojanto submitted to a pretrial process, there was no guarantee that the judges' decision would be fair, and it would likely be used against him. Then Widjojanto would be considered guilty and have no other legal recourse or appeals process. Given his status and networks, Widjojanto attempted a political resolution of the case. Most ideal solutions were impossible because the system was unreliable and corrupt: in highly politicized cases it was unlikely that any judge would be able to rule without political interference. The activists' finely honed skills in legal drafting, policy review, and other domains of law on paper could not control law in practice.

The kriminalisasi campaign showed that a system that should work to combat impunity—law and law enforcement—had become an archipelago-wide infrastructure to further impunity. From legal aid trainings and other meetings and demonstrations it became clear that in Indonesia, other avenues of political protest were not working, precisely because activist leaders were being stigmatized as criminals, which extended a key component of the infrastructure of impunity into the present.

By 2020, Budi Gunawan, who was confirmed as the head of the national police at the same time that Bambang Widjojanto was forced to step down from his post with the Corruption Eradication Commission, had risen to the position of head of the State Intelligence Agency and allegedly had been "indirectly involved in the discussion of numerous laws in parliament, including legislation that [had] weakened the KPK."[27] The Corruption Eradication Commission (KPK), an institution that once challenged the corrupt practice of law, has been thoroughly undermined legislatively and through the criminalization of its most powerful commissioners and the besmirching of the reputations of others involved with it. Regional autonomy laws designed to counter the centralization of the New Order regime have created decentralized opportunities for corruption and the politicization of regional and local bureaucracies. Not only has the infrastructure of impunity stymied efforts to address past violations, but, through criminalization, law has become an accomplice to eviscerate post–New Order reform and democratization gains. Activists have noted that under Jokowi, state authorities and private companies have turned to legal instruments to silence critics rather than physical threats and intimidation.[28] Impunity for past cases has not only emboldened hard-liners and military and intelligence figures but has also left an infrastructure with multiple elements that extend impunity into the present and can continually be used to silence dissent. Practices of stigmatization, and the bureaucracies designed to enforce them, now target advocates for women's and gender rights, environmental issues, and the urban poor. Citizens whose religion does not conform to the six state-recognized religions, especially Shia Muslims, are denied protections guaranteed by the constitution and other laws. Instead, hard-line groups attack them with impunity, which echoes past patterns. Like defamation laws, blasphemy and pornography laws have become powerful tools for silencing and criminalizing those who advocate for gender or religious minorities. As Jokowi seeks to expand physical infrastructure and foreign investment, indigenous, agrarian, and rural communities are sidelined from their land and criminalized, along with environmentalist allies.

Out of the affective power of narratives about the events of 1965 and subsequent laws and cases of gross violations of human rights, Indonesia's powerful figures have built a multifaceted infrastructure of impunity. Elements of authoritarianism endure beyond the false histories that can be countered with truth, or legal cases that can be won with evidence in court, or social campaigns that can create change with narratives and images of injustice.

Social attitudes built through media, culture, experience, memory, propaganda, and habituation to the infrastructure of impunity cause citizens to tolerate imperfect law enforcement and ignore stigmatizing practices and the unfair application of law enforcement, all in the name of social order, development, and stability. The infrastructure of impunity relies on visible but unseen and ordinary forms of human rights violations. It draws on legal, bureaucratic, social, and affective elements that accrete over time. And for this reason, impunity is not readily debunked by truth and law, since law itself is one of its sites. On the contrary, the kriminalisasi campaign suggests that efforts to pass new laws and law enforcement proliferate the opportunities and spaces to deepen impunity.

Human rights and transitional justice practices have assumed that the exposure of past abuse prevents repetition, but the kriminalisasi case demonstrates how affect, social practice, bureaucracy, and law come together to produce an infrastructure of impunity that thwarts activist efforts to draw on laws on paper, new institutions, and other legal reforms to further justice and reconciliation and end impunity. Efforts to eradicate corruption and increase law enforcement rather than strengthening the rule of law may in fact be deployed to further impunity.

Looking beyond Indonesia, the kriminalisasi campaign raises questions about the future of justice projects where the following conditions exist: excessive police, a legal apparatus dominated by politics and corruption, a creeping return of authoritarian policies and practices, suppression of free association and the press, rampant hoaxes in the media, and a durable infrastructure of impunity. Nevertheless, it is important to see how actors on this landscape of impunity attempt to engage with ambiguous and double-edged instruments of law and advocacy, how they aggregate cases to find patterns, and how they disaggregate law on paper and practice, to develop nimble strategies to navigate a complex and shifting terrain where the law, however flawed, is necessary for those seeking justice.

The next chapter turns to another innovative approach to seeking justice: namely, the Kamisan Thursday silent protests that try to disrupt the infrastructure of impunity with techniques that move beyond the fact-finding and truth-telling suppositions of human rights literature. At Kamisan, victims, family members, and activists persistently demand justice (most often defined in legal terms) despite repeated failures to achieve accountability. Their consistent and creative demands may ultimately subvert the infrastructure in the realm of affect rather than law.

6

THE RED THREAD

Every Thursday at four o'clock in the afternoon since January 18, 2007, family members and victims of state violence, their supporters, and others have gathered and stood silently in front of the state palace in Jakarta, sheltered from heat and rain by black umbrellas stenciled with slogans that demand the resolution of particular past cases and an end to impunity. On the side of the road, they stand behind concrete barriers draped with long banners that feature photos of the missing or photos of suspected perpetrators. A long line of police officers in brown uniforms stand at attention between the barricade and the road. Supported by various NGOs and activists, this weekly Thursday action, called Aksi Kamisan and referred to as Kamisan, was initiated by a group of self-described victims of authoritarian-era violence and their families. Nevertheless, the action is not about their suffering or victimization.

Each week a letter to the president outlines their requests for attention to past cases in technical, legal, and affectively powerful terms. Maria Caterina Sumarsih, as one of the initiators and members of the presidium of the Solidarity Network for the Families of Victims (Jaringan Solidaritas Keluarga Korban), which also includes Munir's widow, Suciwati, and Bedjo Untung, (a victim of 1965), signs the letter, which is then walked across the street and given to the gatekeeper at the palace in exchange for a receipt. At approximately a quarter to five, the group circles up and the reflection begins. Early in the action, Sumarsih typically asks newcomers or others from outside Jakarta or those who have contacted her if they will reflect. These individuals are called to the center of the circle and given the microphone by the facilitator (usually a young person from one of the supporting NGOs). Many individuals from outside Jakarta came to the capital to advocate for their cases, and often they were turned away at all the relevant state institutions they visited, but they could come to Kamisan and be heard and supported. Having a place to come and be heard, to ask questions or to be treated as part of a community that seeks justice, is important to many people who attend. Sometimes they share what they have learned by being there and talking to individuals the state has branded as threats to national security. Others express disbelief and sadness that the state can act with impunity. Participant comments indicate that what is inspiring here is Sumarsih herself, and her consistency.

The circle is inclusive and welcoming; anyone can attend. Some weeks feature music or performance, and anniversary weeks typically feature multiple performances and activities. One week the pantomime artist Wanggi Hoed acted out the effort of an individual struggling against the "red thread" that connects past cases and ongoing injustices, much as the individuals gathered at Kamisan struggle against the infrastructure of impunity.

A short discussion of the theme for the next week's letter and a request for volunteers to work on drafting it with Sumarsih follows the reflection time. Finally, someone leads the group in a short prayer and everyone is asked to pray (silently) in their own way. When the spoken prayers draw on religious language, they usually ask that God support their struggle for justice. Some weeks, donated boxes of sweet tea or snacks are distributed. The event ends with the group chanting "Long live victims" (*Hidup korban*), or "Eradicate impunity" (*Hapus impunitas*). To close, everyone moves from the circle to pose for a group photo, with the palace in the background.

Kamisan has now spread from Jakarta to sixty other sites,[1] as individuals initiate the ritual near local sites of power.

Kamisan has created an important space of confronting impunity and engaging youth with performance activism.[2] Unlike other place-based activism and memorialization of sites of past violence,[3] in this case the place is symbolically linked to the president and nation, and to the overall problem of impunity rather than to particular cases. Locating the action across from the palace (in regional iterations, protesters have selected sites that seem closest to state power), Kamisan emphasizes the state's responsibility to provide justice and accountability. Repeated actions at a place selected for its proximity to power can give new meaning to a place as a site not for memorializing the past but for acting for the present and future. These repeated actions at a particular location at a specific time create sites for justice. After years of Kamisans in Jakarta, the site itself has become symbolic and a site for a wide range of protests. Most memorably, perhaps, the women of Kendang protested the construction of a cement mine by sitting with their feet shackled in blocks of cement in March 2017.

The power of the site is indicated by the government's efforts to prohibit protest there and to relegate free speech, literally, to sites on the city's margins.[4] Notwithstanding these threats, Kamisan has continued in this spot (one week participants even wore signs to protest the relocation order). Sumarsih told me that one of the police officers said it was fine for Kamisan to continue at the site, since they were right (*benar*). For the most part, the Kamisan protest does not disrupt city center traffic, but it is visible to those in cars, taxis, buses, and motor-cycles stuck in the ubiquitous traffic jams that define life in Jakarta.

Kamisan started as a protest in the tradition of all street protests in Indonesia: almost ten years after the end of Suharto's rule, its initiators followed the tradition of public mobilization that had worked in the past. Memories of reformasi are heroic and masculine, but Kamisan provides a more inclusive and complex memory. Kamisan builds on the practices of performance and occupation of

FIGURE 6.1.   Suciwati (left) and Sumarsih (center) stand firm as they are instructed to leave the Kamisan site on March 10, 2016. The police and protesters coexisted, but occasionally men from other units, sometimes in army uniforms or suspected intelligence agents, would arrive at the site. Photo by the author.

public space established by the student activists that toppled the New Order in 1998, but over more than fifteen years it has also become a stage for new aesthetic and affective responses to injustice, and in so doing it has created new forms of public space and political subjectivities. It includes embodied learning and engagement, interactions with victims of past and present cases, and commemorations of past cases, and is a constant to which anyone can show up, to experience, engage, learn, connect, reflect, remember, and protest injustice. Kamisan shows how the demand for legal justice for past human rights violations has evolved away from documentation, testimony, and truth telling about facts—facts that were never fully denied to begin with—toward more affective, embodied, and aesthetic practices that engage youth and condemn ongoing impunity.

Providing a stage and audience, Kamisan also hosts multiple artistic performances that address impunity. The embodied and performative element of Kamisan is emotionally powerful. Writing about the case of South Africa, Catherine Cole, a scholar of English and dance, analyzes the importance of the work of performance artists in addressing the incomprehensible excess of unresolved histories of apartheid that surpass "our ability to do something productive in the face of them, at least in a linear fashion." She writes, "As their art disorders the toxic real, they wedge open spaces where necessary new fictions can take root, gestate, and become sentient, living, breathing realities in the now."[5]

Kamisan subverts an impunity so persistent that it threatens to become normalized, inevitable, or unchangeable. The action provides a way to act by standing in silent solidarity with others who have been stigmatized and demanding that the state fulfill its promises and follow its laws. At the same time, it celebrates the repetition of showing up and persevering. The inclusive circle and the belief that truth and law will ultimately prevail become a new reality—ephemeral but also reliable, as the circle returns every week. Kamisan's nonlinear circular time provides a way to challenge the state's historical narratives and justifications, and standing in the circle acts as a counterweight to the state-mandated educational trips to sites such as Lubang Buaya, described in chapter 1.

Ibu Sumarsih (Ibu, or Mother, is used as title of respect) is an iconic figure of Kamisan.[6] She is hailed as its founder and attends every week, and she also engages with young people on social media. Sumarsih's long tenure as a civil servant gives a depth and precision to Kamisan's work at the same time that she is attached to the martyred students and the promise of reform.

Sumarsih is the mother of Bernardinus "Wawan" Realino Norma Irmawan. Wawan was one of the students shot with live bullets as he was helping a wounded student on campus, in what became known as the Semanggi 1 tragedy on November 13, 1998. At the time, Wawan was in his second semester at the Catholic

University of Atma Jaya, located near a busy traffic cloverleaf (Semanggi) in central Jakarta, and Sumarsih was a secretary for Golkar (Suharto's functional group), working at the Parliament building not far from the university. Sumarsih took notes at the session where Suharto announced he would step down in May 1998. She was also the personal secretary who often accompanied Suharto's family. She explained to me that she had prioritized her children and time at home rather than her career, and hence had remained a secretary.

Their family was close. Her son came home for dinner every night, and after Suharto stepped down they talked about politics and students' responses. Wawan was active in the Catholic church and social organizations, especially the Volunteers for Humanity team (TRuK) with Father Sandyawan, which investigated the violence against Chinese women in May 1998. Wawan worked with street children to improve their literacy skills and economic opportunities. Sumarsih asked her son to be careful, urging him to finish his studies quickly so he could get a job and donate part of his wages to social causes. He reduced his activities, focusing on a planned seminar. He was told by a "friend" that he was on the intelligence lists and was a target. In what is known as the Semanggi 1 tragedy, Wawan was shot by security forces on campus as he helped a friend who had been shot moments before.[7]

Justice for Sumarsih's son has been difficult to achieve. Despite investigations by Komnas HAM that determined that this and two other shootings (Trisakti and Semanggi 1 and 2) were cases of gross violations due to policies on handling demonstrations,[8] representatives in Parliament, including the faction Sumarsih served, determined that the Semanggi 1 case should be resolved by criminal court or a military tribunal.[9] In 2001, the representatives did not recommend the retroactive use of the human rights tribunal law. Demonstrating both her anger and her cunning, Sumarsih attended the meeting where this conclusion was announced, with eggs to throw at the representatives who had determined this. She admitted to throwing the eggs, but those in charge said they understood her anger and outrage. She told me that one of them (later convicted in a large corruption case) confessed he did not know how he would live if his child had been killed. Kamisan works from this space. In 2001, victims' families successfully demanded that Komnas HAM investigate the links between the three cases in which protesters were killed by the security forces (Trisakti, Semanggi 1, and Semanggi 2); the team determined it was a gross violations case and urged the attorney general to follow up, so that an ad hoc Human Rights Tribunal could be established. A legal framework exists but has not been implemented for political reasons. Sumarsih and others have for decades struggled for judicial accountability for the case using every legal means available. Their struggle demonstrates the ways in which politics intersects with law to extend impunity.[10]

Sumarsih carefully documents official statements on past cases—when I first met her in 2007, she gave me photocopies of spreadsheets of newspaper stories and other documentation. As a former secretary at Parliament, she has an excellent sense of how the bureaucracy works. In certain weeks she would call the cell phones of various staff members in the palace to ascertain who had seen the letters from Kamisan.

Unlike many victims of New Order violence, Sumarsih has not been stigmatized, but she has also not become involved in politics, as many of the student activists have. Sumarsih has said the Kamisan action would not continue if only three people showed up, but since the first Kamisan in January 2007, people have always come.

Kamisan is linked to and featured in broader campaigns to #eradicateimpunity and #resistforgetting. A regular attendee said Kamisan was like a "pocketbook of history" that contained the essential highlights that people must know: "The dark events of history must be acknowledged. . . . It is evidence that we are not just fine [*baik baik aja*]." Kamisan's count of the number of Thursdays is a different historical intervention than the "straightening of history" sought by the early postauthoritarian activists. The information presented about cases repeats past statements by the government or officials rather than uncovering new testimonies from victims. In drawing on publicly circulated information, Kamisan subtly highlights the problem of complicity and the distance between action and stated ideals.

Performances and artistic works that address unresolved violence and injustice provide innovative ways of addressing haunting past violence that continues in the present.[11] There have been a variety of artistic responses to past cases and impunity in recent years, but I focus on Kamisan because it creates sites for justice, repeated moments in time and space for reflection, action, engagement, and performances related to past cases. In the infrastructure of impunity, the past continues in stigmatizing policies and is compounded by multiple forms of discrimination, and it shapes the futures that people can imagine. The infrastructure of impunity includes a temporality that recalls past violence to justify present and future mistreatment; over decades, these affectively powerful narratives have transformed political and state violence into social and legal stigmatization and have produced ongoing economic and structural violence. Kamisan subverts the infrastructure of impunity's temporality through repeated, embodied creative acts that reset perceptions, possibilities, and imaginations about social belonging, political subjectivity, and national identity.

Kamisan's relationship to time is innovative—circular time, characterized by repetition and consistency. Circular time is about the past seamlessly connected to the present and future: what could happen to anyone and is happening to many ordinary people across Indonesia has already happened to others. Circular time underscores how the time of waiting, uncertainty, lack of justice, and ongoing impunity extends backward and forward. The past, present, and future blur into persistent impunity, reinforced appointment by appointment, failed promise by failed promise. At the same time, the action and related works of art and performance create a community in the present and the space to imagine futures where the nation's ideals are upheld, impunity is eradicated, and the law functions without political interference. This space centers victims for celebration, engagement, and inclusion, and resists the imposition of temporal frames that ignore intergenerational harm and ongoing suffering. Creative acts, art, and performance, like those featured at Kamisan, collapse linear time—the past and present—into circular time to demonstrate the effects of past atrocity in the present (and future).

Circular time emphasizes repetition and consistency through its measures of time, which are thematized in actions and works of visual and performance art. Kamisan measures time in two specific ways. Anniversaries of incidents of particular past cases and the first Kamisan are commemorated during the week in which they occurred. This measure occurs in years and follows calendar dates; for example, twenty years since Semanggi 1, or eleven years since the first Kamisan action. Commemorating the anniversaries of disparate incidents of violence that occurred in the same week, but in different years or on different dates, unifies otherwise disparate events into one circular narrative: Bloody September commemorates the victims of the supposed coup attempt of September 30, 1965, along with the killing of Muslim protesters in the Tanjung Priok case in 1984, the second Semanggi protest in 1999, and the murder of Munir in 2004. May Mourning commemorates the 1993 murder of the labor activist Marsinah, the 1998 Trisakti killings, and the mass rapes and violence of the transition described in chapter 3. National holidays and international days of recognition, such as Indonesian Youth Pledge, Independence Day, and International Women's Day, are also incorporated into these cycles, becoming part of a narrative of past violence and ongoing impunity. The memory work—resisting forgetting (*melawan lupa*)—recalls named cases as moments in a cycle of state violence.

In the second measure of time, each Kamisan is counted and recorded. As of April 14, 2023, the number was 771 (Kamisan does not occur on national holidays). The numbers convey the value of persistence for those who have stood there, facing uncertainty and nonresponsiveness by the state. Organizers also note the number of Kamisans in their letters to the president and in graphics circulated on social media that proclaim how many weeks they have been unheard and unseen, or their demands ignored. Kamisans that mark every hundredth

FIGURE 6.2. On May 18, 2017, multiple cases of violence that occurred in May were commemorated with a painting created throughout the afternoon by artists from the SERRUM art collective based in Jakarta. Youths and older victims posed for a photo with the completed image at the end of the action. Several people wore aprons naming the different cases that had occurred in May. Photo by the author.

Kamisan action, and anniversaries, are usually celebrated by large gatherings, extended by an extra hour, that feature orations, music, and drama or panto-mime performances, and other art installations and activities. Intervening weeks also feature such performances but at a smaller scale.

These special Kamisans are distinct from quieter intervening weeks, attended by a much smaller core group of older victims (and family members) and members of human rights organizations in Jakarta. Older victims often meet at KontraS on Thursday morning and spend time in the courtyard, where they store umbrellas and a megaphone, talking to younger people, and then ride together to the action. In the many weeks I attended Kamisan, the circle was small and had gaps, but the older victims were always there. If they were not, it was usually due to health issues, and in smaller conversations protesters would share news of illness and health concerns, which usually appeared later on social media.

A core community of civil society and human rights organizations in Jakarta supports and facilitates Kamisan. For different anniversaries of cases or of the first Kamisan or other significant weeks, a group of representatives from different cases and organizations will meet in advance to brainstorm themes, slogans, and activities. Meetings strengthen networks of organizations and integrate Kamisan into other campaigns against past and ongoing impunity. Different individuals contact bands and artists to schedule performances. Others coordinate various activities, such as a board for notes to the president. For the eleventh anniversary of Munir's murder (September 10, 2015), organizers provided paper for notes to hang on trees made from branches potted in concrete. Individual notes expressed the individuals' demands and hopes, in the spirit of Munir's encouraging victims to speak. Thus, by the end of the day, branches had filled with diverse sentiments.

FIGURE 6.3.   Kusnendar holds his umbrella at the Kamisan commemorating the eleventh anniversary of Munir's murder. Those present wrote messages on cards and hung them on tree branches potted in cement to stand at the site. Kusnendar wrote, "Our hope is that immediately, quickly, a presidential decree will be issued that rehabilitates the victims of 1965–1966. Until now this is not yet resolved. Faster is better. Please, President Jokowi, quickly!" Photo by the author.

One week in March 2016, I planned to meet Atnike, who was finishing her PhD research on the topic of social services for the 1965 victims at Kamisan. We had known each other through research and advocacy related to transitional justice since the early 2000s. The circle that day was very sparse. She took the megaphone for a reflection, turning to face each part of the circle. She said that it was important to come each week even if it was boring, and that the older victims were there each week and did not care about boredom.

"Boredom" is an important element of Kamisan, in several respects. In 2017, I met Hariwcahyo Utomo, known as Hariwi, a young filmmaker who attended Kamisan every week with a Sony PXW-X70 camera balanced on his shoulder. Hariwi told me he originally came to interview Sumarsih as an expert for his film on Munir in 2013, but he felt something "essential" in that moment and knew he had to continue. Hariwi appreciated the quieter weeks in 2017. He told me he felt the essence of Kamisan more deeply in these weeks, and that the bustle of other weeks was like a fog that obscured the value of the action. His film aspired to convey the very boredom of Kamisan. He decided he would attend each week, even though he lived an eight-to-ten-hour train ride away in Yogyakarta. He took the train to Gambir station, which was close to Kamisan, filmed the action, and then returned home by the next night's train. He finished the editing each week so that he did not have to go back over it. The idea of the film was to not have a plot, and to highlight circularity and repetition. He wanted viewers to understand what it was like to stand in front of the state palace each and every week, demanding justice that never came and standing up against a seemingly impervious impunity.

When I talked to him two years later in late July 2019, I was curious about the film, wondering how the boredom theme had worked out. It was "too boring," he said. The concept was boredom, but he was not aspiring to be boring. And his mentors had thought Kamisan was a silent protest, but in fact it was noisy in 2017. There were too many bands (about one every two months) and this made it harder to feel the boredom or sense the circular time that Kamisan evokes. He saw the music as a great gimmick to get more people to the action, but for him it risked compromising the value of Kamisan, which came from the quiet. In the past, he explained, the people holding the umbrellas did not care if they were hot or uncomfortable; they were still there. Although a millennial himself, he noted that most his age seemed incapable of witnessing something quiet.

He lingered on the importance of emotional moments, where young people who were not part of an NGO (whose members were encouraged to attend) but were appearing for the first time would tear up as they spoke to him about why they were there or what they felt being there, or how they felt if Sumarsih hugged them. Another time he had filmed Kamisan during a heavy rain. A group of five young men had come from the neighboring city of Bogor. The men were dripping wet, but they were there. He described the participants' singular focus, not looking to the left or the right and not caring about the material inconveniences (sun, heat, rain, transportation costs each week), as part of the original Kamisan's value.

Hariwi thought he might need two more years of filming when we spoke in 2019. I asked what he was looking for or what he needed. He had a hard time translating that into language. He said he needed to get the true meaning. The ending would have no climax. He saw the repetition and he knew it could go on this way for twenty years. Of the older victims he said, "Their hearts are tired. There is nothing that guarantees that the cases will be resolved by the time they die," and in fact there are many victims who have died during the years of Kamisan.

Technically, Hariwi would not be able to find a venue if his film went beyond an hour and a half. To convey the boredom theme, he suggested it was one thing to see the scale of years, but it was another thing to see it in the shorter scale. Hariwi wondered, Could the audience go to Kamisan for a month? Could his audience stand the boredom for the hour and a half of the film? In the film, he hoped to convey the embodied aspect of Kamisan to achieve some of the affect of boredom and uncertainty. He wondered whether the audience could remain standing on their feet as they watched the film. Boredom is very closely related to consistency, and to circular time, and to legal justice itself—doing something steadfastly in the same way, even if it is not fun, useful, or personally beneficial, and even if it doesn't get an immediate response. Boredom dramatizes impunity's empty space of inaction, but the "boring" ritual also transforms it into an affective intervention, a performance of the consistency that the law should embody.

The five hundredth Kamisan was spectacular, and, as the filmmaker noted, it was not silent. It was embodied and visceral but did not present boredom. Rather, it demonstrated the momentum of all those weeks in between with the stalwarts present, which amplified the injustice and consistency of the demands. To affectively engage participants, it had embodied activities in addition to performances. It occurred on July 27, 2017, coinciding with the twenty-first anniversary of the 1996 attack on Megawati's supporters at PDI headquarters, which began the abductions of prodemocracy activists, thirteen of whom remain missing, as described in chapter 3. This made it a particularly haunting collapse of past and present, as the fate of the disappeared and the hope that others would not be disappeared were thematized in activities.

As with other special Kamisans, the gathering started an hour earlier than usual. Rather than the usual megaphone, the five hundredth Kamisan used sound equipment. A stage was created by a thin red carpet spread on the pavement in front of a standing, printed banner detailing the history and purpose of Aksi Kamisan, which would appear in photos taken of celebrity musicians. The cloth covering the concrete barricades was black with white handprinted letters that read, "500 KAMISANS ONLY SWEET PROMISES. JOKOWI HAS ALMost [HAM-pir] FORGOTTEN." The first three letters of "almost" spelled out the acronym for human rights (HAM), while the remaining letters ("pir") were lowercased to emphasize that acronym, and suggested that Jokowi had almost forgotten human rights. Recalling promises made during campaigns that had not yet come to fruition focuses attention on what the president himself had promised he would do and what appeared possible at the moment he was seeking election.

Other slogans made specific demands: for example, to fire Wiranto, who was minister of defense and commander of the armed forces in 1998 and is implicated in several of the cases of gross violations. He had been appointed by Jokowi to serve as coordinating minister for political, legal and security affairs, which included coordinating the response on past cases.[12] In pointing to specific appointments that furthered impunity, Kamisan highlighted not only how the past cases became unresolvable but also what was in the power of the president to do now. In another example of circular time, the past, present, and future blur into a persistent infrastructure of impunity, reinforced appointment by appointment of alleged perpetrators to positions of power in the present, failed promise by failed promise.

The circle was large and linked stalwarts and curious newcomers. As he was most weeks, Asih Widodo, called Pak Sigit in honor of his son who was one of the students killed at Semanggi 1, attended on his motorcycle with signs that read, "Looking for justice while looking for a living." This slogan emphasized not his victimization in the past but his agency in the present and highlighted the ways in which past violence translates into socioeconomic challenges in the present for families of victims. He provided the facts: "My son was killed by TNI and my forehead was struck by the butt of a police automatic rifle [keningku popor polisi]." Families of most major cases were represented: the women whose children (dismissed as looters) were incinerated in the mall set on fire by security forces in May 1998; 1965 victims, including some who had been on Buru and women who had been imprisoned as Communists and were still stigmatized; the daughter of a victim of Tanjung Priok; and activists from Papua, whose communities were still under threat. Many of the student activists from the 1998 generation, including one who worked across the street for Jokowi, and other human rights activists were also scattered through the crowd. Many of the older victims who attended each week wore commemorative T-shirts of other Kamis-ans over their regular clothes, materially layering the repetition of their actions on their bodies. The crowd was at least ten people deep: over three hundred people huddled under shared umbrellas or stood or sat on the ground in black attire, and most were young (approximately in their twenties).

The pantomime artist Wanggi Hoed, who initiated a parallel Kamisan in the nearby city of Bandung, traveled to Jakarta to perform a pantomime and parody focused on President Jokowi. Wanggi appeared as the president, dressed in his trademark white shirt and wearing a black *peci* (a cap shaped in a long oval with tall straight sides). Before he began his pantomime, Wanggi started with a short dialogue that mimicked Jokowi's recent public events, where bicycles were given to those who correctly answered questions.

Wanggi, as president, stated that he was deaf (echoing the feeling of many of the victims that their pleas have not been heard). He stammered that there were victims in the attack on Megawati's headquarters, and noted that the perpetrators "are comfortable, all are comfortable, enemies have become friends in one interest."[13] As the military and political elite closed ranks, it was harder to believe that political processes would yield justice for past cases. The satire highlighted the positions and power of certain individuals in the present, as opposed to the near-universal condemnation of their role in violence in 1998.

The performance emphasized the theme of resisting forgetting. Behind the mask, Wanggi continued to read from his phone: "Do you remember, I remember, I am the President. I was selected by the people. Because I am for the people, not the state apparatus [*aparat*]." He sighed that he should work but was tired from the campaign, underscoring the sense of many activists that Jokowi and other politicians cared only for their reelection and did not work to follow through on their campaign promises. The satire allowed the audience to laugh at the president rather than despair about how he had failed to fulfill campaign promises.

Wanggi then moved away from the microphone and dropped the mask to reveal his pantomime appearance: with his face covered in white makeup and a black peci on his head, he still looked like Jokowi. A large red silk scarf fluttered behind him as he unbuttoned his white shirt and put the red scarf through it and put it behind him. Beneath the white shirt he wore a black T-shirt with a white woodcut print that proclaimed, "Resolve the Cases of Human Rights Violations" (Tuntaskan Kasus Pelanggaran HAM). He removed his peci and his long hair flowed free behind him, embodying the look of activists and others who were stigmatized by the regime in the past. He mimed laboring under the weight of dragging the burdens of the white shirt and red scarf behind him. Finally, he laid the red scarf and white shirt under the umbrella stenciled with cases of eviction of the urban poor, an ongoing and acute problem in large cities like Bandung and Jakarta, especially as Jokowi pursued his infrastructure and development agendas.

FIGURE 6.4. Pantomime artist Wanggi Hoed pulling the red thread that connects past and present injustice and impunity at the five hundredth Kamisan performance on July 27, 2017. Photo by the author.

FIGURE 6.5. Wanggi Hoed crouches down before he places the red scarf and stenciled umbrella on the ground at the conclusion of his performance. The audience watches and many take photos. Photo by the author.

When we discussed the performance much later, he said that while the scarf could represent bloodshed in the past, he called it a "red thread." This is an expression often used in Indonesia to describe connections between multiple events—in this case, that past cases were connected to present problems, much like the infrastructure of impunity that the performance and others like it at Kamisan make visible. He said that by taking off his shirt and peci, he wanted to emphasize that all people are the same in God's eyes. Without the shirt and peci (symbols of Jokowi in Wanggi's appearance as president), he "struggled with his own blood" (emphasizing his embodied efforts and personal sacrifices) and his efforts as an ordinary person for victims' rights, and also to voice injustice itself, which he said created anxiety for all Indonesians. The red thread, or the infrastructure, overwhelmed the symbols of Jokowi, the white shirt fluttering on the long red fabric, unable to escape it. As an individual, he was able to act. The performance modeled and inspired the efforts that ordinary people must make for justice, at the same time that it sought to undermine the stigmatization and marginalization of the urban poor and others that had occurred since 1965. The stigmatization drew on policies but also on social attitudes that could be changed by individuals. His umbrella named the forced evictions of poor residents as a present-day version of decades of dehumanization of ordinary people; these evictions were linked with the same red thread to past cases and continued to occur. His T-shirt's woodcut illustration recalled the popular leftist artwork of the past as applied to a current issue.

Kamisan draws on the arts for social justice and creates a space for reviving formerly prohibited, politically engaged arts. Rather than focus on victimization, these artistic practices emphasize the struggle for justice. Other performances linked to traditional forms. The dancer and cultural theorist Diyah Larasati, a former Indonesian national troupe dancer and descendant of women stigmatized for their political role in 1965, performed a dance that had been co-opted by the New Order and reconnected it to resistance.[14] A popular indie band, Efek Rumah Kaca, played songs with lyrics about Kamisan's struggle for justice. Kamisan reforges the bond between the arts and justice that was severed in 1965. The art forms at Kamisan engage and disseminate the feeling of justice and hope for change; they also circulate beyond the sites of Kamisan. They provide an affective and fun way for participants to engage in the struggle for memory against impunity.

There were also embodied activities that allowed those attending Kamisan to take part, actions that engaged them more deeply than standing and observing and that would create further images that would circulate on social media. Participants posed for selfies in front of a wooden backdrop that proclaimed, "We will continue to struggle because we do not want our children to be kidnapped, killed or poisoned." These embodied activities ground participants in the present, which differs from the past but requires ongoing struggle to avoid returning to a time where children might be kidnapped. Inserting themselves into a larger "we" linked to victims challenged practices of stigmatizing and isolating victims. Nonvictims could demonstrate that they were not complicit with practices of social stigmatization of victims and amplify their solidarity on social media.

Another more embodied activity asked participants to literally dirty their hands and join the struggle by making black handprints, with the ink normally used by police to fingerprint suspects, on a long, meter-wide white cloth with "Aku Kamisan" (I am Kamisan) written in thick letters at the top. This activity recalled the criminalization of activists, but here individuals had the power and became visible to the state through their statements and participation in Kamisan. Participants added their messages and handprints. One read, "Where did you put the corpses of the disappeared activists in 1998?" Jokowi was not president then, but the direct address contracted time and connected him to the victims. Emphasizing the intergenerational aspect of the struggle and extending it beyond the present into the future, one child-sized set of handprints was captioned, "Small hands remember the past." Older generations, such as the long-term Buru detainee who wanted to replenish the land with fruit trees (see chapter 1), also participated. Ordinary people did not have to be full-time human rights defenders to participate; they could come, engage in activities, be part of the circle, learn from actual "agents" of history, and be part of an action in the face of the past injustice and betrayals that had been perpetrated by the state.

Kamisan creates a context for all individuals to practice citizenship by demanding rights for justice and addressing the president. The five-hundredth-anniversary event provided opportunities to share demands, experiences, and desires directly with the president on a large chalkboard, with "Dear Mr. President" spelled out (in English) on multicolored fluorescent sticky notes across the top. The black space beneath filled up over the course of the afternoon. Several notes spoke to the importance of ending practices of dehumanization, the ongoing problems of discrimination, and a failure to honor the rights of all citizens, including the urban poor (evicted in the name of infrastructure and development) and the LGBTQ community. Some messages were personal and pointed to the unresolved fate of the disappeared, such as "Where are our children" and "Please return my little brother." Among the slang or more trendy phrases and handwriting, there were also letters that disclosed the slight tremble of an older hand and the struggle of writing; these were printed in all capital letters. These messages were straightforward: for example, "Resolve the past violations of human rights." One emphasized that ongoing violence was not acceptable even as Jokowi created high-profile infrastructure projects: "Souls and blood cannot be traded for asphalt and development. Investigate Papua."[15] Others demanded, "Make those who are marginal part of humanity [*manusiakan marginal*]" and "Human Rights are for everyone not just a few." These notes and the rhetoric of humanization that NGOs use in other contexts call out the infrastructure of impunity and its stigmatization of marginal groups. As participants addressed notes to the president, they also acted against stigmatization. Many other messages reiterated the importance of a judicial solution for past cases and demanded that Indonesia respect the rule of law (in the present).

As daylight faded, small candles like those placed on graves were passed out, with small paper squares below them to catch the dripping wax, and people leaned together to light from candle to candle. Many of those stigmatized in the past, especially those killed in 1965–66 and suspected criminals extrajudicially killed in the 1980s, were denied proper burial rights. Lighting candles was a way to mourn the victims and include them in cultural practices that asserted their humanity and inclusion in the community.

The five hundredth Kamisan event was widely covered in the media, including several videos produced by a major newspaper with the caption "They demand the state shows up to create the values of humanitarianism with their commitment to resolve past cases of gross violations of human rights."[16] The aesthetic performances conveyed the problem of injustice for past cases in intriguing and compelling, or at least novel, ways in order to interest an audience that might otherwise have tired of repetitive and seemingly futile demands. The audience, mostly dressed in black, also became part of the action: they had a chance to express their grievances and hopes in writing, take selfies, listen to songs, laugh as the powerful were parodied, and lean together feeling the heat as candles were lit and passed the light through the crowd. They were able to do something in the face of the knowledge that the state narratives were lies and that what they grew up believing was wrong. This betrayal by the state prompted anxiety and apathy in many accounts, but Kamisan provided a way to act in the face of it. The audience for this event was too young to have experienced many of these cases firsthand, which indicates that the struggle had resonance beyond its direct victims and would not quietly disappear as older victims aged and died. The boring and sparsely attended weeks of Kamisan, as well as the spectacular, noisy weeks, are both embodied and experiential. In addition to regenerating the movement for the future beyond the direct victims, the count and the celebration of numbered Kamisans also promise consistent actions in the future until the cases are resolved.

Kamisan has become a training ground for students and activists, human rights defenders, and artists to experience demonstrating as well as engaging with individuals who have been stigmatized by state propaganda. The Legal Aid Institute and KontraS offer training programs for students to become public lawyers and activists, respectively. Each offers an intensive training program in Jakarta, and Kamisan is one of the key field trips for these programs. Often the group of students (more than thirty in each program, each year) will attend one or more Kamisans. Frequently they make signs to emphasize a particular issue or anniversary. Some will return to their homes in other cities and initiate a Kamisan there. And Kamisan connects youth to international solidarity movements as well: visitors from neighboring Southeast Asian countries have attended and discussed cases in their countries in the reflection circle.

Participation at Kamisan ensures that the human rights and legal aid trainees go forward to do the work with the foundation of seeing victims in their full humanity and learning the details of their individual stories, which includes their current daily struggle, issues of social justice and structural violence, and legal uncertainty and the arbitrary exercise of power by the state apparatus (bureaucrats as well as police and military). The affective exchanges and human bonds supplement legal skills to ensure that the future human rights workers will proceed from a place of caring and humanity, which is required to achieve justice for the past cases and to build a nation in which ideals can be realized. Contact with survivors-victims at Kamisan is part of the intergenerational transmission of resistance and the regeneration of critique.

Training youth and regenerating movements for justice has symbolic and practical dimensions. The way that circular time emphasizes the cycle of national holidays and past violence provides an opportunity for Kamisan to directly address nationalist myths and challenge official narratives that justify violence in the past and present. The Youth Pledge anniversary celebrates the role of youth from across the archipelago in founding the Indonesian nation and struggling for independence against colonial powers. The reformasi Generation 98 has claimed its place in the lineage of revolutionary Indonesian youth.[17] Kamisan has a strong link to the slain heroes of reformasi, especially Sumarsih's son, but it also offers a more generationally inclusive and dynamic approach, as demonstrated by a Youth Pledge anniversary in 2015 with a performance by uniformed high school students coordinated by Theological Academy Drikarya. "YOUTH CARE ABOUT HUMAN RIGHTS" was spelled out in white tape on umbrellas arranged after a silent dance performance in which three students acted out the important contributions that youth had made to the nation in different eras. The weekly letter was printed in a very large format and positioned for all to read. It linked their generation, "the future continuity of the nation, and the elders along with those brothers and sisters who have become victims and families of victims of human rights violations in Indonesia." The weekly letter critiqued commemorations of the Youth Pledge that did not engage in justice projects in the present and linked their struggle in the present to historical rhetoric and the spirit of the original pledge. The letter also recalled first president Sukarno's statement: "Don't bequeath [*mewarisi*] the dust or ashes of the Youth Pledge, but pass down the fire of the Youth Pledge. If you pass on the ashes of the Youth Pledge you will be satisfied with Indonesia as it is now with one language and one nation and one fatherland, but that is not the final goal."

The letter stated that in the eighty-seven years since the pledge, the youth participants writing the letter had learned deep lessons about the history of the nation and that "truth and justice are very expensive in this state." They expressed their hope that past crimes against humanity would not be repeated and then pled, "We hope that Jokowi can become the first president of the nation of Indonesia who is brave enough to resolve a few cases of past human rights

FIGURE 6.6.   On October 29, 2015, in celebration of the Youth Pledge day after the pantomime and dance performances, young people arranged umbrellas to spell out "YOUTH CARE ABOUT HUMAN RIGHTS." Journalists and TV media were present at this Kamisan. The black cloth banner with images of victims that usually hangs on the concrete barricades to the road is visible in the lower left corner. Photo by the author.

violations in this state [*negeri*] so that later, one moment in the future, we can be proud that we once had a president who was brave and on the side of truth and justice."

Highlighting the importance of affect, they moved beyond the facts of cases or legal procedures to demand that Jokowi demonstrate bravery not through violence but through siding with truth and justice. In contrast to the histories that justify the state violence, the letter detailed consistent failures of the state to follow through on truth and justice. It took a nationalist symbol of pride that has been claimed by Generation 98 and transformed it from something to be nostalgic for into something that must be fulfilled in the present. The letter and performance emphasized that those standing at Kamisan are the pioneers (youth, *pemuda*) and heroes of the future. Not all Kamisans are this directly historical, but all of them share a pedagogical experience of nationalism and hope for a state that follows through on its ideals.

Kamisan has generated diverse visual and performative works that amplify its themes and extend its presence, unified with the iconic black umbrella. It creates a context for youth to experience national solidarity through creative work that circulates and links actions at sites of justice across the archipelago. Through images and art, Kamisan has spread the message of justice more effectively than earlier documentaries, reports, documents, and testimonies. Social media have provided a network with which to circulate images of Kamisan and create connections across the different sites. WhatsApp is a social media app that allows users to send short messages and files of various formats. Importantly, it uses Wi-Fi rather than purchased units of data. Thus, it is accessible and used not only in Jakarta but also to connect national and regional groups and individuals. WhatsApp helps keep count of different Kamisan actions and attendance numbers, as well as letters submitted in Jakarta to the president. Social media take the ephemeral Kamisan experience and circulate it, continuously update it, and transform it into content that can be amplified and shared.

The Aksi Kamisan WAG (WhatsApp group) was an exciting and dynamic forum for communication and often shared "Black Umbrella Greetings" (Salam Payung Hitam). In this space, Sumarsih interacted with groups formed outside Jakarta, which shared graphics and images of their Thursday protests. The WAG forum communicated national and regional weekly themes. The graphics discussed here were shared on WhatsApp as well as on Instagram and Facebook. The group also shared media stories about impunity and, more often, about Kamisan. When victims of the gross violations (often 1965 victims, but more recent cases as well) fell ill, passed away, or suffered various calamities, prayers and sometimes information on donations appeared. Members shared petitions, news of urgent human rights cases, and notices for gatherings, discussions, films, events, and TV shows that featured Kamisan or the cases.

The actions in other cities were typically initiated by one person—often someone who had attended in Jakarta, or sometimes a student from one of the Jakarta human rights training programs that attended Kamisan. They worked with their networks to find a core group and select a site for the weekly protest. Different sites kept their own count of actions. These linked sites of justice created a counterweight to the infrastructure of impunity's ubiquitous sites, at the same time that they linked local actions to simultaneous actions across the archipelago. The WhatsApp group allowed individuals across the archipelago to coordinate themes for the actions, especially the graphics, that were then circulated through social media, amplifying and connecting local and national issues related to impunity. The graphics succinctly conveyed the infrastructure. For example, Lampung's graphic for its sixth Kamisan in September 2019 proclaimed, "DEMOCRACY HAS DIED" and featured headstones that named the "dead" components of democracy, such as the draft criminal code and the Corruption Eradication Commission. The same week, several other cities listed all the cases that had occurred in September across Indonesia.

The circulation of the graphics from different regions created a new sense of national solidarity as regions worked together to highlight particular issues. For example, in November 2017, Bandung created a graphic that looked like a white stucco wall with a black stencil of a child's silhouette, holding an umbrella above the child's head. The text commemorated World Children's Day and offered a tribute to the twenty-eight children who were killed in Kalimantan in a mining hole.[18] The graphic from Kalimantan that week featured the same text on a light background, but the black figure of the prone child had a hand reaching up for help, under the word "drowned." The resonance between the visuals emphasized the connections and solidarity across the nation.

As Kamisan spreads to other cities, a range of related forums have developed in Jakarta itself. A bookstore on the outskirts of the city, operated by Kamisan regulars, holds launch events for books by or about survivors and began a discussion series on Wednesday nights (in the Indonesian language, this is phrased as the night before Thursday, so it keeps the word *Kamis*, or Thursday, in the title). Individuals from civil society organizations that support Kamisan (including KontraS and Amnesty International) are often featured as speakers, and the format is typically a roundtable discussion related to ongoing issues of injustice or the New Order past cases. Kamisan initiators and victims are often invited guests on television talk shows, which then generate new links and content for circulation on social media. Kamisan has also become a research site for undergraduate and master's theses. I periodically met individuals who came to Kamisan to interview Sumarsih and other survivors as well as to experience the action.

KontraS, the organization founded by the slain human rights activist Munir and discussed in chapter 3, was at the forefront of developing the opportunity for interactions with and among victims, and also the artistic and aesthetic elements of Kamisan and the struggle against state violence more broadly. Its current office features large-scale murals and an installation of Kamisan photos framed in large tins traditionally used to store deep-fried crisps, which were originally exhibited at Kamisan. Any visitor to the office would see the moments of Kamisan over the last decade but presented in an everyday object, and as part of daily life. The krupuk tins assemble shards of history into one installation without reference to chronology or number—a repetitive aesthetic that captures the equally continuous and ongoing nature of impunity that Kamisan addresses.

In addition to linking groups and sites throughout the archipelago, graphics and images also connect past and present. The cultural theorist Kaitlyn Murphy points to the importance of visual works that "render visible specific memory narratives in order to create a context for publics to see and feel past and present injustices."[19] During the period I was observing Kamisan, its graphics interleaved newspaper clippings, photos, statements, and slogans from the past with contemporary images to create visuals that merged the past and present as they circulated and reiterated the unmet demands of reform. Circular time and repetition underscore the persistence of impunity, through changes in governments and rhetorics.

Images from the past juxtapose shifting public sensibilities, especially as the promises of reform remain unfulfilled. This is especially true of the images that circulate around anniversaries, particularly the shootings of students and others protesting at the end of the New Order. For example, the graphic for the twenty-year anniversary of the Semanggi 2 incident featured an image of mass protests from 1999 that was overlaid with an image of almost identical mass protests in the present, with a black flag with white lettering stating "Reform has been corrupted." The caption states, "Not only have the cases not been resolved, in fact, the sequel has been produced."[20] In the infrastructure of impunity, the harms of past cases extend into the present.

Images connecting past and present make visible the networks of suspected and acknowledged perpetrators in key positions of power that allow the infrastructure of impunity to function through the institutions that should promote accountability, visible but unseen. For example, a graphic for Kamisan

FIGURE 6.7.   A graphic for the twenty-year anniversary of Semanggi 2 emphasizes the reproduction and extension of corruption and impunity in the present and also highlights the consistency of 603 Kamisan protests with the iconic umbrellas.

607 proclaimed, "Dark day for Human Rights," printed over newspapers from 1998 that reported the dismissal of Suharto's own son-in-law, Prabowo, for his involvement in the case of the kidnapped activists.[21] In the center, a color image showed Jokowi shaking Prabowo's hand as he was appointed minister of defense the day before. An earlier graphic had already warned that the authoritarian regime had returned.[22]

Similarly, another graphic stated that "Reconciliation without a process of law is impunity," using images to highlight the links between the cabinet minister charged with addressing the past cases and suspected perpetrators that undermined processes of law.[23] The same slogan also appeared in another graphic for the same week, with images of kidnapped activists from the Kamisan banner, and emphasized the painful costs to families that have lost loved ones. Taken together,

FIGURE 6.8.   Graphic for Kamisan 607 highlights the impunity that perpetrators of past human rights violations enjoy as they take on new positions of increased power, extending the infrastructure into the present.

the graphics serve to demonstrate how a plan of reconciliation engineered by the perpetrators will further expand the infrastructure of impunity and undermine the rule of law.

The new laws of reformasi were intended to promote accountability in these gross cases of human rights violations; however, over more than two decades, as this book has shown, these new laws have not resulted in accountability or justice. In some cases, the new laws have actually become instruments of impunity and neoauthoritarian practices. Kamisan counts the repeated failures in its slogans, graphics, letters, and demands. Performances, letters, graphics, and orations point to the decisions (appointments, policies, and statements) of the current government that extend impunity. They implicitly highlight how politics and law are elements of the infrastructure of impunity, rather than the means for achieving accountability and national ideals.

Kamisan makes visible that the law is part of the infrastructure of impunity, at the same time that its demands suggest a faith in the system to function and deliver justice if only there are good people and enough political will to activate the system for justice. In several examples, the letters noted that the legal apparatus to resolve the cases existed and asked the president what he was waiting for, before making an emotional appeal for the president to be brave. In another example, a letter explicitly described the failure of law, with a subject line that stated, "Law has become a tool of repression."[24] As the commemoration of the Seventy-Second National Independence Day approached, the letter conveyed to the president the demands of "we victims and citizens who hope to strengthen human rights via Kamisan Actions." The letter reflected on independence and inserted Kamisan into the national symbolic realm, noting that "we still see that the commitment of Indonesia as a state of law [negara hokum] as stated in the 1945 Constitution . . . has yet to be realized [terwujud]." It further pointed out the contrast with the authoritarian past: "When the New Order was in power, law was only interpreted and used for the interest of the powerful using institutions of the armed forces (including military and police) [ABRI (TNI and POLRI)],[25] while in the era of reformasi, legal supremacy became one of the foundations for the nation and state."

The letter writers reminded Jokowi that the constitution guarantees rights for all, then enumerated violations of those human rights and observed that "the institutions of the state are often used to discriminate and give punishments to groups that are seen as minorities" in religious beliefs, sexuality, or politics. Highlighting the infrastructure of impunity, they noted that perpetrators were still the same as in the past—the military and police, plus the judicial institutions, including the prosecutor and courts. To establish legal supremacy, they urged the president to implement the process to form an ad hoc Human Rights Tribunal according to Law 26/2000 (UU 26/2000) for the cases investigated by Komnas HAM;[26] fire those suspected of committing, being involved in, or otherwise bearing some responsibility for the human rights violations; and support the work of commissions and civil society organizations.

The rhetoric of law was extremely important to the New Order, but letters from Kamisan are about reconciling the law on paper with law in practice. The nation has fallen short of its ideals and constitution. Indirectly, letter 502's recommendations expose the infrastructure of impunity and how the state uses law to discriminate against ostensibly "minority" groups, failing to provide equal rights for all, particularly in terms of due process. The letter collapses time, connecting the authoritarian era, the failed legal reforms, and the ongoing lack of legal supremacy in the present.

The Kamisan weekly letters and other messages addressed to the president also demonstrate how politics are part of the infrastructure of impunity. Jokowi campaigned on his status as an outsider and a promise to resolve past cases. As the letters point out, the work of the student activists and the changes of reformasi are what enabled him, as someone not from the political or military elite, to be elected by the voters (the people) who believed in his vision. Kamisan demonstrates that the political system has failed to enforce accountability, even around issues featured prominently in campaigns. In calling attention to the repetition of impunity, Kamisan disrupts the causal links in dominant political rhetoric about what is possible and why cases have not proceeded.

Kamisan's circular time links victims' families to the martyrs of the student reform movement. Unlike the former student activists, who have established political careers and forsaken the purity of the movement's goals, Sumarsih embodies profound integrity and consistency absent political or self-interest. Sumarsih and others at Kamisan advocate for a corresponding implementation of law and national ideals. Other than their references to voters who selected Jokowi, their demands articulate a system without "politics" in the sense of political parties, haggling, interests, opportunism, and inconsistency. The ad hoc Human Rights Tribunals that they seek do require a legislative mandate to implement, and those in power are able to block it because of the impunity that has allowed past perpetrators and beneficiaries to retain their political power, even after reformasi. The focus on the appointments made by Jokowi emphasizes how he could operationalize differently the power vested in him by the democratic vote. The specific demands to fire Wiranto, or to order the attorney general to follow up on investigations, are actions that he could take without the legislature.

Politics became a key element of the infrastructure of impunity through a problem that the political scientist Dan Slater calls "party cartelization Indonesian-style." Slater describes how "promiscuous power-sharing . . . in which parties express or reveal a willingness to share executive power with any and all other significant parties after an election takes place, even across a country's most important political cleavages," has undermined opposition in Indonesian democracy. This, he says, has created a situation in which "accountability relations between voters and parties remain surprisingly tenuous in Indonesia, nearly 20 years after democracy started taking root."[27] In 2014, many activists thought that the election and democracy could be used to seek accountability and end impunity; however, by 2017, Jokowi—consumed with reelection—had moved from his original vision to an appeasement of majority interests (especially particular versions of Islam) and political factions (especially the military and oligarchs).

The 2019 presidential elections bitterly divided civil society activists. Some favored Prabowo for his populist or Islamic credentials, justifying their preference by arguing that his past involvement in human rights abuses had been addressed through his discharge from his position in the Special Forces. Others continued to favor Jokowi because of his stated commitment to human rights, even though they recognized his failures to fulfill promises and, worse, his appointment of intelligence agents implicated in Munir's murder to key positions. This led many to argue for a boycott of the elections, reviving a strategy used to contest the lack of choice under the New Order. The political situation is such that democratic processes cannot easily be used in the service of ending impunity, and polarizing elections tend to divide civil society, even as the elite remain united.

Where other efforts have become ensnared in technicalities and strategic evasions of law or other elements of the infrastructure of impunity, Kamisan—while seeming to do the same thing, and to advocate for the legal resolution of past cases based on victims' voices—has focused on the problem of impunity and highlighted key elements of the infrastructure that are visible but perhaps also unseen. Kamisan recreates the expectations that democracy and rule of law should work and demands justice. It does this by making impunity and its infrastructure visible through affective and technical messages and by dramatizing the idea that impunity is a crime not only against the victims but also against the laws and national principles. Pointing to impediments to the realization of justice through the rule of law also conveys a hope and a plan to make the system work.

Kamisan letters and demands name concrete actions to remedy the impunity and in so doing undermine the infrastructural inevitability of impunity. By its repeated and expanding presence, Kamisan demonstrates that past cases won't simply be forgotten, and that cases affect the nation, not just victims and their families. Kamisan is an emergent countermovement and practice that reveals the state's bad faith and makes demands to reclaim the law. As Kamisan spreads and succeeds, political and legal elements of the infrastructure of impunity extend and repeat efforts to foreclose the visions of law and justice connected.[28]

The consistency—the "boring" sameness and repetition—of Kamisan attendees, especially Sumarsih, itself challenges the regime's claims to legality and nationalism with a new logic of steadfast, consistent fidelity to national principles and the rule of law. In a sense, Kamisan performs the political and ideological correctives to impunity: an unwaveringly constant and fair application of law, a boring consistency. After more than ten years, its repetition has become symbolically important in a context where political discourses, alliances, and promises shift rapidly, and where politics is dominated by military and elites. The Kamisan practice is for the future and not the past; more precisely, it has a circular time where the past, present, and future follow continuously. As Sumarsih put it in a message to a newer member of the group outside of Jakarta, "We resist [lawan] impunity so there is a guarantee that the past cases of gross violations of human rights won't be repeated in the future."[29]

Hariwi, the filmmaker, recalled a dialogue between Sumarsih and a police officer one week. It was a light and jovial conversation but, for him, a very meaningful one. The policeman said that he was exhausted by the large demonstration. Hariwi thought his comments were humane and understandable—and Sumarsih replied that it was tiring. But then she reminded the police officer, "You are paid to be here." Hariwi recalled that Sumarsih was not paid to be at the event and she had shown up every week for more than a decade.[30] Her consistency was made all the more meaningful because she got nothing out of the time and investment,[31] nor did she want anything other than justice—invitations to meet with the president and even apologies did not impress her.

Boredom is the feeling of consistency, and consistency is the standard of legal supremacy. The tedium of showing up every week, even if it is likely that a case won't be solved, has been embraced by youth, despite claims that millennials cannot tolerate boredom. It is about imagining a different future where all the victims of small cases are heard and respected, where justice is done for past cases, and where these injustices are seen as wrong and contrary to national values.

Kamisan chips away at one of the most powerful elements of the infrastructure of impunity: the emotionally powerful, deeply resonant narratives of stigmatization and danger. It does this not through typical human rights representations of the harm suffered by victims. Such images can fail to resonate because the state's powerful stigmatizing propaganda persists, and it is difficult to undo its unconscious, affective power over bystanders and society. Instead, Kamisan offers an affective counterweight to the stigmatizing propaganda. The experience of being at Kamisan reverses and undermines the experience of being at the monument and museum (see chapter 1) because at Kamisan the stigmatized are humanized and approachable, and the violence of the past is not justified as a defense against the betrayal and corruption of the nation. Instead, impunity is exposed as the force that corrupts national ideals.

For individuals attending who have never met a 1965 victim, the experience can be surprising. They discover that in real life, these victims are not dangerous or bad people. The humanizing process of Kamisan is not limited to those stigmatized for 1965 but extends to others who may be painted as criminals or "othered" in the media. And all who attend have a chance to ask questions to learn from those involved.

The New Order blatantly co-opted the political, nationalist symbols, rhetoric, and law in Indonesia. The system has been held together by the repeated mobilization of symbols and a pretext of law and democracy to justify and conceal extralegal and undemocratic practices. Kamisan performs alternative commemorations and exposes the misuse of law. It reverses the stigmatization of victims and critics by allowing them to claim the symbols and values of the nation. Even after participants leave, there is the sense that they could come to this circle any-time. It will be there every week. The unwavering consistency and the dedication to showing up at Kamisan are slowly undermining the affective power of the dehumanizing narratives and policies that feed the infrastructure of impunity. Kamisan takes the impunity "in plain sight,"[32] names it, and protests its persis-tence. Kamisan makes the infrastructure of impunity *felt* as well as seen. It creates a performative space for young people, especially, to come and do what they can, even if they are not full-time human rights workers. Kamisan offered, and still offers, a glimpse of how things could be different.

INFRASTRUCTURES OF IMPUNITY BEYOND INDONESIA

This book has explored a general question in the specific context of postauthoritarian Indonesia: why do truth telling and the revelation of historical facts fail to produce justice and accountability? It has answered this question by describing an "infrastructure of impunity" in Indonesia. This infrastructure is built out of a variety of elements: bureaucratic, legal, political, educational, social, and affective. Although some of these elements are occasionally dormant and others have been used at different times and in different cases, they can be described as a unified entity whose elements, both singly and in concert, help explain and account for the persistence of impunity.

The domain of law and law enforcement supports impunity in several ways. The legal apparatus made the regime's initial usurpation of power and subsequent discrimination legal, and dissent illegal or subversive. Those in power have pervasive opportunities to practice corruption and bribery, and conflicts of interest remain uninvestigated (often shielded by political appointments that obstruct implementation of accountability and a politicized process for determining which cases to investigate). An appearance that the law "works" and that justice is indeed delivered is created through occasional disciplinary actions against individual state agents who are found to have acted criminally, without any examination or interrogation of the systemic practices of militarism and state-sanctioned violence. Laws and policies are selectively enforced to benefit powerful individuals and corporations and shield law enforcement from accountability. Finally, campaigns against nebulous and ever-renewable threats of "Communists," "instability," and "criminality," and the promotion of exaggerated threats of the same, effectively justify the suspension of due process and the rights of targeted, stigmatized groups in the name of order and security for the dominant population. In its legal dimensions, the infrastructure of impunity relies on the creation of policies and laws on paper as well as on their interpretation and implementation in practice by decentralized elements of the state. In some cases, as we have seen, critics score victories and achieve minor accountability. Nevertheless, without an excavation of more systemic violence, the infrastructure persists.

Bureaucracy is another key element of the infrastructure of impunity. Through "clean environment letters," identification cards branding ex-prisoners, requirements to report to authorities, procedural requirements for accessing rights and state services, the bureaucracy identifies, isolates, formally stigmatizes, and limits the rights of certain citizens. And in Indonesia the decentralization of bureaucratic practices of stigmatization enlists and implicates families and communities as participants. Bureaucracy and its practices tie order and security to the rewards of economic development, and enforce economic marginalization and deprivation for critics and stigmatized groups, expanding outward to their families and allies. Extensive bureaucratic appointments that are distributed through political deals and power-sharing arrangements undermine opposition and create, through bureaucracy, conditions in which politics serve the elite and the parties rather than the citizens.

Affectively powerful historical narratives and exculpatory rationalizations and logics are at the heart of the infrastructure of impunity. They justified the initial genocide and the subsequent stigmatization of targeted groups, such as "Communists." And as these narratives are repeated and amplified across both time and space, they create chronic and perpetual conditions of fear and insecurity to enforce widespread compliance. Affectively powerful narratives, such as the one promulgated in the state's propaganda film, are then woven through and reinforced by putatively more "factual" and historical sites, such as the 1965 museum and monument and public commemorations. These spaces renew the narrative and its visceral elements throughout the country. School curricula and field trips further reinforce them, and tie them consequentially to contemporary citizenship and national identity. Meanwhile, aggressive suppression and censorship of alternative historical materials and analyses fortify the affective narrative.

If we conceptualize impunity as an infrastructure that combines elements of law on paper and law in practice, bureaucracy and governance, and propaganda and affective manipulations, then we can better understand how all of these elements, in concert, deflect the transformative potential of truth telling and the deliberate efforts toward justice by determined individuals of high integrity who work variously within the system. Even as regimes change, these interlaced elements perpetuate impunity, despite declared (and perhaps sincerely held) intentions to seek justice.

The concept of an infrastructure of impunity is applicable to other contexts, including those that lack discrete events such as genocides, overt authoritarianism, and regime changes.[1] Even when it does not develop suddenly after a succinct, dramatic event, an infrastructure of impunity can develop with dispersed and distributed violence over long periods of time, and in established democracies. Within the apparatus of democracy there are opportunities to create impunity through the deliberate creation of laws and policies that support it, the shirking of democratic obligations and responsibilities, and the selective application of democratic values by those in power, their beneficiaries, and bystanders. Checks and balances that might guard against impunity can fail through bureaucratic technicalities and loopholes and when individuals fail to act with integrity and in the interest of all citizens. Laws that undermine the citizenship of some citizens based on race are one example. Even after such laws are revoked, systemic inequity and economic disparity remain and compound over generations. Failure to acknowledge these legacies and the practices that extend them is a feature of the infrastructure of impunity. Without understanding past impunity, those wishing to uphold the status quo can reject efforts to redress it using, for example, the rhetoric of reverse discrimination. The censorship of critical discussions of history (and race) in public schools also helps to accrete impunity over the generations. Individual police officers may be disciplined for widely publicized acts of violence against citizens and labeled bad officers; however, discourses of public safety and the fear of criminal "others" can derail efforts to review more systemic problems, such as the militarization of the police or their role in society. Similarly, in established democracies the judiciary is an ambivalent institution. Individual judges can be at the vanguard of enforcing individual liberties and rights, or they can reinforce corporate or party interests. In these cases, it can appear that the law has been followed, but the law itself is part of the infrastructure of impunity. This effectively undermines democracy while maintaining its facade.

Truth is frail. Illusions and national fables can be obstinately persistent. The United States, even as a settled democracy, seems to be in a postfact and a posttruth era, where the affective power of stories and narratives endures and withstands any attempt to "correct" the record with facts or tell the truth against these narratives. Why is this so? Why does the truth no longer rebut these narratives? Does "truth" have any power or sway in correcting injustice? The preceding chapters have demonstrated that the recitation of facts or the compilation of documents can't offset an affectively powerful narrative. The Kamisan protests work differently from tribunals and legal cases because the protests and works of art presented there counteract affectively the force of lies and narratives. The pro-testers recall past statements by those in power not to "set the record straight" but rather to galvanize justice by bearing witness, day in and day out, and through a visceral, embodied rebuttal to the historical narratives of impunity.

Because falsehoods, distortions, and propaganda often establish or extend impunity, truth is seen to be an important antidote, or a first step toward justice and accountability. Establishing and acknowledging the truth about past vio-lence and impunity is indeed critical, but it is also insufficient, especially in cases of protracted impunity in which many facts are not in dispute. Widely acknowl-edged details and official statements can be undermined and reversed over time, so "common knowledge" is not stable and must continually be defended from the erosions of truth, public amnesia, and resignification. Impunity often rewrites the meaning of the past as much as its details. And acts of capitulation, small and large, that can also take the form of nonactions or failures to act or speak are not direct renunciations of democracy but nonetheless contribute to its attenu-ation. The cumulative effect of repeated distortions, glossed as aberrations or dismissed as merely the hypocrisy of particular individuals, creates opportunities for an infrastructure of impunity to develop even within the parameters of an established democracy.

Acts of direct and indirect violence, outrageous re-narrations of widely witnessed and broadcast events, and lies and distortions cannot be addressed through official accountability apparatuses that can be activated only through political processes, and thus they become nothing more than material for late-night comedy skits and cynicism, apathy, or despair. Nor do these multiple elements that enable impunity and lack of accountability for violations of demo-cratic ideals, even if not technically violations of particular laws, get named as such, and they do not activate transitional justice processes, occurring as they do in a settled democracy. Rather, politics becomes the terrain of struggle, and this further obscures the extent to which politics also *contributes* to the infrastructure of impunity. The same might be said of the law, which is both an element of impunity and presented as its remedy.

Like other infrastructures, impunity is invisible when it is working smoothly and uncontested. In Indonesia, the infrastructure disperses the work of impu-nity, which makes it harder to see or to prosecute. This is especially true when impunity derives from technically correct uses of laws and policies on the books, or where changes to bureaucracy are debated in technical and arcane terms and justified by narratives that inspire visceral fears. Key cases may break through the apparatuses that silence, distract, and rationalize impunity, but they often remain just that—individual, specific cases, handled as such. It is difficult to demonstrate the systemic, sprawling, and pervasive infrastructure of impunity and ongoing injustice. Reform of laws that disenfranchise particular groups requires more than revelations of the truth that these laws are unjust. Again, narratives and logics play important roles in preserving the infrastructure of impunity. In some cases, celebrating moments of change and transition actually obscures how the infrastructure continues to function: racial injustice persists in a supposedly and self-congratulatorily color-blind society, and impunity endures even after political transitions and legal reforms.

Even where the truth is made obvious and undeniable, fear and complicity create conditions in which it is difficult for such truths to change the system and the elements that keep the infrastructure of impunity functioning. Occasional legal efforts to address particular cases can provide specific truths as they obscure the larger truths of how impunity works. In cases where institutions, and their representatives, are the arbiters and authorizers of truth, it can be particularly difficult to reveal or recognize truth. In a democracy, various aspects of the electoral system and even affectively powerful untruths can be used to undermine truth and systems for acting on it. Truth and justice are important, but infrastructures of impunity, built through both action and inaction, are obdurate: they bend truth to impunity rather than the reverse.

The creation of an infrastructure of impunity to shield perpetrators of a relatively undiscussed genocide may seem to be a problem of elsewhere, the so-called Third World—a place that still suffers the legacies of corrupt dictators. Or the infrastructure of impunity may seem like an intangible accomplice to the more literal and tangible infrastructure of development, investment, or opportunities to exploit natural resources or create an emerging market for consumer goods in developing nations. In Indonesia the infrastructure of impunity supported and still supports the economic infrastructure—the allocation of land, resources, and wealth to beneficiaries of the system. We in the United States may have secured the luxury of thinking of impunity and injustice of the sort described in this book as a distant problem or a vestige of the Cold War. But the conditions of dispersed, historic, and ongoing violence and injustice, disregard for truth and democratic institutions, and persistent systemic injustice may already have created conditions in which such an infrastructure could take root—one comprised not of gross violations of human rights but of a multitude of ordinary impunities. A lesson from the Indonesia case is that such an infrastructure of impunity, once established, is difficult to eradicate.

The preceding chapters have explored Indonesia in the context of global discourses and practices of transitional justice and have demonstrated that legal trials and tribunals alone have not eradicated, and will not eradicate, a system of impunity lodged in affectively powerful narratives and dispersed social practice. Bypassing politics and even formal legal processes and consistently naming impunity *as* impunity—as happens every week at Kamisan—is a start toward denaturalizing it. Labeling appointments and processes, even where technically legal, as abetting impunity is one way to highlight individual elements of the system that often appear overwhelming and are normalized and tolerated as "just the way it is." The arts and local citizen-based actions can address affective elements of impunity and begin to undermine the stigmatization that allows individuals to feel that they are modern, civilized, and cultured and living in a nation governed by the rule of law, even when rights are not upheld equally for all citizens. As the Indonesia case makes clear, it is important to move beyond the hope that the law or political system will address impunity, especially since both the legal and political systems are implicated in impunity. In the end, the demise of impunity requires the consistent actions of individuals to act with integrity to demand justice in the present and to imagine a future in which the law functions, politicians answer to voters, all human beings are treated with dignity and care, and individuals resist the affective manipulations of the powerful.

Notes

INTRODUCTION

1. Teitel, *Transitional Justice*.
2. There is extensive scholarly and political debate regarding the definition and application of the term "genocide," especially to the Indonesian case. The most recent legal review by the International People's Tribunal for 1965 has concluded that this was a case of genocide (IPT 1965, *Final Report*). Furthermore, the affective and social processes over multiple generations that are the core of the infrastructure of impunity resonate with Alexander Hinton's expansive definition of genocide as "the more or less coordinated attempt to destroy a dehumanized and excluded group of people because of who they are." Hinton, "Critical Genocide Studies," 10. For a review of the term "genocide" as applied in Indonesia, see Roosa, *Buried Histories*, 23–26.
3. Jokowi's vision was called Nawa Cita. For all nine points of the Nawa Cita, see "Jadikan Indonesia mandiri, berkepribadian, dan berdaulat," Kementerian Komunikasi dan Informatika Republik Indonesia. February 2015, https://kominfo.go.id/index.php/content/detail/5629/NAWACITA%3A+9+Program+Perubahan+Untuk+Indonesia/0/infografis.
4. Felman, *Juridical Unconscious*, 146.
5. Feitlowitz, *Lexicon of Terror*, 22.
6. Feitlowitz, *Lexicon of Terror*, 22.
7. Feitlowitz, *Lexicon of Terror*, 22.
8. Feitlowitz, *Lexicon of Terror*, 23.
9. Teitel, "Human Rights Genealogy"; Moyn, *Last Utopia*.
10. Teitel, "Human Rights Genealogy," 317.
11. Keenan, "Mobilizing Shame."
12. The legal scholar Priscilla Hayner notes that what constitutes the truth sought by commissions varies and is often open to interpretation by those individuals serving as commissioners, but that these temporary bodies share several key elements: a focus on past events and patterns occurring during a period of time, engagement with affected populations, a final report, and their having been authorized by the state under review. Hayner is also one of the founders of the International Center for Transitional Justice, an NGO that has provided training, funding, expertise, and advocacy for transitional justice interventions around the world. See Hayner, *Unspeakable Truths*, 11.
13. Hayner, *Unspeakable Truths*, 92.
14. Rotberg and Thompson, *Truth v. Justice*.
15. Hayner, *Unspeakable Truths*, 92.
16. Rowen, *Searching for Truth*, 11.
17. Hayner, *Unspeakable Truths*. On historical justice, see Teitel, *Transitional Justice*, chap. 3.
18. Arendt, *Eichmann in Jerusalem*; Douglas, *Memory of Judgment*.
19. Teitel, *Transitional Justice*, 73.
20. Teitel, *Globalizing Transitional Justice*, 110.
21. Leebaw, *Judging State-Sponsored Violence*.
22. Miller, "Effects of Invisibility."

23. Hinton, *Transitional Justice*; Shaw, Waldorf, and Hazan, *Localizing Transitional Justice*.

24. On gender, see Ross, *Bearing Witness*; Theidon, *Intimate Enemies*. On violence and memory, see Shaw, "Memory Frictions"; Ferme, *Out of War*. On public secrecy, see Ferme, *Underneath of Things*; Taussig, *Defacement*. On social forgetting, see Ferme, *Out of War*; Theidon, *Intimate Enemies*. On betrayal, see Thiranagama, *In My Mother's House*; Thiranagama and Kelly, *Traitors*.

25. Hamber and Wilson, "Symbolic Closure."

26. Hinton, *Justice Facade*, 7.

27. Engle, Miller, and Davis, *Anti-impunity*, 1.

28. Moyn, "Anti-impunity," 68.

29. Moyn, "Anti-impunity," 69–70.

30. Moyn, "Anti-impunity," 72–75; see also Clarke, *Affective Justice*.

31. Nesiah, "Doing History with Impunity," 96.

32. Haberkorn, *In Plain Sight*, 5.

33. Larkin, "Politics and Poetics," 328.

34. Larkin, "Politics and Poetics," 333.

35. On indirect violence, see Rodgers and O'Neill, "Infrastructural Violence." On abjection and abandonment, see Anand, "Pressure." See also O'Neill, "Camps, Gulags and Extraordinary Renditions."

36. Rodgers and O'Neill, "Infrastructural Violence," 404.

37. Ferguson, "Structures of Responsibility," 559.

38. The territorial command was created under Sukarno's Guided Democracy, but it was mobilized by Suharto's New Order to further both repression and impunity.

39. Caton and Zacka, "Abu Ghraib," 206.

40. Huggins, Haritos-Fatouros, and Zimbardo, *Violence Workers*, 3.

41. Melvin, *Army and the Indonesian Genocide*.

42. Roosa, *Buried Histories*, 41.

43. Roosa, "State of Knowledge"; Ryter, "Pemuda Pancasila."

44. Indonesian human rights lawyer Yap Thiam Hien, quoted in Robinson, *Killing Season*, 247.

45. On the spectacular, see Mrázek, *Engineers of Happy Land*; Barker, "Engineers and Political Dreams." On visibility, see Starr, "Ethnography of Infrastructure."

46. In the case of trafficking infrastructures, Shaylih Muehlmann argues that invisibility "allows [infrastructures] to function as clandestine channels" that "depend on making something knowable (a route, mode of exchange, or path of communication, for example) at the same time that it remains concealed." Muehlmann, "Clandestine Infrastructures," 49.

47. The idea of affect has generated extensive theorization; it is beyond the scope of this text to fully engage these debates. Scholars who have used affect as part of understanding genocide and international justice will be discussed below.

48. Whigham, *Resonant Violence*.

49. Brennan, *Transmission of Affect*.

50. On felt realities, see Million, "Felt Theory." On connections, see Clarke, *Affective Justice*; Massumi, "Future Birth."

51. Murphy, *Mapping Memory*, 36.

52. For an analysis of another case in which silence does not indicate resolution, and an exploration of the complex dynamics surrounding memory after intracommunal violence, especially in conjunction with the senses, see Theidon, *Intimate Enemies*.

53. For a discussion of the belatedness of traumatic memory and how it continues to reappear in the present context, see Ferme, *Out of War*, chap. 1.

54. Clarke, *Affective Justice*, 7.

55. My analysis is grounded in long-term fieldwork experience in Indonesia since 1996. In 2014–17, I spent twenty-five months in Indonesia conducting research on history, human rights, and transitional justice, with follow-up research in 2019. From 1998 to 2001, I spent over thirty months conducting research on Indonesia's authoritarian transition, including work as a policy analyst. In 2003 and 2004, I conducted research in Indonesia and Timor Leste on transitional justice and the legacies of Indonesian state violence in Timor Leste.

56. Cole, *Afterlives of Injustice*; Kurze and Lamont, *New Critical Spaces*.

57. Ramírez-Barat, "Path to Social Reconstruction," 242.

1. BUILDING THE FOUNDATION FOR IMPUNITY

1. Like many Indonesians, Sukarno is known by one name only.

2. Farid, "Legacies of Bandung," 14.

3. Sukarno, "Tahun 'Vivere pericoloso' Tavip."

4. Feith, *Indonesian Elections of 1955*, 83–87.

5. Demokrasi Terpimpin, or Guided Democracy, was in place from 1959 until the beginning of the New Order in 1966.

6. Roro Sawita notes that although this policy is remembered as a PKI action, it was in fact passed by the legislature. Sawita, "Connection," 90.

7. In January 1965, Sukarno withdrew from the United Nations in protest of the seating of Malaysia on the Security Council, and made this statement. "Defiance of U.S. Repeated," *New York Times*, May 4, 1964.

8. Sukarno resisted the name G30S and instead called it Gestok, the October 1st Movement, after the date on which it actually occurred. See Kammen and McGregor, *Contours of Mass Violence*, 19.

9. Roosa, *Pretext for Mass Murder*.

10. In 2007, books without the */PKI* were banned by the attorney general. See Roosa, "September 30th Movement," 27.

11. "Amok" explanations also appeared in the international press: e.g., "Vengeance with a Smile."

12. Wieringa and Katjasungkana, *Propaganda*; Roosa, *Pretext for Mass Murder*; Robinson, *Killing Season*, 63–69.

13. Anderson and McVey, *Preliminary Analysis*.

14. Roosa, *Pretext for Mass Murder*, 42.

15. Robinson, *Killing Season*, 67.

16. Dake, *Sukarno File*.

17. Wertheim, "Untung Coup"; Latief, *Pledoi*.

18. Robinson, *Killing Season*, 75.

19. Kahin and Kahin, *Subversion as Foreign Policy*. Schaefer and Wardaya, *1965*, examines international involvement in Indonesia in 1965 beyond the United States.

20. Robinson, *Killing Season*, 77–78.

21. "Vengeance with a Smile."

22. For the official history, see Notosusanto and Saleh, *Coup Attempt*.

23. Herlambang, *Kekerasan budaya pasca 1965*; Heryanto, *State Terrorism*.

24. Latief, *Pledoi*; Roosa, *Pretext for Mass Murder*; Katoppo, *Menyingkap kabut Halim 1965*; Roosa, Ratih, and Farid, *Tahun yang tak pernah berakhir*; Adam, *Soeharto*; Sulistyo, *Palu arit di ladang tebu*.

25. Hutabarat, *Stigma 65*.

26. Whigham, *Resonant Violence*, 5.

27. Marching and Nicholls, *End of Silence*.

28. Wieringa and Katjasungkana, *Propaganda*; Robinson, *Killing Season*.

29. On the contributions of the Left, see Yatmaka, *Sejarah gerakan kiri Indonesia*; on the experiences of exiles, see Aleida, *Tanah Air yang hilang*; Saptari, "Persecution."

30. Anderson, "How Did the Generals Die?," 111; Roosa, *Pretext for Mass Murder*, 65; Anderson and McVey, *Preliminary Analysis*; Wieringa, *Sexual Politics*, 303.

31. For the official history, see Notosusanto and Saleh, *Coup Attempt*; on how the propaganda was developed in falsified media reports, see Wieringa, *Sexual Politics*, 303–11; Wierenga and Katjasungkana, *Propaganda*, 102; Roosa, *Buried Histories*, 63.

32. Pancasila, though coined by Sukarno, was modified by Suharto to be less socialist and less internationalist. The principles in effect to the present are defined as belief in one god, a just and civilized society, national unity, representative democracy based on consensus, and social justice for all Indonesian people. Under Suharto, it was used to criminalize activists and critics, especially those accused of not being monotheistic or organizations claiming Islam, rather than the state ideology, as their basis. President Jokowi attempted to draw on it as a unifying nationalist symbol in the "I am Indonesia, I am Pancasila" campaign in 2017.

33. Scholars have suggested that Konfrontasi was caused by a security threat or by a revolutionary ideology, or was a way of unifying opposed political forces in Indonesia. The conflict was resolved when Suharto seized power, though as the Indonesian scholar Budiawan notes, despite Suharto-era efforts to paint Konfrontasi as an example of Sukarno's effort to distract popular attention from the economic conditions of the time, in popular memory discourses after the fall of Suharto, there was nostalgia for the national pride embodied by Sukarno. Budiawan, "How Do Indonesians Remember Konfrontasi?"

34. *Buku panduan Monumen Pancasila Sakti, Lubang Buaya, Jakarta*, revised edition, 2013.

35. The booklet refers to the building as the torture house (rumah penyiksaan), while the English signs in the park refer to it as the "Torturing Verandah." On the history of Gerwani and other women's movements and their relationship to the PKI, see Wieringa, *Sexual Politics*.

36. Damm, "Lubang Buaya," 109.

37. Rubin argues for an infrastructural approach to memory politics in Spain that decenters the work of human actors in contesting narratives about the past to explore the ways in which "material, institutional, and nonliving actants affect people's experiences of the past and their expectations of the future." Rubin, "Francisco Franco," 224.

38. Whigham, "Reading the Traces," 16.

39. The film was made in the early 1980s (and was released in 1984), taking two years and 800 million rupiah (some of which was government funding) to make. Originally to be titled *The History of the New Order*, it is the dramatization of New Order narratives about the past. It was retitled *Treachery of the September 30th Movement/PKI*. ("6 fakta"). Krishna Sen and David Hill note that the Suharto government feared the commercial failure of the film, and therefore released it through different channels and made it required viewing; they also note that with the advent of the internet, there were critical readings of the film in anonymous postings. Sen and Hill, *Media, Culture and Politics*, 147.

40. Heryanto, *State Terrorism*, 7. Sen, *Indonesian Cinema*, situates the film in a wider context.

41. For example, in September 2017, an episode of the popular television talk show *Indonesian Lawyers Club* titled "PKI: Hantu atau nyata" (PKI: Ghost or reality) featured scenes from the film as if they were documentary footage of historical events.

42. *Buku panduan*, ii.

43. James Siegel analyzes how the state claims vengeance for itself. Siegel, *New Criminal Type*, 5.

44. *Buku panduan*, i.

45. *Buku panduan*, i.

46. Robinson, *Killing Season*, 36; Wieringa and Katjasungkana, *Propaganda*, 66.

47. Robinson, *Killing Season*, 36.

48. Wieringa and Katjasungkana, *Propaganda*, 71.

49. Wieringa and Katjasungkana, *Propaganda*, 67.

50. Wieringa and Katjasungkana, *Propaganda*, 77.

51. Wieringa and Katjasungkana, *Propaganda*, 71.

52. Wieringa, *Sexual Politics*, 311.

53. Roosa, *Buried Histories*, 60–61, describes the army's control of the media.

54. Herlambang, *Kekerasaan budaya pasca 1965*; Scott, "Overthrow of Sukarno."

55. Wieringa, *Sexual Politics*, 288.

56. Suseno, "People and the Wayang."

57. On sexual slander, see Wieringa, *Sexual Politics*, 288. On Bali, see Robinson, *Dark Side of Paradise*.

58. Roosa, *Buried Histories*, 60.

59. For a discussion of how the bronze relief images demonstrate this through their depiction of women, see Wieringa, "Sexual Slander," 556.

60. Anderson, "How Did the Generals Die?"

61. Roosa, *Buried Histories*, 74–76.

62. Roosa, *Buried Histories*, 74–75; Wieringa, *Sexual Politics*, 296–316.

63. This recollection is actually inaccurate. It was Panjaitan's daughter, Catherine, who did this. Nasution's five-year-old daughter, Ade Irma, was not depicted with her father's blood.

64. Daughtry, *Listening to War*, discusses the affective power of sound and the vulnerability of listeners to trauma.

65. Very few official documents were made available to Komnas HAM, which relied on victim testimony.

66. IPT 1965, *Final Report*, 82.

67. "6 fakta."

68. Also at issue was the failure to note the 1948 Madiun Incident. Tan, "Teaching and Remembering."

69. The 2012 feature film *The Act of Killing* follows several of the gangster executioners from the 1965 killings that took place in Medan as they make their own film about the killings. In one scene, two of the executioners discuss the G30S film. See Morris, "Murders of Gonzago."

70. "6 fakta."

71. "6 fakta."

72. "6 fakta."

73. On the critical role of student movements over time, see Lee, *Activist Archives*.

74. Interview by the author, July 2, 2019.

75. Jessica Widartha, "Dari aku yang kau sebut apatis," Ingat 65, September 6, 2017, https://medium.com/ingat-65/dari-aku-yang-kau-sebut-apatis-bfd0715506e8.

76. Widartha, "Dari aku."

77. Widartha, "Dari aku."

78. Emont, "Propaganda Precursor."

79. The president's remarks followed the violent attack on a seminar of 1965 survivors at the Legal Aid Institute the day before. He reiterated that Communism remained illegal, citing the TAP MPRS regulation, but discouraged people from taking the law

into their own hands and encouraged them to contact the authorities if they suspected a resurgence of Communism. Wishnugroho Akbar, "Jokowi sarankan film G-30 S/ PKI dibuat versi baru," CNN Indonesia, September 18, 2017, https://www.cnnindo nesia.com/nasional/20170918195220-20-242583/jokowi-sarankan-film-g-30-s-pki-dibuat-versi-baru.

80. Addi M. Idhom, "Wiranto jelaskan maksud Jokowi soal film G30S/PKI versi baru," Tirto Id, September 22, 2017, https://tirto.id/wiranto-jelaskan-maksud-jokowi-soal-film-g30spki-versi-baru-cw6J; and Felix Nathaniel, "Wiranto: Revisi film G30S PKI tak bermaksud ubah sejarah," Tirto Id, September 24, 2017, https://tirto.id/wiranto-revisi-film-g30s-pki-tak-bermaksud-ubah-sejarah-cxcQ.

81. "Panglima TNI: Silakan nonton film G-30S/PKI," Liputan 6.com, September 26, 2018, https://www.liputan6.com/news/read/3652810/panglima-tni-silakan-nonton-film-g-30spki.

82. IPT 1965, *Final Report*, 28–29; Robinson, *Killing Season*, 58–63.

83. Tanter, *Intelligence Agencies*, 214.

84. Tanter, *Intelligence Agencies*, 214.

85. In 1988, Suharto closed Kopkamtib and created the Agency for the Coordination of Support for the Development of National Stability (Badan Koordinasi Bantuan Pemantapan Stabilitas Nasional, or Bakorstanas).

86. For a detailed discussion, see Robinson, *Killing Season*, 65.

87. Danusubroto and Adam, *Memoar Sidarto Danusubroto*. Robinson, *Killing Season*, 65, confirms that the document has not been found.

88. As the fourth president of Indonesia (1999–2001), Abdurrahman Wahid apologized to PKI victims of Nahdlatul Ulama violence; observers suggest that his formal proposal to rescind MPRS Resolution No. 25 of 1966 may have been partly responsible for his being forced out of the presidency. The legislature passed further legislation (Law No. 27 of 1999, Undang-Undang Hukum Pidana yang berkaitan dengan kejahatan terhadap keamanan negara), which, in the name of state security, criminalizes disseminating "Communist-Marxist-Leninist" ideas or opposing Pancasila.

89. The Legal Aid Institute estimated that three million individuals who were members of the PKI or other social organizations were killed, while seventeen million sympathizers of the PKI and related organizations, supporters of Sukarno, and their descendants were affected by the policies and had their rights violated. Those whose economic rights were violated included several groups as described in the class action suit: those who were fired from their jobs; those who did not receive their pensions as civil servants, police, or military; those who were victims of the special screenings and clean environment policies and were not able to get work or whose careers were obstructed; those who lost their status as veterans or heroes; those who were expelled from school; and those who were obstructed from creating art or publishing their works. Hutabarat, *Stigma 65*, xi–xii. In November 1965, an official fact-finding mission estimated that seventy-eight thousand people had been killed to date. In mid-1966, Kopkamtib suggested one million, with eight hundred thousand deaths occurring in Bali and Java. On his deathbed, one of the primary perpetrators, Sarwo Edhie, suggested three million. This number has not been confirmed and is doubted; however, the figure is important to victims. The Australian scholar Robert Cribb ("Genocide in Indonesia") analyzed the numbers, concluding that a scholarly estimate would be around five hundred thousand, but it could be much higher or lower. Annie Pohlman ("Massacres of 1965–66") revisited the issue later in light of new studies, and Siddharth Chandra ("New Findings") provided new analysis based on census figures. And yet there remains no conclusive figure.

90. For a discussion of violence in eastern Indonesia, see Kolimon and Wetangterah, *Memori-Memori terlarang*.

91. In East Java the army's Kodam (Regional Military Command) had *bina mental*, or mental management teams, to carry out indoctrination. Roosa, *Buried Histories*, 61.

92. Roosa, *Buried Histories*, 93. See also Robinson, *Killing Season*, and Melvin, *Army and the Indonesian Genocide*.

93. Roosa, *Buried Histories*, 68.

94. Roosa, *Buried Histories*, 61.

95. Robinson, *Killing Season*, 170n105.

96. Melvin, *Army and the Indonesian Genocide*; Robinson, *Killing Season*.

97. Roosa, *Buried Histories*, 83.

98. Roosa, "State of Knowledge."

99. Oppenheimer's film *The Look of Silence* describes this.

100. Robinson, *Killing Season*, 208–36. For accounts of specific killings based on oral testimonies, and on the use of torture, see Roosa, *Buried Histories*, especially 88–90. For a demonstration of the army's systematic involvement, see Melvin, *Army and the Indonesian Genocide*.

101. Kartika, "Politicization of Psychology," 24. Abdul Wahid, "Campus on Fire," analyzes how screenings affected Indonesian universities.

102. Quoted in Robinson, *Killing Season*, 219.

103. Robinson, *Killing Season*, 219.

104. IPT 1965, *Final Report*, 79–80.

105. Jaksa Agung Republik Indonesia, Nomor instr-007/J.A/11/1973, "Tentang penylesaian perkara pembunuhan oknum2 G.30.S/PKI," quoted in IPT 1965, *Final Report*, 49.

106. *Bahaya Laten Komunisme di Indonesia*, Jilid ke-5, *Penumpasan pemberontakan PKI dan sisa-sisanya* (Jakarta: Markas Besar Angkatan Besar Republik Indonesia, Pusat Sejarah dan Tradisi ABRI, 1995), 119, cited in IPT 1965, *Final Report*, 40.

107. "Three More Long-Term Political Prisoners Executed."

108. For a discussion of its changes and persistence, see Tanter, "Intelligence Agencies," and Robinson, *Killing Season*, 58–59.

109. Lestario was an official in the East Java Provincial PKI. He worked clandestinely to try to rebuild the party near Blitar in 1967 and was captured in 1969 with two associates. He was tried in 1975 for subversion and sentenced to death in 1976. As Vanessa Hearman notes, Lestario's correspondence with grassroots transnational solidarity networks created emotional solidarity and increased awareness of what was occurring in Indonesia. Hearman, "Letter-Writing and Transnational Activism."

110. According to Hearman, the 1975 speech was smuggled out of prison and circulated among exiles, as evidenced by the inclusion of copies of it in their papers. It was also translated into English and published in the *TAPOL Bulletin* in 1985, and circulated among activists in Indonesia. Hearman, "Letter-Writing."

111. "Gatot's Defence Statement," 6.

112. "Gatot's Defence Statement," 9.

113. John Roosa notes how these statements cannot be retracted and produce truth in torture. Roosa, "Truths of Torture."

114. "Gatot's Defence Statement," 6. The South Blitar Affair was a subsequent rebellion by "remnants" of the PKI in 1967–68. For a discussion of these events, see Hearman, *Unmarked Graves*, 138–94.

115. "Gatot's Defence Statement," 8.

116. John Roosa describes how this pattern of extralegality (with elite complicity) worked during the chaotic period leading up to Sukarno's declaration of Guided Democracy. Roosa, *Buried Histories*, 35.

117. "Gatot's Defence Statement," 9.

118. Mira, "'G30S/PKI' Symbol," 3.

119. Prisoner accounts describe the harsh conditions of life on Buru; for examples, see Pramoedya Ananta Toer's memoir, *The Mute's Soliloquy*, and Hersri Setiawan's *Memoar pulau Buru*. Recent films such as *Pulau Buru tanah air beta* (Buru island, my homeland), by Rahung Nasution, demonstrate the hard work of clearing the land and building their barracks, the difficulty of growing sufficient food, the starvation and deprivation, the difficulty of being isolated from family, and the inability to read or write. Accounts from other locations include Lamasitudju et al., *Sulawesi bersaksi*.

120. To preserve the man's confidentiality, I have not named the organization here.

121. For a discussion of victimhood, see Hearman, "Contesting Victimhood."

122. Interview by the author, July 6, 2017.

123. Ahmad, "South Sulawesi."

124. IPT 1965, *Final Report*, 41–42.

125. Sawita, "The Connection between Land Reform and the 1965-66 Tragedy in Bali," 94-96.

126. The film can be viewed online at the Transformative Memory Digital Archive, last accessed March 22, 2023, https://omeka.irshdc.ubc.ca/s/Transformative-Memory/item/31.

127. Keputusan Presiden RI No. 28 Tahun 1975 tentang Perlakuan terhadap mereka yang terlibat G30S/PKI Golongan C., quoted in Hutabarat, *Stigma 65*, 2.

128. Robinson (*Killing Season*, 253–54) lists the various regulations used to implement the clean environment campaign and details the screening questions, which include "Communism is said to be a latent danger. Why?" and "What is your opinion of the New Order?"

129. Keputusan Presiden RI No. 16 Tahun 1990 tentang Penelitian Khusus bagi Pegawai Negeri RI, changed the official description and terminology from *mental ideology screening* to *special review*, known by the abbreviation *litsus*. "Sebuah upaya menghapus" documents the uncertainty and anxiety over the efforts to clean the government and military of those from the G30SPKI environment.

130. Presidential Decree No. 38/2000 regarding Bakorstanas, and Presidential Decree No. 39/2000 regarding litsus, dissolved Kopkamtib.

131. Conroe, "Efficacy of 'Dangerous' Knowledge."

132. The primary source of information used was the KKPK report described in chapter 4.

133. Ikatan Pemuda dan Pelajar Indonesia (Indonesian League of Youth and High School Students).

134. The group was awarded the Gwangju Human Rights Prize in 2019; it was also the subject of the documentary film *Rising from the Silence* in 2016.

135. Robinson, *Killing Season*, 247; Van Der Kroef, "Indonesia's Political Prisoners."

136. Robinson notes that approximately one million people were affected by the policy to mark "ET" on state identity cards (Kartu Tanda Penduduk). Robinson, *Killing Season*, 251. The class action suit estimated that twenty million people (three million as members of the PKI and seventeen million as sympathizers, Sukarnoists, and members of related organizations, including children and grandchildren) had been affected by the stigma of 1965 in all its forms. Hutabarat, *Stigma 65*, 13.

137. Robinson, *Killing Season*, 247n34.

138. December 1, 1976, press statement by Sudomo, quoted in Robinson, *Killing Season*, 248n35.

139. Quoted in Robinson, *Killing Season*, 248n36.

140. These occupations included the civil service, the armed forces, and strategic industries; depending on interpretation, former prisoners were also restricted from

teaching, working in corporations, being journalists, working at universities, or serving as lawyers. For a full list, see Robinson, *Killing Season*, 251.

141. Wardaya, *Suara di balik prahara*. Wardaya directs PUSDEMA (the Centre for Democracy and Human Rights Studies), Sanata Dharma University, Yogyakarta.

142. Tjiptaning, *Aku bangga*.

143. Tjiptaning, *Aku bangga*, v.

144. Suriyanto, "Ribka Tjiptaning yang tak pernah malu jadi anak PKI," CNN Indonesia, September 30, 2015, https://www.cnnindonesia.com/nasional/20150929180907-20-81660/ribka-tjiptaning-yang-tak-pernah-malu-jadi-anak-pki.

145. The PDI-P was founded in 1999 by Sukarno's daughter Megawati. In 1996, Megawati was forced out of her leadership role in the Indonesian Democratic Party (PDI), one of the parties formed under the New Order, leading to riots in Jakarta on July 27, 1996, and the kidnapping of many prodemocracy activists, which is another one of the cases of gross violations further discussed in chapter 3.

146. Secretary General of PDI Perjuangan Hasto Kristiyanto, in Glery Lazuaradi, "Polemik Ribka Tjiptaning anak PKI, PDIP: Garis politik tidak diturunkan," *Tribune News* (Jakarta), February 7, 2018.

147. Wisnu Nugroho, "Jokowi: Kalau PKI nongol, gebuk saja," Kompas.com, May 17, 2017, https://nasional.kompas.com/read/2017/05/17/16433321/jokowi.kalau.pki.nongol.gebuk.saja.

148. Her story has been featured in a number of collections and films; she also testified anonymously behind a curtain at the International People's Tribunal. I met with her in November 2015 and spoke with her about the process of testifying and her work for justice with other survivors in the organization Kipper. For the wider context of her story and events in Yogyakarta, see Wandita, Yuniar, and Easton, *Bertahan dalam impunitas*.

149. The student league was Ikatan Pemuda dan Pelajar Indonesia (Indonesian League of Youth and High School Students).

150. Bedjo Untung, interview by the author, Jakarta, March 10, 2016.

151. Nani Nurani, interview by the author, Jakarta, December 16, 2015.

152. Army psychological warfare teams operating in different areas included Tim Penerangan Operasi Mental (Operation Mental Information Teams), Tim Komando Operasi Mental (Operation Mental Command Teams), and Tim Indoktrinasi (Indoctrination Teams). See Robinson, *Killing Season*, 170 and Roosa, *Buried Histories*, 61–62.

153. Wierenga, *Sexual Politics*, 327.

154. Soe Tjen Marching writes that her mother saved her father's life by burning his documents, especially appointment letters from the PKI. Her own and other testimonies in Marching and Nicholls, *End of Silence*, describe changing names on documents.

155. "Civil death" is an expression coined by the pioneering human rights advocate Yap Thiam Hien to describe restrictions on former prisoners after release. Quoted in Robinson, *Killing Season*, 247.

156. See the website Ingat 65 (https://medium.com/ingat-65) for multiple cases of individuals finding out about family members' relationships to 1965.

157. *Surat dari Praha*, a 2016 film written by Mohammad Irfan Ramly and directed by Angga Dwimas Sasongko, was very popular and well regarded by those working on 1965 for its telling the story of exiles to a young generation who did not know why family members had not returned.

158. Multiple interviews by the author with victims and NGO workers noted this issue.

159. Marching and Nicholls, *End of Silence*, 189.

160. Interviews by the author, Jakarta, especially July 19, 2017; April 25, 2016.

161. This issue was frequently raised in discussions with groups of victims, especially the Wednesday afternoon discussions organized in conjunction with the IPT, as well as in individual conversations.

162. Interviews by the author, especially May 16, 2016.

163. "Apology," Marching and Nicholls, *End of Silence*, n.p.

164. Marching and Nicholls, *End of Silence*, 18.

165. Marching and Nicholls, *End of Silence*, 18.

166. Roro Sawita, interview by the author, September 15, 2015.

167. Chambert-Loir, "PKI Stroganoff."

168. See, for example, Nadia Fourina, "Tragedi 1965 di mata saya: Terima kasih kepada novel 'Pulang,'" October 18, 2017, https://medium.com/ingat-65/tragedi-1965-di-mata-saya-terima-kasih-kepada-novel-pulang-79a94e654120.

169. Leila Chudori, interview by the author, July 26, 2019.

170. Saskia Wierenga notes that, ironically, the sexual and moral depravity that the regime accused the Gerwani of embodying was perpetrated on victims by the army, especially in its extensive use of sexual torture and humiliation in interrogations and detentions. Wierenga, "Sexual Slander."

171. Conroe, "Efficacy of 'Dangerous' Knowledge," describes the complexity of how children of victims (*anak korban*) acquire knowledge and make claims about 1965.

172. Chudori, *Home*, 352. I have quoted from John McGlynn's translation of the novel, as it has been authorized by Chudori.

173. When I lectured on human rights in Indonesia, many students would accept that being arrested was a human rights violation for those who were innocent (not PKI); however, some were puzzled about whether the idea of human rights applied to those who were "actually, truly" Communists, so deeply had the narrative and logic of an evil, threatening Communist Party permeated their consciousness and sense of national endangerment. In 2015–16, a number of initiatives examined the Left more positively and considered the rights of those who were actually PKI; nevertheless, there was strong backlash and protest regarding many of these discussions.

174. Chudori, *Home*, 352.

175. Chudori, *Home*, 355.

176. Chudori, *Home*, 362–63.

2. THE FORGOTTEN MYSTERIOUS KILLINGS

1. For a range of figures, see Van Der Kroef, "'Petrus.'"

2. "Itu untuk shock therapy. Supaya orang banyak mengerti bahwa terhadap perbuatan jahat masih ada yang bisa bertindak dan mengatasinya." Dwipayana and Ramadhan, *Soeharto*, 389–91.

3. Bourchier and Hadiz, *Indonesian Politics and Society*, 9.

4. Suharto's version of Pancasila democracy was elaborated in his speech to the Interim People's Representative Council on August 16, 1967, quoted in Bourchier and Hadiz, *Indonesian Politics and Society*, 38. The Pancasila includes belief in monotheism, commitment to civilized humanitarianism (or internationalism in some iterations), commitment to the unity of Indonesia, governance by consultation and consensus, and a commitment to social justice. Morfit, "Pancasila," describes the Pancasila and its translation into policies and institutions. The military was also considered part of the national family and had a social and political role, as described by Reeve, *Golkar of Indonesia*.

5. Suharto, speech to the Interim People's Representative Council on August 16, 1967, quoted in Bourchier and Hadiz, *Indonesian Politics and Society*, 38.

6. Moertopo, "The Acceleration and Modernization of 25 Years' Development," 1972, published by the Jakarta-based Centre for Strategic and International Studies in English in 1973, quoted in Bourchier and Hadiz, *Indonesian Politics and Society*, 48.

7. Morfit, "'Pancasila,'" describes the school curriculum as related to the Pancasila Democracy and national family. In the previous chapter, I discussed the propaganda regarding the coup attempt and the ever-renewing threat of Communism making a comeback.

8. Moertopo, "Acceleration and Modernization," quoted in Bourchier and Hadiz, *Indonesian Politics and Society*, 35.

9. Suharto, speech, August 16, 1967, quoted in Bourchier and Hadiz, *Indonesian Politics and Society*, 40.

10. Suharto, speech, August 16, 1967, quoted in Bourchier and Hadiz, *Indonesian Politics and Society*, 41.

11. Ryter, "Pemuda Pancasila," 55.

12. After a meeting with President Suharto about the process of "training the former political prisoners of G-30S/PKI," the interior minister Amirmachmud told the press that "criminal acts which occurred recently and political symptoms in the lead-up to the last election were the work of ex-PKI who were manipulating things." Y, "Mendagri: Eks PKI ikut main dalam tindakan kejahatan dewasa ini," *Merdeka* (Jakarta), August 12, 1982.

13. Amirmachmud, quoted in L-1, "Tidak keberatan ratusan penjahat harus dikorbankan: Amirmachmud pribadi setuju penembakan misterius," *Sinar harapan* (Jakarta), July 21, 1983; and SEL, "Amirmachmud setuju penembak misterius: Kejahatan secara nekad merupakan usaha PKI," *Kompas* (Jakarta), July 22, 1983.

14. HT, "Operasi Gabungan akan kurang bermakna, jika praktek 'upeti' masih berlangsung," *Kedaulatan rakyat* (Yogyakarta), April 6, 1983.

15. LHD, "'Gali' yang mau insyaf tidak akan dipersulit: 'OPK' terus berlangsung dan tanpa pandang bulu!" *Kedaulatan rakyat*, April 15, 1983.

16. BL, "Pangdam V Jaya Mayjen Try Sutrisno: Tidak ada perintah tembak di tempat," *Pos kota* (Jakarta), May 20, 1983.

17. WK/AMD, "Diskusi operasi pemberantasan kejahatan model Yogyakarta," *Kompas*, May 28, 1983.

18. Yogyakarta commander, Military Engineering Corps (CZI), M. Hasby, in LHD-TW, "Operasi Anti Kejahatan tidak terbatas pada fisik," *Kedaulatan rakyat*, April 30, 1983.

19. *Sinar pagi* (Jakarta), May 19, 1983, quoted in confidential document, copy in the author's possession.

20. L-1, "Pangab/Pangkokamtib: Penanggulangan kejahatan selalu berlandas hukum," *Sinar harapan*, May 21, 1983; SEL, "Pangab: Aparat keamanan tidak main tembak saja," *Kompas*, May 22, 1983. A month later, Moerdani also suggested that there was not a policy of petrus—that the term came from the media. JL, "Pangab tentang penembak misterius," *Kompas*, June 22, 1983; A-2, "Pangab: Persaingan antar gang menambah korban penembakan misterius," *Sinar harapan*, June 22, 1983.

21. SEL, "Pangab: Aparat keamanan tidak main tembak saja," *Kompas*, May 22, 1983.

22. Ali Said, quoted in B-5, "Menteri Kehakiman: Penembakan gelap tidak berdiri sendiri," *Sinar harapan*, May 23, 1983. The head of the MPR/DPR, Amirmachmud, stated his agreement; see L-1, "Tidak keberatan ratusan penjahat harus dikorbankan: Amirmachmud pribadi setuju penembakan misterius," *Sinar harapan*, July 21, 1983.

23. The head of the MPR/DPR, Amirmachmud's agreement with the killings was clarified as a personal opinion in OS, "Pernyataan Amirmachmud pribadi, bukan Dewan," *Kompas*, July 23, 1983. On Islam, see *Kedaulatan rakyat*, April 18, 1983, quoted in confidential document, copy in the author's possession. On the rights of the society to peace,

see S-6/M-2, "Marzuki Darusman tentang penembakan terhadap penjahat," *Suara karya* (Jakarta), May 24, 1983.

24. *Sinar pagi*, May 16, 1983 quoted in confidential document, copy in the author's possession.

25. *Antara* (Jakarta), June 18, 1983, quoted in confidential document, copy in the author's possession.

26. In one example, for providing legal aid to accused criminals, the Legal Aid Institute in Yogyakarta was accused of supporting crime and disregarding the humanity of the victims of crime. See Mac, "Plakat-plakat gelap di sekitar rumah Ketua LBH," *Kedaulatan rakyat*, April 19, 1983.

27. "Jangan beri vonis sebelum dijatuhkan pengadilan: Amirmachmud tidak setuju koruptor jadi sasaran penembakan misterius," *Sinar harapan*, July 29, 1983.

28. B-3, "Wk. Ketua DPA Ali Murtopo: Penembakan misterius dapat dipertanggung-jawabkan," *Sinar harapan*, July 28, 1983; SEL, "Wakil Ketua DPA Ali Moertopo: Penembakan misterius dapat dipertanggungjawabkan," *Kompas*, July 28, 1983.

29. B-5, "Menteri Kehakiman."

30. B-5, "Menteri Kehakiman"; S-6/M-2, "Marzuki Darusman."

31. The stories were collected and published in 1993 (Ajidarma, *Penembak misterius*) and published in translation as *The Mysterious Marksman*. Because Suyenaga's translation has been reviewed by Seno, I have quoted from it unless otherwise indicated.

32. Forché, *Against Forgetting*, 31; Gordon, *Ghostly Matters*, 32.

33. Ajidarma and Bodden, "Fiction, Journalism, History," 164; see also Ajidarma, *Ketika jurnalisme dibungkam*.

34. Ajidarma, *Mysterious Marksman*, xvii.

35. Keenan, "Mobilizing Shame," 435.

36. Teitel, *Globalizing Transitional Justice*, chap. 6.

37. Dube, "Transitional Justice," 185.

38. Originally published as "Keroncong pembunuhan," *Kompas*, February 3, 1985.

39. Ajidarma, *Mysterious Marksman*, 5.

40. Ajidarma, *Mysterious Marksman*, 7.

41. Ajidarma, *Mysterious Marksman*, 9.

42. Ajidarma, *Mysterious Marksman*, 9.

43. Ajidarma, *Mysterious Marksman*, 9.

44. Ajidarma, *Mysterious Marksman*, 10.

45. BM's story has been published in several media outlets. He also worked with the National Human Rights Commission (Komnas HAM) and victims' organizations as the case was investigated (2008–12). We talked several times by phone but were never able to meet; by the time I contacted him, he was very involved in campaigning for his daughter in a local election. The investigations that he had contributed to had not produced any significant results.

46. Manangka, "Dendam politik seorang 'preman' terhadap sejumlah jenderal," RMOL Kantor Berita Politik Republik Merdeka, April 3, 2018, https://rmol.id/read/2018/04/03/333680/dendam-politik-seorang-preman-terhadap-sejumlah-jenderal.

47. Manangka, "Dendam politik"; see also Triyana, "Petrus."

48. "Jegar jeger petrus."

49. Triyana, "Petrus."

50. Manangka, "Dendam politik."

51. "Jegar jeger petrus"; also see Suyono and Kalim, *Benny Moerdani*, 150–51.

52. "Jegar jeger petrus."

53. "Jegar jeger petrus."

54. Suyono and Kalim, *Benny Moerdani*, 150–51.

55. Suyono and Kalim, *Benny Moerdani*, 150–51.

56. "Penembak misterius massa lalu," *Kompasina humanoria* (Jakarta), September 27, 2015.

57. Suyono and Kalim, *Benny Moerdani*, 150.

58. Human rights advocacy relies on innocent victims (as Meyers, *Victims' Stories*, demonstrates), and the petrus victims did not all fit into this category.

59. "Pengakuan Kentus." Also see the case of Abu Santoso, in "Perintah dor Sang Jenderal," in Suyono and Kalim, *Benny Moerdani*, 146–52.

60. Witness statements made to Komnas HAM investigators.

61. "Bagus lanjutkan," in Suyono and Kalim, *Benny Moerdani*, 153–55. The identity card policy was part of the Operation to Eradicate Criminality (Operasi Pemberantas Kejahatan) and was frequently featured in the media, especially in Yogyakarta; see, for example, *Kedaulatan rakyat* during April 1983.

62. Originally published as Seno Ajidarma Gumira, "Bunyi hujan di atas genting," *Kompas*, July 28, 1985.

63. Ajidarma, *Mysterious Marksman*, 12.

64. Ajidarma, *Mysterious Marksman*, 12.

65. Ajidarma, *Mysterious Marksman*, 12.

66. See, for example, "Korban penembakan misterius di Jawa Barat mencapai 127 orang," *Sinar harapan*, June 22, 1983, which describes the criminals who have been killed and notes that it is now safe.

67. Ajidarma, *Mysterious Marksman*, 13.

68. Ajidarma, *Mysterious Marksman*, 13.

69. Ajidarma, *Mysterious Marksman*, 14.

70. Ajidarma, *Mysterious Marksman*, 15.

71. Ajidarma, *Mysterious Marksman*, 17.

72. Ajidarma, *Mysterious Marksman*, 11.

73. NAD, "Memories of 'Petrus' Resurface after Three Decades," *Jakarta Post*, July 26, 2012, http://www.thejakartapost.com/news/2012/07/26/memories-petrus-resurface-after-three-decades.html.

74. Many "ex-criminals" were denied permission letters to have tattoos removed. In one instance a person used an iron to remove his tattoos for fear of becoming a "fugitive from the mysterious killings." See U-2, "Polisi tolak berikan surat hilangkan rajah di badan," *Sinar harapan*, June 22, 1983.

75. Yosep Adi Prasetyo, interview by the author, Jakarta, February 12, 2014.

76. *Pos kota* (Jakarta), June 28, 1983, quoted in confidential document, copy in the author's possession.

77. Officials publicly stated that the operations to eradicate crime had three stages: shock therapy, registration, and guidance. *Suara merdeka* (Semarang), July 26, 1983, quoted in confidential document, copy in the author's possession.

78. P-1, "Polri Kodak Metro ringkus 928 penjahat," *Suara karya*, July 1, 1983.

79. SEL, "Pangab: Aparat keamanan tidak main tembak saja," *Kompas*, May 22, 1983.

80. Komnas HAM investigations have detailed the suffering of victims' family members. Legal aid organizations raised concerns about the social-consequences aspects of the policy, see "Direktur LBH Yogyakarta: Masyarakat jangan hina istri gali," *Suara merdeka*, July 6, 1983; and PR/U-1, "Yayasan LBH: 'Penembakan Misterius' merusak nilai & sendi sebagai Negara Hukum," *Sinar harapan*, July 27, 1983. According to the chairman of an Islamic nongovernmental organization (PP Muhammadiyah), the policy was not forbidden according to Islam "if the target was security, order, and peace for the society." *Kedaulatan rakyat*, April 18, 1983, quoted in confidential document, copy in the author's possession.

81. Interview by the author, Jakarta, July 16, 2016.

82. NAD, "Memories of 'Petrus.'"

83. Seno Gumira Ajidarma, "Grrh!," *Kompas*, January 18, 1987.

84. Ajidarma, *Mysterious Marksman*, 21–22.

85. Ajidarma, *Mysterious Marksman*, 22.

86. Ajidarma, *Mysterious Marksman*, 23.

87. Ajidarma, *Mysterious Marksman*, 26.

88. Ajidarma, *Mysterious Marksman*, 27.

89. Ajidarma, *Mysterious Marksman*, 27. The sentence "The slaughter was a big mistake, sir!" was removed by *Kompas* when the story was first published but was restored in the anthology of the stories.

90. Amel Widaya, "Penembak Misterius and Seno Gumira Ajidarma," *Kompasina*, August 9, 2018, https://www.kompasiana.com/amelwidya92/5b6b54045e137349ee5e9ab2/penembak-misterius-dan-seno-gumira-ajidarma?page=all.

91. This story was not originally published in a newspaper but appeared for the first time in the collection *Penembak misterius*.

92. Ajidarma, *Mysterious Marksman*, 78.

93. Ajidarma, *Mysterious Marksman*, 80.

94. Ajidarma, *Mysterious Marksman*, 83.

95. Ajidarma, *Mysterious Marksman*, 84.

96. The emptiness of the New Order values is taken up more specifically in different stories. In one story, all that remains of family bonds and affection is to care for a potted jasmine plant that is handed down in the fragmented, but wealthy, family. Caring for the potted plant is the only meaningful and connecting activity. No one remembers why the plant is important.

97. Ryter, "Pemuda Pancasila," 64–70.

98. Ryter, "Pemuda Pancasila," 67.

99. Ryter, "Pemuda Pancasila," 68–69.

100. Bakker, "Organized Violence," 260.

101. For example, a history seminar organized by 1965 victims on September 17, 2017, was attacked. See "Buntut Seminar 1965," *Tempo*, September 17, 2017.

102. Wilson, *Politics of Protection Rackets*.

3. RESIST FORGETTING

1. McCoy, *Scandal and Democracy*.

2. Ashadi Siregar, quoted in McCoy, *Scandal and Democracy*, 71.

3. Lee, *Activist Archives*, chap. 1.

4. Lee, *Activist Archives*, chap. 1.

5. Komisi Penyelidik National (National Commission of Inquiry) and Dewan Kehormatan Militer (Council of Military Honor).

6. The Council of Military Honor report led to the disciplining, transfer, dismissal, or prosecution of nineteen officers. Of those prosecuted, the longest sentence was eighteen months for shooting into a crowd. Those who were responsible for killings after the demonstration, as well as for the cover-up of the incident, were not prosecuted. See Asia Watch, "East Timor: Asia Watch Criticizes Commission Report" and Asia Watch, "East Timor: The Courts Martial."

7. Aspinall, "Students and the Military," 36.

8. It indicated that unauthorized agencies had been involved in the case, that the Criminal Procedure Code (Kitab Undang-Undang Hukum Acara Pidana) had been violated in many ways, including failing to provide suspects lawyers, that there was evidence

of physical and psychological torture that violated the Criminal Code (Kitab Undang-Undang Hukum Pidana), and finally that there might be other (military) suspects involved. In retaliation, the military banned commissioners from speaking at an event in East Java, citing their lack of a permit.

9. In January 1994, the decree authorizing military interference in labor disputes was repealed, but in practice the military continued its interventions. During this period there were numerous cases demonstrating that Indonesian workers were denied the right to free association. The infrastructure of policies and regulations does not allow for resolution of labor concerns in contexts other than public demonstrations, which are often met with violence by the security forces.

10. Jones and McClintock, *Limits of Openness*, 4.

11. Lee, *Activist Archives*.

12. Lee, *Activist Archives*, 89–95.

13. Personal observation of multiple discussions in 1998.

14. These commodities are rice, sugar, cooking oil and margarine, chicken and beef, chicken eggs, milk, corn, iodized salt, and kerosene.

15. McCoy, *Scandal and Democracy*, 73–74.

16. For discussion of these cases, see Davidson, *From Rebellion to Riots*; Duncan, *Violence and Vengeance*.

17. Drexler, *Aceh, Indonesia*.

18. McCoy, *Scandal and Democracy*, 88–90, provides several examples.

19. The armed forces' name was changed to TNI (Tentara Nasional Indonesia) from ABRI (Angkatan Bersenjata Republik Indonesia) in 1999 to reflect the separation of the armed forces and the police.

20. "Akhirnya, pemerintah tunda RUU PKB," *Kompas* (Jakarta), September 25, 1999.

21. While East Timor was an important issue, Habibie had also failed to demonstrate sufficient effort in holding Suharto accountable for graft. For details of the politics behind Habibie's downfall, see Jeremy Wagstaff, "Dark before Dawn: How Elite Made a Deal before Indonesia Woke Up," *Wall Street Journal*, November 2, 1999; for a review of the role of scandal in reformasi, see McCoy, *Scandal and Democracy*.

22. Lee, *Activist Archives*, 25–29.

23. For an excellent overview of legal developments related to transitional justice, see Wahyuningroem, *Transitional Justice*.

24. The capitalized *S* at the end of the name is deliberate. Some say that it was a reference to Suharto and their opposition to him. Different dates are remembered for KontraS's founding. Usman Hamid notes that it was made public in *Kompas* on April 16, 1998.

25. The formal document establishing KontraS was signed by Munir (YLBHI), M. M. Billah (CPSM), Lukas Loewarso (AJI), Abdul Hakim GN (ELSAM), H. J. Princen (LPHAM), Toeti Herati, Franz Magnis Suseno, Ade Rostina Sitompul, Todung Mulya Lubis, Ibrahim Gibrah Zakir, Trimulja D. Soerjadi, Eros Djarot, Karlina Supelli, Hermawan Soelistyo, Mulyana W. Kusuma (KIPP), and NU's student organization Persatuan Mahasiswa Islam Indonesia (PMII), represented by Chatibul Umam Wiranu. Usman Hamid, "Merosotnya demokrasi, hak asasi dan lahirnya gerakan korban di Indonesia: Reformasi dan legacy dua dasawarsa KontraS."

26. ELSAM, *Pulangkan mereka*.

27. Dempster, *Transitional Justice*, 25. For further discussion on the politics and harms of disappearance, see De Alwis, "'Disappearance' and 'Displacement'"; and Robins, "Victim-Centred Transitional Justice."

28. Hamid, "Merosotnya demokrasi," 16.

29. Hamid, "Merosotnya demokrasi," 16.

30. Eklöf, *Power and Political Culture*.

31. In April 1998, the badly damaged corpse of one was found.

32. Quoted in Hamid, "Merosotnya demokrasi," 28.

33. Quoted in Panggabean, *Keberanian bernama Munir*, 71.

34. Quoted in Panggabean, *Keberanian bernama Munir*, 72.

35. Hamid, "Merosotnya demokrasi," 32.

36. Interview by the author, Jakarta, August 27, 2015.

37. Muchdi was later tried for his implication in Munir's murder. "KontraS akan gugat panglima TNI dalam kasus penculikan," *Kompas*, August 2, 1999.

38. Armed Forces of the Republic of Indonesia Headquarters, Military Court (Markas Besar Angkatan Bersenjata Republik Indonesia, MABES ABRI, Mahkamah Militer).

39. "Penculikan untuk pertahankan 'status quo.'" *Kompas*, December 23, 1998.

40. "Penculikan untuk pertahankan 'status quo.'"

41. "Dakwaan oditur kecewakan korban penculikan," *Kompas*, December 24, 1998.

42. "Dakwaan oditur kecewakan korban penculikan."

43. "Dakwaan oditur kecewakan korban penculikan."

44. "Dakwaan oditur kecewakan korban penculikan."

45. "Selidiki ulang kasus penculikan," *Kompas*, April 8, 1999.

46. "Selidiki ulang kasus penculikan."

47. "Selidiki ulang kasus penculikan."

48. Indonesia's opening came later than that of most countries in Latin America, but the international human rights toolkit was nevertheless widely known, and gathering data for future investigations and transitional justice processes was key to the promise of justice in the future. There have been very few found caches of documents such as the case described by Kirsten Weld in *Paper Cadavers*. See also Dawes, *World May Know*; Neier, *International Human Rights Movement*.

49. Keenan, "Mobilizing Shame."

50. The antisubversion law (Presidential Decree No. 11/1963) was established by Sukarno prior to the mass killings and was frequently used by the Suharto regime. In addition, the *haatzaaiartikelen*, or Articles 154–56 of the criminal code against "sowing hatred," were deployed against free speech and protest of the government. In later years, these articles were also invoked to punish blasphemy. Additional articles also punish insults to the president or vice president (Article 134), public insults to government authorities (Article 207), and incitement of violence or disobedience (Article 160). The articles are vague and have been invoked against critics.

51. Lev, "Between State and Society."

52. Nusantara, *Politik hukum Indonesia*, 19.

53. Widjojanto, "Seandainya hukum gagal."

54. In one example, a poem by the activist Beathor Suryadi uses the lowering informal form of "you" to address Suharto. See Lee, *Activist Archives*, 27.

55. Currently these groups often refer to themselves as civil society organizations (CSOs), but at the time, the terms *nongovernmental organizations* (NGOs) or LSM (*lembaga swadaya masyarakat*) were more widely used.

56. Further complicating the investigations was the narrow definitions of rape and of evidence for it under Indonesian law. See Strassler, "Gendered Visibilities."

57. Purdey, "Problematizing," 606.

58. Strassler, "Gendered Visibilities," 714.

59. Purdey, "Problematizing," 611.

60. TGPF, *Laporan akhir*, executive summary, 24.

61. "MENNEG UPW: Belum ada data akurat tentang pemerkosaan," *Kompas*, June 14, 1998; "Menperta tentang berita perkosaan: Kami sangat peduli," *Kompas*, June 28, 1998; "Data korban perkosaan masih misterius," *Republika* (Jakarta), August 22, 1998.

62. Coomaraswamy, *Report of the Special Rapporteur*. The document has also been translated into Indonesian and is available from Komnas Perempuan as part of their series of "key documents."

63. Presidential statement by B. J. Habibie on July 15, 1998, reproduced in Sadli, *Saatnya meneguhkan rasa aman*, 30.

64. As the news of the sexual violence spread and was increasingly denied and doubted in the media by the military and others, a consortium of women in civil society lobbied for a meeting with President Habibie to convince him that the rapes had occurred and that it was sound and accepted practice internationally to not insist that victims testify in public. In October 1998, Habibie established the National Commission on Violence against Women, which has worked to support the victims of May violence, to advocate for changes in legislation and institutions to support victims of sexual violence, and to ensure that international mandates that Indonesia has signed are effectively implemented. While it does not handle individual cases, it reviews past cases, especially the May rapes, and evaluates the progress that has or has not been made on the recommendations from the commission. It was established with Presidential Decree No. 181/1998 and renewed through Presidential Decree No. 65/2005.

65. Sadli, *Saatnya meneguhkan rasa aman*.

66. Strassler, "Gendered Visibilities," 702.

67. Lawmakers recognizing the popular support for reform passed significant legislation to create a strong human rights framework, including ratifying conventions that protected freedom of association and the right to organize. Previously ratified conventions were strengthened with the adoption of optional protocols (the Convention on the Elimination of All Forms of Discrimination against Women and the Convention on the Rights of the Child). In addition, legislators seeking to establish their distance from the past also ratified the Convention against Torture and Other Cruel, Inhuman or Degrading Treatment or Punishment; the International Covenant on Economic, Social and Cultural Rights, with the note that the right to self-determination did not apply to peoples living in a sovereign nation; the International Covenant on Civil and Political Rights, excluding the optional protocols that would allow for investigation of complaints and abolishing the death penalty; the Convention on the Rights of Persons with Disabilities; and the Convention on the Elimination of All Forms of Racial Discrimination. In addition, child protection, domestic violence, disability, and antidiscrimination laws were enacted and supported by establishing commissions on violence against women as well as child protection. For a reflection on these, see Susanti, "Constitution and Human Rights Provisions."

68. Clause 104 of Law 39/1999 defines gross violations of human rights as mass murder (genocide), arbitrary or extrajudicial killing, torture, forced disappearance, slavery, and systematic discrimination. See ICG, *Indonesia*, 13.

69. Butt and Lindsey, *Indonesian Law*, 253. For an earlier discussion of tensions on the issue of nonretroactivity, see ICG, *Indonesia*.

70. Stockmann, *Indonesian Reformasi*; Butt and Parsons. "Judicial Review."

71. Butt and Lindsey, *Indonesian Law*, 255.

72. Butt and Lindsey, *Indonesian Law*, 260.

73. Wahyuningroem, *Transitional Justice*, 164.

74. KPP HAM Timor Timur, *Executive Summary Report*.

75. Confidential interviews by the author.

76. KPP HAM Timor Timur, *Executive Summary Report*.

77. ELSAM, *Failure of Leipzig*.

78. Cohen, *Intended to Fail*.

79. Cohen, *Intended to Fail*, 12–14.

80. Drexler, "Failure of International Justice."

81. Cohen, *Intended to Fail*, 15.

82. The major general was Adam Damiri. Cohen, "Seeking Justice on the Cheap," 14.

83. The Islamic Defenders Front (Front Pembela Islam) was a paramilitary group that evolved out of the voluntary troops Wiranto had organized to defend the extraordinary sessions of parliament, known as *pamswakarsa*.

84. The minister of law and legislation and chairman of the Muslim Crescent and Star Party, Yusril Ihza Mahendra, accused Komnas HAM of applying double standards. ICG, *Indonesia*, 9.

85. "Jenazah Munir dipulangkan secepatnya," *Kompas*, September 9, 2004; "Pemerintah harus beri penghargaan untuk Munir," *Republika*, September 14, 2004; "Mahkamah Konstitusi nilai Munir layak dapat Bintang Jasa," *Media Indonesia* (Jakarta), September 14, 2004; "Jenazah Munir Sabtu sore tiba, Pemerintah layak beri penghargaan," *Kompas*, September 11, 2004.

86. For example, Todung Mulya Lubis, a senior human rights advocate, stated that "the sharp criticisms put forth by the deceased, both directed to the government and to TNI, caused him to be accused as a person who was not nationalist or, even more dangerously, 'selling out' the state [*'menjual' negara*]. I know who Munir was, I know that his struggle did not know limits of race, ethnicity, religion, or gender, to the point that that accusation is mistaken [*salah kaprah*]." Quoted in Partogi et al., *Bunuh Munir*, 41.

87. Partogi et al., *Bunuh Munir*, 127.

88. Presidential Decree 111/2004, regarding the formation of a Fact-Finding Team for the Munir Case (Keputusan Presiden [Keppres] No. 111 tentang Pembentukan Tim Pencari Fakta Kasus Munir), December 23, 2004.

89. The term used, NKRI (Negara Kesatuan Republik Indonesia), refers to the unitary state of Indonesia projected back to the founding constitution. "NKRI Harga Mati" (Live or die for NKRI) is a slogan often used to provoke violence toward those who question the centralized (as opposed to federalist) state, especially in East Timor and more recently in Papua. See Krisnamughni, "Nationalism Failure, NKRI Harga Mati, & the Land of Papua," Medium, June 13, 2020, https://medium.com/@krisnamughni24/nationalism-failure-nkri-harga-mati-the-land-of-papua-30ea28d0b61f.

90. Usman Hamid and Rachland Nashidik were the members of the fact-finding team who were investigated by the police for defamation.

91. *Laporan akhir*. This was the final report of the fact-finding team investigating Munir's death.

92. Arbi Sumandoyo, "Jejak pembunuhan Munir dan 'Ikan Besar' di Singapura," Tirto.id, October 17, 2016, https://tirto.id/jejak-pembunuhan-munir-dan-ikan-besar-di-singapura-bUWg.

93. "Wiranto sebut tidak mudah."

94. "Wiranto sebut tidak mudah."

95. "15 Tahun pembunuhan Munir 'Membongkar pemufakatan jahat pembunuhan berencana terhadap Munir,'" KontraS press release, September 11, 2019, https://kontras.org/2019/09/11/15-tahun-pembunuhan-munir-aeoemembongkar-pemufakatan-jahat-pembunuhan-berencana-terhadap-munirae%C2%9D/.

96. "15 Tahun pembunuhan Munir."

97. The report is TGPF, *Laporan akhir*.

4. NARRATING WHAT IS KNOWN

1. Manneke Budiman, "An Introduction to the Literature of Indonesia, 2015 Frankfurt Book Fair's Guest of Honour," The Conversation, October 13, 2015, https://theconversation.com/an-introduction-to-the-literature-of-indonesia-2015-frankfurt-book-fairs-guest-of-honour-47274.

2. "Indonesian Writers' Festival Forced to Cancel Events Linked to 1965 Massacre," *Guardian* (US edition) October 23, 2015.

3. "Festival Belok Kiri dilarang."

4. Rekoleksi Memori: Museum Temporer, December 7–12, 2015, Taman Ismail Marzuki, Jakarta. The temporary museum was supported by the National Human Rights Commission and civil society groups that were involved in a wide range of initiatives related to past cases.

5. Ati Nurbaiti, "May 1998 Monument Hailed as a 'Sign of State Responsibility,'" *Jakarta Post*, May 15, 2015.

6. For a discussion of this process, see Robet, *Politik hak asasi*; Wahyuningroem, *Transitional Justice*.

7. Aceh has a separate Truth and Reconciliation Commission, as provided by the law on governing Aceh negotiated as part of the Peace Agreement. Wiratraman et al., "Taking Policy Seriously," 27.

8. The younger sister of the director of the KKPK worked on the Commission for Reception, Truth, and Reconciliation in East Timor (CAVR). Initially the term *victim* was widely used, but I began to hear the word *survivor* in 2014 and after. The PRD activists who were kidnapped did not use this term to refer to their case.

9. Pohlman, "Year of Truth."

10. Wahyuningroem, "Seducing for Truth and Justice."

11. KKPK, *Menemukan kembali Indonesia*.

12. KKPK, *Menemukan kembali Indonesia*.

13. Galuh Wandita, interview by the author, Jakarta, August 20, 2015.

14. Wandita, interview.

15. One such institution was the Institution for the Protection of Witness and Victims (Lembaga Perlindungan Saksi dan Korban).

16. Interviews by the author, Jakarta, August 2015.

17. Oppenheimer's subsequent film, *The Look of Silence* (2014), highlighted the experience of victims as they navigated living alongside perpetrators. It was screened in various public contexts but was not as significant in shifting public attitudes.

18. Intan Paramaditha points to the global power relations inherent in crediting Oppenheimer with "(re)discovery" of "secrets" of violence in Indonesia, noting how this framing obscures frictions and dissonances in post-Suharto Indonesia. Paramaditha, "Narratives of Discovery." See also Roosa, "State of Knowledge."

19. See, for example, special issues of *Critical Asian Studies* in 2014.

20. On the absence of the army, see Cribb, "Act of Killing"; Hearman, "Missing Victims." On misinterpretation, see Roosa, "Who Knows?"

21. Ariel Heryanto argues that this criticism is misplaced and that the film cannot show everything. Heryanto, "Great and Misplaced Expectations."

22. Morris, "Murders of Gonzago."

23. "Academic Responsibility and Past Human Rights Violations," panel discussion moderated by the author, Department of Anthropology, University of Indonesia and American Indonesian Exchange Foundation, May 27, 2016.

24. Some analysts have pointed to Anwar's performance of remorse as part of what convinces them that the film is ethical. See van Klinken, "*Act of Killing* Is Not Unethical." For Oppenheimer's response to this issue, see Morris, "Murders of Gonzago."

25. Paramaditha, "Tracing Frictions."

26. In October 2012, *Tempo* did a seventy-two-page special report from the perspective of perpetrators, with corroborating evidence and fact checking sources, titled "Algojo"; Tyson, "Multiple Acts of Killing," reflects on these reports and their relationship to the film.

27. Paramaditha, "Tracing Frictions," 47.

28. Paramaditha, "Tracing Frictions," 49.

29. Tyson notes that while the connections to the current middle class and elite are apparent in the film, the tone and representation do not invite reflection. Tyson, "Multiple Acts of Killing."

30. Paramaditha, "Tracing Frictions," 46.

31. On youth attention, see Paramaditha, "Tracing Frictions," 47. The state apparatus failed to protect screenings from disturbances by social organizations in some cases.

32. "Algojo." See also Heryanto, "Great and Misplaced Expectations."

33. Paramaditha, "Tracing Frictions," 47.

34. Wandita, in "*PREMAN* Nation," notes that watching *The Act of Killing* was difficult for victims, but in one analysis of responses from children of 1965 victims living in exile, it also "produced an affective atmosphere capable of evoking embodied memories of intergenerational experiences of historical violence." Dragojlovic, "Violent Histories," 271.

35. Examples of this type of film include Robert Lemelson's *Forty Years of Silence* (2009) and Lexy Rambadeta's *Mass Grave* (2001).

36. International People's Tribunals are community initiatives that review evidence of past violence in a fashion similar to formal courts but outside mechanisms of state governments or international institutions such as the UN. As the IPT notes on its website, "Its authority comes from the voices of the victims, as well as that of civil society, both national and international." "F.A.Q.," International People's Tribunal 1965, accessed March 31, 2023, https://www.tribunal1965.org/en/faq/. For scholarly discussion of recent tribunals, see Zunino, "Subversive Justice."

37. Wieringa, Melvin, and Pohlman, *International People's Tribunal*, 3. Scholars and advocates were commissioned to prepare reports based on archival materials and scholarly analysis as well as testimonies. The Indonesian human rights lawyer Todung Mulya Lubis and a team of Indonesian legal activists then prepared an indictment for the hearings. At the same time, members of the IPT team worked to prepare victims for traveling to the Netherlands to give their testimony. A panel of seven international legal experts was convened to judge the tribunal. See IPT 1965, *Final Report*, 1.

38. *Surat dari Praha* (Letter from Prague) (2016) was directed by Angga Dwimas Sasongko and written by Mohammad Irfan Ramly. See also Aleida, *Tanah air yang hilang*.

39. "Kisah Tom Iljas."

40. Muhyiddin, "Taufik Ismail: PKI memang sudah tidak ada, tapi PKI bangkit," *Republika* (Jakarta), March 7, 2018, https://www.republika.co.id/berita/p56kpr396/taufik-ismail-pki-memang-sudah-tidak-ada-tapi-pki-bangkit.

41. The Indonesian political scientist Sri Lestari Wahyuningroem describes similar victims' organizations in Java and Sulawesi and contextualizes their work within local politics and past variations in patterns of violence. Wahyuningroem, "Working from the Margins."

42. For further analysis of sexual violence as crimes against humanity, see Pohlman, "Two Women's Testimonies."

43. Documents related to the Komando Operasi Pemulihan Keamanan dan Ketertiban (Operational Command for the Restoration of Security and Order), IPT researcher, interview by the author, January 7, 2016.

44. Melvin, *Army and the Indonesian Genocide*.

45. Linton, "Accounting for Atrocities," 225. Wandita, Fernida, and Campbell-Nelson, "Mass Torture in 1965–66," notes that as important as the genocide ruling was, systematic torture was particularly devastating and extended intergenerationally. ELSAM, *Pulangkan mereka*, found that forced disappearances in 1965 and after were likewise systematic and damaging.

46. Luhut Panjaitan, coordinating minister for political, legal, and security affairs, quoted in Juliet Perry, "Tribunal Finds Indonesia Guilty of 1965 Genocide; US, UK

Complicit," CNN, July 21, 2016, https://www.cnn.com/2016/07/21/asia/indonesia-genocide-panel. For a detailed account of state reactions to the IPT, see Santoso and van Klinken, "Genocide."

47. There were smaller art exhibits and historical reenactments done on many campuses, as well as other films, including *Buru tanah air beta* (Buru, my homeland).

48. Sutojo, *Kenangan tak terucap.*

49. Comissão Verdade e Amizade, or the Indonesia–Timor Leste Commission for Truth and Friendship, was established jointly by the governments of Indonesia and Timor Leste in August 2005 and after three years produced a final report (*Per memoriam ad spem* [Through memory to hope], available at http://www.chegareport.org/profil-of-ctf/). Similar to the symposium, the commission was designed to review existing evidence from Indonesia's Human Rights Commission's investigations, the CAVR, the Jakarta ad hoc Human Rights Tribunals, and the UN-supported hybrid tribunals (the Special Panels for Serious Crimes in Timor Leste). In addition, it heard from select witnesses. Critics feared the commission existed only to exercise its power to clear the names of those wrongfully accused and grant amnesty to perpetrators, but it did not use those two powers and focused on issues of institutional responsibility.

50. The organization was originally named Forum Silaturahmi Anak Bangsa; the name was changed to Forum Solidaritas Anak Bangsa and the acronym remained FSAB.

51. Danusubroto, Simanjuntak, and Tarigan, *Bicara dengan sejarah*; Danusubruto, *80 tahun Sidarto Danusubroto*; and Danusubroto and Adam, *Memoar Sidarto Danusubroto.*

52. "Kerangka Acuan," 1.

53. "Kerangka Acuan," 1.

54. "Kerangka Acuan," 2.

55. "Kerangka Acuan," 2.

56. "Kerangka Acuan," 2.

57. "Kerangka Acuan," 2.

58. "Kerangka Acuan," 3.

59. This same logic is deployed in discussions of cases where religious and sexual minorities are attacked.

60. "Kerangka Acuan," 3.

61. This is a contentious issue. At a press conference sponsored by the KKPK, Usman Hamid, longtime KontraS coordinator, student activist during reformasi, and current head of Amnesty International Indonesia, shared that his father was born in 1918 and had been a local religious leader. When Hamid began to work with victims, including those from the 1965 case at KontraS in the early 2000s, his mother had reminded him that his father's life had been threatened and asked how he could be doing this work. His siblings were similarly shocked, but he kept on and eventually they accepted it. He emphasized that the PKI had done bad things and been violent prior to the genocide, but that did not mean that they should have been killed. He emphasized that people needed to understand that it was wrong that the actions of some PKI were used as a justification for further violence. He was one of the few people to make this statement so clearly and did so on a panel with Imam Aziz, then the head of the Nahdlatul Ulama, one of the largest Muslim organizations in Indonesia, whose youth wing was mobilized to participate in the killings.

62. Observation at the symposium; also quoted in CNN Indonesia live updates: "We will not apologise. We are not that stupid. We know what we did, and it was the right thing to do for the nation." "Live National Symposium on the 1965 Tragedy Updates," CNN Indonesia, April 16, 2016, https://www.cnnindonesia.com/nasional/20160418085757-20-124594/live-simposium-nasional-tragedi-1965.

63. Wieringa and Katjasungkana, *Propaganda*, 93.

64. Herlambang, *Kekerasan Budaya Pasca 1965.*

65. "Jokowi perintahkan Luhut cari kuburan massal korban peristiwa 1965," *Kompas* (Jakarta), April 25, 2016, https://nasional.kompas.com/read/2016/04/25/11502191/Jokowi.Perintahkan.Luhut.Cari.Kuburan.Massal.Korban.1965.

66. "Komnas HAM diminta bentuk satgas untuk kumpulkan data kuburan massal Tragedi 1965," *Kompas*, May 2, 2016. https://nasional.kompas.com/read/2016/05/02/19164231/Komnas.HAM.Diminta.Bentuk.Satgas.untuk.Kumpulkan.Data.Kuburan.Massal.Tragedi.1965.

67. Febriana Firdaus, "Bagaimana nasib rekomendasi Simposium 1965 pasca acara tandingan?," *Rappler*, June 2, 2016, https://www.rappler.com/world/indonesia/135037-bagaimana-nasib-rekomendasi-pasca-simposium-tandingan/.

68. Febriana Firdaus, "Symposium tanding 1965 fokus kritisi kebangkitan PKI," *Rappler*, May 30, 2016, https://www.rappler.com/world/simposium-tandingan-fokus-kritisi-kebangkitan-pki.

69. Firdaus, "Bagaimana nasib."

70. "Ini sembilan rekomendasi dari symposium anti PKI," *Kompas*, June 2, 2016, https://nasional.kompas.com/read/2016/06/02/17575451/ini.sembilan.rekomendasi.dari.simposium.anti.pki.

71. Sidarto Danusubroto (Anggota Dewan Pertimbangan Presiden), "Refleksi Simposium Nasional Membedah Tragedi 65: Pendekatan Kesejarahan," Jakarta, April 18–19, 2016. Document read at the symposium; copy in the author's possession.

5. LAW WITHOUT JUSTICE

1. Latour, *Down to Earth*, 23.

2. For a detailed review of the KPK and associated institutions, see Butt, *Corruption and Law*.

3. The individuals worked at organizations including PSHK (Pusat Studi Hukum dan Kebijakan Indonesia), LeIP (Lembaga kajian dan advokasi Independensi Peradilan), LBH Jakarta (Lembaga Bantuan Hukum Jakarta), MAPPI UI (Masyarakat Pemantau Peradilan Indonesia Universitas Indonesia), YLBHI (Yayasan Lembaga Bantuan Hukum Indonesia), KPA (Konsorsium Pembaruan Agraria), LBH Masyarakat (Lembaga Bantuan Hukum Masyarakat), KontraS (Komisi untuk Orang Hilang dan Tindak Kekerasaan), WALHI (Wahana Lingkungan Indonesia).

4. All of the organizations represented in the group conducted legal and policy-based analysis as well as campaigned for raising public awareness. Two of the organizations were based only in the capital city and were research and policy oriented; the balance of the organizations had branches located across Indonesia. The legal aid organizations provided legal services to numerous clients, and the environmental, agrarian, and human rights organizations all documented numerous cases of violations of various rights by the state apparatus.

5. "Ungkap rekayasa kasus Bibit-Chandra, MK beber rekaman pembicaraan," *Jawa Pos* (Surabaya), November 2, 2009.

6. KontraS et al., "Kriminalisasi," 8.

7. PSHK et al., *Kriminalisasi*, 3.

8. KontraS et al., "Kriminalisasi," 4.

9. KontraS et al., "Kriminalisasi," 6.

10. KontraS et al., "Kriminalisasi," 35.

11. Larkin, "Politics and Poetics," 329.

12. On haunting, see Gordon, *Ghostly Matters*; and Sharpe, *In the Wake*. Kriminalisasi resonates with anthropological analyses of criminalization that map how states and power holders have defined particular groups and/or practices as criminal. For works that

point to how structural and political conditions rather than intent have prompted criminal behavior, as well as works that indicate the ambiguous relationships between states
and criminality, see Bourgois, *In Search of Respect*; Comaroff and Comaroff, *Truth about
Crime*; Barker, "State of Fear."

13. Legal aid workers drew on cases from fair trial advocacy, and in legal aid trainings
they discussed the problem of kriminalisasi as linked to the importance of the right to a
fair trial for all. Nevertheless, the group framed the issue as a problem not of the presumption of guilt of the suspect, but of the malicious use of law enforcement.

14. On the problem of strategies highlighting the innocence of victims, see Ralph,
Torture Letters, 22.

15. International media also used the term "presumption of guilt": for example, Australian media said that Indonesia had a presumption of guilt in reference to the case of
Corby Schapelle, an Australian woman arrested and imprisoned for smuggling marijuana
into Bali. Lindsey and Butt, *Indonesian Law*, 239, analyze this case and argue that the
Indonesian legal system does recognize the presumption of innocence.

16. Derrida, "Force of Law."

17. Asad, *On Suicide Bombing*.

18. Comaroff and Comaroff, "Law and Disorder," 30.

19. Telle, "Faith on Trial."

20. Clarke, *Fictions of Justice*.

21. Sharma, "New Brooms and Old," S81.

22. The annual program is called Kalabahu.

23. The Legal Aid Foundation has a tradition of "structural legal aid," addressing
problems beyond the individual case, and this exercise was designed to help the students
move from casework to structural analysis and advocacy.

24. The sessions took place in Jakarta on April 12, 2016.

25. The "Grounding Democracy" series of discussions followed the series of Belok Kiri
festival events and was in response to increasing encroachments on democracy perceived
by the activists, including the use of mass or social organizations and vigilantism to shut
down discussions and forums related to 1965.

26. For a longer discussion of the possibility of a pretrial mechanism in Widjojanto's
case, which reflects much of what this activist explained, see Lindsey and Butt, *Indonesian
Law*, 297.

27. Hamid, Birks, and Indriansyah, *Protection of Social Justice Leaders*, 22.

28. Hamid, Birks, and Indriansyah, *Protection of Social Justice Leaders*, 41.

6. THE RED THREAD

1. On April 13, 2023, Aksi Kamisan number 771 took place in Jakarta. A livestreamed
video of the action can be seen at Jakartanicus, "Live on Location: Aksi Kamisan 771—
Greenpeace & TrendAsia," YouTube video, April 13, 2023, https://www.youtube.com/
watch?v=J1r67dNsbx0. On the sixteen-year anniversary (or 760 actions) of the first
Kamisan action in Jakarta, *Kompas* featured a series of infographics that documented
the number of letters sent and the sixty sites to which Kamisan actions have spread.
"Aksi Diam yang menuntut pemerintah tidak diam," *Kompas interaktif*, January 19, 2023,
https://interaktif.kompas.id/baca/aksi-diam-yang-menuntut-pemerintah-tidak-diam/.
According to unpublished documents from Amnesty International Indonesia, a total of
1,961 Kamisan actions had taken place across these sites as of January 2019.

2. On youth activism and place, see Kurze, "#WarCrimes #PostConflictJustice
#Balkans."

3. Kurze and Lamont, *New Critical Spaces*; Murphy, *Mapping Memory*.

4. Kurnia Sari Aziza, "Ahok keluarkan Pergub, Demo di Jakarta hanya bisa di tiga lokasi ini," *Kompas* (Jakarta), October 30, 2015, https://megapolitan.kompas.com/read/2015/10/30/09290341/Ahok.Keluarkan.Pergub.Demo.di.Jakarta.Hanya.Bisa.di.Tiga.Lokasi.Ini?page=all.

5. Cole, *Afterlives of Injustice*, 219–20.

6. Sumarsih coordinates Jaringan Solidaritas Keluarga Korban (Solidarity Network for the Families of Victims) with support from various civil society organizations, including KontraS, LBH Jakarta, and Amnesty International Indonesia.

7. This discussion draws on multiple interviews from 2014 through 2017.

8. The National Human Rights Commission (Komnas HAM) determined that Trisakti (May 12, 1998, when police snipers opened fire on demonstrators, killing four inside the campus), Semanggi 1 (November 13–14, 1998, when seventeen people, including students, were killed by the security forces during protests over the Special Parliamentary Session related to the transition of power), and Semanggi 2 (September 23–24, 1999, when twelve civilians were killed as they protested the state security bill) together represented a gross violation of human rights. Komnas HAM concluded that systematic killing over a long period of time, persecution to break up demonstrations (including tear gas, kicking, hitting, shooting, and bites from tracking dogs), rape and sexual violence, forced disappearances, and restrictions to freedom of movement occurred because of policies regarding how to handle demonstrations. Komnas HAM, *Ringkasan eksekutif*, 334–35.

9. Between 1998 and 2003 there were military tribunals for individual incidents focused on low-ranking soldiers.

10. In January 2020, the attorney general stated to the legislature that Semanggi 1 and Semanggi 2 did not qualify as gross violations of human rights. According to Komnas HAM, the attorney general had failed in his investigative responsibilities and had obstructed the case. In a case brought by Sumarsih and other family members, the administrative court (Pengadilan Tata Usaha Negara) in Jakarta ruled that his statement was in violation of the law. The attorney general, however, immediately appealed this decision, and the Supreme Court ruled in his favor, against the victims' families, thus foreclosing all paths to a judicial solution through an ad hoc tribunal for gross violations of human rights.

11. The claims made for art processes that focus on local participation and engagement include their ability to "contribute to individualized and collective healing, make the invisible visible, extend social responsibility, restore collective memory, repair the social fabric, reclaim truths and foster collective change." Shefik, "Reimagining Transitional Justice," 314. In addition, artistic processes address temporal complexity and "how the past is recalled in the future." McLeod, Dimitrijcvic, and Rakocevic, "Artistic Activism," 25.

12. Wiranto served as coordinating minister following the National Symposium (July 27, 2016 –October 20, 2019), and in December 2019 he was appointed head of the Presidential Advisory Council. In March 1998, Suharto appointed him minister of defense, a position he held until October 1999. He has been investigated by the UN for his role in facilitating violence in East Timor during the referendum vote; in addition, he was allegedly implicated in human rights violations that occurred during the transition and other violations in Aceh.

13. Jokowi's victory over Prabowo in 2014 was interpreted as a vote for his campaign promise to resolve the past. Activists focused on the past were bitterly divided by their rematch in the 2019 election; while the elite consolidated, civil society remained fragmented.

14. Larasati, *Dance That Makes You Vanish*.

15. The "trade" involves not pursuing accountability and giving perpetrators key positions in the state apparatus, where they can block or selectively implement policies. But

the trade is also literal, because in many cases the infrastructure and extractive development have displaced the urban poor, overridden indigenous rights to territories, criminalized and attacked environmental advocates, and ignored military violence in Papua, where an estimated sixty to one hundred thousand people are displaced due to violence, according to the UN. United Nations Human Rights, Office of the High Commissioner, "Indonesia: UN Experts Sound Alarm on Serious Papua Abuses, Call for Urgent Aid," press release, March, 1, 2022.

16. Fabian Januarius Kuwado, "Photos and Videos: Aksi Kamisan ke 500 masih menagih janji Jokowi," *Kompas*, July 27, 2017, https://nasional.kompas.com/read/2017/07/27/20332441/berita-foto-dan-video—aksi-kamisan-ke-500-masih-menagih-janji-jokowi.

17. Lee, *Activist Archives*, 11.

18. Graphic produced for Aksi Kamisan in Bandung, number 215.

19. Murphy, *Mapping Memory*, 8.

20. Kamisan 603, September 26, 2019.

21. Prabowo was also indicted by Interpol for war crimes in East Timor in 1999.

22. Kamisan 602, September 19, 2019.

23. Graphics for Kamisan 611 (November 21, 2019) featured two photos, both with the coordinating political, legal and security affairs minister, Mohammad Mahfud, MD, who was charged with coordinating the response for past cases. In the top image he was pictured with Prabowo. In the bottom image, he shook hands with his predecessor in the security post, Wiranto, who had been promoted to head of the Presidential Advisory Council (Dewan Pertimbangan Presiden, or Wantimpres) for the term of 2019–24.

24. Kamisan 502, August 10, 2017.

25. The original text uses ABRI and follows with the acronyms TNI and POLRI to emphasize that this includes the Indonesian National Armed Forces and the Indonesian National Police.

26. The cases included the May 1998 Riots (Kerusuhan Mei 1998), Trisakti-Semanggi 1 and 2, forced disappearances (*penghilangan paksa*), Talangsari 1989, mysterious killings (*penembakan misterius*) 1982–85, the events of 1965–66 (Peristiwa 1965–66), and recent cases after reformasi, including the Papua 2001 case (Peristiwa Papua 2001, listed here by its geographic sites, Wasior Wamena), and the KKA intersection in Aceh case (Kasus Simpang KKA-Aceh).

27. Slater, "Party Cartelization, Indonesian-Style," 26.

28. As this book was going into production, the infrastructure of impunity gained another element. In his annual speech to the legislature on August 16, 2022, President Jokowi announced that he had signed a presidential decree (Keppres 17/2022) creating a Team for the Non-judicial Resolution of Past Gross Violations of Human Rights (Tim Penyelesaian Non-Yudisial Pelanggaran HAM Berat Masa Lalu). Details of the team were publicized in September, and the team was given a mandate to work until the end of 2022. The members of the implementation team included two human rights figures who had worked in government for many years, as well as cabinet ministers and military figures. Their tasks were to reveal and analyze the facts of the past cases based on the data and recommendations from Komnas HAM; suggest steps for healing (*pemulihan*) victims and/or their families; suggest recommendations for preventing similar human rights violations from occurring in the future; and finally to create a final report. Activists including Sumarsih, Suciwati, and other Kamisan regulars, as well as the Indonesian Legal Aid Foundation (YLBHI) and multiple branches of the Legal Aid Institute (LBH) from across Indonesia, have demanded that the decree be revoked, calling it an "illusion," "empty rhetoric," and nothing more than a "facade" for the Jokowi government to appear as if it had fulfilled its promises while in fact it had provided impunity for the perpetrators. (YLBHI,

"Tanpa proses hukum dan tindakan konkrit, pengakuan dan penyesalan presiden sekedar retorika dan ilusi," press release, January 12, 2023, https://ylbhi.or.id/informasi/siaran-pers/tanpa-proses-hukum-dan-tindakan-konkrit-pengakuan-dan-penyesalan-presiden-sekedar-retorika-dan-ilusi/.) They criticized the lack of transparency, norms, and standards in creating the decree, and Kamisan protested the team in actions and letters. Sumarsih highlighted the team's incompetence, citing an example in which it had invited a student who had been killed in 1998 to serve as an expert on the Trisakti, Semanggi 1, and Semanggi 2 case. The Kamisan letter stressed that the initiative was an attempt to whitewash the past and to "subscribe" to impunity, as well as an effort to appear to have resolved the past cases, when the team's work really amounted only to social assistance (Kamisan 754 letter, November 24, 2022). Sumarsih and others have also highlighted the background of team members, including military figures who were possibly involved in the assassination of Munir and crimes against humanity in East Timor.

29. Ibu Sumarsih, message on social media, February 4, 2020.

30. Hariwi, interview by the author, August 1, 2019.

31. Hariwi distinguished himself from individuals who attended because they were encouraged by their places of work (typically civil society organizations). I said, "But you need to be here for your film," and he replied that no one had paid him to be there. This relates to the problem of paid protesters in 1998, as well as to the current jockeying by former activists to gain positions in Jokowi's government.

32. Haberkorn, *In Plain Sight*.

CONCLUSION

1. I am grateful to John Davis for valuable conversations that helped me to articulate the relevance of the infrastructure in other contexts, especially the United States.

Bibliography

Adam, Asvi Warman. *Soeharto: Sisi gelap sejarah Indonesia*. Yogyakarta: Ombak, 2006.

Ajidarma, Seno Gumira. "Keroncong pembunuhan." *Kompas*, February 1985.

Ajidarma, Seno Gumira. *Ketika jurnalisme dibungkam: Sastra harus bicara*. Yogyakarta: Bentang, 2005.

Ajidarma, Seno Gumira. *The Mysterious Marksman*. Translated by Joan Suyenaga. Jakarta: Lontar Foundation, 2019.

Ajidarma, Seno Gumira. *Penembak misterius*. Jakarta: PT. Pustaka Utama Grafiti, 2007.

Ajidarma, Seno Gumira, and Michael H. Bodden. "Fiction, Journalism, History: A Process of Self-Correction." *Indonesia* 68 (1999): 164–71.

Ahmad, Taufik. "South Sulawesi: The Military, Prison Camps and Forced Labor." In Kammen and McGregor, *Contours of Mass Violence*, 156–81.

Aleida, Martin. *Tanah Air yang hilang: Wawancara dengan orang yg "Klayaban" di Eropa*. Jakarta: Penerbit Buku Kompas, Gramedia, 2017.

"Algojo." *Tempo*, October 1, 2012.

Anand, Nikhil. "Pressure: The PoliTechnics of Water Supply in Mumbai." *Cultural Anthropology* 26, no. 4 (2011): 542–64. https://doi.org/10.1111/j.1548-1360.2011.01111.x.

Anderson, Benedict. "How Did the Generals Die?" *Indonesia* 43 (1987): 109–34. https://doi.org/10.2307/3351215.

Anderson, Benedict, and Ruth T. McVey. *A Preliminary Analysis of the October 1, 1965 "Coup" in Indonesia*. Ithaca, NY: Modern Indonesia Project, Cornell University, 1971.

Appel, Hannah, Nikhil Anand, and Akhil Gupta. "Introduction: The Infrastructure Toolbox." Theorizing the Contemporary, *Fieldsights*, September 24, 2015. https://culanth.org/fieldsights/introduction-the-infrastructure-toolbox.

Arendt, Hannah. *Eichmann in Jerusalem: A Report on the Banality of Evil*. New York: Penguin Books, 1994.

Asad, Talal. *On Suicide Bombing*. New York: Columbia University Press, 2007.

Asia Watch. "Asia Watch Criticizes Commission Report on East Timor." *News from Asia Watch* 4, no. 1 (January 3, 1992). https://www.hrw.org/sites/default/files/media_2021/08/202108asia_timorleste_asiawatch.pdf.

Asia Watch. "East Timor: The Courts Martial." *News from Asia Watch* 4, no. 19 (June 23, 1992). https://www.hrw.org/sites/default/files/reports/INDON ESI926.PDF.

Aspinall, Edward. "Students and the Military: Regime Friction and Civilian Dissent in the Late Suharto Period." *Indonesia* 4 (1995): 21–44.

Bakker, Laurens. "Organized Violence and the State." *Bijdragen tot de taal-, land- en volkenkunde/Journal of the Humanities and Social Sciences of Southeast Asia* 172, no. 2–3 (2016): 249–77. https://doi.org/10.1163/22134379-17202001.

Barker, Joshua. "Engineers and Political Dreams: Indonesia in the Satellite Age." *Current Anthropology* 46, no. 5 (2005): 703–27.

Barker, Joshua. "State of Fear: Controlling the Criminal Contagion in Suharto's New Order." *Indonesia* 66 (1998): 6–43.

Bourchier, David, and Vedi R. Hadiz, eds. *Indonesian Politics and Society: A Reader.* New York: Routledge, 2003.

Bourgois, Philippe. *In Search of Respect: Selling Crack in El Barrio.* Cambridge: Cambridge University Press, 1995.

Boyer, Dominic. "Infrastructure, Potential Energy, Revolution." In *The Promise of Infrastructure,* edited by Nikhil Anand, Hannah Appel, and Akhil Gupta, 223–43. Durham, NC: Duke University Press, 2018.

Brennan, Teresa. *The Transmission of Affect.* Ithaca, NY: Cornell University Press, 2004.

Budiawan. "How Do Indonesians Remember Konfrontasi? Indonesia–Malaysia Relations and the Popular Memory of 'Confrontation' after the Fall of Suharto." *Inter-Asia Cultural Studies* 18, no. 3 (2017): 364–75. https://doi.org/10.1080/146 49373.2017.1345349.

"Buntut Seminar 1965, Seratusan orang kepung LBH Jakarta malam ini." *Tempo,* September 17, 2017. https://nasional.tempo.co/read/910004/ buntut-seminar-1965-seratusan-orang-kepung-lbh-jakarta-malam-ini.

Butt, Simon. *Corruption and Law in Indonesia.* London: Routledge, 2017.

Butt, Simon, and Tim Lindsey. *Indonesian Law.* Oxford: Oxford University Press, 2018.

Butt, Simon, and Nicholas Parsons. "Judicial Review and the Supreme Court in Indonesia: A New Space for Law?" *Indonesia* 97 (2014): 55–85.

Caton, Steven, and Bernardo Zacka. "Abu Ghraib, the Security Apparatus, and the Performativity of Power." *American Ethnologist* 37, no. 2 (May 2010): 203–11. https://doi.org/10.1111/j.1548-1425.2010.01250.x.

Chambert-Loir, Henri. "PKI Stroganoff: Leila Chudori's Novel *Pulang* (Revisited)." In *Traditions Redirecting Contemporary Indonesian Cultural Productions,* edited by Jan van der Putten, Monika Arnez, Edwin P. Wieringa, and Arndt Graf, 67–98. Newcastle upon Tyne, UK: Cambridge Scholars, 2017.

Chandra, Siddharth. "New Findings on the Indonesian Killings of 1965–66." *Journal of Asian Studies* 76, no. 4 (2017): 1059–86. https://www.jstor.org/stable/26572404.

Chudori, Leila S. *Home: A Novel.* Translated by John H. McGlynn. Jakarta: Lontar, 2015.

Chudori, Leila S. *Pulang: Sebuah novel.* Jakarta: PT Kepustakaan Populer Gramedia, 2012.

Clarke, Kamari. *Affective Justice: The International Criminal Court and the Pan-Africanist Pushback.* Durham, NC: Duke University Press, 2019.

Clarke, Kamari. *Fictions of Justice: The International Criminal Court and the Challenge of Legal Pluralism in Sub-Saharan Africa.* Cambridge: Cambridge University Press, 2009.

Cohen, David. *Intended to Fail: The Trials before the Ad Hoc Human Rights Court in Jakarta.* Edited by Paul Seils. New York: International Center for Transitional Justice, 2003.

Cohen, David. "Seeking Justice on the Cheap: Is the East Timor Tribunal Really a Model for the Future?" *AsiaPacific Issues* 61 (August 2002): 1–8.

Cole, Catherine. *Performance and the Afterlives of Injustice.* Ann Arbor: University of Michigan Press, 2020.

Comaroff, Jean, and John L. Comaroff. "Law and Disorder in the Postcolony: An Introduction." In *Law and Disorder in the Postcolony,* edited by Jean Comaroff and John L. Comaroff, 1–56. Chicago: University of Chicago Press, 2006.

Comaroff, Jean, and John L. Comaroff. *The Truth about Crime: Sovereignty, Knowledge, Social Order.* Chicago: University of Chicago Press, 2016.

Conroe, Andrew. "The Efficacy of 'Dangerous' Knowledge: 'Children of Victims' in Indonesia after 1965." In McGregor, Melvin, and Pohlman, *Indonesian Genocide of 1965,* 199–214.

Coomaraswamy, Radhika. *Report of the Special Rapporteur on Violence against Women, Its Causes and Consequences.* Geneva: United Nations, 1999.

Cribb, Robert. "The Act of Killing." *Critical Asian Studies* 46, no.1 (2014): 147–49. https://doi.org/10.1080/14672715.2014.867621.

Cribb, Robert. *Gangsters and Revolutionaries: The Jakarta People's Militia and the Indonesian Revolution, 1945–1949.* Honolulu: University of Hawaii Press, 1991.

Cribb, Robert. "Genocide in Indonesia, 1965–1966." *Journal of Genocide Research* 3, no. 2 (2001): 219–39.

Dake, Antonie. *The Sukarno File, 1965–1967: Chronology of a Defeat.* Leiden: Brill, 2006.

Damm, Muhammad. "Lubang Buaya, kuburan para pahlawan: Abjeksi dalam historiografi peristiwa 1 Oktober 1965." *Antropologi Indonesia* 38, no. 2 (2017): 105–24.

Danusubroto, Sidarto. *80 tahun Sidarto Danusubroto: Jalan terjal perubahan dari Ajudan Soekarno sampai Wantimpres Joko Widodo.* Jakarta: Kompas, 2016.

Danusubroto, Sidarto, and Asvi Warman Adam. *Memoar Sidarto Danusubroto, ajudan Bung Karno: Sisi sejarah yang hilang; Masa transisi di seputar Supersemar.* Jakarta: Ombak, 2013.

Danusubroto, Sidarto, Togi Simanjuntak, and Sudiman T. Tarigan. *Bicara dengan sejarah, damai melalui rekonsilias.* Jakarta: PT Multazam Mitra Prima, 2005.

Daughtry, J. Martin. *Listening to War: Sound, Music, Trauma, and Survival in Wartime Iraq.* New York: Oxford University Press, 2015.

Davidson, Jamie. *From Rebellion to Riots: Collective Violence on Indonesian Borneo.* Madison: University of Wisconsin Press, 2008.

Dawes, James. *That the World May Know: Bearing Witness to Atrocity.* Cambridge, MA: Harvard University Press, 2007.

De Alwis, Malathi. "'Disappearance' and 'Displacement' in Sri Lanka." *Journal of Refugee Studies* 22, no. 3 (September 2009): 378–91.

Dempster, Lauren. *Transitional Justice and the 'Disappeared' of Northern Ireland.* Abingdon, Oxon: Routledge, 2019.

Derrida, Jacques. "Force of Law: The 'Mystical Foundations of Authority.'" *Cardozo Law Review* 11, no. 5–6 (1990): 919–1046.

Douglas, Lawrence. *The Memory of Judgment: Making Law and History in the Trials of the Holocaust.* New Haven, CT: Yale University Press, 2005.

Dragojlovic, Ana. "Violent Histories and Embodied Memories: Affectivity of 'The Act of Killing' and 'The Look of Silence.'" In McGregor, Melvin, and Pohlman, *Indonesian Genocide of 1965*, 269–85.

Drexler, Elizabeth F. *Aceh, Indonesia: Securing the Insecure State.* Philadelphia: University of Pennsylvania Press, 2008.

Drexler, Elizabeth F. "The Failure of International Justice in East Timor and Indonesia." In *Transitional Justice: Global Mechanisms and Local Realities after Genocide and Mass Violence*, edited by Alexander Hinton, 49–66. New Brunswick, NJ: Rutgers University Press, 2010.

Dube, Siphiwe Ignatius. "Transitional Justice beyond the Normative: Towards a Literary Theory of Political Transitions." *International Journal of Transitional Justice* 5, no. 2 (July 2011): 177–97.

Duncan, Christopher. *Violence and Vengeance: Religious Conflict and Its Aftermath in Eastern Indonesia.* Ithaca, NY: Cornell University Press, 2013.

Dwipayana, G., and K. H. Ramadhan, eds. *Soeharto: Otobiografi, pikiran, ucapan, dan tindakan saya.* Jakarta: PT Citra Kharisma Bunda, 1988.

Eklöf, Stefan. *Power and Political Culture in Suharto's Indonesia: The Indonesian Democratic Party (PDI) and Decline of the New Order (1986–98).* Copenhagen: NIAS, 2004.

ELSAM (Lembaga Studi dan Advokasi Masyarakat). *The Failure of Leipzig Repeated in Jakarta: Final Assessment of the Human Rights Ad Hoc Tribunal for East Timor.* Jakarta: ELSAM, 2003.

ELSAM (Lembaga Studi dan Advokasi Masyarakat). *Pulangkan mereka: Merangkai ingatan penghilangan paksa di Indonesia.* Jakarta: ELSAM, 2012.

Emont, Jon. "The Propaganda Precursor to 'The Act of Killing.'" *New Yorker*, October 24, 2015. https://www.newyorker.com/news/news-desk/the-propaganda-precursor-to-the-act-of-killing.

Engle, Karen, Zinaida Miller, and D. M. Davis, eds. *Anti-impunity and the Human Rights Agenda.* Cambridge: Cambridge University Press, 2016.

Evanty, Nukila, and Annie Pohlman. "After 1965: Legal Matters for Justice?" In McGregor, Melvin, and Pohlman, *Indonesian Genocide of 1965*, 311–34.

Farid, Hilmar. "Rethinking the Legacies of Bandung." *Inter-Asia Cultural Studies* 17, no. 1 (2016): 12–18. https://doi.org/10.1080/14649373.2016.1133387.

Feith, Herbert. *The Indonesian Elections of 1955.* Ithaca, NY: Modern Indonesia Project, Cornell University, 1957.

Feitlowitz, Marguerite. *A Lexicon of Terror: Argentina and the Legacies of Torture.* Oxford: Oxford University Press, 2011.

Felman, Shoshana. *The Juridical Unconscious.* Cambridge, MA: Harvard University Press, 2002.

Ferguson, James. "Structures of Responsibility." *Ethnography* 13, no. 4 (December 2012): 558–62.

Ferme, Mariane. *Out of War: Violence, Trauma, and the Political Imagination in Sierre Leone.* Berkeley: University of California Press, 2018.

Ferme, Mariane. *The Underneath of Things: Violence, History, and the Everyday in Sierra Leone.* Berkeley: University of California Press, 2001.

"Festival Belok Kiri dilarang, ini kronologinya." *Tempo*, February 27, 2016. https://metro.tempo.co/read/748759/festival-belok-kiri-dilarang-ini-kronologinya/full&view=ok.

Forché, Carolyn. *Against Forgetting: Twentieth-Century Poetry of Witness.* New York: W. W. Norton, 1993.

"Gatot's Defence Statement." *TAPOL Bulletin*, no. 71 (September 1985): 6–10.

Gordon, Avery. *Ghostly Matters: Haunting and the Sociological Imagination.* Minneapolis: University of Minnesota Press, 2008.

Gusterson, Hugh. "Drone Warfare in Waziristan and the New Military Humanism." *Current Anthropology* 60, no. S19 (2019): S77–86.

Haberkorn, Tyrell. *In Plain Sight: Impunity and Human Rights in Thailand.* Madison: University of Wisconsin Press, 2018.

Hadiprayitno, Irene Istiningsih. "Defensive Enforcement: Human Rights in Indonesia." *Human Rights Review* 11 (2010): 373–99.

Hamber, Brandon, and Richard Wilson. "Symbolic Closure through Memory, Reparation and Revenge in Post-conflict Societies." *Journal of Human Rights* 1, no. 1 (March 2002): 35–53.

Hamid, Usman. "Merosotnya demokrasi, hak asasi dan lahirnya gerakan korban di Indonesia: Reformasi dan legacy dua dasawarsa KontraS." Unpublished manuscript, 2018.

Hamid, Usman, Teresa Birks, and Naufal Rofi Indriansyah. *Protection of Social Justice Leaders in Indonesia.* Jakarta: Public Virtue Institute, 2021.

Hayner, Priscilla. *Unspeakable Truths: Transitional Justice and the Challenge of Truth Commissions.* New York: Routledge, 2010.

Hearman, Vanessa. "Contesting Victimhood in the Indonesian Anti-Communist Violence and Its Implications for Justice for the Victims of the 1968 South Blitar Trisula Operation in East Java." *Journal of Genocide Research* 19, no. 4 (2017): 512–29.

Hearman, Vanessa. "Letter-Writing and Transnational Activism on Behalf of Indonesian Political Prisoners: Gatot Lestario and His Legacy." *Critical Asian Studies* 48, no. 2 (2016): 145–67. https://doi.org/10.1080/14672715.2016.1157954.

Hearman, Vanessa. "Missing Victims of the 1965–66 Violence in Indonesia: Representing Impunity On-screen in *The Act of Killing*." *Critical Asian Studies* 46, no. 1 (2014): 171–75. https://doi.org/10.1080/14672715.2014.863586.

Hearman, Vanessa. *Unmarked Graves: Death and Survival in the Anti-Communist Violence in East Java, Indonesia*. Singapore: NUS Press, 2018.

Herlambang, Wijaya. *Kekerasan budaya pasca 1965: Bagaimana Orde Baru melegitmasi anti-Komunisme melalui sastra dan film*. Serpong, Indonesia: Margin Kiri, 2013.

Heryanto, Ariel. "Flaws of Riot Media Coverage." *Jakarta Post*, July 15, 1998.

Heryanto, Ariel. "Great and Misplaced Expectations." *Critical Asian Studies* 46, no. 1 (2014): 162–66.

Heryanto, Ariel. *State Terrorism and Political Identity in Indonesia: Fatally Belonging*. London: Routledge, 2006.

Hinton, Alexander Laban. "Critical Genocide Studies." *Genocide Studies and Prevention: An International Journal* 7, no. 1 (2012): 4–15.

Hinton, Alexander Laban. *The Justice Facade: Trials of Transition in Cambodia*. Oxford: Oxford University Press, 2018.

Hinton, Alexander Laban, ed. *Transitional Justice: Global Mechanisms and Local Realities after Genocide and Mass Violence*. New Brunswick, NJ: Rutgers University Press, 2010.

Huggins, Martha Knisely, Mika Haritos-Fatouros, and Philip G. Zimbardo. *Violence Workers: Police Torturers and Murderers Reconstruct Brazilian Atrocities*. Berkeley: University of California Press, 2002.

Hutabarat, Restaria F. *Stigma 65: Strategi mengajukan gugatan class action*. Jakarta: Yayasan Pustaka Obor Indonesia and LBH Jakarta, 2011.

ICG (International Crisis Group). *Indonesia: Impunity versus Accountability for Gross Violations of Human Rights*. Jakarta: ICG, 2001.

"Indonesia: Vengeance with a Smile." *Time*, July 15, 1966.

IPT 1965 (International People's Tribunal for 1965). *Final Report of the International People's Tribunal on Crimes against Humanity in Indonesia, 1965*. Bandung: Ultimus, 2017.

Isnur, Muhamad, ed. *Rentang jejak LBH Jakarta, kisah-kisah penanganan kasus*. Jakarta: Lembaga Bantuan Hukum Jakarta, 2015.

Jeffery, Renee. "The Role of the Arts in Cambodia's Transitional Justice Process." *International Journal of Politics, Culture, and Society* 34 (2021): 335–58.

"Jegar jeger Petrus." *Tempo*, October 6, 2014. https://majalah.tempo.co/read/laporan-khusus/146479/jegar-jeger-petrus.

Jones, Sidney, and Michael McClintock. *The Limits of Openness: Human Rights in Indonesia and East Timor*. New York: Human Rights Watch, 1994.

Kahin, George McT., and Audrey Kahin. *Subversion as Foreign Policy: The Secret Eisenhower and Dulles Debacle in Indonesia*. New York: New Press, 1995.

Kammen, Douglas, and Katharine McGregor, eds. *The Contours of Mass Violence in Indonesia, 1965–68*. Singapore: NUS Press, 2012.

Kartika, Dyah Ayu. "The Politicization of Psychology: The Role of Psychologists in Indonesia's Detention Camps during New Order Era." MA thesis, International Institute of Social Studies, 2016.

Katoppo, Aristides. *Menyingkap kabut Halim 1965*. Jakarta: Pustaka Sinar Harapan, 1999.

Keenan, Thomas. "Mobilizing Shame." *South Atlantic Quarterly* 103, no. 2/3 (2004): 435–49.

"Kerangka Acuan, Simposium Nasional Membedah Tragedi 1965, pendekatan kesejarahan, Jakarta, 18–19 April 2016." Unpublished manuscript, also referred to as the symposium's terms of reference (TOR). Copy in the author's possession.

"Kisah Tom Iljas, Diusir dari Indonesia karena ziarah ke makam orang tua." *Tempo*, October 18, 2015. https://nasional.tempo.co/read/710584/kisah-tom-iljas-diusir-dari-indonesia-karena-ziarah-ke-makam-orang-tua/full&view=ok.

KKPK (Koalisi Untuk Keadilan dan Pengungkapan Kebenaran). *Menemukan kembali Indonesia: Memahami empat puluh tahun kekerasan demi memutus rantai impunitas*. Jakarta: Koalisi Untuk Keadilan dan Pengungkapan Kebenaran, 2014.

Kolimon, Mery, and Liliya Wetangterah, eds. *Memori-memori terlarang: Perempuan korban & penyintas tragedi '65 di Nusa Tenggara Timur*. Kupang: Yayasan Bonet Pinggupir, 2012. Translated and republished as Kolimon, Mery, Karen Campbell Nelson, and Liliya Wetangterah, eds. *Forbidden Memories: Women's Experiences of 1965 in Eastern Indonesia*. Translated by Jennifer Lindsay. Herb Feith Translation Series. Clayton, Australia: Monash University Press, 2015.

Komnas HAM (Komisi Nasional Hak Asasi Manusia). *Ringkasan eksekutif: Laporan penyelidikan pelanggaran HAM yang berat*. Jakarta: Komnas HAM, 2014.

KontraS (Komisi untuk Orang Hilang dan Tindak Kekerasan), PSHK (Pusat Studi Hukum dan Kebijakan Indonesia), YLBHI (Yayasan Lembaga Bantuan Hukum Indonesia), LeIP (Lembaga kajian dan advokasi Independensi Peradilan), MAPPI UI (Masyarakat Pemantau Peradilan Indonesia Universitas Indonesia), LBH Jakarta (Lembaga Bantuan Hukum Jakarta), LBH Masyarakat (Lembaga Bantuan Hukum Masyarakat), WALHI (Wahana Lingkungan Indonesia), KPA (Konsorsium Pembaruan Agraria), et al. "Kriminalisasi: Modus dan kasus-kasusnya di Indonesia." Unpublished report, 2016.

KPP HAM (Komisi Penyelidik Pelanggaran Hak Asasi Manusia) Timor Timur. *Executive Summary Report on the Investigation of Human Rights Violations in East Timor*. Jakarta: Komnas HAM, 2000. https://reliefweb.int/report/indonesia/executive-summary-report-investigation-human-rights-violations-east-timor.

Kurze, Arnaud. "#WarCrimes #PostConflictJustice #Balkans: Youth, Performance Activism and the Politics of Memory." *International Journal of Transitional Justice* 10, no. 3 (November 2016): 451–70. https://doi.org/10.1093/ijtj/ijw014.

Kurze, Arnaud, and Christopher K. Lamont. *New Critical Spaces in Transitional Justice: Gender, Art, and Memory*. Bloomington: Indiana University Press, 2019.

Lamasitudju, Alamsyah A. K., Muhammad Abbas Gagarisman, Nurlaela A. K. Lamasitudju, Nurhasanah, and Putu Oka Sukanta. *Sulawesi bersaksi*. Jakarta: Lembaga Kreatifitas Kemanusiaan, 2013.

Laporan akhir tim pencari fakta kasus meninggalnya Munir. Established by Presidential Decree 111/2004. Copy in the author's possession.

Larasati, Rachmi Diyah. *The Dance That Makes You Vanish: Cultural Reconstruction in Post-genocide Indonesia*. Minneapolis: University of Minnesota Press, 2013.

Larasati, Rachmi Diyah. "Reclaiming the Aesthetic of Women: De-colonizing land ownership." *Cultural Studies* 33, no. 3 (2019): 550–69.

Larkin, Brian. "The Politics and Poetics of Infrastructure." *Annual Review of Anthropology* 42 (2013): 327–43.

Latief, Abdul. *Pleidoi Kol. A Latief: Soeharto terlibat G30S.* Jakarta: Institut Studi Aus Informasi, 2000.

Latour, Bruno. *Down to Earth: Politics in the New Climatic Regime.* Translated by Catherine Porter. Medford, MA: Polity, 2018.

Lee, Doreen. "Absolute Traffic: Infrastructural Aptitude in Urban Indonesia." *International Journal of Urban and Regional Research* 39 (2015): 234–50. https://doi.org/10.1111/1468-2427.12212.

Lee, Doreen. *Activist Archives: Youth Culture and the Political Past in Indonesia.* Durham, NC: Duke University Press, 2016.

Leebaw, Bronwyn. *Judging State-Sponsored Violence, Imagining Political Change.* Cambridge: Cambridge University Press, 2011.

Lev, Daniel S. "Between State and Society: Professional Lawyers and Reform in Indonesia." In *Indonesia: Law and Society*, edited by Tim Lindsey, 48–67. Sydney: Federation, 2008.

Lev, Daniel S. "Judicial Authority and the Struggle for an Indonesian Rechtsstaat." *Law and Society Review* 13 (1978): 37–71.

Lev, Daniel S. "Judicial Institutions and Legal Culture in Indonesia." In *Culture and Politics in Indonesia,* edited by *Claire Holt,* 246–318. Ithaca, NY: Cornell University Press, 1972.

Lev, Daniel S. *Legal Evolution and Political Authority in Indonesia: Selected Essays.* The Hague: Kluwer International, 2000.

Lev, Daniel S. *The Transition to Guided Democracy: Indonesian Politics, 1957–59.* Ithaca, NY: Modern Indonesia Project, Cornell University, 1966.

Lindsey, Tim, ed. *Indonesia: Law and Society.* Sydney: Federation. 2008.

Linton, Suzanne. "Accounting for Atrocities in Indonesia." *Singapore Year Book of International Law* 10 (2006): 199–231.

Marching, Soe Tjen, and Angus Nicholls. *The End of Silence: Accounts of the 1965 Genocide in Indonesia.* Amsterdam: Amsterdam University Press, 2017.

Massumi, Brian. "The Future Birth of the Affective Fact: The Political Ontology of Threat." In *The Affect Theory Reader*, edited by Melissa Gregg and Gregory J. Seigworth, 52–70. Durham, NC: Duke University Press, 2010.

McCoy, Mary E. *Scandal and Democracy: Media Politics in Indonesia.* Ithaca, NY: Cornell University Press, 2019.

McGregor, Katharine E. *History in Uniform: Military Ideology and the Construction of Indonesia's Past.* Honolulu: University of Hawaii Press, 2007.

McGregor, Katharine, Jess Melvin, and Annie Pohlman, eds. *The Indonesian Genocide of 1965: Causes, Dynamics and Legacies.* Cham, Switzerland: Palgrave Macmillan, 2018.

McLeod, Laura, Jovana Dimitrijević, and Biliana Rakočević. "Artistic Activism, Public Debate and Temporal Complexities: Fighting for Transitional Justice in Serbia." In *The Arts of Transitional Justice: Culture, Activism, and Memory after Atrocity*, edited by Peter Rush and Olivera Simić, 25–42. Springer Series in Transitional Justice, vol. 6. New York: Springer, 2014.

Melvin, Jess. *The Army and the Indonesian Genocide: Mechanics of Mass Murder.* New York: Routledge, 2018.

Meyers, Diana Tietjens. *Victims' Stories and the Advancement of Human Rights.* New York: Oxford University Press, 2016.

Miller, Zinaida. "Effects of Invisibility: In Search of the 'Economic' in Transitional Justice." *International Journal of Transitional Justice* 2, no. 3 (December 2008): 266–91. https://doi.org/10.1093/ijtj/ijn022.

Million, Dian. "Felt Theory: An Indigenous Feminist Approach to Affect and History." *Wicazo Sa Review* 24, no. 2 (2009): 53–76.

Mira. "The 'G30S/PKI' Symbol Is the Major Obstacle to Democracy." *TAPOL Bulletin*, no. 71 (September 1985): 1–3.

Morfit, Michael. "Pancasila: The Indonesian State Ideology According to the New Order Government." *Asian Survey* 21, no. 8 (1981): 838–51.

Morris, Errol. "The Murders of Gonzago." Slate, July 10, 2013. https://www.slate.com/articles/arts/history/2013/07/the_act_of_killing_essay_how_indonesia_s_mass_killings_could_have_slowed.html.

Moyn, Samuel. "Anti-impunity as Deflection of Argument." In Engle, Miller, and Davis, *Anti-impunity*, 68–94.

Moyn, Samuel. *The Last Utopia: Human Rights in History*. Cambridge, MA: Harvard University Press, 2010.

Mrázek, Rudolf. *Engineers of Happy Land: Technology and Nationalism in a Colony*. Princeton, NJ: Princeton University Press, 2002.

Muehlmann, Shaylih. "Clandestine Infrastructures: Illicit Connectivities in the US-Mexico Borderlands." In *Infrastructure, Environment, and Life in the Anthropocene*, edited by Kregg Hetherington, 45–65. Durham, NC: Duke University Press, 2019.

Murphy, Kaitlin M. *Mapping Memory: Visuality, Affect, and Embodied Politics in the Americas*. New York: Fordham University Press, 2019.

Neier, Aryeh. *The International Human Rights Movement: A History*. Princeton, NJ: Princeton University Press, 2012.

Nesiah, Vasuki. "Doing History with Impunity." In Engle, Miller, and Davis, *Anti-impunity*, 95–122.

Notosusanto, Nugroho, and Ismail Saleh. *The Coup Attempt of the September 30 Movement in Indonesia*. Jakarta: Pembimbing Masa, 1971.

Nusantara, Abdul Hakim Garuda. *Politik hukum Indonesia*. Jakarta: Yayasan Bantuan Hukum Indonesia, 1988.

O'Neill, Bruce. "Of Camps, Gulags and Extraordinary Renditions: Infrastructural Violence in Romania." *Ethnography* 13, no. 4 (2012): 466–86.

Panggabean, Meicky Shoreamanis. *Keberanian bernama Munir: Mengenal sisi-sisi personal Munir*. Bandung: Mizan Pustaka, 2008.

Paramaditha, Intan. "Narratives of Discovery: Joshua Oppenheimer's Films on Indonesia's 1965 Mass Killings and the Human Rights Discourse." *Social Identities* 25, no. 4 (2019): 512–22.

Paramaditha, Intan. "Tracing Frictions in *The Act of Killing*." *Film Quarterly* 67, no. 2 (2013): 44–49.

Partogi, Edwin, Haris Azhar, Indria Fernida, Papang Hidayat, and Usman Hamid. *Bunuh Munir*. Jakarta: KontraS, 2006.

"Pengakuan Kentus, target Petrus yang selamat." *Tempo*, July 31, 2012. https://nasional.tempo.co/read/420361/pengakuan-kentus-target-petrus-yang-selamat.

Pohlman, Annie. "The Massacres of 1965–1966: New Interpretations and the Current Debate in Indonesia." *Journal of Current Southeast Asian Affairs* 32, no. 3 (2013): 3–9.

Pohlman, Annie. "Two Women's Testimonies of Sexual Violence during the 1965–66 Indonesian Massacres." In McGregor, Melvin, and Pohlman, *Indonesian Genocide of 1965*, 115–32.

Pohlman, Annie E. "A Year of Truth and the Possibilities for Reconciliation in Indonesia." *Genocide Studies and Prevention: An International Journal* 10, no. 1 (2016): 60–78.

Pompe, Sebastiaan. *Indonesian Supreme Court: A Study of Institutional Collapse.* Ithaca, NY: Southeast Asia Program Publications, 2005.

PSHK, LEIP, LBH Jakarta, MAPPI, YLBHI, KPA, LBH Masyarakat, WALHI. *Kriminalisasi* (brochure). Jakarta, 2015.

Purdey, Jemma. "Problematizing the Place of Victims in Reformasi Indonesia: A Contested Truth about the May 1998 Violence." *Asian Survey* 42, no. 4 (2002): 605–23.

Ralph, Laurence. *The Torture Letters: Reckoning with Police Violence.* Chicago: University of Chicago Press, 2020.

Ramírez-Barat, Clara. "The Path to Social Reconstruction: Between Culture and Transitional Justice." *International Journal of Transitional Justice* 14, no. 1 (March 2020): 242–50. https://doi.org/10.1093/ijtj/ijz035.

Rappert, Brian. "Leaky Revelations: Commitments in Exposing Militarism." *Current Anthropology* 60, no. S19 (February 2019): S148–157. https://doi.org/10.1086/700649.

Reeve, David. *Golkar of Indonesia: An Alternative to the Party System.* Singapore: Oxford University Press, 1985.

Robben, Antonius C. G. M. *Political Violence and Trauma in Argentina.* Philadelphia: University of Pennsylvania Press, 2005.

Robet, Robertus. *Politik hak asasi manusia & transisi di Indonesia.* Jakarta: ELSAM, 2014.

Robins, Simon. "Towards Victim-Centred Transitional Justice: Understanding the Needs of Families of the Disappeared in Postconflict Nepal." *International Journal of Transitional Justice* 5, no. 1 (March 2011): 75–98.

Robinson, Geoffrey. "Break the Rules, Save the Records: Human Rights Archives and the Search for Justice in East Timor." *Archival Science* 14 (2014): 323–43.

Robinson, Geoffrey. *The Dark Side of Paradise: Political Violence in Bali.* Ithaca, NY: Cornell University Press, 1998.

Robinson, Geoffrey. *The Killing Season: A History of the Indonesian Massacres, 1965–66.* Princeton, NJ: Princeton University Press, 2018.

Rodgers, Dennis, and Bruce O'Neill. "Infrastructural Violence: Introduction to the Special Issue." *Ethnography* 13, no. 4 (December 2012): 401–12. https://doi.org/10.1177/1466138111435738.

Roosa, John. *Buried Histories: The Anticommunist Massacres of 1965–1966 in Indonesia.* Madison: University of Wisconsin Press, 2020.

Roosa, John. *Pretext for Mass Murder: The September 30th Movement and Suharto's Coup d'État in Indonesia.* Madison: University of Wisconsin Press, 2006.

Roosa, John. "The September 30th Movement: The Aporias in the Official Narratives." In Kammen and McGregor, *Contours of Mass Violence,* 25–49.

Roosa, John. "The State of Knowledge about an Open Secret: Indonesia's Mass Disappearances of 1965–66." *Journal of Asian Studies* 75, no. 2 (2016): 281–97.

Roosa, John. "The Truths of Torture: Victims' Memories and State Histories in Indonesia." *Indonesia* 85 (2007): 31–49.

Roosa, John. "Who Knows? Oral History Methods in the Study of the Massacres of 1965–66 in Indonesia." In "Confronting Mass Atrocities," edited by Erin Jessee and Annie Pohlman, special issue, *Oral History Forum d'histoire orale* 33 (2013): 1–28.

Roosa, John, Ayu Ratih, and Hilmar Farid. *Tahun yang tak pernah berakhir: Memahami pengalaman korban 65; Esai-esai sejarah lisan.* Jakarta: ELSAM bekerja sama dengan Tim Relawan Untuk Kemanusiaan [dan] Institut Sejarah Sosial Indonesia, 2004.

Ross, Fiona. *Bearing Witness: Women and the Truth and Reconciliation Commission in South Africa*. London: Pluto, 2003.

Rotberg, Robert, and Dennis Thompson, eds. *Truth v. Justice: The Morality of Truth Commissions*. Princeton, NJ: Princeton University Press, 2000.

Rowen, Jamie. *Searching for Truth in the Transitional Justice Movement*. Cambridge: Cambridge University Press, 2017.

Rubin, Jonah S. "How Francisco Franco Governs from beyond the Grave: An Infrastructural Approach to Memory Politics in Contemporary Spain." *American Ethnologist* 45, no. 2 (2018): 214–27.

Rush, Peter, and Olivera Simić, eds. *The Arts of Transitional Justice: Culture, Activism, and Memory after Atrocity*. Springer Series in Transitional Justice, vol. 6. New York: Springer, 2014.

Ryter, Loren. "Pemuda Pancasila: The Last Loyalist Free Men of Suharto's Order?" *Indonesia* 66 (1998): 45–73. https://doi.org/10.2307/3351447.

Sadli, Saparinah. *Saatnya meneguhkan rasa aman: Langkah maju pemenuhan hak perempuan korban kekerasan seksual*. Jakarta: Komnas Perempuan, 2008.

Santoso, Aboeprijadi, and Gerry van Klinken. "Genocide Finally Enters Public Discourse: The International People's Tribunal 1965." *Journal of Genocide Research* 19, no. 4 (2017): 594–608.

Saptari, Ratna. "Persecution through Denial of Citizenship: Indonesians in Forced Exile Post-1965." In *The International People's Tribunal for 1965 and the Indonesian Genocide*, edited by Saskia Wieringa, Jess Melvin, and Annie Pohlman, 115–34. London: Routledge, 2019.

Sawita, Roro. "The Connection between Land Reform and the 1965–1966 Tragedy in Bali." In McGregor, Melvin, and Pohlman, *Indonesian Genocide of 1965*, 89–114.

Schaefer, Bernd, and Baskara T. Wardaya, eds. *1965: Indonesia and the World; Indonesia dan dunia*. Bilingual ed. Jakarta: Gramedia Pustaka Utama, 2013.

Scott, Peter Dale. "The United States and the Overthrow of Sukarno, 1965–1967." *Pacific Affairs* 58, no. 2 (Summer 1985): 239–64.

"Sebuah upaya menghapus dosa turunan bersih diri tentang pki." *Tempo*, May 12, 1990.

Sen, Krishna. *Indonesian Cinema: Framing the New Order*. London: Zed Books, 1994.

Sen, Krishna, and David T. Hill. *Media, Culture and Politics in Indonesia*. Melbourne: Oxford University Press, 2000.

Setiawan, Hersri. *Memoar pulau Buru*. Magelang: IndonesiaTera, 2004.

Sharma, Aradhana. "New Brooms and Old: Sweeping Up Corruption in India, One Law at a Time." *Current Anthropology* 59, no. S18 (2018.): S72–82.

Sharpe, Christina. *In the Wake: On Blackness and Being*. Durham, NC: Duke University Press, 2016.

Shaw, Rosalind. "Memory Frictions: Localizing the Truth and Reconciliation Commission in Sierra Leone." *International Journal of Transitional Justice* 1, no. 2 (2007): 183–207.

Shaw, Rosalind, Lars Waldorf, and Pierre Hazan, eds. *Localizing Transitional Justice: Interventions and Priorities after Mass Violence*. Redwood City, CA: Stanford University Press, 2010.

Shefik, Sherin. "Reimagining Transitional Justice through Participatory Art." *International Journal of Transitional Justice* 12, no. 2 (July 2018): 314–33. https://doi.org/10.1093/ijtj/ijy011.

Siegel, James T. *A New Criminal Type in Jakarta: Counter-revolution Today*. Durham, NC: Duke University Press, 1999.

"6 fakta tentang film G30 S PKI wajib diketahui." *Tempo*, September 17, 2017. https://nasional.tempo.co/read/910003/6-fakta-tentang-film-g-30-s-pki-yang-wajib-diketahui.

Slater, Dan. "Party Cartelization, Indonesian-Style: Presidential Power-Sharing and the Contingency of Democratic Opposition." *Journal of East Asian Studies* 18, no. 1 (2018): 23–46. https://doi.org/10.1017/jea.2017.26.

Starr, Susan Leigh. "The Ethnography of Infrastructure." *American Behavioral Science* 43, no. 3 (1999): 377–91.

Stockmann, Petra. *Indonesian Reformasi as Reflected in Law: Change and Continuity in Post-Suharto-Era Legislation on the Political System and Human Rights.* Hamburg: Institut fur Politische Wissenschaft, Universitat Hamburg, 2004.

Stoler, Ann Laura. "Colonial Archives and the Arts of Governance." *Archival Science* 2 (2002): 87–109.

Strassler, Karen. "Gendered Visibilities and the Dream of Transparency: The Chinese Indonesian Rape Debate in Post-Suharto Indonesia." *Gender and History* 16, no. 4 (2004): 689–725.

Sukanta, Putu Oka. *Cahaya mata sang pewaris: Kisah nyata anak-cucu korban tragedi '65.* Bandung: Ultimus, 2016.

Sukarno. "Tahun 'Vivere pericoloso' Tavip." Speech on August 17, 1964. Jakarta: Department of Information, 1964.

Sulistyo, Hermawan. *Palu arit di ladang tebu: Sejarah pembantaian massal yang terlupakan, Jombang-Kediri, 1965–1966.* Jakarta: Pensil-324, 2011.

Susanti, Bivitri. "Constitution and Human Rights Provisions in Indonesia: An Unfinished Task in the Transitional Process." In *Constitutions & Human Rights in a Global Age: An Asia-Pacific Perspective*, edited by Tessa Morris-Suzuki, 5–14. Canberra: Australian National University, 2003.

Suseno, Franz Magnis. "The People and the Wayang." Translation and introduction by Verena Meyer. *International Journal of Dharma Studies* 4, no. 3 (2016). https://doi.org/10.1186/s40613-016-0028-6.

Sutojo, Nani Nurrachman, and Imelda Bachtiar. *Kenangan tak terucap: Saya, ayah, dan tragedi 1965.* Jakarta: Penerbit Buku Kompas, 2013.

Suyono, Seno Joko, and Nurdin Kalim. *Benny Moerdani: Yang belum terungkap.* Seri Buku Tempo (Tempo Book Series). Jakarta: Kepustakaan Popular Grammedia, 2015.

Tan, Paige Johnson. "Teaching and Remembering." *Inside Indonesia* 2 (April–June 2008).

Tanter, Richard. "Intelligence Agencies and Third World Militarization: A Case Study of Indonesia, 1966–1989, with Special Reference to South Korea, 1961–1989." PhD diss., Monash University, 1991.

Taussig, Michael T. *Defacement: Public Secrecy and the Labor of the Negative.* Stanford, CA: Stanford University Press, 1999.

Teitel, Ruti. *Globalizing Transitional Justice: Contemporary Essays.* New York: Oxford University Press, 2014.

Teitel, Ruti. "Human Rights Genealogy." *Fordham Law Review* 66, no. 2 (November 1997): 301–18.

Teitel, Ruti. *Transitional Justice.* New York: Oxford University Press, 2000.

Telle, Kari. "Faith on Trial: Blasphemy and 'Lawfare' in Indonesia." *Ethnos* 83, no. 2 (2018): 371–391.

TGPF (Tim Gabung Pencari Fakta). *Laporan akhir peristiwa kerusuhan tanggal 13–15 Mei: Jakarta, Solo, Palembang, Lampung, Surabaya dan Medan.* Jakarta: Government of Indonesia, 1998. Copy in the author's possession.

Theidon, Kimberly. *Intimate Enemies: Violence and Reconciliation in Peru.*
    Philadelphia: University of Pennsylvania Press, 2012.
Thiranagama, Sharika. *In My Mother's House: Civil War in Sri Lanka.* Philadelphia:
    University of Pennsylvania Press, 2011.
Thiranagama, Sharika, and Tobias Kelly, eds. *Traitors: Suspicion, Intimacy, and the
    Ethics of State-Building.* Philadelphia: University of Pennsylvania Press, 2010.
"Three More Long-Term Political Prisoners Executed." *TAPOL Bulletin,* no. 71
    (September 1985): 3.
Tjiptaning, Ribka. *Aku bangga jadi anak PKI.* Jakarta: Cipta Lestari, 2002.
Toer, Pramoedya Ananta, and Willem Samuels. *The Mute's Soliloquy.* New York:
    Hyperion, 1999.
Triyana, Bonnie. "Petrus: Kisah gelap Orba; Bertato saja sudah cukup untuk dijadikan
    alasan pembunuhan." *Majalah historia,* December 20, 2010. https://historia.id/
    politik/articles/petrus-kisah-gelap-orba-PyXNv.
Tyson, Adam. "Multiple Acts of Killing." *Critical Asian Studies* 46, no. 1 (2014): 157–61.
Valverde, Mariana, Fleur Johns, and Jennifer Raso. "Governing Infrastructure in the
    Age of the 'Art of the Deal': Logics of Governance and Scales of Visibility."
    PoLAR: Political and Legal Anthropology Review 41, no. S1 (2019): 118–32.
Van Der Kroef, Justus M. "Indonesia's Political Prisoners." *Pacific Affairs* 49, no. 4
    (1976): 625–47.
Van Der Kroef, Justus M. "'Petrus': Patterns of Prophylactic Murder in Indonesia."
    Asian Survey 25, no. 7 (1985): 745–59.
van Klinken, Gerry. "No, *The Act of Killing* Is Not Unethical." *Critical Asian Studies* 46,
    no. 1 (2014): 176–78.
Wahid, Abdul. "Campus on Fire: Indonesian Universities during the Political Turmoil
    of 1950s-1960s." *Archipel* 95 (2018): 31–52.
Wahyuningroem, Sri Lestari. "Seducing for Truth and Justice: Civil Society Initiatives
    for the 1965 Mass Violence in Indonesia." *Journal of Current Southeast Asian
    Affairs* 32, no. 3 (2013): 115–42.
Wahyuningroem, Sri Lestari. *Transitional Justice from State to Civil Society:
    Democratization in Indonesia.* London: Routledge, 2020.
Wahyuningroem, Sri Lestari. "Working from the Margins: Initiatives for Truth and
    Reconciliation for Victims of the 1965 Mass Violence in Solo and Palu." In
    McGregor, Melvin, and Pohlman, *Indonesian Genocide of 1965,* 335–56.
Wandita, Galuh. "*PREMAN* Nation: Watching *The Act of Killing* in Indonesia." *Critical
    Asian Studies* 46, no. 1 (2014): 167–70.
Wandita, Galuh, Indria Fernida, and Karen Campbell-Nelson. "Mass Torture in
    1965–66: A Continuing Legacy." In *The International People's Tribunal for 1965
    and the Indonesian Genocide,* edited by Saskia Wieringa, Jess Melvin, and Annie
    Pohlman, 60–79. London: Routledge, 2019.
Wandita, Galuh, Dodi Yuniar, and Matt Easton. *Bertahan dalam impunitas: Kisah
    para perempuan penyintas yang tak kunjung meraih keadilan.* Jakarta: AJAR and
    Komnas Perempuan, 2015.
Wardaya, Baskara T., ed. *Suara di balik prahara: Berbagi narasi tentang tragedi '65 di
    Indonesia.* Yogyakarta: Galangpress, 2011.
Wardaya, Baskara T., ed. *Truth Will Out: Indonesian Accounts of the 1965 Mass Violence.*
    Translated by Jennifer Lindsay. Clayton, Australia: Monash University, 2020.
Weld, Kirsten. *Paper Cadavers: The Archives of Dictatorship in Guatemala.* Durham,
    NC: Duke University Press, 2014.
Wertheim, W. F. "Suharto and the Untung Coup—the Missing Link." *Journal of
    Contemporary Asia* 1, no. 2 (Winter 1970): 50–57.

Whigham, Kerry. "Reading the Traces: Embodied Engagement with the Past at Three Former Nazi Concentration Camps." *Holocaust Studies: A Journal of Culture and History* 26, no. 2 (2019): 1–20.

Whigham, Kerry. "Remembering to Prevent: The Preventive Capacity of Public Memory." *Genocide Studies and Prevention: An International Journal* 11, no. 2 (2017): 53–71.

Whigham, Kerry. *Resonant Violence: Affect, Memory, and Activism in Post-genocide Societies*. New Brunswick, NJ: Rutgers University Press, 2022.

Widjojanto, Bambang. "Seandainya hukum gagal." In *Indonesia di tengah transisi*, edited by Stanley, 87–91. Jakarta: Propatria, 2000.

Wieringa, Saskia. *Sexual Politics in Indonesia*. New York: Palgrave Macmillan, 2002.

Wieringa, Saskia. "Sexual Slander and the 1965/66 Mass Killings in Indonesia: Political and Methodological Considerations." *Journal of Contemporary Asia* 41, no. 4 (2011): 544–65. https://doi.org/10.1080/00472336.2011.610613.

Wieringa, Saskia, and Nursyahbani Katjasungkana. *Propaganda and the Genocide in Indonesia: Imagined Evil*. New York: Routledge, 2019.

Wieringa, Saskia, Jess Melvin, and Annie Pohlman, eds. *The International People's Tribunal for 1965 and the Indonesian Genocide*. London: Routledge, 2019.

Wilson, Ian Douglas. *The Politics of Protection Rackets in Post–New Order Indonesia: Coercive Capital, Authority and Street Politics*. London: Routledge, 2017.

"Wiranto sebut tidak mudah ungkap dalang pembunuhan Munir." *Tempo*, September 11, 2017. https://nasional.kompas.com/read/2017/09/11/21564081/wiranto-sebut-tidak-mudah-ungkap-dalang-pembunuhan-munir.

Wiratraman, Herlambang P., Sri Lestari Wahyuningroem, Manunggai K. Wardaya, and Dian P. Simatunpang. "Taking Policy Seriously: What Should Indonesian Government Do to Strengthen Aceh Truth and Reconciliation Commission?" *Petita jurnal kajian ilmu hukum dan Syariah* 5, no. 1 (2020): 14–32.

Yatmaka, Yayak I. *Sejarah gerakan kiri Indonesia: Untuk pemula*. Bandung, Indonesia: Ultimus, 2016.

Zunino, Marcos. "Subversive Justice: The Russell Vietnam War Crimes Tribunal and Transitional Justice." *International Journal of Transitional Justice* 10, no. 2 (July 2016): 211–29. https://doi.org/10.1093/ijtj/ijw007.

Index

Page numbers in *italics* refer to figures.

Sukanta, Putu Oka, 156–57

Sukarno: 1965 coup attempt and, 21, 28, 36, 55, 151; army-controlled media discrediting, 34; emergency laws of, 110–11; Extraordinary Military Tribunals' trials for allies of, 50; as first president (1950–67), 19–20; Madiun Incident and, 35; Pancasila (Five Principles) of, 24–25; political engagement of masses and, 74; protesting UN seating of Malaysia, 215n7; Taufiq on, 156; territorial command, creation of, 214n38; transfer of power to Suharto, 50; on Youth Pledge, 195

Sukarnoputri, Megawati, 100, 103–4, 106, 187

Sukmawati (Sukarno's daughter), 159–60, *160*

Sumarmiyati, Christina "Mamik," 64, 221n148

Sumarsih (Ibu), *179*, 180–82, 186, 194, 196, 202–4, 236n6, 236n10, 237n28

Superman Is Dead (band), 138–39

Supreme Court of Indonesia, 111; affirming attorney general's finding of no gross violations in Semanggi 1 and Semanggi 2, 236n10; co-optation by New Order, 111; on discrimination against Category C families, 58

survivor testimony, 1, 2, 6, 12; on arrest and detention of PKI supposed members, 52; criminalization attached to, 62–63; infrastructure of impunity diminishing, 32; in kidnappings case, 100, 110, 125; in KKPK "Year of Truth," 136–39; KontraS encouraging, 106–8; lack of PKI leaders giving, 54; Lestario's defense statement, 54–56; murder of victim about to testify, chilling effect of, 113; stigmatization's long-term effects, 65. *See also specific cases and violent historical events*

Susilo Bambang Yudhoyono, 134

Sutoyo, Nani Nurachman, 149

Sutrisno, Try, 78

Tanjung Priok case (1984), 118, 120–21, *121*, 183, 188

Tanter, Richard, 49–50

TAP MPRS 25/1966 (parliamentary order), 50, 62

TAPOL Bulletin, political prisoner on long-term effects of false narrative, 56

Team for the Non-judicial Resolution of Past Gross Violations of Human Rights (Tim Penyelesaian Non-Yudisial Pelanggaran HAM Berat Masa Lalu), 237n28

Teitel, Ruti, 4, 5

Telle, Kari, 169

Tempo (magazine): on *The Act of Killing* (Oppenheimer film), 142; on coerced confession of witness to murder, 171; on *Treachery* film, 41

Tendean, Pierre, 36, 38

TGPF. *See* Joint Fact-Finding Team

Thalib, Munir Said. *See* Munir

Theological Academy Drikarya, 194

Thursday silent protests. *See* Kamisan

Timor Leste. *See* East Timor

Tjidurian 19 Rumah budaya yang dirampas (Seized culture house; film), 58

Tjiptaning, Ribka: *I Am Proud to Be the Child of PKI*, 62–63

torture cases, 167–68

transitional justice interventions, 1–6; anthropologists on, 6; assumptions about effectiveness of, 3, 14; at end of New Order regime (1996–98), 22, 97; interviews on IPT's role, 143–44; practice of criminal law and, 169; role of, 1; shortcomings of, 2, 5; truth produced in, 5; universal human rights as standard in, 4. *See also specific commissions and administrative bodies*

Treachery of the September 30th Movement/ PKI (Pengkhianatan G30S/PKI) (film): as affectively powerful narrative, 207; background, 216n39; as collective memory of 1965 attempted coup, 41, 46–47, 96, 152; compared to Oppenheimer's *The Act of Killing*, 142; Gerwani's role, 34–35; link to Lubang Buaya Monument and Museum, 47; Madiun role of PKI and, 33–34; mandatory viewing, 27–28, 41, 45, 47; students viewing, 38–41, 45; updating to reinforce dangers of Communism, 47

Trisakti Tragedy (May 12, 1998), 101–2, 181, 183, 236n8

Truth and Reconciliation Commission bill (Rancangan Undang Undang Komisi Kebenaran dan Rekonsiliasi), 135–36

truth commissions: as institutionalization of truth telling, 5, 80; quasi-judicial nature of, 5; what constitutes truth, variances in, 213n12

truth telling: assumptions about effectiveness of, 3–5, 14, 97, 209; in Cold War literature, 14, 80, 91; of disappearances, 106; failure to redress human rights violations, 1, 12, 153, 158–59, 163, 175; false narratives vs., 22–23, 41, 112–16, 175, 207; speaking truth to power in Cold War, 4, 110

Turn Left Festival (Belok Kiri Fest, Jakarta 2016), 135, 147–48
Tuti (Ibu), 106–7

Ubud Readers and Writers Festival (Bali 2015), 134
Uciwati (Uci), 59–60, 62, 139
United Development Party (Partai Persatuan Pembangunan; PPP), 74, 84
United Nations: conventions for human rights, 229n67; East Timor tribunal, 119; Security Council, 103; special rapporteur on rapes (1998), 114
United States: 1965 coup attempt against Sukarno, possible role in, 21, 140, 152; arms sales and military aid to repressive governments, 4; congressional testimony of Indonesian kidnapping victim, 108; infrastructure of impunity's ability to enter into, 210; in post-truth era, 208
Untung, Bedjo, 64, 177
Utomo, Hariwcahyo. *See* Hariwi

vengeance: danger of Communists seeking, 51, 59; overcoming common sense and morality, 43; PKI descendants accused of (1998), 102
violence: historical violence, 5; indirect violence, 7, 10, 13, 209; link between law and, 169; residual violence after genocide, 23; revelations of state violence, 99. *See also* genocide and campaign against PKI; infrastructure of impunity; mysterious

killings of mid-1980s; structural violence; *other specific acts of violence*
Volunteers for Humanity team (Tim Relawan untuk Kemanusiaan; TRuK), 112–13, 115, 181

Wahyuningroem, Ayu Sri Lestari, 118
Wandita, Galuh, 137–38
Wardaya, Baskara T., 61–62
Wawan (Bernardinus Realino Norma Irmawan), 180–81
Wayang adaptations of Sanskrit epics, 34–35
Weber, Max, 8
WhatsApp group of Kamisan (Aksi Kamisan WAG), 196–97
Whigham, Kerry, 11, 23, 26
Widartha, Jessica, 45–46
Widjojanto, Bambang, 111, 164–65, *166*, 173–74
Widjojo, Agus, 149, 154–55
Wieringa, Saskia, 33–35, 143, 222n170
Wilson, Ian, 95
Wiranto (general), 47, 103, 112, 127, 188, 202, 230n83, 236n12, 237n23
World Children's Day commemoration, 197

Yatamak, Yayak, 147
Year of Truth (KKPK), testimonies offered during, 136–39
Youth Pledge (Sumpah Pemuda), 101, 183, 194–96, *195*
Yudhoyono, Susilo Bambang, 58, 123, 134

Zacka, Bernardo, 8

www.ingramcontent.com/pod-product-compliance
Lightning Source LLC
Chambersburg PA
CBHW020843270326
41928CB00006B/528